OXFORD STUDIES IN AFRICAN AFFAIRS

General Editors
JOHN D. HARGREAVES *and* GEORGE SHEPPERSON

COLONIST OR UITLANDER?

COLONIST
OR
UITLANDER?

A Study of the British Immigrant in South Africa

BY

JOHN STONE

CLARENDON PRESS · OXFORD

1973

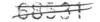

Oxford University Press, Ely House, London W.1

GLASGOW   NEW YORK   TORONTO   MELBOURNE   WELLINGTON
CAPE TOWN   IBADAN   NAIROBI   DAR ES SALAAM   LUSAKA   ADDIS ABABA
DELHI   BOMBAY   CALCUTTA   MADRAS   KARACHI   LAHORE   DACCA
KUALA LUMPUR   SINGAPORE   HONG KONG   TOKYO

PRINTED IN GREAT BRITAIN
BY RICHARD CLAY (THE CHAUCER PRESS) LTD.,
BUNGAY, SUFFOLK

Preface

THE WHEEL has turned full circle: one hundred and fifty years ago the question of British emigration to South Africa was a subject of sharp controversy, and so it is today. During the intervening years the debate in Britain about the desirability of a stream of settlers sailing off towards the Southern hemisphere was muted, a matter of indifference or of mild approval. In South Africa, the controversy has rarely ceased ever since five thousand British settlers arrived on the stormy shores of the Eastern Province at a point called Algoa Bay, the site of present-day Port Elizabeth. Since then the flow of British immigrants has waxed and waned, reaching peaks when the balance of economic advantage turned against life in Britain, subsiding again either when conditions at home improved or when periodic booms, induced by the discoveries of gold and diamonds and the demands of industrial development, lost their initial momentum. This migration, like every other in human history, has been intimately shaped by the social structure of the host society, in this particular case one of immense complexity and interest. Despite most immigrants' understandable belief to the contrary, it is this strange environment, rather than any extraordinary characteristics of the migrants themselves, that makes this case study different from others.

In the book I have attempted to answer a sociological problem posed by the British immigrant in South Africa—what accounts for his rapid integration into the structure of South African society, and his still more rapid acculturation into its norms and dominant values? The problem has been approached from four different ways: it has been seen in the light of sociological theory; viewed in terms of a comparative analysis of race relations in Britain and South Africa; considered from the standpoint of the historical evidence; and, finally, assessed against the findings of a sample survey of post-war British immigrants.

Three basic explanations have been considered: (1) that there is a process of extensive self-selection on racial and political grounds, (2) that differences in the social structures and dominant value systems of British and South African society have been grossly exaggerated, (3) that there are certain characteristics of the 'immigrant situation', particularly combined with the structure of South African society, that are exceptionally conducive to conformity and hence to a change in racial attitudes. While there may be an element of truth in the first two propositions, the central theme of this book is an elaboration and demonstration of the third.

From the point of view of social science—social anthropology excepted—South Africa is an underdeveloped country. There is only one major sociological study of South Africa as a whole,[1] and the writing of the historical section of the book virtually entailed a reconstruction of the history of British immigration to South Africa during the twentieth century. Fortunately, access to the documents, files, and memoranda of the 1820 Memorial Settlers' Association provided an invaluable source of information with which to attempt the task. The fact that this is an exploratory study in a new field is also reflected in the research strategy employed in the empirical section of the work, the stress on 'open-ended' rather than closed questions and the use of qualitative as much as quantitative data.

It may be asked whether a migration on this comparatively modest scale over the past hundred and fifty years really merits detailed study. There are at least three main reasons why this is so. First, because immigration into any society is likely to focus attention on the key social structural characteristics of that society and to high-light sources of actual or potential cleavage within it. This is as true for Britain as it is for South Africa.

The second argument is related to the specific South African situation, for the balance of power within the 'white' community, between English-speaking South African and Afrikaner, is such that immigration on a severely limited scale could quite easily affect the relative size of each ethnic group. This simple equation has been fully appreciated throughout South African history and has been the motivation behind crucial policy decisions. At the macro-societal level, however, what might have been a simple political choice has been immensely complicated by the second major axis of conflict within South African society—that between black and white. If political power among the white group had remained with those South Africans of British origin, or if the major source of immigrant recruitment had been from countries of the non-English-speaking world, then this problem would not have arisen. Even the ability of South Africa in more recent years to attract increasing numbers of

[1] P. L. van den Berghe, *South Africa: A Study in Conflict* (1965).

immigrants from Southern European countries has not solved the Afrikaner Nationalist's dilemma, for by steering clear of the Scylla of an international language, he has landed himself in the Charybdis of an international church.

The third justification for such a study is that it makes an interesting contrast from the more familiar case in which British people have formed a host society into which many other diverse groups have attempted to integrate. It is interesting to consider the British as a migrant group, for this will help to isolate those characteristics that are general to all migrations and those that are specific to this particular case. An added interest is provided by the fact that this is the only significant example of British immigration into a society in which the dominant political power is held by a group of non-British origin.

To conclude, the reason why it is worth studying a relatively small number of British migrants to South Africa is that in this case the question of numbers is not of primary importance, a small numerical significance belies an intrinsic relevance to wider sociological problems and to an understanding of the society as a whole. Africa is a fascinating continent and South Africa has its own fascination. The sociologist must surely agree with Pliny's verdict of two millennia ago: 'Ex Africa semper aliquid novi'.

Acknowledgements

THE PRESENT study was started some five years ago and during the intervening period many debts have been contracted. I would particularly like to acknowledge the constructive criticism and enthusiastic guidance of Professor Kenneth Kirkwood of St. Antony's College, Oxford. The substance of the book is based on a D.Phil. thesis submitted to the University of Oxford, and I would like to thank the Warden and Fellows of St. Antony's for my election to a Research Fellowship in order to convert the thesis into this book. My thesis examiners, Dr. A. H. Halsey of Nuffield College and Dr. Percy S. Cohen of the London School of Economics, made some helpful comments on the original manuscript as have several of my colleagues in the Department of Sociology at Columbia University. In South Africa, many sociologists and historians at the Universities of the Witwatersrand, Cape Town, and Natal made useful suggestions at every stage of the research. Peter Johnston of the Institute for Social Research (Durban) generously allowed me to read the draft manuscript of his M.A. thesis on the British immigrant in Durban. The officers and members of the 1820 Memorial Settlers' Association, both in London and in all the major centres in South Africa, played an indispensable role in providing access to their unique collection of documents on twentieth-century immigration, and assistance in securing a sample of present-day British immigrants. My wife and Peter Brugman helped in translating books and articles from Afrikaans and Dutch, and Mrs. Judy Lay, on the staff of the Science Research Council's Atlas computer at Chilton, supervised the operation of the M.V.C. program. My sincere appreciation goes to the five hundred British immigrants and their families who submitted themselves to the formal interview with such good grace, and to all the other immigrants and South Africans who informally contributed to the study. Finally, I would like to express my debt to Mr. and Mrs. Erroll Baker who first introduced me to South African society; to my parents in both continents for their encouragement; and, above all, to Roleen who apart from everything else provided a delightful vocal accompaniment to the task of research and writing.

Contents

List of Abbreviations/List of Illustrations   xii

PART ONE
THE THEORETICAL AND COMPARATIVE SETTING

   I. Problems and Perspectives   3
   II. Emigration as a Sociological Process   11
   III. Race Relations and Sociological Theory   33
   IV. Comparative Intergroup Relations   45
   V. Initial Conclusions and Hypotheses   83

PART TWO
THE HISTORICAL BACKGROUND

   VI. The Settlers and the Frontier   91
   VII. The Uitlanders and Imperialism   110
   VIII. The Artisans and Apartheid   122
   IX. Social Structure, Immigration, and Intergroup Relations   143

PART THREE
THE SURVEY EVIDENCE

   X. The Basic Variables   149
   XI. The First Stage of Migration   162
   XII. The Process of Integration: (1) The Economic Dimension   180
   XIII. The Process of Integration: (2) The Social Dimension   190
   XIV. The Process of Integration: (3) The Political-Cultural
         Dimension   208
   XV. Total Integration   230
   XVI. Testing the Hypotheses   233

PART FOUR
SUMMARY AND CONCLUSIONS

XVII. Colonist or Uitlander?—Towards a Reassessment   247

PART FIVE
APPENDICES

   A. A Note on Methods, Terms, and Values   257
   B. The Interview Schedule   261
   C. Case Studies and Samples   274
   D. Migrant Statistics   276
   E. Chronology of Dates   278

   Select Bibliography   281
   Index   307

List of Abbreviations

A.S.R.	American Sociological Review
A.J.S.	American Journal of Sociology
B.J.S.	British Journal of Sociology
C.A.R.D.	Campaign Against Racial Discrimination
I.E.A.	International Economic Association
N.A.S.	National Association of Schoolmasters
N.I.E.S.R.	National Institute of Economic and Social Research
S.A.B.R.A.	South African Bureau of Racial Affairs
S.A.I.R.R.	South African Institute of Race Relations
S.A.J.S.	South African Journal of Science
P.E.P.	Political and Economic Planning
P.M.B.	Pietermaritzburg

List of Illustrations

A Cartoonist's assessment of two hundred and seventy years of British immigration policy   46

'Emigration to the Cape of Forlorn Hope', or 'All Among the Hottentots capering ashore' (1819)   *facing page* 87

'The Ideal Immigrant' (1967)   87

PART ONE

The Theoretical and Comparative Setting

TARLETON: 'You mean Jinghis-
kahn? Ah yes. Good thing the
Empire. Educates us. Opens our
minds. Knocks the Bible out of
us. And civilizes the other chaps.'

LORD SUMMERHAYS: 'Yes it civilizes them. And it uncivilizes
us. Their gain. Our loss,
Tarleton, believe me, our loss.

TARLETON: 'Well, why not? Aver-
ages out the human race. Makes
the nigger half an Englishman.
Makes the Englishman half a
nigger.'

LORD SUMMERHAYS: 'Speaking as
the unfortunate Englishman in
question, I don't like the process.
If I had my life over again, I'd
stay at home and supercivilize
myself.'

(SHAW, *Misalliance*, 1910)

CHAPTER I

Problems and Perspectives

SOUTH AFRICAN society is pre-eminently a society of groups. Ethnic or 'racial' groups determine the life chances and life styles of their members to as great a degree as classes in other societies.[1] This is not to deny the reality of class in the South African social system, but to emphasize its secondary importance.[2] Among these groups, English-speaking 'white' South Africans might appear to be the least exotic section of a society that is a veritable racial mosaic, and yet, from a sociological point of view, they are of particular interest.[3] Balanced precariously near the apex of the South African power 'triangle', their position is unique in its economic dominance yet apparent political impotence, a resultant of the forces acting between Bantu, Boer, and Briton.[4] It is into this social situation that the British immigrant arrives; it is into this group that he will probably integrate; and it is against this background that his assimilation must be considered. The purpose of our study is to explore the processes involved in the assimilation and adjustment of these immigrants in South Africa.

Before proceeding with the investigation, it is essential to clarify the precise meaning of the terminology employed in the study. An exact definition of pluralism[5] raises many problems as most societies

[1] H. Gerth and C. W. Mills, *From Max Weber: Essays in Sociology* (1948), pp. 180–1.
[2] A study of class perceptions among white South Africans was undertaken by the Institute for Social Research (University of Natal) during 1967–8. For class among South African Africans see L. Kuper, *An African Bourgeoisie: Race, Class and Politics in South Africa* (1965).
[3] Cf. J. Bond, *They were South Africans* (1956), p. 1; on the same theme see G. Butler's introduction to *A Book of South African Verse* (1959), pp. xvii–xviii, and 'The Cultural and Political Future of English-speaking South Africa', *New Nation* (Feb. 1968).
[4] I. D. MacCrone, *Group Conflicts and Race Prejudice*, Hoernlé Memorial Lecture (1947), p. 24. Perhaps 'impotence' is a little misleading: J. Lewin, *Politics and Law in South Africa* (1963), p. 11; but see also D. Brown *Against the World: a study of White South African attitudes* (1966), p. 10. W. M. Macmillan, *Bantu, Boer and Briton* (1963).
[5] Cf. J. Rex, 'The Plural Society in Sociological Theory', *B.J.S.* 10 (1959), 114–24 and 'The Plural Society: The South African Case', *Race*, 12, no. 4 (1971)

exhibit some pluralistic features, but the term refers basically to a situation in which several different communities, with independent institutional structures and often, though not always, distinct cultures, coexist within the same overarching political system. In the context of a plural society, of which South Africa is a prime example, the term 'integration'[6] is a more appropriate description of the immigrant's experience after his entry to the country than the term assimilation, with its implicit assumption of a homogeneous host society.

My assumption that South African society is pluralistic, according to the previous definition, can be illustrated from a number of different sources. While defending the concept of 'separate development', Pienaar writes of safeguarding the 'nations' of South Africa, and in a book by the 'verkrampte' intellectual Dr. J. Raubenheimer it is argued that South Africa has only a geographical and constitutional meaning, and that there is no such thing as a South African nation.[7] In a similar vein, both the journalist Calpin and the historian Hancock have raised the question of whether in fact there are any 'South Africans'; while the editors of a recent volume of South African historical studies stress that group focus, the product of the social milieu in a plural society, has biased the intellectual perspective of previous historians.[8] The point is most clearly illustrated in a sociological study of Jewish refugees[9] who escaped to Southern Africa from the persecution of Hitler's Europe during the 1930s. The authors argue that social integration of the refugees should be considered complete once they join or identify themselves with existing Jewish

---

401–13, where Rex makes valid criticism of certain restricted definitions of pluralism and their applicability to South Africa. For more recent discussion of the concept; see P. L. van den Berghe, *Race and Racism* (1967), pp. 132–49, *South Africa: A Study in Conflict* (1965), pp. 268–70; M. Banton, *Race Relations* (1967), pp. 282–92.

[6] R. Taft, *From Stranger to Citizen* (1965), p. 4; E. J. B. Rose *et al.*, *Colour and Citizenship* (1969), pp. 23–7.

[7] S. Pienaar and A. Sampson, *South Africa: Two views of Separate Development* (1960), pp. 1–29. J. Raubenheimer, *Boer, Brit en Bantoe* (Potchefstroom, Pro Rege-Pers, 1968); and the related points in E. S. Munger, *Afrikaner and African Nationalism: South African parallels and parameters* (1967), p. 1; W. H. Vatcher, *White Laager: the Rise of Afrikaner Nationalism* (1965), p. ix.

[8] G. H. Calpin, *There Are No South Africans* (1946). W. K. Hancock, *Are there South Africans?*, Hoernlé Memorial Lecture (1966). M. Wilson and L. Thompson (eds.), *The Oxford History of South Africa*, vol. I *South Africa to 1870* (1969), p. v.

[9] F. H. Sichel, *From Refugee to Citizen* (1966), p. 54; see also S. N. Eisenstadt, *The Absorption of Immigrants* (1954), p. 19.

institutions in South Africa and are accepted as part of this group. Thus 'pluralistic integration' rather than 'unitary assimilation' is a more suitable model on which to base an analysis of the experience of British immigrants in South Africa.

The process of integration includes a number of analytically distinct yet interrelated stages. What are the motives for migration and how do they affect the later stages of integration? What are the main variables involved in the integration process itself? What accounts for the speed of acculturation? How can we explain the drastic changes in attitudes,[10] values, and behaviour which appear to take place in the space of a relatively short time? These are some of the questions posed by our central problem and they must, therefore, be included within the scope of our theoretical framework.

That attitudes and behaviour can change dramatically in certain situations is a fact that has been observed not merely in the case under study, but in many other instances described in the literature of sociology and social-psychology.[11] American race relations studies have shown that when Northern students are transplanted into a Southern environment their attitudes seem to change towards those prevailing among their Southern contemporaries.[12] Whether this change is a result of contact with the Negro or with the general Southern atmosphere cannot be clearly determined but, apart from the influence of a changed social structure or the power of conformity, an alternative explanation could be the operation of self-selection, either positively attracting racialist Northerners to the South or discouraging liberal Northerners from studying there. A related observation was noted by Myrdal, that while the white Northerner who settled in the South rapidly adopted the stronger race prejudice of his new surroundings, the Southerner going North was more likely to keep his race

[10] The author's observation among a group of British university students, visiting South Africa for four months during 1964, revealed an almost laboratory case study of such attitude change. Cf. P. L. van den Berghe, *Race and Racism*, p. 39 n. 28.

[11] An interesting South African example of possible attitude change among soldiers as a result of wartime experience is described by E. G. Malherbe, *Race Attitudes and Education*, Hoernlé Memorial Lecture (1946); for a classic study of traumatic socialization see B. Bettelheim, 'Individual and Mass Behaviour in Extreme Situations', *J. Abnormal Psych.* 38 (1943), pp. 417–52.

[12] V. M. Sims and J. R. Patrick, 'Attitude towards the Negro of Northern and Southern College Students', *Journal of Social Psychology*, 7, no. 2 (1936), 203; see also E. Katz and P. F. Lazarsfeld, *Personal Influence: the part played by people in the flow of mass communications* (1955), p. 49.

B

prejudice unchanged. He attributed this discrepancy to the fact that the Northerner in the South would find the whole community intent upon his conforming to local patterns, in contrast to the Southerner who would meet with no such concerted action.[13]

The implication of this, that race attitudes and behaviour are more flexible in the one direction, towards greater intolerance, than in the reverse is possibly correct, but it is by no means certain. An investigation of the effects of Southern white workers on race relations in Northern plants revealed that not only did the Southern whites work with Negroes, but they also shared the same rest rooms and dressing rooms, and were able to make a peaceful accommodation to the norms of the new situation.[14] It is not even necessary for the transition from one system of race relations to another to be gradual or complete, for in the contrasting social systems of Panama and the Canal Zone during the late 1940s it was found that Panamanian Negroes conformed to discriminatory practices when they went to the Zone side of the street, while white Americans tended to accept equality when they crossed to the Panamanian side.[15] Even within a small community individuals appear to be able to tolerate and accept a racially schizophrenic existence. An interesting example of this situation was discovered in the Pocahontas coal field where whites and Negroes integrated below ground and segregated on the surface, and it was estimated that some sixty per cent of the miners were able completely to reverse their roles without any difficulty.[16]

Whether the evidence cited above justifies the position taken by Thomas and Znaniecki is questionable, for they seem to overstate the case when they argue that:

It would be superfluous to point out by examples the degree to which society has in the past been able to impose its scheme of attitudes and

[13] Crijns's study of African intellectuals revealed a minority who were sceptical about the unprejudiced attitudes of the white man from overseas. It was alleged that as soon as he came to settle down permanently in South Africa, and thus became subject to the pressure exerted upon him by South African whites, he rapidly conformed to their norms. A. G. J. Crijns, *Race Relations and Race Attitudes in South Africa* (1959), p. 139. G. Myrdal, *An American Dilemma: The Negro Problem and Modern Democracy* (1944), p. 79.

[14] L. M. Killian, 'The Effects of Southern White Workers on Race Relations in Northern Plants', *A.S.R.* 17, no. 3 (1952), 328–30.

[15] J. Biesanz and L. M. Smith 'Race Relations in Panama and the Canal Zone', *A.J.S.* 62 (1951), p. 7; J. Biesanz, 'Race Relations in the Canal Zone', *Phylon*, 2 (1950), 23–30.

[16] R. D. Minard, 'Race Relations in the Pocahontas Coal Field', *Journal of Social Issues*, 8, no. 1 (1952), 29–44.

values on the individual. Professor Sumner's volume 'Folkways' is practically a collection of such examples, and, far from discouraging us as they discourage Professor Sumner, they should be regarded as proofs of the ability of the individual to conform to any definition, to accept any attitude, provided it is an expression of the public will or represents the appreciation of even a limited group.[17]

However, the investigations of Rogers and Frantz, and Holleman in Rhodesia,[18] and those of van den Berghe and Lever in South Africa[19] describe a situation in which this extreme contention about attitude and behavioural change is approached. It will be a central part of our study to isolate some of the key variables responsible for such change, and to relate them to the overall question of integration.

Recent studies have repeatedly emphasized the sociologist's unique contribution to an understanding of the development and dynamics of race relations.[20] The significance of the 'situation'—the structuring of both prejudiced attitudes and discriminatory behaviour by specifically social forces—concentrates attention on changing social structures and institutions as an essential complement to the study of 'attitudes' in a more restricted social-psychological sense.[21] To establish the perspective most suitable for analysing our problem we must go beyond a consideration of attitudes themselves. Attitudes do not develop in a vacuum, and it is precisely the structural and cultural aspects of the situation that can be more revealing than a study based on the individual as the unit of analysis.[22]

[17] W. I. Thomas and F. Znaniecki, *The Polish Peasant in Europe and America* (1919), vol. 1, p. 73.

[18] C. A. Rogers and C. Frantz, *Racial Themes in Southern Rhodesia* (1962), and 'Length of Residence and Race Attitudes of Europeans in Southern Africa', *Race*, 3, no. 2 (1962), 46–54. J. F. Holleman, J. W. Mann, and P. L. van den Berghe, 'A Rhodesian White Minority Under Threat', *Journal of Social Psychology*, 57 (1962), 315–38.

[19] P. L. van den Berghe, *Race and Racism*, p. 27. H. Lever, 'The Ethnic Preferences of Immigrants', *Journal for Social Research*, 17, no. 2 (1968), 1–14.

[20] J. Rex and R. Moore, *Race, Community and Conflict* (1967), p. 12; and G. E. Simpson and J. M. Yinger 'The Sociology of Race and Ethnic Relations' in R. K. Merton, L. Broom, and L. S. Cottrell, *Sociology Today* (1959), p. 380.

[21] For a discussion of the place of attitude studies in sociology see P. S. Cohen, 'Social Attitudes and Sociological Enquiry', *B.J.S.*, 17, no. 4 (1966), 341–52.

[22] The role of structure and culture in immigration studies is assessed in S. A. Weinstock, 'A Note on the Value of Structural Explanations in the Study of Acculturation', *B.J.S.*, 17, no. 1 (1966), 60–3, and the 'Rejoinder' by R. J. Silvers, ibid., 64–9.

Many examples can be found to support the value of this interpretation. Lohman and Reitzes have argued that a view of race relations centred upon individual attitudes is severely limited, not because there are no situations in which the behaviour of persons towards others can be explained as individual *qua* individual in terms of specific attitudes, but rather because this conception is entirely inadequate when dealing with the major and significant areas of social life, namely at work and in the community.[23] The same is true with respect to studies of immigrant assimilation and integration, where concentration on the nature of group life should not be interpreted as a dismissal of the relevance of individual psychological states, but rather as an attempt to achieve the correct balance between social and psychological forces.[24] MacCrone makes a similar point in his discussion of the early development of South African race relations and argues that since colour prejudice, as a social attitude, can have no reality outside the existence of the group, special attention must be paid to the formation of social groups and the circumstances under which social contacts take place.[25]

The design of this study does not attempt to substitute a sociological imperialism for the exclusive psychological orientation associated with the 'Authoritarian Personality' type of investigation,[26] but it aims rather to steer a middle course between the two extremes. It is a valid criticism of the traditional psychoanalytical outlook that, despite Freud's comments on civilization and its discontents, few psychoanalysts have been prepared to venture outside the individual's mind in order to assess the influence of society and culture on the development of personality.[27] Perhaps the most balanced contribution to the debate has been provided by Thomas Pettigrew's comparative studies of intergroup attitudes and his attempt to estimate the changing weight of personality and socio-cultural factors in different social settings. Neither the personality of the bigot nor his

[23] J. D. Lohman and D. C. Reitzes, 'Note on Race Relations in Mass Society', *A.J.S.*, 63, no. 3 (1952), 241; see also A. H. Richmond, 'Sociological and Psychological Explanations of Racial Prejudice', *Pacific Soc. Rev.*, 4, no. 2 (1961), 63–8.

[24] M. M. Gordon, *Assimilation in American Life* (1964), p. 233.

[25] I. D. MacCrone, *Race Attitudes in South Africa* (1937), p. 131.

[26] T. W. Adorno, E. Frenkel-Brunswik, D. J. Levinson, and R. N. Sanford, *The Authoritarian Personality* (1950).

[27] B. Bettelheim and M. Janowitz, *Social Change and Prejudice* (1964), p. 52. For a notable exception see E. H. Erikson, *Childhood and Society* (Penguin Books, Harmondsworth, 1965).

cultural milieu is assumed to be paramount in every situation, but the comparative evidence drawn from surveys in South Africa and in the Southern States of America leads to the conclusion that in such areas, where racial intolerance is rooted in history, cultural norms, rather than externalizing personality factors, are fundamental.[28] While it is possible, then, to make a strong case for concentration on the sociological as opposed to the psychological aspects of the situation, particularly with reference to South Africa, this is essentially an artificial distinction which can be justified only as a heuristic device. The multi-causality of prejudice must never be forgotten.[29]

Race relations and the processes of migration and integration represent fields of study and are not 'disciplines' in their own right.[30] There is no 'pure theory' of race relations but rather a set of problems attracting the attention of students from a wide variety of academic perspectives. It is this 'problem-orientation'[31] which frequently provides the motivation for fruitful study in the social sciences, though not in a purely empirical sense; for while it is unrealistic to have theory without facts, equally it is unscientific to collect facts unrelated to a relevant theoretical foundation. For these reasons a theoretical sociological framework needs to be kept at the centre of our analysis.

A final introductory consideration involves a brief discussion of the concept of race in sociological theory. The key issue involved here is the extent to which race relations situations can be analysed in terms of conventional sociological theory and particularly those aspects of it relating to social stratification. To what degree are race and class attitudes, and racial and class relations, essentially similar?[32] Clearly there are many parallels between the two 'patterns of

[28] T. F. Pettigrew, 'Personality and Socio-cultural Factors in inter-Group Attitudes', *Journal of Conflict Resolution*, 2, no. 1 (1958), 29–42.
[29] G. W. Allport, *The Nature of Prejudice* (1958 edn.), p. 212, and 'Prejudice: A Problem in Psychological and Social Causation' in T. Parsons and E. Shils (eds.), *Towards a General Theory of Action* (1962 edn.), pp. 365–87. See also: I. D. MacCrone, 'Race Attitudes: An Analysis and Interpretation' in E. Hellmann (ed.), *Handbook of Race Relations in South Africa* (1949), p. 670.
[30] M. Banton, 'Sociology and Race Relations', *Race*, 1, no. 1 (1959), 3; P. L. van den Berghe, *Race and Racism*, pp. 6, 22.
[31] E. C. Hughes, 'Race Relations and the Sociological Imagination', *A.S.R.*, 28, no. 6 (1963) 879; R. Dahrendorf, 'Out of Utopia: Toward a Re-orientation of Sociological Analysis', *A.J.S.*, 64 (1958), 115–27; C. W. Mills, *The Sociological Imagination* (1959).
[32] H. M. Blalock, *Towards A Theory of Minority Group Relations* (1967), p. 201.

dominance',[33] but it is possible to claim that there are some distinguishing characteristics of race relations situations. Some sociologists point to the societal definition of group membership, the peculiar criteria for prejudice and discrimination, and the special 'folk theory' of the determination of behaviour.[34] Others stress the relationship to social stratification—the unequal distribution of power and privilege —but still emphasize the ascriptive criteria based on physical and cultural distinctions, and the over-all justification derived from a deterministic philosophy or set of beliefs.[35] While it is interesting to recognize these special features, it remains true that race relations lie firmly in the study of society itself and require few, if any, special sociological concepts for their analysis.[36]

[33] P. Mason, *Patterns of Dominance* (I.R.R., Oxford University Press, London, 1970).

[34] P. L. van den Berghe, *Race and Racism*, p. 24.

[35] J. Rex, *The Concept of Race in Sociological Theory*, paper delivered to the British Sociological Association 26 Mar. 1969, p. 12, and *Race Relations in Sociological Theory* (1970).

[36] D. Lockwood, *Some Notes on the Concept of Race and Plural Society*, paper delivered to B.S.A. 26 Mar. 1969, p. 9, reprinted as 'Race, Conflict and Plural Society' in S. Zubaida (ed.), *Race and Racialism* (1970), pp. 57–72. R. E. Park came to a similar conclusion when considering the field in 1939: quoted in E. C. Hughes *A.S.R.*, op. cit.

CHAPTER II

Emigration as a Sociological Process

TWO MAJOR themes, which are in practice closely related, form the basis of our theoretical problem. Both themes may be illustrated by a classic study in American sociology. On the one hand, emigration has to be considered as a sociological process in the manner of Thomas and Znaniecki's *Polish Peasant in Europe and America*.[1] On the other, and superimposed on this, is the second theme of race relations as a problem in sociological theory, with particular reference to the conflict between values and actions exemplified by Myrdal in *An American Dilemma*.[2] In the following two chapters an attempt will be made to combine theoretical aspects of these two themes to account for the major factors affecting acculturation and attitude change—both crucial elements in over-all integration— among British immigrants in South Africa. From this analysis some tentative hypotheses will be formulated in order to explain our central problems, and these will be tested against the survey findings described in a later section of the book.

One point must be stressed in the following discussion. In Thomas and Znaniecki's study the authors emphasize that they are dealing not only with immigration alone, but also with the related spheres of racial prejudice, cultural assimilation, and the development of new attitudes.[3] This is, in fact, inherent in the nature of the type of investigation which inevitably involves the two related fields of immigration and race relations,[4] though some social scientists would emphasize the former and others the latter.[5] So although we may isolate certain aspects of the immigration process for the sake of clarity, it must be remembered that all these factors are closely interconnected.

---

[1] First published in 1919; for a useful critique see J. Madge, *The Origins of Scientific Sociology* (1963), pp. 52–87.
[2] (1944); see Madge, ibid., pp. 255–83.
[3] Thomas and Znaniecki, op. cit., vol. 1, p. 1.
[4] A. H. Richmond, *Colour Prejudice in Britain* (1954), p. v.
[5] For the former approach in the British context see S. Patterson, *Dark Strangers* (1963), and *Immigrants in Industry* (1968).

a: A MACRO-SOCIAL THEORY OF MIGRATION: EISENSTADT'S APPROACH

Perhaps the most influential attempt to formulate a purely sociological analysis of migration has been provided by Eisenstadt in *The Absorption of Immigrants*. In this study Eisenstadt defines migration as 'the physical transition of an individual or group from one society to another',[6] and emphasizes the manner in which this transition involves the abandonment of one social setting and the entrance into a new and different one. He then breaks down the migratory process into a series of distinct stages:

(i) the motive to migrate;
(ii) the social structure of the actual migratory process;
(iii) the absorption of immigrants within the sociocultural framework of the new society.

The first stage, the motivational basis of migration, is particularly important because of its crucial influence on the subsequent stages. This includes such elements as the immigrant's initial attitudes and behaviour patterns, his image of the new society, and his orientation towards and degree of readiness to accept change. Following Talcott Parsons, Eisenstadt divides motivation into 'economic' and 'cultural' sub-categories. The former comprises: (i) 'a lack of adaptation for the requirements of minimum physical existence' and (ii) 'the inability to attain instrumental goals' such as the maximization of economic gains; and the latter: (i) 'inadequate expectations of solidarity' as in the case of political refugees who fail to identify with a society, and (ii) 'the inability to develop a progressive social theory'. Despite its tortuous terminology, this scheme does suggest a guide to the possible motives for migration which recognizes both material and ideological factors, and appreciates that their influence may operate on the basis of either absolute or relative deprivation. However, it is difficult to see the need for the 'progressive' qualification to Eisenstadt's second cultural sub-category, particularly if our aim is to achieve general validity. For the Voortrekkers, as witnessed by the letter of Piet Retief to the Grahamstown Journal and the comments of Anna Steenkamp on the eve of the Great Trek, or in the clauses of

---

[6] S. N. Eisenstadt, *The Absorption of Immigrants*, p. 1.

the Grondwet of 1858, provide a classic example of a *retrogressive* social theory partly motivating a migration.[7]

The second stage is concerned with the migratory process itself. This leads to a narrowing of the immigrant's sphere of social participation,[8] with the consequent development of a non-structured, incompletely defined situation[9] resulting in insecurity and anxiety. According to Eisenstadt, this type of social change which is common to all migrations not only involves the achievement of specific goals, but also 'a resocialization of the individual, and the reforming of his entire status image and set of values'.[10] It is precisely this result, the 'resocialization' of the immigrant, that is a central focus of our study.

The third and final stage in Eisenstadt's attempt to develop a sociology of migration is the process of absorption, which is equivalent to 'integration' in our use of terms. Absorption includes both the 'institutionalization of the immigrant's role' and the 'transformation of his primary group'. However, these developments are usually complicated by the fact that the immigrants' expectations and the social demands of the host society rarely coincide.[11] In other words, conflict within the individual immigrant and (or) between the immigrant group and the host community is an inseparable feature of most migrations.

Although the general applicability of the Eisenstadt scheme has been criticized on the grounds that it is biased towards group analysis,[12] which cannot adequately account for the psychological strains inherent in more individualistic types of migration, this is neither completely true nor directly relevant to our own particular

---

[7] E. A. Walker, *A History of Southern Africa* (1957), p. 199. J. Bird, *The Annals of Natal* (1888), 1, p. 459. G. W. Eybers, *Select Constitutional Documents illustrating South African History, 1795–1910* (1918), p. 364; J. A. I. Agar-Hamilton, *The Native Policy of the Voortrekkers* (1928), p. 89.

[8] S. N. Eisenstadt, op. cit., p. 6.

[9] L. A. Coser and B. Rosenberg, *Sociological Theory* (2nd. edn., 1964), pp. 231–59.

[10] Eisenstadt, loc. cit. Allport writes: 'from the point of view of attitude change, this state of "unstructuredness" is a necessary stage. A wedge has been driven. While the individual may be more uncomfortable than before, he has at least a chance of recentering his outlook in a more tolerant manner.' (*The Nature of Prejudice*, p. 469). In our case the direction of attitude change is towards intolerance, but the mechanism remains the same.

[11] Eisenstadt, op. cit., p. 10.

[12] A. H. Richmond, 'Immigration as a Social Process: the case of Coloured Colonials in the United Kingdom', *Social and Economic Studies*, 5, no. 2 (1956), 186.

problem. The group nature of Jewish immigration to Israel[13] is reflected in the group structure of South African society, in spite of their radically different dominant value systems. It would seem appropriate, therefore, to analyse both situations in similar sociological terms.

b: THE FIRST STAGE OF MIGRATION:
    TOWARDS A 'VALUE-ADDED' PERSPECTIVE

This over-all sociological framework suggested by Eisenstadt provides a basis on which to proceed, but it needs to be supplemented by a more detailed consideration of each stage of migration. The first stage of the migratory process—that which operates in the 'home' society as opposed to the 'host' society—comprises a large number of interacting variables which must be ordered in a logical fashion. In the approach that follows we shall adapt the 'value-added' concept of the economist and apply it to the social process of migration, in a manner similar to that of Smelser in his theoretical study of collective behaviour.[14] Smelser argues that collective behaviour is a result of social mobilization based on those beliefs which 'redefine social action',[15] but the distinctive characteristic of this behaviour is that it meets unstructured and undefined situations. In several ways there is a similarity between migratory movements and the types of collective behaviour, in particular those associated with the 'value-orientated' movement,[16] considered by Smelser. The Great Trek, for example, can be regarded as an alternative to a rebellion or a revolution as a mode of adjustment to frustrations, and so it may be studied with the same concepts.

Two basic propositions underlie the value-added approach: first, that we require a unique combination of determinants to yield a unique outcome, and secondly, that the sufficient condition to produce this result is the combination of every necessary condition according to a definite pattern.[17] This pattern can be reduced to a set of six

[13] A. Weingrod, *Israel—Group Relations in a New Society* (1965).

[14] N. J. Smelser, *Theory of Collective Behaviour* (1963).

[15] Ibid., p. 8.

[16] Ibid., pp. 313–81; other sociologists of migration have pointed to the possibility of applying Smelser's schema to an analysis of motives: R. C. Taylor, 'Migration and Motivation' in J. A. Jackson (ed.), *Migration* (Cambridge University Press, Cambridge, 1969), pp. 132–3.

[17] Smelser, op. cit., pp. 13–14. The value-added approach bears a certain resemblance to the perspective adopted in two other studies. In trying to account for the emergence of democracy in an American trade union use is made of

stages in which the occurrence of any one particular type of collective behaviour emerges out of a successive narrowing of possible alternatives as one moves from the first stage towards the last. The six stages are:

1. 'structural conduciveness'—a permissive factor
2. 'structural strain'
3. 'growth and spread of generalized beliefs'—making the structural strain meaningful to potential actors
4. 'precipitating factors'
5. 'mobilization of participants for action'—the role of leaders
6. 'social controls'—(a) to minimize (1) and (2): 'prevention'
      (b) to act after the event: 'cure'.

It is now possible to modify this framework and apply it towards a theory of migration in the migrant's home society. This presents a scheme similar in many respects to that used by Richardson to classify the variables relevant to voluntary migration to Australia,[18] although there is one significant difference in emphasis which will be discussed later. The stages in this scheme, with some reservations as to their 'correct' order, are as follows:

1. 'means'—physical and financial
2. 'incentive'—(a) 'positive' factors (i) 'objective' element
     (b) 'negative' factors (ii) 'subjective' element
3. 'awareness'—of emigration opportunities
4. 'precipitating factors'
5. 'mobilization'
6. 'social controls'.

The physical and financial means to migrate, which makes up the first stage in the process, is essentially the same as Smelser's 'structural conduciveness', and it is equally a permissive factor. Without certain basic preconditions emigration is impossible, but

---

Weber's dice-throwing analogy: S. M. Lipset, M. Trow, and J. S. Coleman, *Union Democracy* (1956); see also the 'funnel of causality' formulation in A. Campbell, P. E. Converse, W. E. Miller, and D. E. Stokes, *The American Voter* (1960), and the critical comments in W. G. Runciman, *Social Science and Political Theory* (1963), pp. 189–90.

[18] A. Richardson 'Some Psycho-Social Aspects of British Emigration to Australia', *B.J.S.*, 10 (1959), 328–9.

the fact that these conducive elements are present in a given social situation is a totally inadequate explanation of the causes of migration; they are a necessary not a sufficient condition of emigration. It is the 'incentive', as opposed to the more superficial 'precipitating factors', that really underlies the motivation for migration, in the same way that 'structural strain'—'strain' being defined as 'an impairment of the relations among the components of action'[19]—forms the basis of collective behaviour.

The incentive factor may be divided into four sub-groups depending on whether the dominant motives for migration can be considered to be 'positive' (i.e. orientated towards the host society) or 'negative' (i.e. orientated towards the home society), and whether they operate on a primary 'objective' or 'subjective' level. Under the 'positive incentive' factors are classified the economic, social, and political-cultural attractions of the new social system, while the 'negative' factors are these same forces repelling the migrant from the old system. In fact, the one may be regarded as simply the inverse of the other as in the conventional 'push-pull' model of migration,[20] but in practice it is essential to make the distinction. For the British immigrant attracted by prospects in South Africa may have an entirely different set of expectations and a radically different outlook from a fellow immigrant moving because of forces operating in Britain, and this could have a significant effect on their relative degree of integration.

Equal weight, or at least conceptual equality, ought to be given to both sets of factors, and Eisenstadt's emphasis on emigration as 'an adjustment process to frustrations' may be misleading. Clearly

[19] Smelser (1963), op. cit., p. 47.

[20] The crudest type of 'push-pull' models are often based on over-simplified assumptions as Petersen argues: 'The fact that the familiar push-pull polarity implies a universal sedentary quality, however, is only one of its faults. The push factors alleged to "cause" emigration ordinarily comprise a heterogeneous array, ranging from an agricultural crisis to the spirit of adventure, from the development of shipping to overpopulation. Few attempts are made to distinguish among underlying causes, facilitative environment, precipitants and motives. In particular, if we fail to distinguish between emigrants' motives and the social causes of emigration—that is, if we do not take the emigrants' level of aspiration into account—our analysis lacks logical clarity. Economic hardship, for example, can appropriately be termed a "cause" of emigration only if there is a positive correlation between hardship, however defined, and the propensity to migrate. Often the relation has been an inverse one; for example, the mass emigration from Europe in modern times developed together with a marked rise in the European standard of living.' ('A General Typology of Migration', *A.S.R.*, 23, no. 3. (1958), 258–9.)

his concentration on negative aspects is a result of focusing on Jewish immigration into Israel and the great American migrations. When we turn to recent migration to South Africa, Australia, Canada, or New Zealand, only 'frustration' in the widest sense of the term seems appropriate to describe the motives of the majority of British immigrants, and it is of a different order to that arising out of massive economic depression or the ravages of political persecution. However, Richardson exaggerates when he moves to the other extreme and claims that without the frustration of any present aspirations an individual merely becomes aware that another society provides easier ways of reaching his goals.[21] For this totally ignores the social definition of much discontent and its origin in comparisons of a relative nature.

The question centres on the second important distinction between the 'objective' and the 'subjective' elements of the incentive factors. The *subjective definition of the situation* is particularly crucial. This partially overlaps with the third stage, especially in Smelser's case, for he stresses that all collective behaviour needs some kind of belief to prepare the participants for action,[22] while in our approach it is also incorporated as an integral part of the incentive factor. Many other illustrations of the importance of the subjective element have been demonstrated in related contexts. The generation of conflict is never a simple dispute over material interests, but always involves the normative definition of the situation;[23] revolutions cannot arise without a related ideology.[24] It was the perceptive Marx who understood that as man's desires and pleasures sprang from society itself, they must also be measured by societal criteria— 'because they are of a social nature, they are of a relative nature'— and de Tocqueville had the same insight when he wrote that the position of the French before the Revolution became 'the more unsupportable in proportion to its improvement'.[25] Precisely the same relationship holds for migration: it is not so much absolute deprivation as relative deprivation that is the key determinant of

[21] Richardson, op. cit., p. 328.
[22] Smelser, op. cit., p. 79.
[23] D. Lockwood, 'Some Remarks on "The Social System"', *B.J.S.*, 7, no. 2 (1956), 140; see also P. Worsley 'The Distribution of Power in Industrial Society', *The Sociological Review*, Monograph no. 8 (1964), 29.
[24] C. Brinton, *The Anatomy of Revolution* (1958), p. 52.
[25] J. C. Davies, 'Towards a Theory of Revolution', *A.S.R.* 6, no. 1 (1962), 5–19.

social action, and it is within this context that 'reference-group' theory becomes important.[26]

The subsequent stages in the value-added scheme are largely self-explanatory and need little elaboration. It is the purpose of the empirical section of the study to determine the actual 'precipitating factors' which may be economic, social, political, or largely of a personal nature, as in the case of divorce. 'Mobilization' may take place through the initiative of formal bodies like the 1820 Memorial Settlers' Association, or by the informal influence of work and family contacts. The last factor, 'social controls', takes the form of restrictions imposed by the Government of the host society: in our case the most notable being that the immigrant should be of 'European race', should possess skills required by the economy, and should not have a background in any way associated with 'communistic activities'.[27]

In his approach Richardson includes an additional variable, that of 'personality', as the final decisive determinant of who will emigrate. This is a result of the chosen perspective of his study and the type of question that he wishes to answer. He focuses his attention specifically on the factors in the experience of the individual that determine the decision to emigrate and in particular the personality differences that exist between those who decide to emigrate and those who do not.[28] Thus, consciously, he employs a social-psychological conceptual framework.

The perspective of the present study, as I have argued before, is primarily sociological—I am concerned with emigrants not so much as individuals but as a social group. The sociology of emigration

[26] On the relationship between relative deprivation and migration, Thomas and Znaniecki write: 'But in modern society dissatisfaction with the given is far more frequently expressed as a desire for the new . . . a typical example is emigration. Thus, in Poland the conditions of the peasant's life are now much better than they were fifty years ago. But the subjective tendencies are not the same. A desire for economic progress has arisen, the opening of new fields for the satisfaction of this desire provokes a latent dissatisfaction with the old life, and the slightest change for the worse, which could be remedied with a little effort, is often enough to make the peasant start to America.' (*The Polish Peasant*, vol. 3, p. 52). For a recent British study see W. G. Runciman, *Relative Deprivation and Social Justice* (1966). Cf. R. K. Merton, *Social Theory and Social Structure* (1957), pp. 225–387; S. A. Stouffer *et al.*, *The American Soldier*, vols. 1 and 2 (1949).

[27] At the 1968 National Party Conference of the Free State Dr. Koornhof, deputy Minister for Immigration, praised the valuable contribution of immigrants to South Africa and assured the congress that no unskilled, Communist, or atheist immigrants were allowed in (*The Star* (Johannesburg), 19 Sept. 1968).

[28] Richardson, op. cit., p. 327.

stands in the same relation to the 'Migrant Personality', if such a psychological character exists, as the sociology of race relations does to the 'Authoritarian Personality'.[29] Following in the tradition stemming from Durkheim's classic studies,[30] we accept the principle that social facts should be explained by other social facts before resort is made to 'reductionist' psychological variables.[31] This is related to the argument that because migration is ubiquitous in human society the propensity to migrate can be taken as 'given', and attention can then be concentrated more on its social structural determinants.[32] However, this in no way suggests that the social-psychological perspective is unimportant, merely that in our study we have decided to focus on a different aspect of social reality.

C: THE SECOND AND THIRD STAGES OF MIGRATION: ADJUSTMENT AND INTEGRATION

So far the discussion has been confined to the processes at work in the emigrant's society of origin, and it is now time to consider the forces involved in adjustment and integration in the new society. The following analysis suggests some of the probable results emerging out of the strains and stresses inherent in the migrant situation. Thomas's and Znaniecki's account of the Polish peasant in America presents a classical description of the problems of disorganization and anomie, and the difficulties of acculturation in a vastly changed environment.[33] In addition, there arise new problems that are interesting not only from the practical standpoint of the relation of immigrants to American society but also in view of their general sociological significance.[34]

An important difference between the study of Thomas and Znaniecki and the present work is related to these more general questions. The work of Thomas and Znaniecki is concerned with the

[29] Above, p. 8; and R. Christie and M. Jahoda (eds.), *Studies in the Scope and Method of 'The Authoritarian Personality'* (1954).

[30] See especially *The Rules of Sociological Method* (1950), and *Suicide: A Study in Sociology* (1951); or for more general assessments: R. A. Nisbet (ed.), *Emile Durkheim* (1965), and C. Lévi-Strauss, *The Scope of Anthropology* (1967), pp. 10–16. For the reaction against 'sociologism' see A. Inkeles, *What is Sociology?* (1964), pp. 47–8; and the related arguments in D. H. Wrong, 'The Over-socialized Conception of Man in Modern Sociology', *A.S.R.* 26 (1961), 184–93; G. C. Homans, 'Bringing Men Back In', *A.S.R.* 29 (1964), 809–18.

[31] D. Lockwood (1969), op. cit., p. 3.

[32] W. Petersen, op. cit., p. 265.

[33] *The Polish Peasant*, vol. 5; *Organization and Disorganization in America*.

[34] Thomas and Znaniecki, ibid., p. viii.

transition from an agrarian-rural society to an industrial-urban environment. This aspect of urbanization is not important in British migration to South Africa, but there is another problem which is in some ways almost the reverse of it and that is the movement from what might be crudely described as an 'achievement-orientated' class society to an 'ascription-orientated' caste society. However, we do not mean to imply that the empirical reality is in exact accordance with these theoretical ideal-types. Clearly the very concept of class has connotations of ascription which may make its juxtaposition with achievement-orientation seem paradoxical; for various class societies, or for that matter 'classless' ones, can vary enormously in their degree of openness.[35] Similarly, the use of 'caste' in a wider context than the Indian social system has been the subject of considerable debate. Some sociologists suggest that the relationship between class and caste will be hopelessly confused if we persist in defining 'caste' as 'nothing more than a peculiarly ossified form of class'.[36] But the use of the term is legitimate provided these difficulties are recognized and care is taken to define the meaning of our categories as they are applied to each situation. The precise elaboration of the differences between the social structures of the two societies will be left to later sections of the book.

A more recent study, *Assimilation in American Life*, gives closer consideration to the role of social structure and culture in the process of integration. This is an important distinction, and in our case we have to answer the question of why there has been so little 'cultural lag' in matters of racial and social attitudes. If culture and social structure are separated conceptually—Parsons's normative and interactional levels of the social system[37]—a clue to the solution of this problem is given by the fact that, while acculturation need not lead to social integration, social acceptance usually results in

[35] In the field of education see, for example, R. H. Turner, 'Contest and Sponsored Mobility: Modes of Social Ascent through Education', *A.S.R.* (1960), 121–39; E. I. Hopper, 'A Typology for the Classification of Educational Systems', *Sociology* 2, no. 1 (1968), 29–45.

[36] E. Leach, 'Caste, Class and Slavery: the Taxonomic Problem' in A. de Reuck and J. Knight (eds.), *Caste and Race: comparative approaches* (C.I.B.A., J. & A. Churchill, London, 1967), pp. 5–17; L. Dumont, 'Caste, Racism and "Stratification": Reflections of a Social Anthropologist', *Contributions to Indian Sociology*, no. 5 (1961), 20–43. My use of the term follows the approach of P. L. van den Berghe, 'The Dynamics of Race Relations: An Ideal-Type Case Study of South Africa', unpublished Ph.D. Thesis, Harvard University (1959), p. 11, and *South Africa, A Study in Conflict* (1965), pp. 52–3.

[37] T. Parsons, *The Social System* (1951), pp. 3–23.

acculturation.[38] The former situation is well illustrated in South African history: the closer Africans have moved towards an adoption of the norms and values of 'Western civilization', the more vigorous has been the demand among the white élite for their social segregation. It is the urban African, not the tribal African, who is the principal target of attack.[39] Similarly the Cape Coloureds share much the same culture as the Afrikaners and yet they are socially excluded from the white group,[40] a fact which emphasizes that it is the social structure of the host society that holds the key to the door of integration. Another important factor is the extent to which a group is orientated towards assimilation, and this is clearly seen in the distinction between West Indian and Pakistani immigrants in Britain, or between the 'School' Xhosa and the 'Red' Xhosa in East London.[41] However, the case of the British immigrant in South Africa is a remarkable example of social acceptance that does result in rapid acculturation.

(i) *The immigrant situation: the role of insecurity and conformity*

In several critical respects the immigrant situation shares common properties with the marginal situation.[42] As Stonequist has argued, anyone in transition from one group to another will possess something of the marginal man's character.[43] Movement not only from one group to another but from one society to another is likely to exaggerate the effects of this marginality and cause it to become a particularly potent factor in the process of attitude change and acculturation.

There are many situations in which such a reaction has been

[38] M. M. Gordon, *Assimilation in American Life*, p. 63; S. N. Eisenstadt, *The Absorption of Immigrants*, p. 17.

[39] P. L. van den Berghe, 'Race Attitudes in Durban, South Africa', *Journal of Social Psychology*, 57 (1962), pp. 55–72 and reprinted in (ed.) *Africa: Social Problems of Change and Conflict* (Chandler, San Francisco, 1964), p. 254; T. F. Pettigrew, 'Social Distance Attitudes of South African Students', *Social Forces*, 38 (1960), 246–53; S. T. van der Horst, *The Effects of Industrialization on Race Relations in South Africa* in G. Hunter (ed.), *Industrialization and Race Relations* (1965), p. 137.

[40] H. F. Dickie-Clark, *The Marginal Situation: A Sociological Study of a Coloured Group* (1966).

[41] E. J. B. Rose *et al.*, *Colour and Citizenship* (1969), pp. 43–62; P. Mayer, *Migrancy and the Study of Africans in Towns* (1962), reprinted in R. E. Pahl (ed.), *Readings in Urban Sociology* (Pergamon, Oxford, 1968), pp. 306–30.

[42] H. F. Dickie-Clark, op. cit., pp. 184–91.

[43] Ibid., p. 9; see also D. Riesman, *Individualism Reconsidered* (1954), pp. 121–78.

C

observed. In a study of university students in South Africa, it was found that those students whose parents were born in South Africa (within the English-speaking group) were more tolerant than those with English parents, while those with one parent born in South Africa occupied an intermediate position.[44] Similarly, among the pupils attending Afrikaans medium schools in Johannesburg, those with foreign-born fathers appeared to exceed the norm of intolerance in an effort to demonstrate their solidarity with the group.[45] It has even been suggested that the overconformity of upwardly mobile individuals may operate in the Coloureds' situation, leading them to display even more prejudice than the whites.[46]

Recognition of these factors underlies Leo Kuper's comments about the British immigrant in South Africa:

> In the absence of research findings, I would like to suggest over-conformity as an unexpected consequence arising in certain cases—an overconformity which may express itself either as an extreme racial prejudice, or as discrimination going beyond the requirements of law and custom.[47]

While a selective process may be involved,[48] attracting immigrants by the prospects of racial domination, this is not necessarily the case. For,

> ... the same consequences may result for immigrants who are relatively free from racial prejudice, but lack the experience of race contact and perhaps deep inner conviction. Just as they conformed with the norms of English society, so they now conform with those of South Africa.[49] Finding themselves consistently in situations of systematic discrimination, they experience an unexpected and intense pleasure in the novel sensation of superiority and domination over their fellow human beings, which needs justification. They are thus given an incentive to acquire the appropriate

---

[44] I. D. MacCrone, 'Parental Origins and Popular Prejudice', *Proceedings of the South African Psychological Association*, vol. 5 (1954), pp. 10–12.

[45] H. Lever, *Ethnic Attitudes of Johannesburg Youth* (1968), p. 158.

[46] H. F. Dickie-Clark, op. cit., p. 150.

[47] 'The Heightening of Racial Tension', *Race*, 2, no. 1 (1960), 29–30.

[48] Selection may be from a particular area or from settlers of a particular psychological type. On the former, Rogers and Frantz write: 'It is perhaps not coincidental that many of the basic differentiating customs of Southern Rhodesia were solidified by legislation in the period 1921–31, when people born in South Africa constituted the largest nationality group among Europeans' (*Racial Themes in Southern Rhodesia*, p. 14). See also O. Mannoni, *Prospero and Caliban: the Psychology of Colonization* (2nd. edn. 1964).

[49] For a 'group norms' theory of prejudice see M. Sherif and C. W. Sherif, *Groups in Harmony and Tension* (1953), p. 218.

supporting attitudes, and parvenu-like, exulting in their new-found wealth, they exaggerate these attitudes—a process assisted by ignorance of other races, the failure to allow for cultural differences and the results of discrimination, and consequent unrealistic expectations of behaviour.[50]

Thus Kuper argues that there are two possible explanations which may account for rapid changes in attitudes and behaviour among immigrants: either a self-selection factor, in which case the 'change' is apparent rather than real, or conformity to group norms from a position previously somewhat free from racial prejudice. Both influences may in fact be working together, but this is not necessarily so, for in a country like South Africa where racialism is deeply ingrained the social pressure towards colour prejudice is such that it will be found among people who have no personality predisposition towards it.[51]

This raises the problem of the complex nature of prejudice. To use Allport's distinction, we are concerned essentially with 'conformity' (i.e. socially determined) prejudice rather than 'functional' (i.e. character conditioned) prejudice[52] which accords with the sociological emphasis of our study. While the division of prejudice into two types is an oversimplification it can be justified for its conceptual convenience. Clearly the two types are closely interrelated, for if ambition, to take an example, can be socially structured, so too can conformity.[53] There can be no doubt that conformity is one of the most powerful forces involved in the development of new racial and social attitudes. A study of South African students revealed a positive correlation between a scale of social conformity and both Authoritarianism and anti-African attitudes.[54] It is well known that these three factors tend to cluster together as products of the same type of personality, but if conformity develops out of the immigrant's

[50] L. Kuper, loc. cit.

[51] P. L. van den Berghe (1962) op. cit., p. 256; In Merton's terminology this would be the case of the 'Unprejudiced Discriminator'. Cf. 'Discrimination and the American Creed' (1949), reprinted in P. I. Rose, *The Study of Society* (1967), pp. 480–98.

[52] G. W. Allport, *The Nature of Prejudice*, pp. 271–5.

[53] Cf. P. L. van den Berghe, 'The Dynamics of Race Relations', Ph.D. Thesis, Harvard University (1959), p. 51, n. 1; A. H. Richmond (1961), op. cit., and M. Banton, *Race Relations*, pp. 293–315. R. H. Turner, *The Social Context of Ambition* (1964); M. Young and P. Willmott, *Family and Kinship in East London* (1957), pt. 2.

[54] T. F. Pettigrew, 'Social Distance Attitudes of South African Students', 246–53.

position in the social structure, and attitudes hostile towards the African are the prevailing norm, it is clear that the two can be linked without Authoritarianism entering the picture.[55]

An example of similar forces at work can be seen in the case of prejudice towards North African Jewish immigrants in Israel.[56] Although the official norms of Israeli society operate strongly against any form of discrimination, research has revealed inter-ethnic strain of sufficient intensity to cause immigrants to accept a negative stereotype of themselves. This self-rejection has been interpreted as an attempt to conform and thereby to gain acceptance into the new society. If immigrants are prepared to accept negative stereotypes of themselves in order to conform and be accepted, how much more likely are they to agree to a positive stereotype of themselves as a member of a superior race entitled to all the advantages of a privileged élite?

The quest for acceptance is a phenomenon well documented in the literature on social mobility and opinion change. Experiments conducted by social-psychologists have shown that persons who are most highly motivated to maintain their membership of a social group also tend to be the most susceptible to influence by other members within the group.[57] Those notorious 'status seekers' are no prerogative of the sociological imagination. Migration can similarly be regarded as a kind of horizontal mobility which raises the same problems of broken group ties and the need to re-establish fresh affiliations in a new environment. The distinction between migration and mere movement, emphasized by Park, shows why this is so, for the former involves, at the very least, a change of residence and the breaking of links with the home environment. For this reason, the movement of gipsies and other pariah peoples, because they bring about no important changes in cultural life, are to be regarded as a 'geographical fact rather than as a social phenomenon'.[58]

In the case of British immigration to South Africa there is also an

---

[55] T. W. Adorno, *et al.*, *The Authoritarian Personality*, pp. 971–2; G. W. Allport, *Personality and Social Encounter* (1960), p. 212.

[56] J. T. Shuval 'Emerging Patterns of Ethnic Strain in Israel', *Social Forces*, 40, no. 4 (1962), 323–30; and *Israeli Annals of Psychiatry* 4 (1966), 101.

[57] C. I. Hovland, I. L. Janis, and H. H. Kelley, 'A Summary of Experimental Studies of Opinion Change' reprinted in M. Jahoda and N. Warren, *Attitudes* (1966), p. 145; cf. in the same volume, A. E. Siegel and S. Siegel, 'Reference Groups, Membership Groups and Attitude Change' pp. 187–95.

[58] R. E. Park, *Race and Culture* (1950), p. 350; W. Petersen, op. cit., p. 258.

important element of social mobility to be considered, though it is of a rather special kind. For 'class-migration' is superimposed on 'national-migration', and this will have the effect of increasing the insecurity of the British manual worker, who represents the modal type of immigrant, in a twofold manner. Perhaps the most exaggerated example of role strain and associated status anxieties can be expected from the position of the manual worker's wife, for it compounds the problems of class with those of sex. From this general situation of insecurity it is possible to imagine the development of 'free-floating' loyalties—in a manner analogous to Eisenstadt's 'free-floating political resources'[59]—which are readily available to be mobilized and channelled into the dominant value system of the new society.

The consequences of the immigrant situation need not be confined to the manual worker,[60] or to the less well educated. All immigrants are likely to be affected to some extent, as Thomas and Znaniecki, writing perceptively about insecurity and its relationship to attitude-change, point out:

If the individual is unable to create his own scheme (of ideas), he is ready to accept any one that is given him and expresses more or less adequately his new way of defining situations. This explains such striking cases as the sudden 'conversion' of individuals whose intellectual level is much above the doctrine to which they are converted, the influence that people of limited intellectual power but of strong convictions can occasionally exercise over much more profound, but doubting personalities, and the incomprehensible social success of self-satisfied mediocrities during periods of intellectual unrest. Anything becomes preferable to mental uncertainty.[61]

(ii) *The social structure of the host society*

The second aspect of the integration process to be considered in more detail is the situation prevailing in the South African 'host' society, particularly the unique and ambivalent attitudes existing there towards the British immigrant. A key to an understanding of this position is, as mentioned earlier, the triangle of forces interacting

[59] S. N. Eisenstadt, *The Political Systems of Empires* (1963).
[60] Cf. T. F. Pettigrew, *Journal of Conflict Resolution*, 34–5.
[61] *The Polish Peasant*, 3, p. 53; on a related theme, M. Banton writes: '. . . when custom is changing the actor has to decide for himself how far he will go in upholding the old norms or in supporting the new ones, and to accept the consequences if he goes too far in either direction. No longer is there any clear guide to conduct; custom has failed him.' (*White and Coloured* (1959), p. 95.)

between the three major power groups in South African society—
Macmillan's trinity of 'Bantu, Boer and Briton'. In his Hoernlé
Memorial Lecture, Hancock alluded to a similar theme when he discussed the importance of what he termed 'Milner's Law', concerning
the crucial relationships between these major South African groups.
Milner made a 'diagnosis of the interplay between the politics of
culture and the politics of colour' and found the 'singular situation
that you might indeed unite Dutch and English by protecting the
black man, but you would unite them against yourself and your
policy of protection'.[62] In other words, Hancock concluded that it is
colour rather than culture that is the fundamental force governing
South African society,[63] and this important fact has had an enduring
influence on the reception of immigrants in the past and in more
recent years.

However, both forces, representing colour conflict and culture
conflict, are significant and should be considered more closely. In
the first place, British immigrants will be favourably received by the
'white community' as a whole—the discussion is in terms of the
dominant values of the group, there may be individual exceptions—in
so far as they are an addition to the 'white laager' and thereby help
to strengthen the power of the white minority against the black
majority. Their arrival will be doubly welcome to the English-speaking
whites, though not to the same degree to the Afrikaans-speaking
group, for the way it affects the crucial numerical balance between
these two language groups. This merely reflects the second great axis
of conflict running through South African history: the struggle
between Boer and Briton exemplified in the hatred of Lord Charles
Somerset's 'anglicizing' policy; the dispute between Kruger and the
Uitlanders; and Milner's grand design to 'open the floodgates' to
British immigrants in order to reverse the relative size of the two
ethnic groups.[64] More recent examples of this Afrikaner ambivalence
can be seen in the dilemma of the Nationalist Government over their
immigration policy.

The debate on the South African Citizenship Act of 1949 is
particularly revealing in this context. After quoting the divergent

[62] W. K. Hancock *Are There South Africans?*; for a similar analysis see
S. Andreski, *Elements of Comparative Sociology* (1964), p. 275.
[63] Hancock, ibid., p. 17.
[64] W. K. Hancock, *Smuts: The Sanguine Years*, vol. 1 (1962), pp. 174–6. For
some contemporary parallels in reverse see the speech of Dr. A. H. Kellerman
to a S.A.B.R.A. youth conference reported in *The Star* 9 Oct. 1967.

views of the two major political parties, Gwendolen Carter comments:

> Behind this exchange lay also two different conceptions of the ideal immigrant. The United Party felt that familiarity with democratic procedures, the parliamentary system, and the values of Western civilization were the most important qualifications. The Nationalists looked instead at attitudes towards South Africa's most pressing problems: the Native question, and what they called 'national-mindedness', which they associated with bi-lingualism.[65]

The Act itself lengthened the time before British immigrants could apply for citizenship from two to five years, and was designed, according to one Natal newspaper, 'to create a new class of voteless "uitlanders" before the next election'.[66]

With the successive increases in the electoral strength of the National Party during the subsequent years, there was a gradual modification of these policies and attitudes. Throughout the 1950s, however, there was a marked reluctance to introduce an assisted passage scheme similar to those already firmly established in other Commonwealth countries.[67] Between 1946 and 1953 Lord Malvern's immigration scheme had increased the white population of Southern Rhodesia by 85,000, that is doubled it in only seven years,[68] which illustrates what might have taken place in South Africa had a different policy been pursued.

Gradually the Nationalist Government, spurred on by the international repercussions of the Sharpeville shootings and the changing political map of Africa north of the Zambesi, accepted the judgement that the positive contribution of British immigrants towards containing the force of African nationalism while sustaining economic expansion outweighed any negative threats, and an assisted passage scheme was introduced in 1961. New efforts were made to encourage immigrants from Britain and other European nations and white settlers from de-colonizing countries. Not that this did not raise protests from the stauncher advocates of Afrikaner purity, but the majority of Nationalists followed Dr. Verwoerd, who considered that the urgency of white survival should take precedence over the

[65] G. M. Carter, *The Politics of Inequality: South Africa since 1948* (1958), p. 54.
[66] *The Natal Daily News* quoted in Carter, ibid., p. 57.
[67] *Report of the Proceedings of the House of Assembly*, 30 Mar. 1955, H. A. Debs, vol. 88 cols. 3451–8 and the *Cape Times*, 31 Mar. 1955.
[68] P. Keatley, *The Politics of Partnership* (1963), p. 283.

possibility of some cultural contamination. There was, however, a vocal dissenting minority.

In 1967 the Federale Raad van Skakelkomittees—the Afrikaans liaison body for cultural associations—published a memorandum which viewed the record level of the inflow of immigrants and its composition as a dangerous challenge to Afrikanerdom.[69] The Raad claimed that as a result of immigration the English-speaking group of the white population was increasing at a rate of 17,600 a year more than the Afrikaans-speaking section and could easily outnumber them within thirty years or less. That such a long-term possibility, in the face of current inter-racial conflict, should produce a vigorous debate is a measure of the persistent influence of inter-ethnic hostility. The memorandum was strongly condemned by English-speaking organizations, such as the Sons of England and the Southern African League, because it posed a dual threat to their colour and to their culture.

The annual congress of the National Party of the Free State held in September 1968 revealed a whole range of fears associated with immigration.[70] One resolution called for stricter control over the selection of immigrants with particular reference to 'their ability to be assimilated by the nation, their Christian philosophy and their intelligence and integrity'. Among the problems raised by delegates were the dangerous consequences of immigrants acquiring key positions; whether they would become naturalized and, if so, whether they would vote for the National Party; whether they would associate themselves with the Afrikaans churches, and what measures were being taken to prohibit or reduce the entry of Roman Catholics.[71]

In reply to these questions, the Minister of Immigration, Dr. C. P. Mulder, and his deputy, Dr. P. Koornhof, defended government policy by claiming that it was the best of three possible choices.

---

[69] Reported in *The Sunday Times* (South Africa), 6 Jan. 1967.

[70] *The Star*, 19 Sept. 1968. Estimates of the effects of immigration on the balance between the white language groups vary dramatically. Dr. P. Koornhof, while chairman of the party's immigration group, analysed statistics for 1961–6 and found that the Afrikaans cultural group gained a total of 367,432 'recruits' while the English cultural group gained only 251,987 (*The Star*, 1 Aug. 1968). In sharp contrast, Dr. H. J. Terblanche, chairman of the Genootskap vir die Handhawing van Afrikaans, claimed that in 1964 the ratio of immigrant recruits to each section was 92 per cent to 8 per cent against the Afrikaner (*The Star*, 31 July 1968).

[71] For the reaction to anti-Catholic statements made at the 1967 Transvaal National Party Congress see *Cape Times*, 14 Sept. 1967.

Mulder estimated that in order to maintain a 'normal' $5\frac{1}{2}$ per cent rate of economic growth, there was a need for an additional 12,000–13,000 skilled workers each year. As a result, South Africa had to choose between an economic recession, the greater use of skilled black labour, or further immigration. Mulder rejected the first two suggestions and, while accepting that the best possible means of maintaining white numbers was 'immigration by way of the cot',[72] felt that the low white birth-rate meant that the introduction of foreign immigrants was essential to make up the deficit. He gave the congress repeated assurances that the Government would not allow the inflow of immigrants to disturb the existing numerical proportions between the English-speaking and Afrikaans-speaking sections of the white community, or between Protestants and Catholics. On the latter, he claimed that between the years 1960–7 the proportion of Roman Catholics had increased from a meagre 6·2 per cent of the white population to 6·4 per cent. Illustrating the dilemma raised by immigration to a Nationalist politician, he pointed out that if Protestants only were eligible to come to South Africa the country would be largely dependent on Britain, and then the 'language people' would start complaining and 'one lands between the devil and the deep blue sea'.

This general situation will have an important influence on the British immigrant arriving in South Africa. As he is not confronted by a solid host society[73] in which he is immediately recognized as an outsider and a stranger, the most probable result of the internal cleavages within South African society is to ease the immigrant's entry and accelerate his integration. He is most likely to be regarded as a new recruit, a potential ally in an insecure environment, and this should promote his admission into the primary groups, organizations, and institutions of the host society—to enhance his 'structural integration'.[74] In addition to this influence, and reinforcing it, is the relative social informality existing within the white community compared with the pervasive class stratification of the United

---

[72] *The Star*, 19 Sept. 1968. This is the optimal policy for any group fearing cultural extinction, but one notoriously difficult to promote. A parallel situation can be seen in Canada where a recent report by The Council on French Life in America called on their women to produce more babies 'if the French race is to survive in North America'. *The Star*, 18 July 1968; for other similarities between the two countries, cf. E. C. Hughes, *French Canada in Transition* (1943) and J. Porter, *The Vertical Mosaic* (1965).

[73] Cf. M. Banton, 'Integration into What Society?', *New Society*, 9 Nov. 1967.

[74] M. M. Gordon, *Assimilation in American Life* (1964), p. 71.

Kingdom, a factor that will further encourage the process of cultural assimilation. The remarkable rapidity of this acculturation, noted in the Rhodesian studies of Dr. Thomas Franck and Rogers and Frantz,[75] can be expected to be equally marked in the South African environment.

(iii) *Social mobility and status discrepancies*

A further aspect of social mobility, mentioned previously in connection with the 'immigrant situation', is concerned with the question of social acceptance. This is a variable of crucial importance, as Lipset and Bendix have suggested in their analysis of the effect of social mobility on the propensity towards political conservatism and radicalism.[76] In emphasizing the varying consequences of social mobility, they point to the contrast between the African in South Africa who obtains a non-manual position and the white American from a working-class family who makes a similar move. While the former is a ready candidate for leadership in a movement of radical protest, the latter tends towards social and political conservatism. They attribute this difference to the impact of status discrepancies.[77]

Now the concept of status discrepancies and the relationship between upward social mobility and racial prejudice are by no means unambiguous. Some empirical tests, using income and education as status variables, have shown situations in which status discrepancies *per se* have had no effect on prejudice.[78] Other sociologists have suggested that it is the individual's social definition of status discrepancies, in terms of relative deprivation, that is the critical explanatory factor involved.[79] The relationship between social mobility and prejudice is also complex, and firm generalizations are dangerous: the extent and direction of movement, the norms of the group to and from which the person is moving, and the general

[75] T. Franck, *Race and Nationalism*, pp. 245–6. C. A. Rogers and C. Frantz, *Racial Themes in Southern Rhodesia*, p. 340.

[76] S. M. Lipset and R. Bendix, *Social Mobility in Industrial Society* (1959), pp. 64–75; and S. M. Lipset, *Political Man* (1960), p. 263.

[77] Lipset and Bendix, op. cit., p. 64; for a discussion of the status discrepancy argument applied to the American Negro, see G. T. Marx, *Protest and Prejudice: a study of belief in the Black Community* (1967), p. 57.

[78] D. J. Trieman, 'Status Discrepancy and Prejudice', *A.J.S.* 71, no. 6 (1966), 651–64.

[79] W. G. Runciman and C. R. Bagley, 'Status Consistency, Relative Deprivation, and attitudes to Immigrants', *Sociology*, 3, no. 3 (1969), 359–75; C. Bagley, 'Relative Deprivation and the Working Class Racialist', *I.R.R. News Letter*, 2, no. 5 (1968), pp. 223–7.

economic and social context of the mobility process are all relevant.[80] In a study of the dynamics of prejudice among war veterans, an interesting minority were isolated who displayed both upward social mobility and outspokenly intolerant attitudes. A tentative explanation has been seen in terms of an association between rapid vertical mobility and a personality characterized by aggressiveness. As Durkheim noted in relation to suicide in Europe, sharp upward mobility involves a radical change in life styles which are liable to produce great stress in the individuals involved. The data on war veterans indicated that though slow upward mobility is closely associated with tolerance, rapid mobility in either direction is positively related to inter-ethnic hostility.[81] A similar study in Elmira, New York, found a correlation between downward mobility and prejudice, and an equal or even greater association with upward mobility, a fact that was interpreted as a manifestation of an effort to enhance or secure hard-won prestige.[82]

The type of upward social mobility experienced by British immigrants in South Africa, the nature of the status discrepancies involved, and the definition of the situation in terms of relative gratification rather than relative deprivation, can be expected to lead to social conservatism and support for the political *status quo*. My analysis should be refined to distinguish between 'positive' and 'negative' status discrepancies, for the comparative example cited by Lipset and Bendix contains two distinct cases. The crucial factor is not the status discrepancies themselves, although they are a necessary feature of the situation, but the way in which they are interpreted in terms of relative deprivation and relative gratification. In the present case, the status discrepancies are in a 'positive' direction—what I later call 'an unachieved rise in status'. It seems plausible that such a situation will produce a strongly conservative bias, in so far as the immigrant does not merely desire to be accepted within the existing order of society, but also feels a certain uneasiness concerning the legitimacy of his mode of access to this new exalted position.

[80] B. Bettelheim and M. Janowitz, *Social Change and Prejudice* (1964), pp. 29–38; G. E. Simpson and J. M. Yinger, *Racial and Cultural Minorities* (3rd edn. 1965).

[81] Bettelheim and Janowitz, p. 165; and H. Lever, *Ethnic Attitudes of Johannesburg Youth*, p. 152.

[82] J. Greenblum and L. I. Pearlin, 'Vertical Mobility and Prejudice: A Social-psychological Analysis', in R. Bendix and S. M. Lipset (eds.), *Class, Status and Power* (1953), pp. 480–91.

Thus, just as the upwardly mobile American worker,[83] being generally accepted in the higher social strata, shows a tendency towards voting for right-wing political parties and attitudes favouring the established structure of society, so in South Africa the British worker enters into the legally protected white élite and consequently does not suffer from the relative deprivation associated with negative status discrepancies. Studies of the assimilation of British immigrants in Australia have revealed a successive progression from 'satisfaction' to 'identification' and thence to 'acculturation'.[84] If upward social mobility and membership of a privileged dominant caste cause the majority of British immigrants to be satisfied with their new environment, then it seems reasonable to anticipate at minimum a passive acceptance of the social *status quo*, or, more likely, a positive identification with the existing order of South African society and an adoption of its racialist dominant value system.

[83] For an analysis of the numerically more important downwardly mobile group in America see H. L. Wilensky and H. Edwards, 'The Skidder: ideological adjustments of downward mobile workers', *A.S.R.* 24 (1959), 215–31, reprinted in N. J. and W. T. Smelser, *Personality and Social Systems* (1963), pp. 330–47.

[84] R. Taft, *From Stranger to Citizen*, p. 64.

CHAPTER III

Race Relations and Sociological Theory

a: A SOUTH AFRICAN 'DILEMMA'?[1]

THE SECOND theme in our theoretical analysis is concerned with the conflict between values and actions exemplified by Myrdal in *An American Dilemma*. Myrdal defines the dilemma as:

the ever ranging conflict between, on the one hand, the valuations preserved on the general plane which we shall call the 'American Creed', where the American thinks, talks and acts under the influence of high national and Christian precepts, and, on the other hand, the valuations on specific planes of individual and group living, where personal and local interests; economic, social, and sexual jealousies; considerations of community prestige and conformity; group prejudice against particular persons or types of people; and all sorts of miscellaneous wants, impulses, and habits dominate his outlook.[2]

The superficial plausibility of Myrdal's concept of a dilemma led to its uncritical acceptance by the majority of American sociologists of race relations. Some early exceptions, however, were the Marxist interpretations of Cox, and Golightly's demonstration that guilt results from the violation of group ideals but that the maintenance of a racial caste need not constitute such a violation.[3] More recently, the fundamental assumptions on which Myrdal based his concept have been re-examined, and to some extent reformulated. In conducting an empirical test of the suggestion that guilt is associated with segregation, Campbell argued that the 'American Creed' was not the only set of relevant norms and that such an assumption represented a drastic simplification of the normative dimensions of the race issue.[4]

---

[1] The term 'dilemma' has been applied to the total situation of South African society; I restrict its use to the case of the British immigrant. For the former see L. M. Thompson, 'The South African Dilemma' in L. Hartz, *The Founding of New Societies* (1964).

[2] Myrdal, vol. 1, p. xliii; for further criticisms of Myrdal's approach see N. Z. Medalia, 'Myrdal's assumptions on Race Relations', *Social Forces*, 40 (1962), 223–7; Bettelheim and Janowitz, p. 14.

[3] O. C. Cox, *Caste, Class and Race: a study in social dynamics* (1948), p. 277. C. L. Golightly, 'Race, Values and Guilt', *Social Forces*, 26 (1947), 125–39.

[4] E. Q. Campbell, 'Moral Discomfort and Racial Segregation: an examination of the Myrdal Hypothesis', *Social Forces*, 39, no. 3 (1961), p. 228.

This confirmed the conclusions of an earlier study of Christian leadership during a racial conflict in which it was found that neither the small sect minister, who was typically a vocal advocate of segregation, nor the denomination minister, who was generally a silent sympathizer with the integrationalist cause, showed significant evidence of guilt.[5] This was explained by the fact that social isolation and a well-defined creed of segregation sheltered the former from communications likely to raise the moral issue; while those ministers who failed to defend a sensed moral imperative during crisis were protected by a set of values and beliefs 'centred around their occupational role obligations'.

Some writers have argued that the concept of a dilemma is totally misconceived; others claim that though it exists, the techniques employed by people to resolve it are quite different from those assumed by Myrdal; and still others shift the focus of ideological contradiction from within the dominant group to a dialectic operating primarily between conflicting racial groups.[6] These qualifications suggest that a more sophisticated reformulation of the concept of a dilemma is necessary when it is applied to America or to the English-speaking white community in South Africa. The salience of mental conflict is likely to be less among Afrikaners than English-speaking South Africans because of their relative cultural isolation, and this may account for the African stereotype of the latter as 'hypocritical'.[7] For the British immigrant, however, it is much more probable that a definite discrepancy will develop, and will be subjectively perceived to develop, between the values derived from British society and the type of behaviour and attitudes necessitated by living in South Africa.

b: CONTRASTING SOCIAL STRUCTURES

Considerable care must be taken to establish the exact nature of the sociological differences between the two societies. It is essentially the political positions that are in the greatest contrast, as seen in the legal systems of the two countries. Laws may be regarded as part of

[5] E. Q. Campbell and T. F. Pettigrew, 'Racial and Moral Crisis: The Role of the Little Rock Ministers', *A.J.S.* 64, no. 5 (1959) 509–16.

[6] C. E. Silberman, *Crisis in Black and White* (1964), p. 10; F. R. Westie, 'An American Dilemma: an Empirical Test', *A.S.R.* 30, no. 4 (1965), 527; P. L. van den Berghe, *Race and Racism*, p. 126.

[7] H. Kuper 'The Colonial Situation in Southern Africa', *Journal of Modern African Studies*, 2, no. 2 (1964), 162–3.

the normative system of society and, though they do not represent a perfect image of the values, beliefs, and codes of behaviour existing within that society, they are, none the less, an important influence on and indicator of these crucial elements of a social system. The extreme Sumnerian doctrine of the complete dominance of 'folkways' and the total irrelevance of laws has long been discredited.[8]

It is not suggested that the contrast between British non-racialism and South African racialism is in any way clear cut. As Freedman warns: 'in the full flower of racialism everything in society and culture is race and all men are to be judged and graded by race; but a touch of the racialist tarbrush may be found in many contexts well short of this position.'[9] There is more than a mere 'touch of the racialist tarbrush' in contemporary British society, as will be documented more extensively in the next chapter. However, this discrimination is not institutionalized into the legal system and, at the quantitative level, is sufficiently different from the position in South Africa to be regarded as a difference in kind. Thus it seems reasonable to suggest that contrasting race relations should exacerbate the normal culture conflict inherent in the process of migration. Once again, this poses the problem of why, under these circumstances, should the acculturation of migrants be so very rapid. If the only feasible alternatives are discounted—either racist self-selection, or an interpretation of racialism in Britain that implies no great contrast in practice from the situation in Southern Africa—then this must be the result of the flexibility of attitudes,[10] which refocuses attention on the social structural factors mentioned previously.

If we accept the premiss that there is a genuine contrast between the situations in Britain and South Africa, then it is necessary to specify these differences in more formal sociological terms. The immigrant moves between what I have termed an 'achievement-orientated class society'[11] to an 'ascription-orientated caste society'.

[8] C. V. Woodward, *The Strange Career of Jim Crow* (Oxford University Press, New York, 1966), pp. 103–9; H. V. Ball, G. E. Simpson, and K. Ikeda, 'Law and Social Change: Summer Reconsidered', *A.J.S.* (1962), 532–40 who argue that Sumner's position has been misrepresented and was, in fact, little different from that of his modern critics.

[9] M. Freedman, 'Some Recent Work on Race Relations: A Critique', *B.J.S.* (1954), 345.

[10] For a discussion of attitudes as dependent and independent variables in sociological studies see P. S. Cohen, 'Social Attitudes and Sociological Enquiry', *B.J.S.* 17, no. 4 (1966), 341–52.

[11] By emphasizing the relative fluidity of the British stratification system I in

This is not to suggest that these represent an ideal-type dichotomy in any strict sense, but the interesting feature from the sociological standpoint is that this transition, from the class- to the caste-stratified end of the Weberian stratification continuum, is against the almost universal trend in the modern world. It is rare to find a movement that is not from 'status' to 'contract',[12] from ascription to achievement, but in many ways quite the reverse; an example of a 'deviant' case which so often has unique sociological value. However, a distinction must be made between the macro- and micro-societal levels: within the white community achievement-orientation and social mobility may be higher in South Africa than in Britain, because of the fluid class system within each caste[13]—one of the 'positive-incentive' factors for emigrating in the first place.

In my attempt to determine the sociological nature of the contrasts between the two societies, I must also assess the relative significance of the various elements composing the stratification systems. Gordon has used the term 'ethclass', a neologism for an individual's ethnic-class position in society, to refer to the 'sub-society created by the intersection of the vertical stratifications of ethnicity with the horizontal stratifications of social class'.[14] Whatever its value in the American context, and one may have doubts about placing 'colour' on the same plane as religion and national origins as a *vertical* division, it clearly needs modification to be applied meaningfully to the South African situation. Here there is a case of 'superimposition'[15]—to borrow the term used by Dahrendorf in an analogous context—of class on ethnic group, giving a minimum of cross-cutting cleavages and leading to a maximum conflict situation. A recognition of this position underlies the analysis of van den Berghe who explicitly describes South African society in terms of a conflict

no way imply that social divisions are unimportant or necessarily diminishing. Cf. W. G. Runciman, *Relative Deprivation and Social Justice*, pp. 151–244; J. H. Westergaard 'The Withering away of Class: A Contemporary Myth' (1965); J. H. Goldthorpe *et al.*, *The Affluent Worker in the Class Structure* (1969).

[12] A major theme in the work of many analysts of social change including Maine, Simmel, Tonnies, Durkheim, Weber and Parsons. It can also be seen in studies of the modernization of traditional societies: D. Silvertsen, *When Caste Barriers Fall: a Study of Social and Economic Change in a South Indian Village* (1963).

[13] P. L. van den Berghe, *South Africa: a study in Conflict*, p. 64.

[14] M. M. Gordon, *Assimilation in American Life*, p. 51.

[15] R. Dahrendorf, *Class and Class Conflict in Industrial Society* (1959), p. 213.

model, in an attempt to provide a theoretical synthesis between the dialectic and functionalism.[16]

C: THE QUEST FOR LEGITIMACY

In contrast with, for example, the British immigrant in North America,[17] the immigrant in South Africa is immediately confronted by a caste-type stratification system in a manner that brooks no evasion. The immigrant manual worker will be in a higher relative position in the new social structure than in the old, without necessarily experiencing 'social mobility' in the conventional sense, simply by virtue of his membership of the dominant white caste. He will have experienced an 'unachieved rise in status' and this will have to be explained, rationalized, or legitimized in some way.[18]

The nature of this migration, whereby immigrants arrive near the top of the social system unlike the more usual case where they arrive near the bottom, is both interesting and important. It is not equivalent to the 'brain drain' type of migration in which individuals in managerial and professional occupations pursue career patterns that transcend national boundaries, a group whose importance, Richmond has suggested, may invalidate our traditional concepts in the sociology of migration.[19] For in this case, social mobility is essentially an 'individually achieved rise in status', whereas in the South African case (though this achieved component may also be present) the most important element of mobility is a 'societally ascribed accretion to status' automatically conferred on the newcomer irrespective of merit. The reason for this pattern is related to Lieberson's distinction between 'migrant' and 'indigenous' superordination:[20] where the former exists, new immigrants from the superordinate group will enter the host society at a high level; where the latter prevails new immigrants will enter at the base of the social pyramid.

[16] Van den Berghe (1965), op. cit., pp. 265–81; 'Dialectic and Functionalism: Toward a Theoretical Synthesis', *A.S.R.* 28 (1963), 695–705, reprinted in N. J. Demerath and R. A. Peterson, *System, Change and Conflict* (1967), pp. 293–305.

[17] For the role of immigration in American history see O. Handlin, *The Uprooted* (1952), and for a penetrating discussion of immigrants in New York City see N. Glazer and D. P. Moynihan, *Beyond the Melting Pot* (1963).

[18] The quest for legitimacy in the industrial sphere is analysed in R. Bendix, *Work and Authority in Industry: ideologies of management in the course of industrialization* (1963).

[19] A. H. Richmond, *Post-War Immigrants in Canada* (1967), p. 28.

[20] S. Lieberson, 'A Societal Theory of Race and Ethnic Relations', *A.S.R.* 26, no. 6 (1961), 903.

D

There are several possible reactions open to the British immigrant placed in this situation:

(a) *rejection:* revealed in a return to Britain, but we must be sure that this is a reaction to racial or political factors;

(b) *neutrality:* which is hard, if not impossible, to define in the South African context;

(c) *ignorance:* (i) 'real' (ii) 'deliberate';

(d) *acceptance:* (i) 'partial' (ii) 'substantial' (iii) 'overconformity'.

The numerical significance of each response can only be established empirically, but the reactions (c) (ii), 'deliberate ignorance', and (d) (iii), 'overconformity', are likely to be of particular interest. On the former, Myrdal has noted in the American context that the ignorance about the Negro is not simply a random lack of interest or knowledge; rather the function of racial stereotypes is to serve as 'intellectual blinds'.[21] Similarly, Moore and Tumin have suggested that the function of ignorance that is most obvious, particularly to the cynical, is its role in preserving social differentials.[22]

The problem of rationalization and the legitimation of both 'unachieved' status and positions of superordination—command without higher justification is rare—is one common to the white immigrant and white native alike. In a similar context Rex claims that 'we grope after anchoring and validating principles which explain why things are as they are and why they should be so. Myth and theology, philosophy and science all provide us with systematic ways of meeting this need.'[23] In the early days at the Cape the distinction between Christian and heathen provided a justification for slavery until there were too many converts.[24] Similarly, in the American South, Henry Hughes and George Fitzhugh provided the first treatises to be graced by the term 'sociology' in explaining that the slave system was 'morally and civilly good' and should remain 'unchanged and perpetual'.[25] Between 1900 and 1920 Frazier argued that the sociological theories which were implicit in the writings on

---

[21] G. Myrdal, *An American Dilemma*, Vol. 1, p. 42.

[22] W. E. Moore and M. M. Tumin, 'The Social Functions of Ignorance', *A.S.R.* 14 (1949); reprinted in Rosenberg, Gerver, and Howton *Mass Society in Crisis* (1964), pp. 516–27.

[23] J. Rex (1969), op. cit. p. 11.

[24] I. D. MacCrone, *Race Attitudes in South Africa*, pp. 6, 41, n. 1.

[25] E. F. Frazier, 'Sociological Theory and Race Relations', *A.S.R.* 12, no. 3 (1947), 265; Fitzhugh's 'Sociology for the South' and 'Cannibals All' have been reprinted in H. Wish (ed.), *Ante-bellum* (1960).

the Negro problem 'were merely rationalizations of the existing racial situation'.[26] And in the African context, there were the views of Smuts on 'trusteeship' and Lugard's 'dual mandate', updated versions of the 'white man's burden', which provided, in the words of Professor Kirkwood, 'the ethical foundation for the Western presence and supremacy throughout the continent'.[27]

The recent British immigrant is faced with the same problem and with the doctrine of apartheid which provides a more acceptable rationalization than its less subtle predecessor, the crude theory of 'baasskap'. What could be more simple, therefore, than to adopt the attitudes and values of the host society, which not only provides a convenient rationalization but also eases his acceptance into the new society? By serving the dual function of easing any moral dilemma[28] while promoting the process of integration, these attitudes become mutually reinforcing.

d: THE ROLE OF ECONOMIC FACTORS

In the previous analysis economic factors have been largely subsumed under more general social structural terms, and they are often best seen as embedded in the over-all social structure and culture. As Richmond argues: 'economic factors also affect attitudes but are likely to be woven into the cultural fabric, for example, as one aspect of status insecurity'.[29] But in South Africa the economic dimension is particularly relevant and needs, at least once, to be dealt with in its own right as a separate and highly influential component of the total position. Cox in his criticism of Myrdal's approach and more recent interpretations of South African history and society[30] have laid particular stress on these economic forces. However, an exclusively economic explanation of the South African social structure is as inadequate as one that ignores the economic factor.

In his study of the political economy of South Africa Horwitz[31]

---

[26] Frazier, ibid., p. 265.

[27] J. C. Smuts, *The Basis of Trusteeship in African Native Policy* (1942); F. Lugard, *The Dual Mandate in British Tropical Africa* (1922); K. Kirkwood, *Britain and Africa* (1965), p. 47.

[28] A. G. J. Crijns, op. cit., p. 70.

[29] A. H. Richmond (1961), op. cit., 67.

[30] E.g. A. Hepple, *South Africa: a political and economic history* (1966).

[31] R. Horwitz, *The Political Economy of South Africa* (1967); this has been criticized by H. Wolpe, *The Sociology of Race Relations in South Africa* (1969). Much of Wolpe's paper is devoted to attacking various writers for employing a 'purely attitudinal level of analysis' rather than 'an analysis of the structural basis

has pointed to the friction between 'market' and 'polity', and demonstrated how the social implications of the two are working in diametrically opposite directions.[32] The latter has been pitted against the former at enormous cost in economic efficiency, and yet the existing social structure has shown remarkable resilience against any revolutionary shift in the balance of power. Some observers of South African society have been too willing to subscribe to what Goldthorpe has referred to as 'evolutionary para-Marxism:'[33] that is, the historicist determinism of the liberal academic. The root of the fallacy seems to lie in too close an attachment to a functionally integrated model of society, in which the economy is seen to have a determining influence over the rest of society, while the polity is relegated to the status of a dependent variable.[34]

---

of both discrimination and racial ideology', p. 17. How van den Berghe, to take just one of these writers, can be accused of such an approach is surprising to say the least. (See *Caneville: The Social Structure of a South African Town* (1964), pp. 123–50; *South Africa: A Study in Conflict*, pp. 73–96; *Race and Racism*, pp. 102–4, etc.) While economic factors have played an important part in the genesis and perpetuation of both race attitudes and race relations in South Africa, there is plenty of evidence to refute a crude Marxist interpretation of monocausal determinism.

[32] A keen appreciation of this theme can be illustrated by many speeches and editorials: in a leading article in the *Transvaler*, 6 Oct. 1967 entitled 'Politics must come before Economics', it is argued: 'The economy only has the present and the individual in mind. It depends on the Whites which force will triumph—economics or politics. It is enough to say that those who rate the economic interests of the individual higher than the political interests of the nation are committing treason against their children and other descendants.' Similar sentiments were expressed by Dr. C. J. Jooste, director of the S.A.B.R.A., in defending the 'policy before profit' theme: *Rand Daily Mail*, 9 Nov. 1967. Compare this with Sir Alec Douglas-Home's belief, faithfully reflecting the view of the organization which sponsored his tour to the country, that: 'there would not be a racial explosion in South Africa, but that economic realities would govern the future development of the Republic's race relations', *The Natal Mercury* (11 July 1968).

[33] J. H. Goldthorpe, 'Social Stratification in Industrial Society', *The Sociological Review: Monograph No. 8* (1964), 117.

[34] For objections to the same type of argument applied to the sphere of race relations see H. Blumer, 'Industrialization and Race Relations', in G. Hunter (ed.), op. cit., pp. 220–53; B. Bettelheim and M. Janowitz, *Social Change and Prejudice*, p. 24; E. C. Hughes and H. M. Hughes, *Where Peoples Meet: racial and ethnic frontiers* (1952), who point to 'the paradox that industry, while claiming to operate on universalistic principles in the name of efficiency, can be shown to discriminate most effectively between different ethnic elements in a population of potential workers'.

Those who see a solution to all South Africa's problems in terms of economics should heed Bryce's warning that: 'even in countries where no race differences intervene, the industrial nexus does not prevent bitter class hatreds and labour wars' (J. Bryce, *Impressions of South Africa* (1900), p. 465).

This approach is exemplified in the writing of Clark Kerr and Talcott Parsons:[35] both seem to take too narrow a view of what constitutes the functional prerequisites of society and look to the maximum efficiency rather than the minimum requirements for the economic basis to sustain a political dictatorship. Just as the monolithic grip of the Party in the Soviet Union is seen to give way before the quietly inexorable counter-revolutionary processes of industrialism, so, it is asserted, the same forces spell the doom of racialism in South Africa. Ironically, the critics of these functionalists arrive at much the same result but through the mechanism of immanent revolution: 'order' and 'conflict' theorists seem to agree on this point at least.[36] In the long run they may well be right—though Keynes's dictum[37] applies to all the social sciences as much as it does to economics—but during the next few decades the argument that 'there is no revolution round the corner'[38] has considerable plausibility. Equally, there is little likelihood of any liberalization as far as the African population is concerned.[39]

South Africa, to paraphrase Pareto, has proved to be the graveyard of revolutionaries, or, to be more exact and less gruesome, the graveyard of revolutionary hopes and predictions. Why has this been the case? We may cite the case of van den Berghe as a recent example of a sociologist whose study of South Africa led him to predict revolution and who was sufficiently incautious to imply a timetable for the process. Van den Berghe's analysis rejects the assumption of value-consensus implicit in the crudest form of Parsonian theory. In its place he suggests that the South African social system is characterized by conflict and an almost complete lack of agreement on the desirable goals of the society. On the other hand, the twin forces of industrialism at home and decolonization to the north were generating sufficient 'contradictions' to precipitate a violent overturning of the ruling régime.

[35] C. Kerr, *et al.*, *Industrialism and Industrial Man* (1962); and Kerr, *Marshall, Marx and Modern Times: The Multi-Dimensional Society* (1969). T. Parsons, 'Evolutionary Universals in Society', *A.S.R.* 29, no. 3. (1964), 339–57; see also the relevant critique: J. D. Y. Peel, 'Spencer and the Neo-Evolutionists', *Sociology*, 3, no. 2 (1969), 173–91.

[36] P. L. van den Berghe, *South Africa: a study in conflict*, p. 263. J. Horton, 'Order and Conflict Theories of Social Problems as Competing Ideologies', *A.J.S.* 71, no. 6 (1966), 701–13.

[37] 'In the long run we are all dead.'

[38] J. Lewin, *Politics and Law in South Africa*, pp. 107–15.

[39] D. Austin, *Britain and South Africa* (1966), p. 12.

It is clear, however, that the [South African] government cannot resist much longer the combination of mounting internal and external pressures, and the political change in South Africa cannot be peaceful. Indeed, all the symptoms of a pre-revolutionary situation are clearly present. The opposing forces of Afrikaner and African Nationalism have become increasingly polarized ideologically, and both have shown an increasing readiness to use violence to achieve their aims. Lack of communication between the antagonists is complete; so are their unwillingness to compromise or negotiate, their disagreement about the 'rules of the game', and their reciprocal denial of legitimacy.[40]

As a result:

A South Africa divided against itself awaits the impending and inexorable catastrophe. The Whites claim a right to survival which hardly anyone denies them. But in claiming to assert that right, they have set themselves against the course of history, and have become an arrogant, oppressive albinocracy. Their pride and prejudice may well be their undoing. Quos vult Jupiter perdere, dementat prius.[41]

This argument represents the rather glib 'conventional wisdom' of the post-Sharpeville era. The massacre in 1960 was viewed as the beginning of a period of mounting revolutionary activity leading to a rapid and decisive conflagration and to the final overthrow of white rule in Southern Africa: an apocalyptic vision of a racial Armageddon. By the end of the decade this outlook had already become dated with most observers agreeing that, as far as South Africa was concerned, the revolutionary potential was probably less explosive than it was ten years previously. Activity there had been, to be sure, but the most active participants in the conflict were the Security Police, crushing, as far as one can ever know in these circumstances, the bases of effective non-white opposition; the ultimate irony being the use of the powers established under the 'Bureau of State Security' Act against the ultra right-wing politicians Hertzog and Marais to harass the development of their breakaway Herstigte Nationale Party—a most eloquent testimony of the realities of the political situation. The patent weakness of economic sanctions to topple the infinitely less secure Smith régime in Rhodesia, and the evident leadership problems among Frelimo after the assassination of Dr. Mondlane, all suggest that the road to revolution in Southern Africa is going to be a much longer and harder struggle than van den Berghe and others have argued.

[40] P. L. van den Berghe (1965), op. cit., p. 182.
[41] Ibid., pp. 262–3.

Many of these predictions fail because they rest on a partial analysis of the relevant sociological variables likely to influence the course of future development in Southern Africa. There is no simple explanation of why South Africa, which appears to be a volcano on the verge of eruption, so persistently fails to erupt. Rather, there are a series of unique factors to which key observers, both inside and outside the country, fail to give sufficient weight. The analogies drawn with the decolonization to the north of the Zambesi are misleading: a closer analogy—yet still only an analogy—is the case of Israel in the Middle East. Notwithstanding radically different aspects in the two cases, of history and of ideology, there are certain common features which may account for both instances of survival despite what have often been considered as impossible social and political odds.

Each society contains minorities steeled by persecution, whether Nazi or British, believing that they fight for their very survival; both command a technology far more sophisticated than their adversaries; and both have powerful and wealthy sources of outside support. In the case of South Africa, the relative numbers of blacks and whites; the political control and independence of the Afrikaner élite; the relative wealth and self-sufficiency of the economy with its massive foreign investment; and the attitude of mind based on the realization that there is nowhere left to run—all these suggest differences from the ex-colonial countries in Africa which makes a direct comparison spurious. No one can accurately predict how far a ruthlessly determined and frightened élite, possessing the most modern sources of social control, can dominate a society by brute force and intelligence. Prejudice may be partly the result of ignorance, but its defence can attract no mean intellects.[42] Of course, the Africans of South Africa have enormous 'potential for control', but they must also display considerable 'potential for unity' to translate this into reality, and Apartheid may be seen as a determined and, so far, highly effective method of divide and rule.[43] It is time that sociologists

[42] In the British–South African context in recent years the names of Verwoerd and Powell come to mind. Cf. A. Hepple, *Verwoerd* (1967) and B. Smithies and P. Fiddick, *Enoch Powell on Immigration* (1969).

[43] This is the terminology used by Dahl in his criticism of C. W. Mills's *The Power Elite*. R. A. Dahl, 'A Critique of the Ruling Elite Model', *American Political Science Review*, LII (1958), 463–9. But see also the principle of 'divide and cohere' discussed by Gluckman in 'Bonds within the Colour Bar' in M. Gluckman, *Custom and Conflict in Africa* (1955).

of South Africa faced up to the realities of 'white power' instead of being obsessed with the potentialities of 'black power'.[44]

Thus the viewpoint of the sociological revolutionaries is as untenable as that which asserts that economic expansion is inherently liberal. Surprisingly, van den Berghe's model of society implies a functional integration which is as exaggerated as the ideological integration posited by Parsons. It underestimates the importance of coercion in maintaining the equilibrium of the political *status quo*; it fails to see that technological forces strengthen the white élite at the same time as they might strengthen the black masses;[45] and it ignores the truth that technology is ethically neutral and its outcome on that score is indeterminate—at least to those who have their reservations about the 'laws of history'.

This exploration of the wider implications of the economic theme rejects those arguments based on monocausal explanations,[46] whether in liberal or neo-Marxist guise. However, the economic factor is extremely important in appreciating the position of the white immigrant in South Africa. It should be remembered that most immigrants, outside the colonial situation,[47] start near the bottom rather than near the top of the stratification pyramid of their adopted society. Hence the strength of the economic forces in maintaining discrimination and prejudice is likely to be much stronger in the South African context than in, for example, North America: the white minority, being relatively small, has much more to lose.[48]

[44] D. Austin, 'White Power?', *Journal of Commonwealth Political Studies*, VI, no. 2 (July 1968), 95–106.

[45] See the related argument focusing on South African labour policies: F. Johnstone, 'White Prosperity and White Supremacy in South Africa Today', *African Affairs*, 69, no. 275 (April 1970), 124–40.

[46] As stressed earlier, there are many types of prejudice—MacCrone (1949), op. cit., p. 673—and many different causes, Allport (1958), op. cit., p. 212.

[47] The comparison between modern South Africa and 'colonial' societies has often been made: H. Kuper, 'The Colonial Situation in Southern Africa', 149–64; G. M. Carter, T. Karis, and N. W. Stultz, *South Africa's Transkei: The Politics of Domestic Colonialism* (1967). The 'bleaching' of the population of Brazil is another case: van den Berghe (1967), op. cit., p. 62; G. Pendle, *A History of Latin America* (1963), pp. 157–8.

[48] S. Andreski, p. 266.

CHAPTER IV

Comparative Intergroup Relations

ONE POSSIBLE objection to my argument so far would be an inter-pretation of race relations in Britain and South Africa that implied little fundamental difference between the two societies. I have already suggested that, though there may be similarities in certain limited respects, the transition for most immigrants represents a movement into a significantly different type of inter-racial contact situation. In terms of the central issues of our study, the most appro-priate level on which to make a comparative study of British and South African race relations would be the 'middle-range', equivalent to Robert Merton's middle-range theorizing.[1] A more abstract formu-lation was presented in the earlier chapters where the movement of the British immigrant was typified as a transition from an 'achievement-orientated' class society to an 'ascription-orientated' caste society. However, such an unqualified and sweeping generali-zation can be a dangerous shorthand, for the bare bones of abstrac-tion need to be covered with some solid documentary flesh. In this chapter will be considered the principal contrasts that an immigrant is likely to encounter in the major sub-systems of the two societies, seen against the background of different historical traditions, different demographic balances, and a different 'racial culture'.[2]

Outsiders frequently prove to have special insight into the work-ings of other societies: a certain emotional and geographical remote-ness may help to offset that abiding curse on the social scientist, the difficulty of freeing himself from the fetters of his own environ-ment. In 1952 the American anthropologist Ruth Landes was able

---

[1] R. K. Merton, *Social Theory and Social Structure*, p. 9; and R. Bendix, 'Concepts and Generalizations in Comparative Sociological Studies', *A.S.R.* 28, no. 4 (1963), pp. 532–9.

[2] Cf. G. A. Almond and S. Verba, *The Civic Culture* (1963), which includes a typology of attitudes towards the political system, and E. A. Nordlinger *The Working Class Tories* (1967), pp. 13–45 for a description of the English 'political culture'. An attempt to develop typologies of 'racial cultures' could be of value provided the interrelation of culture and social structure, is not forgotten, to avoid a repetition of the Parsonian stress on norms at the expense of sub-structure. Most racial typologies are based on power relations rather than on attitude rela-ions, whereas both forces are relevant.

A Cartoonist's assessment of two hundred and seventy years of British immigration policy.

From a cartoon by Gibbard reproduced by permission of *The Guardian*

to contrast race relations between Britain and America in the following terms:

'Prejudice' seemed to muddy up the approach; it did not seem a helpful
assumption in Britain. In America I knew it for a sociological reality,
distinct and compelling. An organized system of values and conduct. . . .
but in Britain I see no such orientation. In this sense, therefore, I would
say there is no prejudice.[3]

Fifteen years later, the American social-psychologist, Thomas
Pettigrew, voiced a very different opinion:

While there are certainly differences in scale, British race relations are
rapidly deteriorating to a point where they more and more resemble those
in the United States, and I would not wish that on any nation.[4]

What accounted for this dramatic deterioration in post-war British
race relations and what parallel changes were taking place in South
Africa?[5]

In June 1948 the *Empire Windrush* brought the first significant
group of coloured immigrants to Britain, a month after the National
Party had swept to power with a narrow and unexpected Parliamentary majority in the South African general elections. Both
events symbolized change, but the nature of the change was not
immediately apparent to people at that time. To the British, the
year 1948 was the beginning of the end of Empire, the early rumblings
of the 'colonial revolution' whose echo was soon to be heard on the
borders of Southern Africa.[6] To South Africans, 1948 appeared to

[3] R. A. Landes, 'Preliminary Statement of a survey of Negro–white relationships
in Britain', *Man* (Sept. 1952).
[4] *The Star* (Johannesburg), 5 Dec. 1967.
[5] Surveys of post-war British race relations can be found in E. J. B. Rose,
Colour and Citizenship, especially chaps. 5–8, 15–16, 29; S. Patterson, *Immigration
and Race Relations in Britain 1960–1967* (1969), a work that makes curiously
selective use of the P.E.P. Report evidence; M. Banton, *Race Relations*, pp.368–
93; and an earlier summary, J. Henderson's chapter in *Coloured Immigrants in
Britain* (1960). See also the *Institute of Race Relations Newsletters* (1960–9) and
Race (1959–70).
South African race relations are well summarized in M. Horrell's annual,
Survey of Race Relations, following from E. Hellmann and L. Abrahams (eds.)
Handbook of Race Relations in South Africa (1949); See also the various publications of the South African Institute of Race Relations and the South African
Bureau of Racial Affairs.
[6] For changing attitudes towards the Empire see G. Bennett, *The Concept of
Empire, from Burke to Attlee* (1962). David Thomson writes: 'The globe, men
realized, had no edges. Of this change the colonial revolution, in all its aspects,
was one great manifestation and one great cause' (*Europe Since Napoleon* (1966
edn.), p. 875).

mark a watershed and yet, ironically, the Afrikaner Nationalists' political mastery over the 'English' had the quality of a Pyrrhic victory, for just at the moment of triumph the cultural enemy became a needed racial friend; the very expression 'race issue' was ceasing to mean the relationship between Englishman and Afrikaner, rather it referred to the renewed struggle between black man and white.[7]

That the arrival of the Afrikaner Nationalist in a position of undisputed political control marked a radical new departure in South African history is a convenient but implausible myth.[8] There was certainly no significant policy change in the relations between black and white; the Apartheid slogan was new, the Apartheid legislation was not.[9] The advocates of 'separate development' could trace its antecedents at least as far back as Shepstone's native reserves[10] and possibly even to Van Riebeeck's almond hedge.[11] To believe that Smuts's United Party was bent on a new era of liberal reform, and to contrast the philosophy of the Fagan and the Sauer reports as evidence of this,[12] seems a little naïve or at least grossly one-sided. For fundamental changes in the social structure, whereby a tribal peasantry was being transformed into an industrial proletariat, and the new value system resulting from increased education combined with the 'demonstration effects' of decolonization to the North, introduced new factors into the situation and made the exact composition of the ruling white élite of less importance. The recent history of Rhodesia should quell the objection that a government representing the majority of English-speaking South Africans would have necessarily followed a radically different path. Thus the successive whittling away of civil liberties cannot be attributed to any personality characteristic of the

[7] This is shorthand for the division in South African terminology between 'Europeans' and 'Non-Europeans'. The analysis in this study is in terms of power groups, which relegates the Coloureds and the Indians to a relatively passive role.

[8] For a different assessment see E. H. Brookes, *Apartheid—a documentary study of modern South Africa* (1968), p. xxvii.

[9] D. W. Kruger (ed.), *South African Parties and Politics, 1910–60* (1960), p. xv.; there is a parallel and equally misleading dichotomy drawn between the two factions of the National Party, the *verligte* and the *verkrampte*. For an interesting analysis see S. C. Nolutshungu, 'Before the Election: Issues of the South African "Enlightenment"', unpublished paper delivered at St. Antony's College, Oxford, 14 May 1970.

[10] E. H. Brookes, *History of Native Policy* (2nd. revised edn. 1927); and Brookes and C. de B. Webb, *A History of Natal* (1965), pp. 56–7.

[11] E. A. Walker, *A History of Southern Africa*, p. 41; see also S. T. van der Horst, *Native Labour in South Africa* (1942), p. 3.

[12] W. K. Hancock, *Smuts: The Fields of Force, 1919–50* (1968), p. 491.

Afrikaner—his history could equally be seen as a breeding ground for anarchists. The simple fact remains that life in the laager does not foster dissent: 'laws which would have aroused the fiercest opposition in 1947, met with sullen acquiescence in 1957, and by 1967 the "nemesis of docility"[13] was all too apparent.'

While in South Africa the rise of the Nationalists resulted in the intensification of legislative activity, in Britain the aftermath of *Empire Windrush* was a period of *laissez-faire*.[14] Any attempt to distinguish in law on the grounds of race or colour would have been regarded as a gross violation of legal tradition. As Deakin explains: 'the point of reference for this doctrine lay not in administrative practice but in the law. That is, the law conceived of as the quintessence of colour blindness: a Diceyan incarnation of idealized opinion.'[15] What then was the importance of this new wave of immigration?

The newcomers were not the first coloured people to come to Britain;[16] they were far less numerous than the continuous flow of alien Irish Catholics and many were no poorer than the Jews, exiles fleeing from the pogroms of Eastern Europe, who crowded into the slums of the East End of London at the turn of the century.[17] As far as the West Indians, forming the vanguard of this movement, were concerned, they differed from the host society only in pigmentation and certain cultural values, they possessed the same citizenship, practised the same religion, and spoke the same language. But coloured immigration acted as a kind of social litmus paper, an acid test of the sincerity with which the ideal of a multi-racial Commonwealth was held in British political circles.[18] Furthermore, like a black dye pumped through the veins of the body politic, these new arrivals set out in sharp relief the crucial bottlenecks in the social system: slum schools, twilight housing, and inadequate social services. It is in these two facts that this particular migration (or to be more accurate migrations) acquires a special relevance to the understanding of contemporary British society.

[13] E. H. Brookes and J. B. Macaulay, *Civil Rights in South Africa* (1958), p. 168. E. G. Malherbe *The Nemesis of Docility*, Presidential Address to the S.A.I.R.R., 30 Jan. 1968.

[14] M. Horrell, *Legislation and Race Relations* (1963); N. Deakin in E. J. B. Rose, *et al.*, *Colour and Citizenship* (1969), pp. 21–3.

[15] Ibid., pp. 199–200.

[16] Cf. K. L. Little, *Negroes in Britain* (1947).

[17] J. A. Jackson *The Irish in Britain* (1963); M. Freedman (ed.), *A Minority in Britain* (1955).

[18] N. Deakin, *Colour and Citizenship*, pp. 605–27.

In the following discussion I will consider some of the more important social sub-systems, compare the British with their South African counterparts, and show how they are related to the arena of political conflict and debate.

a: ECONOMICS AND RACE RELATIONS

Karl Marx's distinctive contribution to sociology is his emphasis, some would say over-emphasis,[19] on the role of economic forces in the genesis, perpetuation, and change of social institutions. Of our two societies, South Africa comes nearer to the Marxist model of a polarized, conflict-ridden battleground of proletariat and bourgeoisie.[20] While neither society can be understood exclusively in economic terms, there is clearly an important economic component in the over-all race relations situation. So without accepting the explicit determinism of the Marxist or the same implicit assumptions of the 'liberal-capitalist',[21] we can proceed to analyse two crucial areas of the economic sub-system, employment and housing.

(i) *Employment—colour bars and stranger bars*

There are three basic facts—historical, legal, and demographic—that most clearly distinguish the two countries in the field of employment. While in South Africa economic history and race relations are synonymous, in Britain the role of class relations in history has been paramount. While in the former, the power of legislation has been mobilized to offset the integrating influence of 'unfettered' market forces,[22] in the latter, a race relations law was only extended to cover the workings of industry in the late 1960s, and with an intention diametrically opposed to the laws operating in South Africa. Behind these differing situations lies the fundamental demographic contrast: white South Africans constitute about twenty per cent of their country's population, black Britons are a minority of less than two per cent.[23]

---

[19] For example, D. G. MacRae in T. Raison (ed.), *The Founding Fathers of Social Science* (1969), pp. 59–67.

[20] For a Marxist analysis of South African history see H. J. and R. E. Simons, *Class and Colour in South Africa, 1850–1950* (1969).

[21] Cf. W. H. Hutt, *The Economics of the Colour Bar* (1964), and more generally, M. Friedman, *Capitalism and Freedom* (1962).

[22] R. Horwitz, *The Political Economy of South Africa* (1967), pp. 298–331, 373–427.

[23] 'Colour and Immigration in the United Kingdom', *I.R.R. Fact Paper* (1968), 1–2.

The origins of the present industrial colour bar in South Africa can be seen to emerge from the earliest days of the Dutch settlement at the Cape and particularly from the introduction of African slaves.[24] With the transition from a 'paternalistic' to a more competitive type of race relations situation as a result of industrialization during the twentieth century, there arose a greater strain towards overt industrial hostility. White workers used their political monopoly to entrench their economic privileges against their black co-workers, and used their numerical monopoly within the white political community to fight capitalist employers, whose profit-consciousness was wont to exceed their colour-consciousness. Against this background, the superficially surprising alliance of Hertzog and Creswell becomes readily intelligible, particularly in the aftermath of the Rand Revolt.[25] 'Swart Gevaar' spelt an equally chilling message to Afrikaner Nationalist and English-speaking artisan.

Before the First World War industrial relations involving both white and coloured workers were or little significance in Britain. Industrial conflict had polarized on the basis of class antagonism only rarely interrupted by friction between different ethnic groups in the work force. The 14,000–20,000 Negroes who were living in London in 1770,[26] whose ambiguous status as 'slaves' was quashed by the Somersett judgement two years later, never became articulated into a rigid two-category system, had no perceptible effect on subsequent industrial relations and attitudes, and presumably merged into the general population by a process of physical amalgamation. With the exception of a handful of coloured students, and these mainly arrived after 1900 from the newly acquired African Empire, the reappearance of the black man in Britain dates from the First World War, the labour demands of the munitions factories, and the increased use of coloured merchant seamen.

In both countries, the early pre-industrial contact between the races seemed to have been guided by 'paternalistic' attitudes on the part of the dominant whites. It was poverty and the 'wrong

---

[24] Among the best studies of the South African colour bar are G. V. Doxey, *The Industrial Colour Bar in South Africa* (1961); S. T. van der Horst, *Native Labour in South Africa*, *The African Factory Worker in Cape Town*; W. H. Hutt (1964), op. cit.; R. Horwitz (1967), op. cit. I. D. MacCrone, *Race Attitudes in South Africa*, p. 73.

[25] N. Herd *1922: The Revolt of the Rand* (1966) and W. K. Hancock, *Smuts: the Fields of Force, 1919–50*, pp. 62–88.

[26] K. L. Little, *Negroes in Britain*, p. 167.

connections,[27] rather than the wrong colour, which accounted for the Negro's low place in British society and the prejudice shown against him, so that until well on in the eighteenth century Englishmen saw nothing extraordinary in a Negro possessing talents equal to their own.[28] A similar situation prevailed in the earliest years of the Dutch settlement at the Cape before colour-caste stratification and related paternalistic attitudes crystallized into a rigid system.[29] Throughout the nineteenth century, while the British coloured population amalgamated itself out of a separate existence, the military conquest and subordination of the Bantu tribes in South Africa reinforced the pattern established at the Cape: as black power diminished, so too did black economic and social status.

The inter-war years of the twentieth century were marked, in both societies, by increasing industrial conflict which coincided with the depressed economic conditions. In South Africa, despite a temporary relaxation in some directions during the First World War, the colour bar became more rigid. This was a result in part of legislation and also of the increased strength of the trade unions composed of white skilled workers.[30] The main laws hardening the colour bar during the period had the effect of hindering the African's advance into skilled trades, and undermining the basis of incipient trade unionism. This trend was reinforced by changes in the ethnic composition of the white mining labour force, so that by 1920, 90 per cent of the mineworkers on the Reef were Afrikaners, compared with the earlier situation in which there were many immigrants from Cornwall and the North of England.[31] Throughout the twenties and the thirties the ever-present spectre of 'poor whiteism' rallied European workers to the platform of 'civilized labour' and firmly established the legal structure of white economic supremacy.

Meanwhile, in inter-war Britain, race relations in the coloured communities of Cardiff and Liverpool reached their 'nadir of disharmony'.[32] Representing only a tiny minority on the periphery of

---

[27] Cf. with Parsons contemporary discussion of the American Negroes' lack of resources that has prevented a 'fitting' into the total society. T. Parsons, 'Full Citizenship for the Negro American?', in T. Parsons and K. B. Clark, *The Negro American* (1966), pp. 709–51.

[28] K. L. Little op. cit., pp. 198, 202.

[29] I. D. MacCrone (1937), op. cit., pp. 70–80.

[30] S. T. van der Horst, *Native Labour in South Africa*, p. 180.

[31] G. V. Doxey, *The Industrial Colour Bar in South Africa*, p. 116.

[32] M. Banton, *White and Coloured*, p. 69.

British society, the domestic colour problem[33] cannot be compared with the turmoil on the Rand, and yet there were race riots in 1919 and responsible public opinion was not free from the most blatant expressions of racialism, the Chief Constable of Cardiff recommending the adoption of South African legislation to prohibit miscegenation.[34] In most of the larger ports the colour bar was an accepted institution and the local coloured populations experienced great difficulties in finding work for their juveniles, and shore work for their men.[35]

Thus, by the 1940s, British and South African industry had in theory followed divergent paths on the question of race relations and employment; in practice the differences were not so great. However, at the time of the 1948 election, the relationship of black and white in industry raged at the centre of South African political controversy, in marked contrast to the British who displayed a 'lack of popular knowledge and interest'[36] about the whole subject.

The post-war years saw the opposing policies of industrial apartheid and industrial *laissez-faire* developed to a greater degree. While the twin forces of industrialization and urbanization continued to gather pace in South Africa, acting as an irresistible magnet to the impoverished rural African, in Britain the labour demands of expanding industry,[37] combined with the effect of the McCarran-Walter Act which diverted West Indian immigrants from America towards the United Kingdom, led to a similar stream of black workers into a predominantly white labour force.

It is difficult to isolate the key legislative aspects of the Apartheid programme as they apply to industry and employment. Nearly every measure affecting the African's freedom of movement, subjection to arbitrary arrest, or rights to permanent residence in urban areas, influences his bargaining power just as much as the illegality

[33] The impact of colonial contacts on domestic attitudes is of great interest. Little points out that the Empire 'enabled British middle class persons to live upper class lives on condition that they went to the Tropics to do so' (K. L. Little, *Negroes in Britain*, p. 216).
However, colonialism is a variable factor. Cf. with the French experience, M. Crowder, *Senegal: a study of French assimilation policy* (rev. edn. 1967).
[34] M. Banton, *The Coloured Quarter* (1955), p. 35; for a recent study of the police role in race relations, see J. R. Lambert, *Crime, Police, and Race Relations: a study in Birmingham* (1970).
[35] K. Little, op. cit., p. 84.
[36] K. Little. *Negroes in Britain*, p. 22.
[37] G. C. K. Peach, *West Indian Migration to Britain* (1968), who argues that 'economic pull' factors were paramount in the case of West Indian immigrants to Britain.

E

of strikes and the other disabilities placed in the way of African trade unionism. The post-Apartheid successors to the 'civilized labour' legislation have spun a web of ever-entangling controls around the African industrial worker,[38] provisions not calculated to enhance labour mobility or to increase the African employee's bargaining power.

Comparing the pre-Apartheid with the post-Apartheid era of the South African colour bar, Doxey argues:

the history of labour legislation thus shows in the beginning a desire to prevent whites from falling below a *white survival line*, measured out by 'civilized standards', gradually giving way to a more negative desire to prevent non-white encroachment above what may be regarded as a *white supremacy line* dictated by traditional prejudice.[39]

Although it is rare for legislation to reflect or mould social practice exactly, there is usually some correspondence between the two. Thus the typical pattern of industry under Apartheid[40] was the result of a policy of centrally inspired discrimination co-existing with some local deviations;[41] informal breaches of formal bureaucratic rules being an essential feature of the efficient working of social institutions.[42]

It was only after the second Race Relations Act (1968) that the reverse situation prevailed in Britain, with locally-inspired discrimination clashing with centralized legal condemnation of such practices. Before this Act, in contrast with the position in South Africa, there was no legislative framework within which to consider the interaction of British race and industrial relations. However, this is not to deny the extent of prejudice and discrimination in industry during the post-war period, of which there was irrefutable evidence.[43]

[38] Specific details of some of these laws are discussed in J. Stone, 'Some Sociological Aspects of the Integration of British Immigrants in South Africa', unpublished D.Phil. Thesis, University of Oxford (1969), pp. 178–9.

[39] G. V. Doxey, *The Industrial Colour Bar in South Africa*, pp. 114–15.

[40] For a study of the work situation of a Johannesburg bus company, see K. G. Hahlo 'A European–African Worker relationship in South Africa', *Race*, 11, no. 1 (1969), 13–35; see also S. T. van der Horst, *The African Factory Worker in Cape Town*, and *The African Factory Worker* (Oxford University Press, Cape Town, 1950), for an earlier study in Durban.

[41] Cf. with Hepple's distinction between 'internal' and 'external' rules in *Race, Jobs and the Law* (1968).

[42] For an extreme example, see Gresham Sykes, *Society of Captives* (Princeton University Press, Princeton, 1958).

[43] S. Patterson, *Dark Strangers*, and *Immigrants in Industry*, refer to field work undertaken in the 1950s. See also the articles: L. Stephens, 'The Employment of

This was an era of transition: the 'dark strangers' of the 1950s had yet to become the 'black British' of the 1970s, and differences of academic interpretation reflected this situation.[44] Some specialists in the field of race relations stressed what they considered to be evidence of widespread colour prejudice,[45] while others preferred to relate discriminatory behaviour either to a 'stranger' hypothesis or to an 'immigrant-host' framework,[46] placing much greater emphasis on the structure of situations than on personality variables. This divergence of views raises important general issues[47] and, as far as industrial relations are concerned, poses the central enigma: what component of discrimination is attributable to 'colour' as distinct from other essentially transitional factors like deficiencies in the immigrants' education, skills, or cultural adjustment compared with the work force of the host population? The crucial limitation of several of these studies is their over-reliance on *ex-parte* evidence, the opinions of white workers and white management,[48] in addition to their inability to disentangle the twisted threads of multi-variate causation.[49]

The relative prosperity of the 1950s resulted in the rapid integration of the coloured worker into the lower echelons of certain British industries and certain types of occupation, usually those shunned by native fellow-workers on account of poor working conditions, low

Coloured Workers in the Birmingham Area', *Institute to Personnel Management Occasional Paper* (1956), and J. Reid, 'Employment of Negroes in Manchester', *The Sociological Review*, 4, no. 2 (1956), and the familiar case studies of Richmond, Banton, and Collins.

[44] Cf. P. L. Wright, *The Coloured Worker in British Industry* (1968), pp. 19–30.

[45] A. H. Richmond, *Colour Prejudice in Britain: a study of West Indian workers in Liverpool, 1942–51*, pp. 40, 170.

[46] M. Banton, *The Coloured Quarter*; S. Patterson, *Dark Strangers*.

[47] Cf. 'A Note on Visibility, Antipathy and Pluralism' in J. Stone, op. cit., pp. 237–44.

[48] D. Nandy, 'Coloured and Immigrant', *New Society*, 19 Dec. 1968, pp. 924–5.

[49] For a quantitative attempt to isolate the importance of 'colour' as a factor causing deprivation for the American Negro, as opposed to the role of education, housing, and income deprivation, by means of multiple regression analysis, see O. D. Duncan and P. M. Blau in a paper presented at Nuffield College, Oxford (1969).

In Britain the P.E.P. report has helped to clarify the position by using a 'matched sample' testing procedure, thus providing the first irrefutable evidence of widespread colour discrimination in employment, housing and insurance: P.E.P., *Racial Discrimination* (1967), and W. W. Daniel, *Racial Discrimination in England* (1968).

pay, and inferior prospects.[50] While no legal colour bar impeded the occupational mobility of these workers and their British-born children, the experience of the 1960s suggested that a mental colour bar, in the minds of white employers and white workers, might reproduce by convention a pattern that in South Africa is sanctified by law. Evidence about future trends and the long-run prospects of industrial integration is as yet inconclusive.[51] However, the balance of opinion could be described as qualified pessimism which recognizes that the forces of inertia, unless vigorously resisted, will condemn the coloured worker to be the 'second class citizen of the industrial world'.[52] In this respect, the British nightmare begins to resemble the South African dream.

The comparative role of trade unions in the two countries must be assessed in order to complete the picture of employment.[53] We have already mentioned the political influence of white South African unions in securing the enactment of the 'civilized labour' policies of the 1930s. Neither movement has accepted a monolithic commitment to racial segregation or to the alternative of non-racial integration. In Britain it was possible to contrast the leadership of Frank Cousins, who on retirement from the T.G.W.U. accepted the chairmanship of the Community Relations Commission, with the more suspicious attitude of William Carron.[54] In South Africa the non-racialism of Solly Sachs[55] makes a more extreme contrast with the segregationalist leaders, D. E. Ellis and Jan Glesiner who, with

[50] P. L. Wright, *The Coloured Worker in British Industry*, p. 219.
[51] Cf. R. B. Davison, *Black British* (1966), p. 81; S. Patterson (1963), (1968) op. cit.; B. Cohen in E. J. B. Rose, *et al. Colour and Citizenship*, pp. 149–81, 296–329; B. Cohen and P. Jenner 'The Employment of Immigrants: a case study within the wool industry', *Race*, 10, no. 1 (1968), 41–55; P.E.P., *Racial Discrimination* (1967), p. 57; B. Hepple, 'The Donovan Report and Race Relations', *I.R.R. Newsletter* (Oct. 1968), 380–2; R. Jowell and P. Prescott-Clarke, 'Racial Discrimination and White-Collar workers in Britain, *Race*, 11, no. 4 (1970) 398–417.
[52] P. L. Wright, op. cit., p. 212.
[53] For brief summaries of the development of South African trade unions, see I. Davies, *African Trade Unions* (1966), pp. 53–70; M. Horrell, *Racialism and the Trade Unions* (1959); E. H. Brookes, *Apartheid*, pp. 112–16; B. Bunting, *The Rise of the South African Reich* (Penguin, Harmondsworth, 1964), pp. 252–78. For 'black' trade unions in the two countries, see S. W. Johns III, 'The Birth of Non-White Trade Unionism in South Africa', *Race*, 9, no. 2 (1967), 173–91; DeWitt John, *Indian Worker's Associations in Britain* (1969).
[54] *Colour and Citizenship*, pp. 116–17; J. Rex, *Labour's Last Chance* (1968), p. 80.
[55] E. S. Sachs, *Rebel Daughters* (1957).

the help of the Nationalist-backed 'reformers', successfully took over the Mineworkers' Union in 1947–8.

During the Depression years, Little assessed the British attitude towards coloured workers as follows:

they were looked upon by the white unions not as a section of the same labouring class striving for a livelihood on exactly the same basis as any other union member, but as the representatives of an altogether different and competitive category, which directly was responsible for keeping white seamen out of work, and forcing down their standard of living.[56]

In the eyes of the rank and file trade unionist a black face and a black-leg were synonymous. The relative prosperity of the fifties[57] and sixties helped to ease relations between unions and coloured workers, although trade union policy often revealed the ambivalence of the ordinary worker 'intensified almost to the point of schizophrenia'.[58] British trade unionists have yet to echo that clarion call of segregationist socialism: 'Workers of the World unite and fight for a White South Africa', the motives of Enoch Powell's dockers being the nearest expression of that sentiment. Nevertheless, there is clear evidence to suggest that many unions are not working to colour-blind rules.[59] While at the national level the T.U.C. and most individual unions have unequivocally condemned any form of industrial colour bar, local practice has often fallen short of these ideals.[60] It would be wrong, however, to exaggerate the rigidity of the situation, and one American research worker discovered, instead of an anticipated picture drawn in black and white, a scene 'painted with a most varied palette . . .'[61]

Modern South African trade unionism reveals a more clear-cut situation. In the 1960s there were four co-ordinating trade union bodies:[62] the South African Confederation of Labour, a right-wing, exclusively white organization with 190,000 members; the Trade

[56] K. Little, *Negroes in Britain* (1947), p. 61.
[57] M. Banton, *White and Coloured* (1959), pp. 165–9.
[58] S. Patterson, *Dark Strangers* (1965), pp. 142–51.
[59] C.A.R.D., *Memorandum of evidence presented to the Royal Commission on Trade Unions and Employer's Associations* (1967); W. W. Daniel, *Racial Discrimination in England* (1968), pp. 132–40.
[60] I.R.R., *Coloured Immigrants in Britain* (1960), pp. 139–46. P. Marsh *The Anatomy of a Strike: Unions, Employers, and Punjabi Workers in a Southall Factory* (1967).
[61] B. Radin, 'Coloured Workers and the British Trade Unions', *Race*, 8, no. 2 (1966), 173.
[62] M. Horrell, *A Survey of Race Relations in South Africa* (1965).

Union Council of South Africa, with a similar sized membership of whom 20 per cent were non-whites; and two much smaller, largely African bodies, the one losing membership to T.U.C.S.A., and the other continually harassed by the security police because of its left-wing political affiliations. An attempt by the Trade Union Council to attract more African unions led to a confrontation with the Minister of Labour, Marais Viljoen, who threatened to cancel the Council's registration. Although the general secretary, Arthur Grobbelaar, received a convincing mandate to proceed with the policy at T.U.C.S.A.'s Cape Town conference in April 1968, it seemed doubtful whether a disunited labour movement would be able to resist concerted government pressure.

The Apartheid concept of industrial relations does not envisage the separate development of African trade unions,[63] it prefers the much more amenable 'works committees' laid down by the Native Labour (Settlement of Disputes) Act of 1953. White trade unionists seem to be polarizing into two camps: those who adhere to a rigid segregation of white and black in the labour force, being predominantly, though not exclusively, Afrikaners working in government employment or on the mines;[64] and those who feel that their security rests on maintaining 'the rate for the job', rather than consigning workers to what economists call 'non-competing' groups.

(ii) *Housing—locations and ghettoes*

At times of full employment it is housing, as much as industrial relations, that is the key factor determining harmonious or hostile race relations. It is not difficult to see why this is so, since where a person lives affects a wider and more diffuse set of social relationships than the more strictly defined, categorical contacts of the work place.

The origins of the modern South African pattern of residential segregation are regarded, conventionally, as a development of the 'Stallard doctrine', enunciated in the *Report of the Transvaal Local Government Commission* of 1922 and embodied in the Native (Urban Areas) Act of 1923.[65] As Davenport bluntly states: 'Most white

[63] S. Uys, 'Now Bantustan Trade Unions?', *Sunday Times* (S.A.), 5 May 1968.
[64] M. Horrell, *A Survey of Race Relations in South Africa* (1966), p. 2.
[65] E. Hellmann, 'The Application of the Concept of Separate Development to Urban Areas in the Union of South Africa' in K. Kirkwood (ed.), *St. Antony's Papers*, no. 10 (1961), pp. 120–46; R. Davenport 'African Townsmen: South African Natives (Urban Areas) legislation through the years', *African Affairs*,

South Africans look upon their towns as places where white people live in by right and black people work in on sufferance.'[66] The 1923 Act established the 'locations' policy which, in conjunction with 'influx control' developed under the Native Laws Amendment Act (1937), set up the legislative corner-stones of the migrant labour policy on which the edifice of residential and territorial segregation rests. Though the United Party began to have second thoughts about the industrial rationality of migrant labour in the 1940s, following the findings of the Smit (1942) and Fagan (1948) reports, the Nationalists had no such reservations. Far from dismantling the existing framework, they tried to build a dam to stem the swelling flood of Africans into the pool of a permanent urban proletariat.

The Group Areas Act (1950),[67] with its subsequent amendments, forms an important part of this attempt to unscramble the trend towards mixed ownership and occupation which was a result of rapid urbanization. This was achieved by designating certain areas as the exclusive property of one 'racial' group. As the power to administer the Act rested in the hands of the white group alone, it was not difficult to predict the consequences. Senator Brookes's claim that the Bill was 'compulsory segregation administered by one race'[68] acquired adequate confirmation in the experience of the Indian traders of Natal and the Coloured community of the Cape Peninsula.[69]

While the Group Areas Acts attempted to strengthen segregation in the towns and cities, the Urban Areas Acts aimed at reducing the number of Africans in the locations to the minimum requirements of industrial efficiency and domestic comfort.[70] Limits were set on the

---

68, no. 271 (1969), 95–109. Of course, these dates are somewhat arbitrary. See M. W. Swanson 'Urban Origins of Separate Development', *Race*, 10, no. 1 (1968), 31–40.

[66] R. Davenport (1969), op. cit., p. 95.

[67] K. Kirkwood, *The Group Areas Act* (1951); M. Horrell, *Group Areas Acts* (1966); E. H. Brookes, *Apartheid* (1968), pp. 131–78; L. Kuper, H. Watts, and R. Davies, *Durban: a study in racial ecology* (1958).

[68] E. H. Brookes (1968), op. cit., p. 161.

[69] The implementation of this Act has been a long and complex process. In January 1969 the famous Coloured Quarter of Cape Town, District 6, was declared a white group area, *Cape Times*, 10 Jan. 1969.

[70] 'Influx control' and the 'endorsing out' of surplus labour to often mythical 'homelands' has been a subject of much criticism: cf. the 1967 'Presidential Address to the Black Sash', *Rand Daily Mail*, 17 Oct. 1967; and the 1969 'Limehill' affair, *The Star*, Mar. 1969.

number of Africans allowed to reside in an urban building, so reducing the inhabitants of the 'locations-in-the-sky', servants lodging in the tops of blocks of flats. In a similar vein, the immensely complicated Bantu Laws Amendment Act of 1964[71] contained, among a welter of other provisions, clauses to limit the housing of domestic servants on private premises and the eventual elimination of permanently based servants in flats. The over-all effect of this legislation on the structure of inter-racial housing is clear; separation must be enforced where breaches in customary segregation have arisen. According to the Apartheid blueprint, the urban African must be contained within the locations, which are not to be regarded as the urban equivalent of the rural Bantustans,[72] but as the temporary resting place of a migrant labour force, a regrettable, yet unavoidable, appendage to the white economy.

There has been no equivalent statutory barrier to determine rigidly the location of coloured residents in Britain, yet the existence of informal colour discrimination is so widely documented as to be beyond dispute.[73] In the early 1950s, it was noted that a 'colour tax'[74] was levied on black students who applied for lodgings in the private market and this has been held to measure 'social disapproval in material terms'.[75] But at least coloured students were able to find accommodation, albeit on discriminatory terms, while coloured workers arriving in the late 1950s and 1960s were faced with difficulties on an altogether different scale. Confronted by a housing situation characterized by 'private sickness and public health'[76]— Galbraith's syndrome in reverse—rebuffed by 'massive discrimination in private letting based solely upon colour', and excluded from council housing by residence qualifications and discriminatory redevelopment schemes,[77] they found themselves forced into the multiple

[71] R. Horwitz (1967), op. cit., pp. 401–8.

[72] G. Carter, T. G. Karis, and N. Stultz *South Africa's Transkei: the politics of domestic colonialism* (1967), pp. 46–69.

[73] See esp., P.E.P. *Racial Discrimination* (1967), pp. 69–99.

[74] A. T. Carey, *Colonial Students* (1956).

[75] M. Banton, *White and Coloured* (1959), p. 47. Burney writes: 'territorial apartheid does not have the force of law and, therefore, can exist only by the limited and inefficient means of social sanctions. These can nevertheless be strong, and carry economic force.' E. Burney, *Housing on Trial* (1967), p. 38.

[76] At least in the rented sector, see Burney (1967), op. cit., chapter 1.

[77] W. W. Daniel, *Racial Discrimination in England* (1968), pp. 164, 180–1; J. Rex and R. Moore, *Race, Community and Conflict* (1967), p. 27.

occupation of lodging-houses in the 'twilight zones'.[78] The slum landlords, predominantly immigrants themselves, were making an 'innovatory' adaptation to a situation where 'colour rather than foreignness'[79] held the key to the door of rented accommodation. Referring sarcastically to the situation prevailing before the passage of the 1968 Race Relations Act, Daniel commented: '"No Coloureds"; "Sorry, no coloureds"; "Europeans only". Such stipulations vie in frequency with "no animals" or "no pets" on cards advertising rented accommodation in newsagents' windows.'[80]

Many immigrants who tried to push their heads out of the twilight zones, having overcome the discrimination of building societies and estate agents,[81] found themselves promptly strangled in the 'suburban noose'. Prospective sellers, fearful of the reaction of neighbours who believed that the advent of coloured householders would herald an automatic fall in values and status, refused to consider coloured purchasers.[82] An analysis of census data for London and the West Midlands between 1961 and 1966 revealed that the 'normal' pattern of suburbanization was being distorted.[83] This was a result both of the private discrimination mentioned earlier, and of the reluctance of local authorities to carry out slum clearance programmes where they involved an obligation to resettle large numbers of coloured tenants. In this manner the process of redevelopment will have the effect of stranding coloured populations between the centres of cities and the suburbs.[84]

While the housing situation in Britain has not the finality of South Africa's 'Group Areas', its trend has been towards the American

[78] Defined by Rex and Moore as 'those areas approaching, but have not yet reached the night of slumdom' (op. cit. p. 29). For criticisms of Rex and Moore, see V. Karn, 'A Note on "Race, Community and Conflict"', *Race*, 10, no. 1 (1967), 101–4; A. H. Richmond, 'Housing and Racial Attitudes in Bristol', *Race*, 12, no. 1 (1970), 49–58; R. H. Ward 'Discrimination, the Market and the Ethnic Colony', Paper delivered to the British Sociological Association, 28 Mar. 1969.

[79] W. W. Daniel (1968), op. cit., p. 163.

[80] Ibid., p. 154.

[81] Ibid., pp. 170–6.

[82] V. Karn illustrates the true complexity of the situation in 'Property Values amongst Indians and Pakistanis in a Yorkshire Town', *Race*, 10, no. 3 (1969), 269–84.

[83] Regional variations are important: E. Burney (1967), op. cit., and E. J. B. Rose *et al.*, *Colour and Citizenship* (1969), pp. 125, 252–6.

[84] E. Burney (1967), op. cit., p. 178.

pattern of incipient ghetto formation.[85] Even a basically optimistic observer like Patterson writes:

> ... but a coloured ghetto is also likely to be self-perpetuating because of its high visibility.[86] Long after Polish, Italian and Jewish ghettos have blurred and merged in the rest of the city, a coloured ghetto can remain, not as an area where temporary migrants or people of a different sub-culture prefer to live, but as a depressed area regarded by the majority of society as suitable for people who, however much they may have come to share the same living patterns and cultural values, are still visibly different and socially unacceptable to that society.[87]

Evidence from the experience of the children of earlier coloured immigrants confirms this assessment: the second and third generations are still confined to quasi-ghettos and denied the opportunities available to white, English-speaking immigrants.[88] Whether the provisions of the 1968 Race Relations Act can be implemented in private and public housing so as to reverse this trend, reducing concentrations of coloured immigrants to communities of choice rather than ghettos of necessity, will depend both on government policy and on the state of the housing market. Each step in this direction will represent a movement away from the situation prevailing in Southern Africa, for if a permanent breach can be driven through the wall of housing discrimination, this may be seen as a valid index of the first stage of the integration of coloured people into the total fabric of British society.

b: POLITICS AND RACE RELATIONS

All politics are the 'politics of inequality',[89] yet not all inequality is characterized by politics. When Gwendolen Carter described the first decade of post-war Nationalist rule in these terms she was

[85] Cf. M. Deutsch and M. E. Collins, *Interracial Housing* (1951); S. Lieberson, 'Suburbs and Ethnic Residential Patterns', *A.J.S.* (1962), 673–81; K. E. and A. F. Taeuber, *Negroes in Cities: residential segregation and neighbourhood change* (1965); *Report of the National Advisory Commission on Civil Disorder* (1968).
[86] Cf. A. Antonovsky in *Mass Society in Crisis* (1964), p. 410; T. Parsons, *The Social System* (1951), p. 172, n. 8; G. Myrdal, *An American Dilemma* (1944), p. 601.
[87] S. Patterson, *Dark Strangers* (1965), p. 195; E. Burney (1967), op. cit., pp. 110–46.
[88] E. J. B. Rose, *Colour and Citizenship* (1969), p. 489.
[89] G. Carter, *The Politics of Inequality* (1959).

referring to a situation in which 'politics',[90] largely restricted to the white minority,[91] was crucially influenced by the overwhelming inequality in the wider society. She was not referring to politics polarized on the fundamental divisions between rich and poor, or even between black and white. By the end of the second decade of Nationalist rule, political 'debate' took the form of a monologue about race relations, not a dialogue between different races. Bantu Affairs, like their predecessor Native Affairs, were a subject of administration rather than discussion, there being no meaningful discourse across the colour line. The objection may be raised that political aspiration is a hydra-headed creature and that the unintended consequences of the Bantustans[92] will result in the re-emergence of the phoenix of African political power from the ashes of government political suppression. But this is to anticipate the remote future, unlike such concrete measures as the Unlawful Organizations Act (1960) or the Prohibition of Improper Interference Act (1968) which serve as a more eloquent testimony to the practice of separate political development than to the practical development of separate political power.

In a curious way, the political discussion about race relations in both countries has often been on a bi-partisan basis. Nicholas Deakin argues that it is not true that there was no official British policy towards immigration and race prior to the 1960s:

. . . both the policies and the practices of the earlier period have been almost entirely covered by the detritus of succeeding epochs, and patient archaeological work is required to uncover the remnants of the structures constructed to deal with what was seen as an incipient problem of some importance.[93]

However, different stances on the subject were far from co-terminous with party divisions. There was to be much more acrimonious debate

[90] For a discussion of the nature of 'political' rule, see B. Crick, *In Defence of Politics* (1964); some African attempts to develop and mobilize political forces are described in L. Kuper, *Passive Resistance in South Africa* (1957); E. Feit, *South Africa: the dynamics of the African National Congress* (1962); M. Benson, *The African Patriots* (1963).

[91] In this context, 'politics' refer to 'legitimate' power struggles *under South African law*. As with Max Weber's definition of authority, the term legitimacy is somewhat ambiguous. It is reminiscent of Harrington's epigram 'treason doth never prosper . . .', and raises the same problems as the teleological implications of functionalist terminology.

[92] Cf. C. R. Hill, *Bantustans: the fragmentation of South Africa* (1964).

[93] *Colour and Citizenship* (1969), p. 207.

surrounding post-war decolonization:[94] Party politics on race were to be fought on foreign fields, the domestic front remaining comparatively quiet until the racist alarms of the 1960s shattered the comfortable consensus of liberal *laissez-faire*.

The political basis of South African race relations has its origins in the earliest years of contact. In the twentieth century, the first crucial turning-point which was to determine, or at least foreshadow, the subsequent course of political events was the terms of settlement of the Act of Union. The 'price of magnanimity' was paid with the franchise of the African voter;[95] had a more parsimonious settlement been reached it might have led to a more generous future. The exclusion of the African from the Union Parliament in 1910, was followed by his exclusion from the common electoral roll in 1936.[96] Smuts, like Campbell-Bannerman's Liberals before him, was prepared to meet the cost of coalition with stolen coin,[97] and as a result a bipartisan policy towards the 'native' was secured once again. Only a few politicians, men like Schreiner, Merriman, and in later years perhaps Hofmeyr, had the insight to foresee the future harvest from this seed-time of disinheritance, but they were regarded as little more than an eccentric minority. The attitude of the majority was well captured by Agar-Hamilton:

... to this day the usual answer of the South African to the problem of the political rights of the native races is to picture the conjunction of the ballot box with the savage from the kraal in all the panoply of his ceremonial dress. The contrast appeals to him as essentially ludicrous.[98]

Even the eloquence and dedication of the 'native representatives', Mrs. Ballinger, Rheinallt-Jones, and Edgar Brookes, could not substitute for the lack of African Members of Parliament elected by African voters on a common roll. The last vestige of African political representation was swept away by the Promotion of Bantu Self-

---

[94] Deakin rightly stresses the link between external decolonization and attitudes towards immigration control in *Colour and Citizenship*, p. 216. In the historical studies it will be shown that the same decolonization was an important factor in changing the Nationalists' aversion to British immigrants.

[95] N. Mansergh, *South Africa 1910–1961—the price of magnanimity* (1961); cf. G. B. Pyrah *Imperial Policy and South Africa, 1902–10* (1955), p. 137; W. K. Hancock, *Smuts: the Sanguine Years, 1870–1919* (1962), p. 218.

[96] The Representation of Natives Act No. 12 (1936).

[97] Cf. Deakin's comment on the 1968 amendment to the Commonwealth Immigration Act: 'the price of progress was once again calculated to be concessions to the unappeasable', in *Colour and Citizenship* (1969), p. 549.

[98] J. A. I. Agar-Hamilton, *The Native Policy of the Voortrekkers* (1928), p. 89.

Government Act (1959),[99] in exchange for certain tribal rights: the white man's concept of the African voter had not changed significantly in thirty years.

The Indians' taste of Parliamentary representation was far more fleeting. As a *quid pro quo* for restrictions on land purchase, resulting from legislation in 1946,[100] they had been offered a limited communal franchise in Parliament and the Natal Provincial Council. This they boycotted as inadequate compensation and found it removed with consummate haste when the incoming Nationalists introduced the Asiatic Law Amendments Act in 1948. Once again, the Indians were cast back into political limbo as 'unassimilable aliens'.

The completion of untainted white political control merely required the removal of the Coloured franchise from the Cape common roll.[101] In the event, this proved to be a controversial and protracted struggle. No amount of political manoeuvring could get the Separate Representation of Voters Bill (1951) passed by the required majority in both Houses. Finally in 1956 the Government 'enlarged' the Senate and were then able to sidestep the two-thirds majority rule entrenched in the South Africa Act.

By the year of the declaration of the Republic, 1961, the non-white voter had virtually ceased to have any influence on the central citadel of political power. The process of disenfranchisement reached its culmination in the Prohibition of Improper Interference Act of 1968, the very apotheosis of political apartheid. Its almost farcical provisions led to the disbandment of the multi-racial Liberal Party and prevented the Progressive Party's bid to extend its Parliamentary representation through an appeal to the Coloureds' communal franchise.

One reason for the breakdown of the bi-partisan front over the question of the Coloureds' franchise was the growing realization that the prize of a white monopoly of power was being bought at the expense of civil liberties,[102] and not just those of the non-whites. Newell Stultz's claim that there was a *qualitative* change in politics after 1961, so that the first five years of the Republic under Verwoerd

[99] E. H. Brookes, *Apartheid* (1968), pp. 126–7.
[100] The Asiatic Land Tenure and Indian Representation Act No. 28 (1946).
[101] H. M. Robertson, *South Africa: Economic and Political Aspects* (1957), pp. 68–119; E. A. Walker, *A History of Southern Africa* (1957), chap. 17.
[102] Leo Marquard writes: 'this mass demonstration was a protest, not against the removal of the Coloured voter from the common roll, but against the threat to the Constitution', *The Peoples and Policies of South Africa* (1962), p. 92.

heralded a new era of the 'politics of security',[103] suggests a misleading discontinuity in recent South African history. Each one of Stultz's 'new' end-values—white unity, anti-Communism, government firmness, and the increasingly hierarchical structure of political authority—evolved as much in the fifties as in the sixties.[104] Without denying the emotional significance of the events of 1961 to Nationalist Afrikanerdom, there is no need to regard the declaration of a Republic as a watershed of mythological proportions. If it signified anything, it was the confirmation of the power structure of the previous decade, rather than the beginnings of a radical new political realignment in the succeeding decade. In spite of this, Stultz's conclusion concerning the relative stability of the present South African political structure, agrees with our analysis in the previous chapter. He concludes that:

. . . stimulated by a continuing, if thus far unavailing challenge to the effectiveness of the régime, and remaining conservative rather than revolutionary in its purpose, the South African 'politics of security' does not exhibit the internal contradictions which Apter believes are characteristic of the 'mobilization system' to which otherwise it bears a likeness.[105]

Thus by 1970 the politics of race in South Africa had followed that part of the apartheid policy which decreed 'separation'; that part which professed 'development' had the election of Chief Matanzima as its lone witness.

I mentioned earlier that there was a certain similarity of response in the manner in which the major political parties of each country reacted to the problems of race relations. Frequently they were regarded as issues that transcended normal political debate and could

[103] N. W. Stultz, 'The Politics of Security: South Africa under Verwoerd' 1961–6', *Journal of Modern African Studies*, 7, no. 1 (1969), 6–20.

[104] To expand my criticism of Stultz on three points:
(a) Surely the bogey of communism was prominent as early as the 1950 Suppression of Communism Act?
(b) A close examination of the new immigration policy would suggest that the Ministers concerned were embarrassingly aware of the 'dangers' of immigration for the Afrikaner's culture, way of life, and political hegemony. Should any of these be seriously threatened, it will be white strength rather than Afrikaner nationalism that will take second place.
(c) While citing the case of the bi-lingual University of Port Elizabeth (1964) as a symbol of 'white unity', he fails to mention the establishment of the Rand Afrikaans University, as a separate entity, across the road from the University of the Witwatersrand, in 1966. Perhaps the promotion of bilingualism in Port Elizabeth has a greater appeal to the Nationalist government than the exposure of Afrikaner youth to the liberalism or 'Wits'.

[105] N. W. Stultz (1969), op. cit., pp. 19–20.

be resolved best by mutual consent. However, a bi-partisan posture was by no means rigid, particularly when the jumps and bends of the apartheid programme began to affect the 'politics of culture' as well as the 'politics of colour'.[106] At Westminster,[107] a high degree of front-bench consensus reigned during both the 'welfare period' (1945–55) and the 'status period' (1956–61),[108] though back-benchers like Cyril Osborne and Fenner Brockway argued for a more positive approach, the former for immigration controls, the latter for a law against the incitement to racial hatred. Ironically, both these members saw their plans accepted by both parties, translated into legislative action, and even extolled as mutually compatible.[109]

At this time back-bench opinion was not sharply divided and it was a Labour member who first pressed for the control of Commonwealth immigrants.[110] This was not surprising for the arrival of coloured immigrants in the poorer parts of urban areas had a more than proportionate impact on Labour-held seats. Only the 'riots' at Notting Hill and Nottingham during 1958 disturbed the surface tranquillity but, unlike the shootings at Sharpeville and Langa two years later, they were not followed by any immediate repercussions. At the turn of the decade, increased pressure on the Home Secretary to introduce controls was given added impetus by the sharp rise in the number of new immigrants from the West Indies and by the ineffectiveness of the bi-lateral voluntary restrictions agreed with India and Pakistan.

As the South African Government withdrew into Republican

[106] Cf. W. K. Hancock, *Are There South Africans?* Hoernle Memorial Lecture (1966).

[107] For the best summaries of the politics of race relations in Britain, see Nicholas Deakin's chapters in *Colour and Citizenship* (1969), esp. pp. 199–232, 492–551, and 605–29; P. Foot, *Immigration and Race in British Politics* (1965); on the 1964 General Election, see D. E. Butler and A. King, *The British General Election of 1964* (1965), App. 3 by A. W. Singham, pp. 360–8; and N. Deakin (ed.), *Colour and the British Electorate 1964* (1965). On the 1966 Election, see D. E. Butler and A. King, *The British General Election of 1966* (1966); N. Deakin, D. Lawrence, J. Silver and M. J. Lelohe, 'Colour and the 1966 General Election', *Race* 8, no. 1 (1966), 17–42. In local politics, see M. J. Lelohe and A. R. Goldman, 'Race in Local Politics: the Rochdale Central Ward Election of 1968', *Race*, 10, no. 4 (1969), 435–47, and for Wolverhampton, see *Race, the Politicians and Public Opinion—a preliminary case study*, N. Deakin mimeo., paper presented at the B.S.A. Conference, 26 Mar. 1969.

[108] E. J. B. Rose, *et al.*, *Colour and Citizenship* (1969), p. 210.

[109] Cf. Hattersley's syllogism: 'without integration, limitation is inexcusable; without limitation, integration is impossible', ibid., p. 229.

[110] That there is no necessary link between party support and racialism has been recognized for some time. See J. H. Robb, '*Working-Class Anti-Semite*' (1955), p. 164, n. 2. N. Deakin, *Colour and the British Electorate 1964* (1965), p. 3.

isolation and took its leave of the multi-racial Commonwealth, so the British Government, by introducing the Commonwealth Immigrants Bill (1961–2), withdrew into its own form of isolation and took leave of a non-racial immigration policy. There can be no doubt that the purpose of the Bill was to check the flow of *coloured* Commonwealth immigrants, for if numbers had been the sole criterion much greater concern would have been shown about the alien Irish and the white Commonwealth citizens who entered the country as 'visitors' and then obtained employment without labour permits. *The Economist* was to comment on the subsequent working of the Act: 'The truth is to be found in Earls Court. Many Australian and New Zealand girls come to Britain to play, and stay to work. Good luck to them—but their presence proves that Britain's bar on immigration is a colour bar.'[111]

The 1964 election, despite the deviant case of Smethwick,[112] was not affected significantly by the factor of colour. Although a sample survey of electors in Brixton claimed that 'immigration' was a more strongly felt issue than pensions, housing, or education, it seemed to have little effect on political attitudes, resulting in a 'low political visibility of coloured immigration as an issue'.[113] While in Bradford it was found that party allegiance made no difference to voters' attitudes on immigrant participation in politics,[114] in the Labour stronghold of Deptford the general rule was confirmed that the parties were still strong enough to prevent the widespread popular hostility towards immigrants and immigration irrupting directly into the political arena.[115] Most politicians were loath to use the immigration issue, and prominent Conservatives like Sir Edward Boyle and Enoch Powell refused to speak in support of the racist campaign being waged at their neighbouring constituency of Smethwick.[116]

Thus 'colour' failed to have a direct impact on the election because it had not become fully articulated into the political system, either in the form of an immigrant 'vote', to be bargained for American-style, or by one major party adopting an overtly anti-immigrant platform.

[111] *The Economist*, 27 May 1967.
[112] P. Foot, *Immigration and Race in British Politics* (1965), pp. 9–79.
[113] N. Deakin (ed.), *Colour and the British Electorate 1964* (1965), p. 17.
[114] Ibid., p. 146.
[115] Ibid., p. 119.
[116] D. E. Butler and A. King, *The British General Election of 1964* (1965), p. 365.

Nevertheless, the shadow of Smethwick was sufficiently dark, and the Labour majority sufficiently precarious, to push government policy firmly in the direction of tighter restrictions. In 1965, as in 1968, the White Paper,[117] drastically cutting labour vouchers to a mere 8,500 a year (of which 1,000 were reserved for the Maltese), and the Race Relations Act,[118] outlawing discrimination in places of public resort and the incitement to racial hatred, represented the coalescence of the divergent streams of thought championed during the fifties by Cyril Osborne and Fenner Brockway.

The 1966 General Election seemed to dispel the 'penumbra of neurotic anxiety that the issue of immigration had cast since Mr. Peter Griffiths' victory at Smethwick in 1964'.[119] Seats significantly affected by immigration recorded a higher swing to Labour than the national average.[120] The Government's White Paper and the Conservative leadership's refusal to exploit the issue during the campaign ensured that consensus reigned supreme.[121] The Wilson Administration's second term of office was marked by the same combination of tighter controls balanced by further attempts at promoting integration. British citizens, who happened to be Asians living in Kenya, found their right of entry removed under the 1968 Amendment to the Commonwealth Immigration Act,[122] while the second Race Relations Act (1968)[123] outlawed discrimination in housing and employment. An embryonic 'urban programme' was inaugurated to funnel resources into regions of acute social deprivation where the largest concentrations of coloured immigrants were to be found.

The year 1968 also marked another development in the politics of British race relations. The Walsall, Birmingham, and Eastbourne speeches of Enoch Powell[124] were important because they represented the first attempt by a major politician, since Oswald Mosley, to reproduce at the national level that which Peter Griffiths had achieved at the local level. By raising the level of racist debate, albeit embellished

---

[117] Cmd. 2739 August (1965).

[118] Cf. *Hansard*, 3 May 1965.

[119] N. Deakin, *et al.*, 'Colour and the 1966 General Election', *Race*, 8, no. 1 (1966), 18.

[120] Ibid., p. 17.

[121] Ibid., p. 20.

[122] D. Steel, *No Entry: the background and implication of the Commonwealth Immigrants Act 1968* (1969).

[123] Cf. *Colour and Citizenship* (1969), pp. 511–49; L. Kushnick, 'The Race Bill Battle', *New Society*, 27 June 1968.

[124] B. Smithies and P. Fiddick, *Enoch Powell on Immigration* (1969).

F

with classical and literary allusions, he effectively legitimized the overt expression of colour prejudice at the highest level of public life.[125] The impunity with which both he and Duncan Sandys—inveighing against 'the breeding of millions of half-caste children [who] . . . will merely produce a generation of misfits . . .'[126]—contravened the incitement clause of the first Race Relations Act, while the Black Power leader, Michael X, was promptly arrested and imprisoned for the reversed brand of racism, shows how a nominally anti-racialist Act was being administered in a blatantly racialist manner. Thus, the situation in Britain at the end of the decade was confused with conflicting forces pulling in opposite directions; in marked contrast to that in South Africa, where the politics of race, along with the economics of race, had been firmly entrenched in an unambiguous legislative framework.

c: SOCIAL INSTITUTIONS AND RACE RELATIONS

(i) *Education:*

The familiar pattern of legislative segregation in South Africa and social segregation in Britain can be seen in the classroom and the university as well as in the polling booth and in Parliament. Education is particularly important in sociology because of its interconnection with the other major social sub-systems;[127] it is a traditional arena of social as well as racial privilege and selection.[128] In spite of the different numerical proportions among the 'races' in the two countries, there is a greater chance of a white and black student meeting in the same institution in the British educational system than in the South African.[129] In the former, a tendency towards segregation is

[125] Cf. J. Rex, *Labour's Last Chance* (1968), p. 75.

[126] *Colour and Citizenship* (1969), p. 544.

[127] T. Parsons, 'The School Class as a Social System', *Harvard Educational Review*, no. 29 (1959), 297–318, stresses the socialization and selection functions.

[128] For the 'class bias' in British education, see A. H. Halsey, J. Floud, and C. A. Anderson, *Education, Economy and Society* (1961); J. W. B. Douglas, *The Home and the School* (1964); B. Jackson and D. Marsden, *Education and the Working Class* (1962); A. Little and J. H. Westergaard, 'Trends of Class Differentials in Educational Opportunity', *B.J.S.* 15, no. 4 (1964), 301–16.

[129] J. Gaitskell in E. J. B. Rose *et al.*, *Colour and Citizenship* (1969), p. 291; however, recent sociometric studies warn us to be cautious in our generalizations (though the Cape Town evidence is atypical): G. Watson, *Passing for White: a study of racial assimilation in a South African school* (1970); S. G. S. Watson and H. Lampkin, 'Race and Socio-economic status as factors in the friendship choices of pupils in a racially heterogeneous South African School', *Race*, 10, no. 2 (1968), 181–4; T. Kawwa, 'Three Sociometric studies of Ethnic Relations in London Schools', ibid., 173–80.

achieved by the complex interaction of socio-cultural deprivation with colour prejudice, in the latter, by legislative decree backed up by social custom.

Although, during the nineteenth century, mixed schooling in the Cape Colony was not uncommon, particularly in the mission schools for Europeans and Coloureds, separation in other parts of South Africa was the rule.[130] This pattern remained and, with the one important exception of the 'open' universities, the focus of educational controversy has been on the content of courses rather than the colour of students. In the white sector, the argument involved the relative merits of dual-medium and single-language schools, and the related debate surrounding Christian National education.[131] In the non-white sector, the sources of conflict are well illustrated by two principal apartheid measures of the 1950s, the Bantu Education Act (1953) and the Extension of University Education Act passed six years later. The architect of the former, Dr. Verwoerd, regarded the transference of control over African education from the Provincial Administration to the Bantu Affairs Department as a necessary step towards the implementation of reforms: 'so that Natives will be taught from childhood to realize that equality with Europeans is not for them. . . . racial relations cannot improve if the wrong type of education is given to Natives.'[132] To one African critic, however, the Act formed the basis of 'education for barbarism'.[133] In essence, it centralized the control of African education by radically reducing the influence of mission schools, greatly increased the use of African languages as a medium of instruction, and raised the proportion of African children attending school but lowered the educational standards, thereby producing a system closely tailored to the apartheid vision of economy and society.

[130] For the classic history of South African education, see E. G. Malherbe, *Education in South Africa, 1652–1922* (1925); for recent developments, see M. Horrell, *Bantu Education* (1964); R. Birley, 'African Education in South Africa', *African Affairs*, 67, no. 267 (1968), 152–8.

[131] L. Marquard, *The Peoples and Policies of South Africa* (1962), p. 211.

[132] A. Hepple, *Verwoerd* (1967), p. 124. This attitude is similar to those of the British upper and middle classes towards the education of the working classes during the eighteenth and much of the nineteenth centuries. Isaac Watts, writing in the 1720s about the role of charity schools, declared that their purpose was to: 'impress upon their tender minds . . . the duties . . . of humility and submission to superiors', quoted in T. Burns and S. B. Saul, *Social Theory and Economic Change* (1967), p. 16.

[133] I. B. Tabata, *Education for Barbarism: Bantu Education in South Africa* (1960).

The Extension of University Education Act of 1959 aimed at removing the few non-white students attending the universities of Cape Town and the Witwatersrand, and as an alternative provided for the foundation of ethnic and tribal colleges. No matter how small the numbers involved, the Nationalist government was aware of the implications of white and non-white meeting in an élite environment of non-racial equality. With very few exceptions such a situation could not arise in the South African educational system of the late 1960s. The 'Mafeje incident' in 1968, where the Minister of Education forced the University of Cape Town to rescind the appointment of an African social anthropologist to a senior lectureship, was a mere tidying up of the principles established earlier.

It was precisely to avoid this pattern of educational segregation that concern began to be shown in British government circles during the sixties.[134] The influx of women and children from non-English-speaking cultures in India and Pakistan—in anticipation of the restrictions imposed by the Commonwealth Immigration Act—and their concentration in limited geographical areas, partly as a result of housing discrimination, had its inevitable reflection in the classroom of the local school. Initially, from 1963 to 1965, the official response was an attempt at dispersal in order to maintain a maximum 30 per cent 'quota' of immigrant to native children.[135] The school's role in the process of integration was defined as a social one, in which immigrant children would be given the maximum opportunity to mix with their English counterparts.[136]

The inadequacy of this simplistic solution was revealed by the example of certain schools, where the importance of teaching English as a second language was shown to be much more significant than the strict adherence to a given quota.[137] By concentrating on the educational needs of children rather than on their colour, the whole problem was gradually subsumed within the wider context of the Plowden Report's 'educational priority areas' and the Government's

[134] E. J. B. Rose et al., *Colour and Citizenship* (1969), pp. 264–96.

[135] Modelled on the American system of 'busing' black children to 'white' schools (rarely the reverse), and aimed at preventing other schools from exceeding the 'tipping point'. Cf. A. L. Stinchcoombe, M. S. McDill, and D. Walker, 'Is there a Racial Tipping Point in Changing Schools?', *Journal of Social Issues*, 25, no. 1 (1969), 127–36.

[136] J. Gaitskell, *Colour and Citizenship* (1969), p. 287.

[137] T. Burgin and P. Edson, *Spring Grove: the education of immigrant children* (1967); *Colour and Citizenship* (1969), p. 292; 'Education and the Immigrants', *N.A.S.* (Apr. 1969).

'urban programme'. Educational deprivation could not be seen in isolation from industrial or housing discrimination,[138] or for that matter unrelated to a common background of working-class deprivation. The same factors tended to retard the academic progress of immigrant children: a pupil's ability was often assessed in the most superficial manner, teachers were not exempt from stereotyped attitudes, and early streaming was particularly detrimental where initial cultural adjustments had to take place.[139] When these disabilities are compounded with the influence of colour prejudice, the prospects of a non-racial system of school education can be seen to depend on the over-all success of integration in other fields and in the wider alleviation of social deprivation. Apart from these school handicaps, race discrimination in the universities was relatively unimportant, for the coloured student, having preceded the main body of coloured workers by more than half a century, had become a familiar part of British academic life.

(ii) *The Family*

Restrictions on intermarriage between black and white have existed in South Africa since the early days of the Dutch settlement in the seventeenth century. A law of 1685 prohibited Europeans from marrying 'freed slaves of full colour', though this did not apply to half-castes.[140] Considerable miscegenation clearly occurred in these early years and produced the present-day Coloured population,[141] although the extent of its subsequent persistence is impossible to determine. At the end of the Anglo-Boer War a Cape law of 1902, which was extended to the other three 'colonies' a year later, laid down severe penalties for prostitution between white women and black men, but not where the colour of the sexes was reversed.[142] It was thus a measure combining both racial and sexual discrimination.

The 'Pact' Government's Immorality Act (1927) prohibited sexual

---

[138] P. M. E. Figueroa, *West Indian School Leavers in London: Prospects and Prejudice*, mimeo. paper to B.S.A. education group, 26 Mar. 1969.

[139] E. Butterworth, 'The Presence of Immigrant Schoolchildren: a study of Leeds', *Race*, 8, no. 3 (1967), 247–62. Cf. B. Jackson, *Streaming: an educational system in miniature* (1964), for a discussion of identical problems from a class perspective.

[140] G. Carter, quoted in E. H. Brookes, *Apartheid* (1968), p. 179; cf. also I. D. MacCrone, *Race Attitudes in South Africa* (1937), pp. 40–6.

[141] P. L. van den Berghe, 'Miscegenation in South Africa', *Cahiers D'Études Africaines*, 4 (1960), 68–84.

[142] J. Lewin, *Politics and Law in South Africa* (1963), p. 87.

intercourse between Europeans and Africans, but it did not apply to intermarriage. This omission was regarded as an urgent task for the Nationalists' post-war apartheid programme, and they set about consolidating the concept of separate development by including both the marital and the sexual spheres. The Prohibition of Mixed Marriages Act (1949) and the amended Immorality Act (1950) outlawed both marriage and extra-marital sexual relations between whites and non-whites.[143]

At the same time that Dr. Donges was applying apartheid to prostitution and marriage, the British Government showed its objection to the mixed marriage of Seretse Khama in neighbouring Bechuanaland. Amid the growing controversy, *Die Burger* noted that while nearly all the whites in Africa would approve of the action taken against the Paramount Chief, an equal percentage in Britain would disapprove, indicating the gulf over racial problems between the British at home and white settlers in Africa.[144] However, such an appraisal would have been incorrect if it implied that there was an absence of strong social and cultural sanctions against violation of the norm of 'racial' endogamy. In his 1956 survey Banton found that at least 45 per cent of his sample 'disapproved' of mixed marriages, while the Gallup polls in 1958 and 1961 showed related figures of 71 per cent and 68 per cent respectively.[145] Patterson's interviews in Brixton gave the impression that the great majority of the local people regarded sexual intercourse between black men and white women as something 'alien and abnormal';[146] a sentiment publicly re-echoed by Duncan Sandys in July 1967. However, taboos on mixed marriages were often shared equally by the immigrant and the host community,[147] but they were particularly important for a group like the West Indians, during the 1950s, which was orientated towards total assimilation. For the process of intermarriage was the only means

---

[143] The Population Registration Act (1950) was an essential prerequisite for enforcing these measures, and was also aimed at preventing Coloureds 'passing' as 'whites'. In deciding borderline cases, it is interesting to note that a social definition of race has been explicitly accepted: one's 'racial' group is decided as much by custom as by colour. Cf. M. Banton, 'Race as a Social Category', *Race*, 8, no. 1 (1966), 7–14.

[144] E. H. Brookes, *Apartheid* (1968), p. 183.

[145] M. Banton, *White and Coloured* (1959), p. 207. S. Patterson, *Dark Strangers* (1965), p. 248; I.R.R., *Coloured Immigrants in Britain* (1960), p. 69.

[146] S. Patterson, *Dark Strangers* (1965), p. 249.

[147] Cf. R. Desai, *Indian Immigrants in Britain* (1963) esp. chap. 8, 'The Deviants: Mixed Marriage and Sex Relations'.

by which a highly visible immigrant group could eventually merge into the host population.[148]

Thus, by the end of the 1960s, the differences between the two countries was as follows: while mixed marriages were tolerated in Britain they certainly carried the stigma of social disapproval, if not outright hostility; in South Africa, at the same time, they were forbidden by law and subject to severe penal sanctions, as was any other sexual excursion across the colour line.

(iii) *Religion*

The first pillar of Anna Steenkamp's vision of the ideal Boer society—that there should be no equality in Church or state between black and white—came to fruition in the Apartheid State.[149] In their turn, many Africans responded by creating Separatist Churches and following Bantu prophets, so that it is no exaggeration to claim that the colour problem 'follows the African up to the gates of heaven'.[150] Sundkler argues that the racial separation of the Churches in South Africa was a direct consequence of segregationalist legislation. Since the Natives' Land Act (1913) each additional measure enforcing segregation has driven a further wedge between black and white co-religionists so that by the late 1940s '"Net vir Blankes—for Europeans only" was figuratively but no less virtually written on many Church doors in the Union'.[151] This customary separation was given legislative support in the 'church clause' of the Native Laws Amendment Act of 1957,[152] which enabled churches to be segregated by Ministerial decree.

Religion has always played an important part in the development of society in Southern Africa. Initially, at the Cape, it was religion rather than race or colour that determined an individual's status in the Dutch settlement.[153] Later the Dutch Reformed Churches distilled from their Calvinist creed[154] a religious sanction for a segregationalist social philosophy. In contrast, many of the missionaries from other Protestant and Catholic Churches developed a more

---

[148] R. B. Davison, *Commonwealth Immigrants* (1964), p. 73; C. R. Hill, *How Colour Prejudiced is Britain?* (1967).

[149] E. A. Walker, *A History of Southern Africa* (1957), p. 199.

[150] B. E. M. Sundkler, *Bantu Prophets in South Africa* (1961), p. 290.

[151] Sundkler, *ibid.*, p. 37; L. Marquand, *The Peoples and Policies of South Africa* (1962), p. 248.

[152] E. H. Brookes, *Apartheid* (1968), pp. 73–85.

[153] I. D. MacCrone, *Race Attitudes in South Africa* (1937), p. 41.

[154] Cf. A. Toynbee, *A Study of History*, 1 (1962), pp. 211–16.

universalistic view of the type of society compatible with Christian teaching. It is tempting to see modern doctrinal differences between the Churches in the same light, though divergent opinions held by Church leaders may not be reflected among their respective congregations. Dr. Albert Hertzog clearly regards those modern religious leaders who have condemned Apartheid as the lineal descendants of Dr. John Philip and the London Missionary Society, but even the Dutch Reformed Church has produced intellectual heretics who question the dogmas of Calvinist Christian political science.[155]

Religion in South Africa has tended to reinforce rather than undermine the social *status quo*.[156] On the one hand, the Dutch Reformed Churches have provided the moral authority and spiritual dynamism underpinning social segregation and political apartheid;[157] on the other, the African Separatist Churches have sublimated political protest by offering a reversed colour bar in heaven as compensation for discrimination on earth.[158] Those in the middle, in spite of the occasional vociferous protest, have made little impact on the two extremes.

Though South Africa and Britain are both nominally Christian countries, the latter has by far the more secular society.[159] Nevertheless, religion, consciously important for a minority, has a less direct (possibly unconscious) influence over the values of the majority, while the position of the practising Christian is akin to that of the active trade unionist, whose universalistic values and particularistic behaviour pose the same moral dilemma. While the Church leadership in Britain has set its face against racialism among its members and in the community at large, the churches have failed to attract many coloured Christian immigrants.[160] Where they have, it has often been

---

[155] A. J. G. Crijns, *Race Relations and Race Attitudes in South Africa* (1959), p. 51. B. B. Keet *Whither South Africa?* (1956), and B. J. Marais, *The Colour Crisis and the West* (1953); L. Marquand (1962), op. cit., pp. 244–5.

[156] Cf. G. T. Marx, 'Religion: Opiate or Inspiration of Civil Rights Militancy among Negroes?', *A.S.R.* 32, no. 1 (1967), 64–72.

[157] The D.R.C. may be seen to combine elements of both the 'religion of the disinherited' and the 'religion of the middle class': H. R. Niebuhr, *The Social Sources of Denominationalism* (1929).

[158] B. E. M. Sundkler, *Bantu Prophets in South Africa* (1961), pp. 295, 304–5.

[159] B. Wilson, *Religion in Secular Society* (1966), p. xi, 233; for an alternative view which we do not share, see D. Martin, 'Towards Eliminating the Concept of Secularization', in J. Gould (ed.), *Penguin Survey of the Social Sciences* (1965), pp. 169–82.

[160] E. J. B. Rose, *Colour and Citizenship* (1969), pp. 370–80; C. Hill, *West Indian Migrants and the London Churches* (1963).

at the expense of alienating white members of the congregation whose beliefs clearly did not 'constrain them to tolerate their coloured co-religionists'.[161]

The existence of Pentecostal sects in Britain, seen by some as the 'embryo of a segregated Church', invites comparison with the Separatist Churches of Southern Africa.[162] While Calley interprets the former as a 'magico-religious refuge from the stresses and strains of settling down in a new country', Sundkler argues that the latter also act as 'psychological safety valves'.[163] In Jamaica many Pentecostal sects have flourished in an environment of extreme poverty, but Pentecostalism has also been popular among migrants,[164] suggesting that it serves as a flexible means of accommodation to frustration. So even if British Pentecostalism is seen in terms of continuity of membership, it is accompanied by discontinuity of frustration: the psychological problems of relative deprivation supersede the more absolute physical hardships, and within this psychological strain the factor of colour prejudice and discrimination (not least among the Churches) plays a central role.

Whether the failure of the British churches to attract coloured worshippers should be regarded as a simple reflection of colour prejudice among the laity is a little doubtful—seen in the wider context of a secular society, the 'failure' could equally well be an index of successful acculturation. The fact that Christian immigrants from the church-going communities of the West Indies[165] so quickly absorb the pagan behaviour of their hosts might suggest a remarkable adaptive power. Nevertheless, there is both the direct evidence that religious institutions and religious people, like their secular

---

[161] J. Rex and R. Moore, *Race, Community and Conflict* (1967), p. 186, though they did find that 'where there is a common class culture mutual acceptance and assimilation was possible', p. 190.

[162] *Colour and Citizenship* (1969), p. 374. The Black Muslims in the U.S.A. also exhibit certain parallels, although they are less 'introverted' and 'other worldly', and with their brother movement, Black Power, strike a more aggressive posture. Together they form the sacred and secular wings of the Negro revolution. Cf. E. U. Essien-Udom, *Black Nationalism: the rise of the Black Muslims in the U.S.A.* (1966); C. E. Lincoln 'The Black Muslim Movement', *Journal of Social Issues*, 19 (1963), 73–85; S. Carmichael and C. V. Hamilton, *Black Power* (1967).

[163] M. J. C. Calley, *God's People* (1965), p. 144. B. E. M. Sundkler, *Bantu Prophets in South Africa* (1961), p. 297.

[164] Calley (1965), op. cit., p. 121; for a more general sociological discussion of this problem, see C. Y. Glock, 'The Role of Deprivation in the Origin and Evolution of Religious Groups', in R. Lee and M. E. Marty (eds.), *Religion and Social Conflict* (1964), pp. 24–36.

[165] E. J. B. Rose, *Colour and Citizenship* (1969), p. 45.

counterparts, are not free from colour prejudice, and the indirect evidence of the sects, to show that the churches are no more than a microcosm of the total society.

d: ATTITUDES, VALUES, AND RACE RELATIONS

The discussion so far has been in comparative structural or institutional terms, while the cultural dimension has only been mentioned implicitly. To complete a picture of the total social system requires the explicit consideration of values, beliefs, and attitudes. The great practical obstacle here is the complete lack of comparative quantitative data; even within one society such data are frequently lacking over time.[166] There is the additional problem of 'time-specific' and 'culture-specific' attitude scales[167]—the relative ordering of items in social distance tests may vary between different cultures—and this will tend to affect international comparisons even more than those confined to a single society.[168]

However, unless the comparative sociologist is to be reduced to a series of Tocquevillian insights, no matter how illuminating these may be, some form of quantification, or at least the development of systematic typologies must be attempted. Other branches of sociology have made tentative moves in this direction: Inkeles and Rossi's study of comparative occupational prestige, and Almond and Verba's typology of 'political cultures' being influential examples.[169] In the field of comparative race relations several writers have attempted to apply Myrdal's 'dilemma' outside the American context,[170] while other studies have sought to measure variations in ethnocentrism, anti-semitism, and social distance between several different countries.[171]

[166] B. Bettelheim and M. Janowitz, *Social Change and Prejudice* (1964), p. 4.
[167] M. Banton, *Race Relations* (1967), pp. 324–5.
[168] Of course, there may be very significant differences within countries too. See T. F. Pettigrew, 'Regional Differences in Anti-Negro Prejudice', *Journal of Abnormal & Social Psychology*, 59 (1959), 28–36.
[169] A. Inkeles and P. H. Rossi, 'National Comparisons of Occupational Prestige', *A.J.S.* 61 (1956), 329–39; R. W. Hodge, D. J. Treiman, and P. H. Rossi, 'A Comparative Study of Occupational Prestige', in R. Bendix and S. M. Lipset, *Class, Status and Power* (1967), pp. 309–21. G. A. Almond and S. Verba, *The Civic Culture* (1963).
[170] Cf. A. H. Richmond, *Colour Prejudice in Britain* (1954), p. 18; P. L. van den Berghe, *South Africa: A Study in Conflict* (1965), p. 237.
[171] H. C. Triandis, E. E. Davis, and S. Tazekawa, 'Some Determinants of Social Distance among American, German and Japanese students', *J. of Personality and Social Psychology*, 2, No. 4 (1965), pp. 540–51.

The first attempt to set British colour attitudes in comparative perspective was the Lapiere study of 1928.[172] In South Africa, largely as a result of the pioneering work of MacCrone, systematic study of race attitudes developed earlier, but attempts to generalize on a cross-national basis have been limited to a few interesting comments by Pettigrew.[173] In fact, studies have been orientated towards detecting internal differences, measuring social distance between groups, so that external generalizations are hard to make. All that can be done in these circumstances is to trace the development of race attitudes within each country during the last two decades, and examine the extent to which their respective 'racial cultures' are congruent with the institutional structures that we have discussed.

The evidence for Britain is meagre. Banton's 1956 survey has limited general value because of the inclusion of atypical areas that bias the sample,[174] and this leaves the various Gallup polls and the surveys conducted by Abrams during 1966–7 for *Colour and Citizenship*[175] as the only available information with a nationwide coverage. A major drawback of the opinion polls on subject-matter as complex and sensitive as race relations is their psychological *naïveté*, while the Abrams study contains certain important methodological inadequacies.[176] Though Abrams is keenly aware of the fact, his study is curiously biased towards the less interesting extremist minorities, the pathologically prejudiced, and the tenaciously tolerant,[177] rather than the intrinsically more interesting masses in the middle. A comparison between 1958 and 1968 showed

---

[172] R. T. Lapiere, 'Race Prejudice: France and England', *Social Forces*, 7 (1928), 102–11; by 1970, no second attempt had been published at the quantitative level although one is in preparation: C. Bagley '*Race Relations and Social Structure in Britain and the Netherlands: A Comparative Study*'.

[173] I. D. MacCrone, *Race Attitudes in South Africa: historical, experimental and psychological studies* (1937), pp. 137–232. T. F. Pettigrew, 'Personality and Socio-cultural Factors in Inter-group Attitudes: a cross-national comparison', *Journal of Conflict Resolution*, 2, no. 1 (1958), 29–42; and 'Social Distance Attitudes of South African Students', *Social Forces*, 38, 246–53.

[174] M. Banton, *White and Coloured* (1959), pp. 197–210; cf. also: A. H. Richmond, 'Sociological and Psychological Explanations of Racial Prejudice' *Pacific Sociological Review*, 4, no. 2 (1961), 66.

[175] *Colour and Citizenship* (1969), pp. 551–88, 592–603.

[176] Cf. letters of J. Rowen and D. Lawrence, *New Society*, 14 Aug. 1969, and Abrams's reply, 4 Sept. 1969; correspondence of A. Marsh and G. C. Kinlock in *Race*, 11, no. 4 (1970); C. Bagley, 'The Prediction of Prejudice in a National Sample', *Race*, 12, no. 2 (1970), 234–6.

[177] The group Lever terms 'poly-centric': '*The Ethnic Attitudes of Johannesburg Youth* (1968), pp. 17–18.

a movement towards 'greater tolerance',[178] but how far this was a true reflection of changing race attitudes or a mere artefact of arbitrarily drawn, and still more arbitrarily labelled, categories, is impossible to determine on the basis of such evidence.

Within the Abrams sample, the finding that British women were slightly more tolerant than men,[179] to select just one example, could have considerable comparative interest seen against Pettigrew's suggestion that it is the female who tends to be the 'carrier of culture' of a society.[180] In South Africa the reverse is true—women are less tolerant than men—and the same pattern is repeated in contrasting the Northern and Southern states of America.[181] However, Abrams' over-all conclusion that tends to relegate social factors to a subsidiary role behind the influence of personality variables,[182] further suggests that his survey has been focused on somewhat extreme, overtly expressed hostility rather than on 'antipathy' of a socially structured or culturally transmitted kind. The reason why personality factors then appear dominant is clear: they are the product, to modify Merton, of a 'self-fulfilling hypothesis'.[183]

Most South African studies of race attitudes exhibit two main characteristics; they are drawn from young, highly educated samples[184] —the perennial 'captive audience' of university students—and they all agree that it is race, and not class membership, that plays the decisive part in determining the individual's attitude and behaviour.[185]

---

[178] *Colour and Citizenship* (1969), p. 593.

[179] Ibid., pp. 553–4.

[180] T. F. Pettigrew, *Social Distance Attitudes of South African Students* (1960), p. 252.

[181] T. F. Pettigrew, *Regional Differences in Anti-Negro Prejudice* (1959), pp. 28–36.

[182] *Colour and Citizenship* (1969), p. 562.

[183] R. K. Merton, *Social Theory and Social Structure* (1957), pp. 421–36.

[184] While being true of most studies, this is particularly relevant in the case of African samples, see A. J. G. Crijns, *Race Relations and Race Attitudes in South Africa* (1959); W. O. Brown, 'Race Consciousness among South African Natives', *A.J.S.* 40 (1935), 569–81; E. A. Brett, *African Attitudes: A Study of the Social, Racial and Political Attitudes of some Middle-Class Africans* (1963). However, industrial studies cover a somewhat wider background: S. Sherwood, 'The Bantu Clerk', *Journal of Social Psychology*, 47 (1958), 285–316; J. C. de Ridder, *The Personality of the Urban African in South Africa* (1961); L. E. Cortis, 'A Comparative Study in the Attitudes of Bantu and European Workers', *Psychologia Africana*, 9 (1962), 148–67.

[185] I. D. MacCrone, 'Race Attitudes: an analysis and interpretation' in E. Hellmann (ed.), *Handbook of Race Relations in South Africa* (1949), p. 703; MacCrone (1937), op. cit., p. 232; K. Danziger, 'Ideology and Utopia in South Africa', *B.J.S.* 14 (1963), 59–76.

Apart from Malherbe's wartime study[186] the only exceptions to this rule are Henry Lever's investigation of the ethnic attitudes of Johannesburg youth[187] and the survey of Hillbrow undertaken by the sociology department of the University of the Witwatersrand.[188] Lever's school (as opposed to university) sample is a far better index of the total white population than most of these other studies, yet his findings are remarkably like MacCrone's, suggesting that the 'hierarchies of social distance . . . have become institutionalized'.[189] In general, these studies reveal a picture of white attitudes in which Afrikaners, as a group, are consistently the most prejudiced of Europeans, Jews are the least prejudiced, and English-speaking South Africans occupy an intermediate position. All three groups display a high 'tolerance–intolerance' threshold separating whites from all non-whites,[190] most studies show women to be more prejudiced than men,[191] and that prejudice is related inversely to social class.[192]

The racial culture viewed from the black side of the colour line revealed a 'Boer-phobia'[193] among educated Africans as a reaction to domination,[194] while the racial attitude of the Coloureds was marked by acute ambivalence. There is no comparable quantitative

[186] E. G. Malherbe, *Race Attitudes and Education* (1946).

[187] H. Lever, *The Ethnic Attitudes of Johannesburg Youth* (1968).

[188] H. Lever, 'Ethnic Preferences of White Residents in Johannesburg', *Sociology and Social Research*, 52 (1968), 157–73; 'The Johannesburg Station Explosion and Ethnic Attitudes', *Public Opinion Quarterly*, 33, no. 2, (1969), 180–9; with O. J. M. Wagner, 'Urbanization and the Afrikaner', *Race*, 11, no. 2 (1969), 183–8.

[189] H. Lever, *The Ethnic Attitudes of Johannesburg Youth* (1968), p. 143.

[190] In some cases antisemitism was almost as significant as colour prejudice: I. D. MacCrone (1949), op. cit., p. 697. (Note: this refers to the early 1940s.)

[191] Though not in MacCrone's sample (1937), op. cit., pp. 215–32.

[192] H. Lever and O. M. Wagner, 'Father's Education as a factor affecting social distance', *Journal for Social Research*, 14 (1965), 21–30; and Pettigrew (1960), op. cit., p. 252; though not MacCrone (1949), op. cit., pp. 700–5 or van den Berghe (1962), op. cit.

[193] I. D. MacCrone, 'Reaction to Domination in a Colour-caste society', *Journal of Social Psychology*, 26 (1947), 68–98; for reaction to oppression by the American Negro, see T. F. Pettigrew, *A Profile of the Negro American* (1964), pp. 27–55. The race attitudes of less well-educated Africans is more difficult to determine. Some 'urban' Africans resist acculturation to an industrial-urban value system, so fitting the apartheid model, others adapt in varying degrees: M. Wilson and A. Mafeje, *Langa: a study of social groups in an African Township* (1963), p. 16; P. Mayer, *Townsmen or Tribesmen?* (1961), pp. 69–70; B. A. Pauw, *The Second Generation* (1963).

[194] H. F. Dickie-Clark, *The Marginal Situation: a sociological study of a Coloured Group* (1966), pp. 143–55.

evidence concerning the racial attitudes of coloured immigrants in Britain, though there is evidence that many are disappointed and keenly aware of discrimination.[195]

Thus, the 'racial cultures'—within which term I include the values of the dominant white societies, the norms governing intergroup behaviour, and the race attitudes of individuals—appear to be largely congruent with the institutional structuring of race relations in the two societies. Comparative social distance tests would certainly show greater outgroup hostility in South Africa, at least for the types of inter-racial contact and intimacy which are forbidden by law. The legislative norms of apartheid tend to increase outgroup rejection across the colour line, but there is no evidence to show that white South Africans are more prejudiced from a personality point of view. The difference lies in the extent to which the society is structured into racially exclusive sectors, and in an ethos resulting from different historical traditions.

[195] W. W. Daniel, *Racial Discrimination in England* (1968), pp. 31–53; H. Tajfel and J. L. Dawson, *Disappointed Guests* (1965).

CHAPTER V

Initial Conclusions and Hypotheses

SOUTH AFRICAN society is a classic example of social and cultural pluralism, while Britain is relatively much more homogeneous in this respect. The implication of these major differences for the British immigrant migrating to South Africa is that he will need to make a specific 'race relations adjustment' within the more general process of integrating into the total society. If we discount the possibility of racist self-selection, which I will consider against the empirical evidence at a later stage, then it seems plausible that a 'dilemma', in the classical Myrdalian sense, could well emerge from the juxtaposition of values and norms derived from British society and the behaviour and attitudes necessitated by living in South Africa. While it would be wrong to exaggerate, for it is clearly not a question of polar extremes, nevertheless the manner in which these significant differences are perceived and resolved is the most interesting aspect of British immigration to South Africa.

From the theoretical analysis five basic factors emerged with possible explanatory power, although their tentative derivation should be emphasized. These are:

 (i) conformity to group norms during the insecurity of the adjustment to a new society;
 (ii) structural factors within the receiving community leading to rapid integration and acculturation;
 (iii) social acceptance producing support for the social and political *status quo*;
 (iv) the need to legitimize and rationalize an 'unachieved' rise in status—the quest for 'personal' legitimacy;
 (v) the need to justify the vast discrepancies in the life styles and life chances between blacks and whites in South Africa—the quest for 'societal' legitimacy.

The next stage is the translation of the basic factors into a set of operational hypotheses for elaboration, re-examination, and testing against the survey evidence. These hypotheses are:

1. that the motives for migration will be economic rather than political or social,[1] and that the only significant exception will be found among the young single group;

2. that the majority of immigrants will experience a significant and rapid change in their attitudes towards social and racial matters from a more 'liberal' to a more 'conservative' position.[2]

3. That the element of 'self-selection' is not of primary importance, the only exception to this being the 'ex-colonial' category[3] and, possibly, a small number of 'racially-propelled' immigrants;

4. that sex is a significant factor in integration,[4] but that it is likely to affect the social rather than the political-cultural dimension;

5. that prior expectations, and prior knowledge, are crucial aspects of the process of integration;

6. that the length of residence,[5] but not the area of residence, in the host society will be significantly related to attitudes and integration;

7. that attitude-change will be more marked among working-class immigrants than middle-class immigrants;[6]

[1] A. Richardson, 'Some Psycho-social aspects of British Emigration to Australia', *B.J.S.* 10 (1959), 333; J. F. Loedolff, *Nederlandse Immigrante, 'n sosiologiese ondersoek van hul Inskakeling in die Gemeenskapslewe van Pretoria* (1960), p. 44; R. T. Appleyard, *British Emigration to Australia* (1964), p. 163; B. J. In den Bosch, 'De Verschillende Aspecten van de Aanpassing der Nederlandse Immigranten in Zuid-Afrika', *Journal for Social Research*, 15, no. 1 (1966), 71; P. Johnston, 'British Emigration to South Africa: a study of their characteristics and a comparison with Australia', M.A. thesis (Univ. of Natal) (1968) chap. 8; A. H. Richmond, *Post-War Immigrants in Canada* (1967), p. 32; 'Anatomy of An Immigrant—Part 2', *The Star* 23 Aug. 1968. (I would like to thank Peter Brugman and my wife for assistance in translating articles from Afrikaans and Dutch.)

[2] Above, p. 7 notes 18 & 19.

[3] Rogers and Frantz (1962), op. cit., p. 22; P. H. W. Johnston, *The Kenyan Immigrant: A Study in Social Adaptation* (1966).

[4] The relationship between sex and prejudice is highly complex and will depend on many factors: I. D. MacCrone (1937), op. cit., pp. 215–32; T. F. Pettigrew, 'Regional Differences in Anti-Negro Prejudice', *J.A.S.P.* 59 (1959), 28–36; Pettigrew (1960), op. cit., p. 252; van den Berghe (1962), op. cit., p. 255; H. Lever, *The Ethnic Attitudes of Johannesburg Youth* (1968).

[5] Rogers and Frantz, 'Length of Residence and Race Attitudes of Europeans', *Race*, 3, no. 2 (1962), 46–54.

[6] This may be more apparent than real on account of the latter's greater ability to rationalize, and greater awareness of intellectual inconsistency.

8. that the upwardly mobile will be the strongest supporters of the *status quo*;

9. That the 'immigrant situation' will give rise to a desire for conformity and be associated with 'deliberate ignorance';

10. that social informality and social acceptance, subjectively perceived, will be associated with support for the *status quo*;

11. that the length, and type, of education will be related to race-attitudes and to support for Apartheid;[7]

12. that those most opposed to Apartheid will also be the least well integrated on the economic and social dimensions;

13. that religion will not be an important influence among immigrants: for the religious minority, the 'conventional' will be stronger supporters of Apartheid and more hostile to outgroups than the 'devout'—an exception possibly being among sectarians;[8]

14. that trade union members in South Africa, rather than British trade unionists, will be significantly stronger supporters of Apartheid and more hostile towards outgroups than non-members,[9]

15. that immigrants will be more apolitical than they were in Britain and that British political party affiliations will be unrelated to support for Apartheid or hostility towards outgroups;[10]

16. that the immigrant's 'outlook on the future' will be related to the degree of his overall integration;[11]

17. that those immigrants who return to Britain do so primarily for non-political motives;[12]

[7] E. G. Malherbe (1946), op. cit., p. 14; H. Lever (1968), op. cit., pp. 151–2.

[8] P. H. W. Johnston (1968), op. cit., p. 24; G. W. Allport, *The Nature of Prejudice* (1958), pp. 413–26, and *Personality and Social Encounter* (1960), pp. 257–67; for attitude change among Catholics: *Cape Argus*, 10 Feb. 1968.

[9] For trade union developments in South Africa, see G. Routh, *Industrial Relations and Race Relations* (1952); M. Horrell, *Racialism and the Trade Unions* (1959); *Sunday Times* (S.A.), 14 Apr. 1968, 5 May 1968.

[10] According to a national survey carried out for the Institute of Race Relations (U.K.), the working-class Tory was *not* found to be any more racialistic than the working-class Socialist. *Report to the B.S.A. Conference*, 28 Mar. 1969.

[11] K. Danziger, 'Ideology and Utopia in South Africa', *B.J.S.* 14 (1963), 59–76; J. M. Gillespie and G. W. Allport, *Youth's Outlook on the Future* (1966); P. L. van den Berghe (1962), op. cit., p. 264.

[12] R. T. Appleyard, 'Determinants of Return Migration' *Economic Record*, 38, no. 83 (1962), 352–68; 'The Return Movement of U.K. Migrants from Australia', *Population Studies*, 15, no. 3 (1962), 214–25; A. H. Richmond, *Post-War Immigrants in Canada* (1967), pp. 229–52.

G

Before I proceed to the survey evidence I will first consider the historical background and development of British immigration to South Africa over the past century and a half. Few if any sociological problems can be described, let alone understood, in isolation from their historical antecedents. The attempt to apply sociology to history is not a plot to usurp the role of the historian, nor a search for the 'laws' of historical development, 'historicism' as attacked by Popper and Berlin,[13] but rather a less ambitious effort aimed at highlighting relatively stable social relationships within societies. Every historical situation is in one sense unique, and yet certain configurations of social structure often coexist with certain patterns of social behaviour. The reinterpretation of historical events in terms of sociological theory may help to reveal parallels between situations previously considered only as discrete historical instances, and the use of historical material can confirm, modify, or destroy what have been regarded as stable social relationships.

Thus the purpose of these historical case studies will be to describe British immigration to South Africa and to relate it to the changing balances of power in the society during the last hundred and fifty years. This will also enable comparisons to be made, though rarely of a quantitative kind, between the reactions, attitudes, and situations of immigrants at different periods of time. It will allow us to sort out what is general from what is particular, to distinguish trends from random fluctuations, and to mitigate some of the fallacies resulting from ethnocentric bias by revealing the 'forgotten alternatives'.[14]

There is another reason why a historical perspective is particularly appropriate for this study. In South Africa history 'lives' with an intensity almost unknown to British society,[15] Ireland being the illuminating exception.[16] Even today, names and events from more

---

[13] K. R. Popper, *The Poverty of Historicism* (1961); *'The Open Society and its Enemies'* (1966), vols. 1 & 2; I. Berlin, *Historical Inevitability*, Auguste Comte Memorial Trust Lecture No. 1 (1954), reprinted in *Four Essays on Liberty* (1969), pp. 41–117.

[14] C. Vann Woodward, *The Strange Career of Jim Crow* (1966), pp. 31–65. This may also reveal former situations that were *less* tolerant than they were currently believed to be: C. R. Boxer, *Race Relations in the Portuguese Colonial Empire: 1415–1825* (1963).

[15] For a discussion of the comparative significance and salience of 'history' in England and France, see Hugh Brogan's introduction to de Tocqueville's *The Ancien Regime and the French Revolution*, Fontana edn. (1966), pp. 7–10.

[16] The historical parallels between Ireland and South Africa have often been noted: '. . . equally interesting was the English penchant, in both Official and Press circles, for seeing Paul Kruger, Jan Hofmeyr, and the Afrikaner Bond in

'Emigration to the Cape of Forlorn Hope', or 'All Among the Hottentots capering ashore' (1819)

A cartoon by George Cruikshank, 1819, reproduced from G. E. Cory, *The Rise of South Africa* (Longmans, 1913)

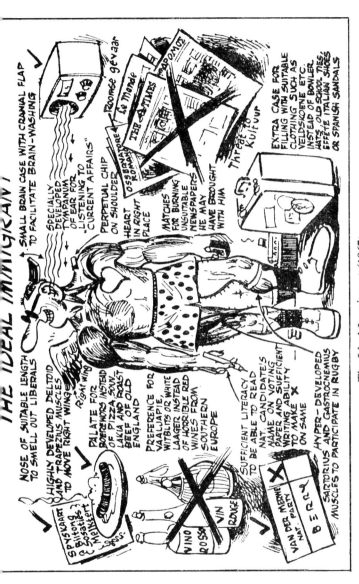

The Ideal Immigrant (1967)

Immigration to South Africa has been a source of satirical comment from the time of Cruikshank to the present day.

than a century ago can evoke antagonistic feelings and serve as meaningful politico-cultural symbols for South Africa's diverse racial and ethnic groups. In Britain, such ghosts of the past have lost their ability to haunt the cleavages of the present; the political debates and controversies they represented, if remembered, have long since ceased to have any emotional impact. So, it is for this additional reason, the impossibility of understanding the current South African social and political structure in isolation from its past, that an appreciation of the historical dimension of the problem forms an indispensable and integral part of this study.[17]

---

terms of Parnell and Fenianism.' In D. M. Schreuder *Gladstone and Kruger: Liberal Government and Colonial Home Rule, 1880–85* (1969), p. xiv.

[17] Another factor is the lack of any comprehensive historical survey of British immigration to South Africa. H. M. Robertson's short article in B. Thomas (ed.), *Economics of International Migration* (1958), pp. 173–84, comes closest to doing this. It is perhaps surprising, though not without significance, that so much attention has been devoted to quite obscure members of the 1820 settlers and yet British settlement throughout the whole of the twentieth century has scarcely received a mention. This may be related to the sociology of knowledge and, in so far as my analysis of power relations is correct, I might predict that now British immigration has become 'respectable' again, much more interest will be shown in it by South African writers. Immigration from the Netherlands, which supplied only 41,039 people from 1924 to 1964, compared with a British total of 196,191, has already been the subject of three major studies: A. P. du Plessis (1956), J. F. Loedolff (1960), and B. J. In den Bosch (1964).

PART TWO

The Historical Background

'The artisans who today come from
Europe adopt the habits of the
country in a few weeks or months.'
(JAMES BRYCE, 1897)

'You ask me what the English
workers think about colonial policy.
Well exactly the same as they think
about politics in general: the same
as the bourgeois think.'
(FRIEDRICH ENGELS, 1882)

CHAPTER VI

The Settlers and the Frontier

FROM THEIR earliest recorded contact with the country British
people have differed in their assessment of South Africa. Sailing
from Lisbon to Goa in 1579, Thomas Stevens left us this account of
his impressions:

We came at length unto the Point, so famous and feared of all men . . .
the waves being exceeding great they rolled us so neere the land, that
the ship stood in lesse than 14 fadoms of water, no more than sixe miles
from the Cape which is called Das Agulias; and there we stood so utterly
cast away . . . the shore so evill, that nothing could take land, and the land
itselfe so full of Tigers and people that are savage and killers of all strangers.
The day of peril was the nine and twentieth of July.[1]

Less than a year later, a sailor on the expedition of Sir Francis Drake
returned with a different picture of a similar area:

We ranne hard aboord the Cape, finding the report of the Portugals to be
most false who affirme that it is the most dangerous Cape of the World,
never without intolerable stormes and present dangers to travailers which
come near the same. This Cape is the most stately thing, and the fairest
Cape we saw in the whole circumference of the Earth, and we passed by it
the 18th of June.[2]

The first Britons to try to establish a settlement in South Africa[3]—
to describe them as 'immigrants' would be misleading—were a small
group of eight men condemned to death at the Old Bailey and set
down in Table Bay in 1615. This was part of a bizarre colonizing
venture devised by the influential seventeenth-century financier
Sir Thomas Smythe. The leader of the group, a Captain Crosse, was
killed in a clash with the Hottentots, and the remainder of his party
fled to Robben Island. Four others were drowned while attempting
to reach a passing ship and the last three survivors were taken back
to England, only to meet their death on the gallows.[4] The experience

---

[1] R. Hakluyt, *Principal Navigations* (1903–5), vol. 1, p. 581; R. Raven-Hart
Before Van Riebeeck (1967), pp. 13–14.
[2] Hakluyt, vol. 4, p. 232 and Raven-Hart (1967), p. 14.
[3] The first Britons to set foot on South African soil were in a party led by
James Lancaster in 1591. E. A. Walker, *A History of Southern Africa* (1957),
p. 24. They engaged in friendly barter with the native inhabitants, G. M. Theal,
History of South Africa, 1486–1691 (1888), pp. 15–16.
[4] J. Cope, *King of the Hottentots* (1967).

of these convicts[5] would seem to lend support to Thomas Stevens's views that the Cape in the early seventeenth century was far from an inviting place to settle.

Five years later, in 1620, the Cape was claimed for the English Crown by two visiting sea captains, Fitzherbert and Shillinge,[6] but possession was not maintained, for English ships preferred to call at the island of St. Helena on their journeys to and from the Orient. During the later part of the seventeenth century, while Van Riebeeck was establishing his Dutch settlement in Table Bay, a number of British vessels were shipwrecked on the Natal coast. Their reception by the indigenous tribes was most friendly. Captain Rogers, in the last decade of the seventeenth century, reported that the natives were 'extraordinary civil to strangers'.[7] Towards the end of the following century shipwrecks became more frequent, so much so that the port of Natal became known to Dutch sailors as the 'Engelsche Logie'—the Englishman's Inn.[8]

It was during the Napoleonic Wars, in 1795, that a British fleet first occupied the Cape and held it initially until 1803,[9] when the resident British population could hardly have exceeded a few score.[10] With the resumption of hostilities, Cape Town was reoccupied in 1806 and finally ceded to Britain by the Treaty of Paris in 1814. The arrival of the 1820 settlers marks the first significant case of British immigration to South Africa. Consisting of nearly five thousand individuals it more than doubled the existing population of the colony, and its impact was out of all proportion to its absolute size.[11]

The 1820 settlement was preceded by three small private colonizing ventures,[12] the most important being the group of 196 Scottish

[5] Cf. later attempts at convict settlement at the Cape in A. F. Hattersley, *The Convict Crisis and the Growth of Unity* (1965).

[6] G. M. Theal (1888), op. cit., p. 18.

[7] E. H. Brookes and C. de B. Webb, *A History of Natal* (1965), p. 5; and Mackeurtan, *The Cradle Days of Natal, 1497–1845* (1930), p. 68.

[8] Brookes and Webb (1965); op. cit., p. 6; C. F. Shuter, *Englishman's Inn* (1963).

[9] An idea of the nature of Cape society at this time can be gained from Lady Anne Barnard's *South Africa a Century Ago* (1913); D. Fairbridge, *Lady Anne Barnard at the Cape of Good Hope, 1797–1802* (1924); J. Hale (ed.), *Settlers: extracts from the journals and letters of early colonists* (1950), pp. 210–99.

[10] J. Bond, *They were South Africans* (1956), p. 5; W. H. Vatcher, *White Laager* (1965), p. 6.

[11] H. E. Hockly, *The Story of the British Settlers of 1820 in South Africa* (1966), pp. 31–2. Cf. L. M. Thompson in L. Hartz, *The Founding of New Societies* (1964), pp. 192–3.

[12] Those of Peter Tait and James Gosling in 1818 were on a smaller scale but were reasonably successful: see C. E. Cory, *The Rise of South Africa* vol. 2

apprentices which set sail from Leith in 1817 under the leadership of Benjamin Moodie.[13] Moodie's own motive for migration was the bankruptcy of his family estate in the Orkneys during the economic crisis following the end of the Napoleonic Wars. Having no profession, he surveyed the various colonies and chose the Cape as the place most likely to 'preserve his feudal and agricultural status'.[14] Although he received no official encouragement, Moodie selected, out of a total of 1,500 applicants from the South of Scotland, a group of young men aged between eighteen and twenty-five years old, who had served apprenticeships and could supply references of good character. These mechanics and labourers signed contracts to work for a fixed period at the Cape in exchange for their passages and subsistence rations. As a whole the scheme benefited most of the apprentices[15] because there was a strong demand for skilled labour in the Colony, which tempted most of them to break their contracts and left Moodie still owing money in 1826.[16] These problems were an exact repetition of the experience of his predecessor, the Dutch colonist Baron van Hogendorp, who had also found it impossible to enforce legal indentures during the rule of the Batavian Republic in 1804.[17]

The initial reaction of the colony to the scheme is most interesting, particularly as it raises some illuminating parallels with later situations. The size of the venture was greatly exaggerated leading to almost universal disquiet from the various sections of the community. According to John Moodie, Benjamin's brother, the Cape Dutch feared for the loss of their identity,[18] slave owners viewed his scheme

---

(1913), p. 7; for a modern counterpart of such schemes for the private recruitment of skilled artisans, cf. the Cyril Lord textile factory near East London and the Zwelitsha scheme. For a critical assessment of the former, see C. and M. Legum, *South Africa: Crisis for the West* (1964), pp. 135–7; *Financial Mail* 23 Aug. 1964, for the latter, see H. J. Van Eck, *Some Aspects of the South African Revolution*, Hoernlé Memorial Lecture (1951), p. 17.

[13] E. H. Burrows, *The Moodies of Melsetter* (1954), chaps. 2–5; for a summary of Scots in South Africa, see G. Donaldson, *The Scots Overseas* (1966), pp. 181–93.

[14] E. H. Burrows (1954), op. cit., p. 24; cf. T. Pringle, *Narrative of a Residence in South Africa* (1966), p. 3.

[15] E. H. Burrows (1954), op. cit., p. 59.

[16] Ibid., p. 79.

[17] C. E. Cory (1913), op. cit., p. 6.

[18] An unfounded fear in this particular case for the apprentices rapidly became proficient in Dutch, and their descendants spoke Afrikaans (E. H. Burrows, op. cit., p. 80).

in terms of the depreciation of their property, and the Colonial Government officials were distressed at the disturbance of their bureaucratic tranquillity and soon 'sighed audibly at the additional plague and bother that the Scottish laird was giving them'.[19] Moodie himself claimed that the only British colonists who were pleased with the prospect were not motivated by altruism or pride in the long-term development of the country, but merely by the chance of acquiring new labour 'without paying for it'.[20]

The move from the wretched poverty of the post-war depression to an area where skilled labour could command a good wage, led to dramatic changes in the apprentices' attitudes and behaviour. Moodie complained that the 'pretensions of all increased in an inordinate degree from the hour they landed'.[21] In addition there was the difficulty of introducing white indentured labour into the stratification system of Cape society,[22] for while black slavery was an accepted and established institution in the Colony, 'white slavery remained an offensive concept to Cape minds, and Captain Moodie's scheme smacked of it'.[23] Nevertheless, the success of these colonizing experiments for the mechanics participating in them, publicized the possibilities of emigration and helped contribute towards the interest aroused in the much larger, government-sponsored venture proposed two years later.

The motivation behind the settlement scheme of 1820 was, like present-day emigration, twofold.[24] For the immigrants themselves, it was largely a result of economic necessity, but for the British Government which planned, encouraged, and financed the scheme, strategic factors played the dominant role in dispelling their earlier

---

[19] Ibid., p. 40; J. W. D. Moodie, *Ten Years in South Africa* (1835).

[20] Ibid., p. 40.

[21] Ibid., p. 53.

[22] As Moodie explained in a letter to England: 'all share in the work, ranks disappear in a new country'. Ibid., pp. 100–1.

[23] Ibid., p. 80.

[24] It should be noted that this chapter consists more of a series of case studies than a general and balanced historical treatment. The choice of the 1820 and Byrne settlers, rather than the equally numerous influx between 1858–62, is dictated simply by the relative availability of detailed information, not because one group was more 'typical' than the other—in fact, the reverse is more probably the case. For major general sources on the 1820 settlement, see G. M. Theal, *History of South Africa* (1913), vol. 2; H. E. Hockly, *The Story of the British Settlers of 1820 in South Africa* (1957); D. E. Rivett-Carnac, *Thus Came the English* (1961), and *Hawk's Eye* (1966); I. E. Edwards, *The 1820 Settlers in South Africa* (1934); W. M. MacMillan, *The Cape Colour Question* (1927), chap. 9.

scepticism.[25] The plan to establish colonists along the western border of the Great Fish river, as a means of defending the Eastern frontier, was first publicized in a report of Colonel Collins in 1808.[26] Five years later, another military officer, Lieutenant-Colonel John Graham,[27] proposed a scheme for settling Highlanders in the same district and had collected several hundred prospective colonists before official permission was refused. Lord Charles Somerset,[28] the Governor of the Cape, urged the Secretary for the Colonies to accept this scheme but it was not until the outbreak of the Fifth 'Kaffir War' in 1819 that government approval and support, in the form of a £50,000 grant, was finally given. Between December 1819 and January 1820, twenty-one emigrant ships left Britain, taking the first major group of British immigrants and confronting them with the peculiar racial conditions of Southern Africa.

That the motives of settlers of all classes were fundamentally economic is revealed in the official correspondence with both the party leaders and other individual settlers. A certain carpenter called Goddard expressed the typical plight of the artisan in a graphic, if somewhat flamboyant, manner:

... had I not been a venturer in life's uncertain lottery and from thence drawn a successive number of blanks, which has reduced me almost to a state of penury and despair—I should not emigrate to this foreign clime to revisit the much loved British shore no more—its necessity, alas, necessity which inspires my pen and which causes me to part with those endearing objects of my native home—to cross the trackless waste and burst the unbroken clods that turfs the wasteland o'er.[29]

Fears of unemployment and debt were widespread during the drastic economic readjustments following in the wake of the Napoleonic Wars.[30] Knowledge about the country, among all classes, was

---

[25] These in turn can be related to economics but 'this "economy" measure, Grey contended, was among the most expensive in the history of the British Empire' (J. S. Galbraith, *Reluctant Empire: British Policy on the South African Frontier, 1834–54* (1963), p. 8).

[26] I. E. Edwards (1934), op. cit., p. 27.

[27] Ibid., p. 40.

[28] 'Somerset had perforce to discover some attraction to entice settlers to this stormy region; and his fertile imagination conjured up a picture of a land flowing with milk and honey' (Ibid., p. 31).

[29] Ibid., pp. 57–8.

[30] Post-war periods have often been associated with a sudden rush of migrants: e.g. Crimean War (1854–6); Anglo-Boer War (1902); First World War (1918) Second World War (1945). For social conditions in post-Napoleonic Britain, see G. M. Trevelyan, *English Social History* (1944), pp. 364–85.

minimal and often ludicrously mistaken,[31] for numerous pamphlets holding diametrically opposed assessments seem to have been circulating at that time. One such pamphlet analysed the causes of distress and displayed a perceptive appreciation of Keynesian economics. It rejected current opinions about technological unemployment, Luddite fears of the early machine age, and also the middle-class diatribes deploring the fecklessness of the working masses, and advocated in their place a 'colonizing system which would preserve the equilibrium in the parent state between the demand and the supply of labour'.[32] The one specific proposal was for the establishment of a whaling industry at Saldanha Bay using unemployed seamen including 'those miserable beings who lately exhibited a deformity shocking to the feelings of humanity in almost every street in the Metropolis'.[33]

Not all the pamphlets stressed the more hopeful side of the picture as may be illustrated from James Griffen's *A Correct Statement of the Advantages and disadvantages attendant on emigration to the new Colony forming near the Cape of Good Hope*.[34] As was the custom in the early nineteenth century, Griffen distinguished sharply between those emigrants who possessed some capital, the middle classes, and those who did not, the working or labouring classes. Summing up the situation for the former, he wrote:

Your advantage then, if successful, may be comprised as follows—A good estate producing everything necessary for the support of yourself and your tenants in comfort, together with wine and several other luxuries; also your storehouse loaded with corn and wool, which you cannot make use of, and for which you cannot find a market.

[31] Examples of this were given by John Centlivres Chase: 'In July 1840, a very celebrated political economist in the House of Commons moved for certain papers regarding the expenditure of the "*island* of the Cape of Good Hope", and the very last Custom House returns of emigration include the Cape of Good Hope among the West India Islands' (J. C. Chase *The Cape of Good Hope and the Eastern Province of Algoa Bay* (1843), p. iv–v). The author, who was referred to disparagingly by one important 1820 settler as 'the cockney Chase'—W. M. MacMillan (1927), p. 116—later became a prominent member of Cape society and a strong defendant of the settlers' point of view. Cf. E. Rosenthal, *Southern African Dictionary of National Biography* (1966), p. 64.

[32] Anon, *Consideration of the means of affording profitable employment to the redundant population of Great Britain and Ireland*, London (1818), pamphlet in Rhodes House Library, Oxford.

[33] Ibid., p. 21.

[34] 2nd. edn. London (1819); cf. the favourable pamphlet: Anon, *An Account of the Colony of the Cape of Good Hope with a view to the information of emigrants* (1819), in Port Elizabeth Public Library.

To produce large quantities of wool, it will be necessary to breed large flocks of sheep; when these become too numerous, you may securely reckon on being eased of the overstock by the incursions of the Caffres and Boshies men, without troubling yourself to find a market for them.

The disadvantages may be enumerated under the following heads:—You give up your country, your friends and all the polish of European society— You give up the education proper for your children, unless the minister becomes schoolmaster which is by no means likely—You are likewise destitute, in case of illness, of any sort of medical assistance; perhaps you may reckon this a blessing—Lastly, no commerce being carried out, and consequently no intercourse kept up with the civilized world, save occasional visitants from the Cape, you have every prospect of beholding your descendants sink so low in point of information as to be distinguished only by their colour from the uncultivated natives.

Quere: Bad as the times are at present in England could not the capital sunk in this enterprise be employed to much more advantage, in every sense of the word, without forsaking your friends, your relatives and your country?[35]

Griffen was even more pessimistic about the prospects for the emigrant who did not possess any capital resources and argued that it was much better to remain at home than to 'throw yourself into the arms of perpetual slavery'.[36] His final assessment was an accurate appraisal of the true purpose of the scheme which, in the opinion of a later historian, was an 'abortive attempt to make the homes of British settlers into the ramparts of an Empire'.[37]

Even acknowledged experts on Southern Africa, like William Burchell and Sir John Barrow, completely disagreed about the merits of the scheme. In June 1819 Burchell was called to give evidence before a Select Committee on the Poor Laws, and strongly supported the idea of an Albany settlement. His evidence was reported in the *Annual Register* and reprinted as a pamphlet entitled *Hints on the Emigration to the Cape of Good Hope. The Quarterly Review* of November 1819 published a scathing retort, dismissing the pamphlet with the comment: 'Mr. Burchell might as well talk of planting a

---

[35] J. Griffen (1819), op. cit., p. 9.

[36] J. Griffen (1819), p. 11; in fact the artisans and labourers did relatively better than the middle-class emigrant, by abandoning the land, to which they had less financial commitment, and moving to the towns. Cf. T. Pringle, *Some Account of the Present State of the English Settlers in Albany, South Africa* (1824), p. 33; H. H. Dugmore *The Reminiscences of an Albany Settler* (1958), pp. 28–9; W. W. Bird, *The State of the Cape of Good Hope in 1822* (1966), p. 240, 377 (note by the editor H. T. Colebrooke); I. E. Edwards (1934), op. cit., p. 81.

[37] I. E. Edwards (1934), op. cit., p. 144.

settlement behind the Himalaya mountains.' But the tone of the reviewer (who was almost certainly Barrow) was undoubtedly sharpened by personal animosity, for he probably felt piqued that he himself had not been invited to give evidence before the Select Committee.[38]

Although opinions were as wide in range as would be found about contemporary South Africa, from sources as diverse as South Africa House or the Africa Bureau, nevertheless the announcement of the scheme brought a flood of 90,000 applications. This gives some indication of the 'emigration temperature' at the time and the generally favourable climate of public opinion. While economic 'push' factors, unemployment and poverty in England, were unquestionably paramount, these were not the only motives. The civil servant, William Bird, suggested that, from the British Government's point of view, political considerations on the home front were not entirely absent. Indeed, Thomas Philipps, one of the most prominent of the 1820 settlers, emigrated partly as a result of political frustration, for a quarrel with his patron, Lord Milford, put an end to his political prospects in England.[39] However, Bird imputed more sinister grievances and suggested that:

Possibly, the Government of England, mindful of the consequences which, in the reign of the first Charles, followed a prevention of the departure to America of Hazelrig, Hampden, Pym and Cromwell, encouraged this emigration of the discontented to a distant part of the globe. To give a straight bias to a ball so impelled, was the difficult task imposed upon ministers.[40]

Another non-materialistic source of motivation was religion and at least one party, according to Pringle, was composed entirely of English Methodists and dissenters who had associated themselves

[38] W. J. Burchell, *Travels in the Interior of Southern Africa* (1967) ed. with introduction by A. Gordon-Brown pp. 12, 20–1, 41.

[39] A. Keppel-Jones (ed.), *Philipps, 1820 Settler* (1960), pp. 12–13.

[40] W. W. Bird (1966), op. cit. p. 179; this is a suggestion strongly denied by J. C. Chase (1843), op. cit. p. 82, who rejected the 'cruel surmise' that the settlers' 'anxiety to leave their native hearths . . . [arose] from political disgust'. Chase comments on Bird: 'we must allow something for disappointment in the early career of his public life, which tinge his panegyric of the Cape' (p. 258) and 'Mr. Bird, it must be recollected wrote in the "Dark Ages" of this settlement, before the influence of the immigration of 1820 had leavened the dead mass of the Colony'; for doubts about Chase's objectivity: G. Nicholson *The Cape and its Colonists with hints to Settlers* (1849), pp. 21, 113.

'like the early American colonists on principles of religious as well as civil communion'.[41] In an address delivered at Bathurst in 1845, another settler, the Revd. John Aycliff, gave his impressions of the many causes which induced the emigration:

With many of the heads of families the grave and serious consideration of the pressing and difficult circumstances of the times; with others a strange romantic idea of trade, wild sports, and the speedy accumulation of riches; with others a strong religious motive; while others for no assignable reason cast in their lot amongst the number of the emigrants.[42]

But whatever other motives may have been present, few could doubt the enthusiasm of both the protagonists and the participants in the scheme.[43]

So far we have considered the motives of the settlers and the sources of information likely to have been available to them. In an earlier chapter we discussed the importance of expectations and the related concept of relative deprivation as factors affecting the initial stages of emigration.[44] There is evidence to suggest that most settlers had entirely unrealistic views about the style of life they would have to endure in their new home, and the traumatic shock based on the subsequent discovery of the true facts can well be imagined. Few had paid much attention to Cruikshank's famous cartoons ridiculing emigration to the Cape of 'Forlorn Hope', or heeded *The Times* warning that the emigrant might soon discover that 'an African climate was injurious to his health'[45] and that by his bargain with the

[41] T. Pringle, *Narrative of a Residence in South Africa* (1966), p. 18.

[42] J. Aycliff, *Memorials of the British Settlers of South Africa* (1845), p. 11.

[43] Bird, in discussing the Parliamentary debate, comments on the former: 'Lord Sidmouth in the House of Lords harangued to the same purport, and fanned the deluding flame, which had been lighted up in the Commons . . . it is strange to relate, such to have been the infatuation that those who disagree on all other subjects, agreed to this alone.' Op. cit., p. 178. And on the latter: 'The eagerness and anxiety of individuals, to be allowed by the colonial secretary of state to emigrate to the sands of South Africa, the "new land of promise", were unbounded. It was hardly, if at all exceeded by the followers of Sir Walter Raleigh, in search of Eldorado, or of Cortes and Pisarro, in their avidity to possess themselves of the gold of Mexico and Peru.' Loc. cit.

[44] Above, pp. 17–18.

[45] In fact, the climate turned out to be the one very favourable element. It is a factor mentioned by many immigrants, but rarely as a prime source of motivation except for those in poor health. Cf. esp. woman emigrants and visitors: e.g. Lucy Grey described in A. F. Hattersley, *A Victorian Lady at the Cape, 1849–51;* and Lady Duff Gordon who wrote some ten years later: 'The glorious African summer is come, and I believe this is the weather of paradise' (*Letters from the Cape* (1921), p. 79).

Parish Officers he had placed himself in a cruel dilemma: 'he may die if he remains, he may starve if he returns'.[46]

Many diaries and reminiscences tell of the exaggerated hopes and ambitions stirred up by the prospect of emigration, and accentuated on the long, monotonous sea voyage:

> ... he ponders by day and dreams by night of the 'promised land' to which he is bound—his imagination runs riot among scenes of arcadian loveliness—he builds castles in the air[47]—and he lays down plans for his future guidance—all of which are dissipated, like the baseless fabric of a vision, when brought into contact with the sober realities of a settler's life.[48]

It was not merely the ignorant masses who were deluding themselves for, as Pringle discovered, a sort of 'Utopian delirium' was somehow excited at that time, and 'the flowery descriptions of superficial observers seem to have intoxicated with their Circean blandishments' not only the 'gullible herd of uninformed emigrants', but also 'many sober men'[49] both in and out of Parliament. This was confirmed by Bird, who attributed the settlers' unbounded expectations to 'injudicious and erroneous statements' in pamphlets and speeches, descriptive of a 'climate and of a fertility known only in romance'.[50] In most of these publications, he claimed, advice was given for the guidance of settlers by 'mere theorists'. On arrival in South Africa, though some were visibly disappointed, Pringle marvelled at the manner in which several of the most intelligent men were carried away by expectations scarcely less extravagant than those of 'our female friends' who fancied they would find 'oranges and apricots growing wild among the thorny jungles of the Zwartkops'.[51]

Some idea of the social composition of the settlers can be derived from a breakdown of their occupations, although these are not aggregated in the most suitable way to differentiate between social classes. Of the 1,455 adult males traced by Hockly, 42 per cent were

[46] D. E. Rivett-Carnac, *Thus Came the English* (1961), p. 23.
[47] Almost the exact words of one returning immigrant from the sample survey: 'They build you up a castle in the air, and then there's the big let down.' (No. 20/98).
[48] R. Godlonton, *Memorials of the British Settlers of South Africa*, compiled by the editor of the *Grahamstown Journal* (1844), pp. vi–vii; see also Pringle's brilliant description of the excitement and anticipation of the settlers before landing, *Narrative of a Residence in South Africa* (1966), pp. 8–9.
[49] T. Pringle, *Some Account of the present state of the English settlers in Albany, South Africa* (1824), pp. 6–7.
[50] W. W. Bird, *The State of the Cape of Good Hope in 1882* (1966), p. 233.
[51] T. Pringle, *Narrative of a Residence in South Africa* (1966), p. 18.

involved in 'farming and country pursuits'; 32 per cent were skilled artisans or mechanics; 12 per cent were in commerce or trade; 5 per cent were ex-army, navy, and merchant seamen; 4 per cent professionals, leaving a further 5 per cent unspecified.[52] A more vivid description of the emigrants on arrival at Algoa Bay is given by Thomas Pringle, and while it is none too flattering it is worth quoting in some detail for the light it sheds on the subject.

I then strolled along the beach to survey more closely the camp of the settlers . . . these were the encampments of some of the higher class of settlers . . . it was obvious that several of these families had been accustomed to enjoy the luxurious accommodations of refined society in England. How far they had acted wisely in embarking their property and the happiness of their families in an enterprise like the present, and in leading their respective bands of adventurers to colonize the wilds of Southern Africa, were questions yet to be determined . . . for they appeared utterly unfitted by former habits, especially the females,[53] for 'roughing it' (to use the expressive phraseology of the camp) through the first trying period of the settlement.
A little way beyond, I entered the Settlers' Camp . . . occupied by the middling and lower classes of emigrants. . . . These consisted of various descriptions of people; and the air, aspect, and array of their persons and temporary residences, were equally various. There were respectable tradesmen and jolly farmers . . . watermen, fishermen, and sailors from the Thames and English seaports . . . pale-visaged artisans and operative manufacturers, from London and other large towns . . . lastly there were parties of pauper agricultural labourers, sent out by the aid of their respective parishes. On the whole they formed a motley and unprepossessing collection of people: guessing vaguely from my observations on this occasion and on subsequent rambles through their locations, I should say that probably about a third were persons of real respectability of character, and possessed of some worldy substance; but that the remaining two-thirds were for the most part composed of individuals of a very unpromising description— persons who had hung loose upon society—low in morals or desperate in circumstances. Enterprise many of these doubtless possessed in an eminent degree; but too many appeared to be idle, insolent, and drunken, and mutinously disposed towards their masters and superiors.[54]

[52] H. E. Hockly, *The Story of the British Settlers of 1820 in South Africa* (1957), p. 31; I. E. Edwards, *The 1820 Settlers in South Africa* (1934). Appendix A. gives the following breakdown: Agricultural = 55 per cent; Artisans = 33 per cent; Army and Navy = 2 per cent; Shopkeepers = 7 per cent; Professions = 2 per cent; Seamen = 2 per cent. (N = 988).
[53] Cf. G. Nicholson, *The Cape and its Colonists with hints to Settlers* (1849), p. 78.
[54] T. Pringle, *Narrative of a Residence in South Africa* (1966), pp. 12–13.
H

The Quarterly Review made an even more devastating character sketch of the settlers, typifying them as 'tavern waiters, broken-down actors, attorney's clerks, pianoforte makers, men and women milliners from Bond Street and ladies' maids'.[55] Although such descriptions are far from objective, they do point to the diversity and class composition of the emigrants.

Another problem that the historical experience of the early settlers helps to illustrate is the effect of the immigrant situation on race attitudes and inter-group relations. In many cases the emigrant's first impression of inter-racial contact revealed the uncertain and unusual nature of the experience for those accustomed to life in the relatively homogeneous society of nineteenth-century Britain. One Victorian lady, Lucy Grey, described her own initial reaction towards her African maid: 'it was a novelty to me and I wondered whether the black would come off when she fastened my dress . . . experience proved not.'[56] Jeremiah Goldswain's encounter with the Hottentots did not leave a favourable impression and he found them 'the most despisable creatours that ever I saw',[57] a sentiment not unlike that of the Revd. Edward Terry who declared, some two centuries earlier, that they were 'beasts in the skins of men, rather than men in the skins of beasts'.[58] While the Hottentots evoked feelings of contempt, the independent and powerful African tribes to the east of the settlement gave rise to fear and hostile stereotypes of an intense kind. The conditions of frontier life[59] and the tendency for race relations, which already bordered on anarchy, to degenerate into open warfare had an enormous effect on shaping these attitudes.

The subsequent events on the Eastern Frontier need not concern us directly but the lasting impact of the frontier wars, preserved in the history books and the collective memory of English-speaking South Africans, has been one factor in the development and perpetuation of race attitudes. This was the time when bitter feelings were expressed against the 'humanitarians', the nineteenth-century equivalent of present-day 'liberals', personified by John Philip of the

[55] Cf. A. W. Tilby, *South Africa, 1486–1913* (1914), p. 102.

[56] A. F. Hattersley, *A Victorian Lady at the Cape*, p. 28.

[57] D. E. Rivett-Carnac (1961), op. cit., p. 47; U. Long (ed.), *The Chronicle of Jeremiah Goldswain* (1946–8).

[58] J. Cope (1967), op. cit., p. 32.

[59] Cf. E. A. Walker, *The Frontier Tradition in South Africa* (1930); but note MacCrone's argument that the key formative period for race attitudes was the eighteenth century in *Race Attitudes in South Africa* (1937), p. 136.

London Missionary Society,[60] because they did not define the situation solely from the settlers' point of view. These attitudes persist as witnessed by the caustic comments of one historian, who clearly sympathizes with the settlers' predicament, that in England 'the philosophy of Rousseau was beginning to be tainted with the sentimentality of Uncle Tom's Cabin'.[61] In contrast, MacMillan exposed the natural tendency to interpret the course of history almost exclusively as it affected the fortunes of the white colonists,[62] and showed that both the rulers and the much harassed colonists utterly failed to see how the increasing disorders arose directly from the 'devastating effects of colonial advance on the social and economic life of the dispossessed Bantu'.[63]

As in the case of Moodie's apprentices, the change of social situation from the conditions prevailing in Britain to those on the Eastern Frontier led to dramatic changes in both attitudes and behaviour. Anticipating Acton's dictum, Pringle wrote of the 'frightful perversion of moral sentiment' found in the dominant class resulting from the 'uncontrolled exercise of arbitrary power'.[64] Only eight years after the foundation of the settlement, the publication of the fiftieth Ordinance provoked a massive protest:

understandable from the ignorant Dutch-African boors . . . but more liberal sentiments might have been naturally expected, one would imagine, from many of the English colonists, and those not of the lowest class, who joined most vociferously in this ungenerous outcry. But the British settlers had now become active competitors with the boors for native labourers, and *in placing themselves in a similar position, the majority had with lamentable facility adopted similar sentiments*.[65]

---

[60] Cf. W. M. MacMillan, *The Cape Colour Problem* (1927), and *Bantu, Boer and Briton* (1929); J. Lewin, *Politics and Law in South Africa* (1963), pp. 72–85. Galbraith has argued that 'the role of Philip in South African history has, I think, been exaggerated by excessive . . . dependence on his own assessment of his contribution. South African historians have collided on the issue of Philip's integrity while agreeing on his influence, for good or ill.' (J. S. Galbraith, *Reluctant Empire* (1963), preface.)

[61] D. E. Rivett-Carnac (1961), op. cit., p. 103.

[62] W. M. MacMillan, *Bantu, Boer and Briton* (1963), p. 43.

[63] Ibid., p. 74.

[64] T. Pringle, *Narrative of a Residence in South Africa* (1966), p. 69; cf. J. H. Hofmeyr's related comments in *Christian Principles and the Race Problem* (1945), pp. 25–6.

[65] T. Pringle (1966), op. cit. p. 250 (my italics); cf. E. A. Walker, *A History of Southern Africa* (1957), p. 157.

It would seem that neither social class[66] nor education were necessary barriers to such changes in attitude.

The attitudes of the majority of British settlers towards the Africans varied, some were midly 'paternalistic' while others developed into the forthright Social Darwinism exemplified by John Mitford Bowker's famous 'springbok speech'.[67] Spokesmen for the settlers' point of view, Chase, Godlonton, and Bowker, were as outspoken as their critics, though the latter were fewer in number. Modern historical scholarship seems to have reached a recognition of the unique features of the social structure which placed both settler and tribesman in an impossible dilemma,[68] and to have abandoned the fruitless effort to apportion blame to one side or the other.

The settlers' relationship with the Boers was generally friendly, for they shared a common predicament, being harassed by the same tribesmen on the east and restricted by the same autocratic government on the west. Before the arrival of the British in the country, ignorance about the Boers among the settlers was widespread: writing in 1850 Napier commented,

strange as it may seem not one person out of ten, with the exception of those who have visited the Cape, is acquainted with the nature, much less the character of the Boer; indeed, we may observe without, we hope, incurring the risk of being accused of exaggeration, that it is commonly believed in England that the Boer is either black, or of a caste between the native tribes and the white settlers.[69]

[66] For the attitudes of the 'lower' classes: 'In England, I know that servants do not object to having a "blackey" in the house with them; but in a colony, where all the white people, even the most humble, consider themselves superior to, and avoid contact with the coloured race, upon equal terms, *ideas on this subject rapidly change . . .*'. (G. Nicholson, *The Cape and its Colonists with hints to Settlers* (1849), p. 163 (my italics).)

[67] 'The day was when our plains were covered with tens of thousands of springbok, they are gone now, and who regrets it? . . . and I begin to think that he too [the African], as well as the springbok, must give place, and why not? . . .' (J. M. Bowker, *Speeches, Letters and Selections* (1864), p. 125.)

[68] Nor should we claim that the officials at the Colonial Office lacked an understanding of the situation. James Stephens noted that most colonists suffered from a 'disadvantage analogous to that of a short-sighted man the strength of whose vision within his own range of sight is compensated for by the narrowness of the horizon over which his eye ranges', (J. S. Galbraith, *Reluctant Empire* (1963), p. 11).

[69] Lt.-Col. E. Napier, *The Book of the Cape, or Past and Future Emigration* (1851), p. 248. From a genetic, as opposed to a social, point of view the latter surmise is not far from the truth. Cf. P. L. van den Berghe, 'Miscegenation in South

The Boers themselves proved to be hospitable and sympathetic neighbours, and the British colonists showed genuine regret at their departure on the Great Trek.

It is now necessary to leave the situation on the Eastern Frontier, around the middle of the century, and consider the development of the colony in Natal. The first permanent settlement, established by Farewell and Fynn in 1824, was little more than a trading post held on sufferance from the Zulu monarch. Conditions during the first ten years were extremely rough. Some new settlers arrived in 1832,[70] and the British, after having occupied Port Natal, temporarily in 1838 and again in 1842, annexed the whole of Natal as a crown colony in 1843. The first emigration of any significance did not begin until the latter half of the 1840s although, as with the Albany settlement, it had been preceded by many plans of varying degrees of plausibility. A certain Dr. Knox of Edinburgh proposed a scheme for colonizing 'the whole of Southern Africa outside the tropics introducing camels and elephants as beasts of burden, and developing trade with central Africa'.[71] But not all the proposals were quite so exotic; Gladstone suggested that convicts might temporarily be sent to Natal, instead of Van Diemen's Land, to prepare the place for future settlers, but this was never actually put into practice.[72] In December 1846 the Lieutenant-Governor set up a commission to report on the best ways to promote immigration, and this eventually paved the way towards the influx of settlers at the turn of the decade. The attention of this study will be focused on the Byrne settlers who represent the most important single group of immigrants arriving in Natal at this time.[73]

Africa', *Cahiers d'études Africaines*, 4 (1960), 68–84. Nor is this confusion confined to past immigrants: cf. the sample survey responses: 'Afrikaners? . . . aren't they the same as Africans?' (No. 3/20); or, 'I thought the Afrikaner was a tribe, a mixture of Coloureds and Bantu' (No. 461/20).

[70] E. H. Brookes and C. de B. Webb, *A History of Natal* (1965), pp. 22–3.

[71] H. M. Robertson, 'The 1849 Settlers in Natal', *S.A. Journal of Economics* 17, no. 3 (1949), 277.

[72] R. E. Ralls, 'Early Immigration Schemes in Natal, 1846–53', M.A. Thesis, University of Natal (*P.M.B.*) (1934), p. 19; The idea of a convict settlement in South Africa has a long history. The first settlement of 1615 was followed by a suggested scheme in 1816 which included the substitution of convicts for slaves, 'an idea that appealed more to England than to South Africa'. A. W. Tilby, *South Africa* (1914), p. 101 n. 1., who quotes Fisher's pamphlet, 'The Importance of the Cape of Good Hope independently of the advantage it possesses as a naval and military station' (1816). A later attempt is described in A. F. Hattersley, *The Convict Crisis and the Growth of Unity* (1965).

[73] Although there were numerous smaller schemes. For those of Irons,

During the period from January 1849 to June 1852, which covers the main Byrne settlement, some 4,800 British settlers came to Natal.[74] Once again, the sources of information about the colony available to prospective immigrants were diverse and of varying reliability. Pamphlets and posters abounded, books like R. J. Mann's *The Colony of Natal* and that of James Erasmus Methley were widely read, but 'more important than the printed page was the personal testimony of one who was trusted locally'.[75] Hopes and expectations, that seem to be as inseparable from the emigrant as they are from the gambler, fed on the exaggerated ecstasy of those with a vested interest in promoting emigration. Even settlers with no axe to grind could be misleadingly lavish in their praise. William Shaw described the country as 'a land flowing with milk and honey, to which the description of an earthly Canaan is literally applicable'.[76] And many immigrants took it as gospel. Byrne himself in his *Emigrant's Guide to Port Natal* gave a deceptive account of both the fertility of the soil and the value of Zulu labour, and while a recent assessment suggests that he was 'over-optimistic' rather than outrightly fraudulent,[77] his optimism certainly gave rein to a vivid imagination.

The types of settlers who came to Natal were very diverse and included representatives from all classes of British society:

Younger sons of the nobility and gentry in search of official appointments, clergymen of the established church to whom the genial climate or the prospects of missionary work among the 'heathen Zoolahs' appealed, yeomen farmers, despairing of a future for their children on British land, stage coach drivers menaced by the competition of the railroad, and small shopkeepers, prepared to brave the hardships of an unsettled colony, their available capital quilted up in the corsets of their wives.[78]

It is interesting to note the almost complete absence of agricultural

---

Christopher, Boast, and the Duke of Buccleuch, see R. E. Ralls (1934), op. cit. pp. 60–70.

[74] A. F. Hattersley, *British Settlement in Natal* (1950), p. 315.

[75] A. F. Hattersley, *Portrait of a Colony* (1940), p. 16; this is an example of role of 'personal influence'. Other sources of information were also available: 'What with exhibitions of African aborigines, the recorded experiences of sportsmen and travellers and the painted scenery of the Leicester Square halls, there was little difficulty in forming impressions of life in the interior of Southern Africa.' A. F. Hattersley, *A Victorian Lady at the Cape, 1849–51*, n.d., p. 15.

[76] A. F. Hattersley (1940), ibid., p. 18.

[77] E. H. Brookes and C. de B. Webb, *A History of Natal* (1965), p. 66.

[78] A. F. Hattersley, *Portrait of a Colony* (1940), pp. v–vi; and *British Settlement in Natal* (1950), p. 176.

labourers among the immigrants—less than one per cent of the total[79] —which, in view of the failure of the land settlement schemes, proved to be a blessing.[80] Like the 1820 settlers before them, they moved to the towns,[81] a fact that enabled Dr. Mann to claim in 1859 'that scarcely a single individual who came out under Mr. Byrne's auspices, can now be pointed to who has not succeeded in making a fair base for future progress'.[82] Although such an assertion fails to mention that about a thousand settlers, all recent Byrne arrivals, left Natal for Australia in 1852, allured by the prospects of gold and following in the wake of Byrne's bankruptcy.[83] These factors, combined with the prosperity of mid-Victorian England and the discouraging letters sent home by dissatisfied emigrants,[84] brought the supply of immigrants to a halt in 1852. The total European population of the colony in 1857 was not much in excess of 8,000 settlers.[85] In that year the problem of emigration was reconsidered by the new Legislative Council and, following the introduction of assisted passages, some 1,300 additional settlers were recruited during the next five years.[86]

Economic factors seem to have been the basic cause of the migration, although the attractive climate was probably a contributory influence.[87] Certain features of the growing settlement are particularly noteworthy: there was an absence of political radicalism;[88] the acquisition of wealth became an easy passport for social mobility,[89] although one visitor to Pietermaritzburg found the colonists to be 'intolerably cliquey';[90] there were opportunities for leisure and

[79] A. F. Hattersley, *The Natalians* (1940), p. 59.
[80] Cf. H. Akitt, 'Government Assisted Immigration into Natal, 1857–62', M.A. Thesis, Univ. of Natal (P.M.B.) (1952), p. 20.
[81] H. M. Robertson, 'The 1849 Settlers in Natal', *S.A.J.E.* 17, no. 4 (1949), 426.
[82] E. Hammond, 'The Settlement of the Byrne Immigrants in Natal, 1849–52', *S.A. Journal of Science* (1927), 604–5.
[83] H. M. Robertson (1949), op. cit., p. 437.
[84] A. F. Hattersley (1950), op. cit., p. 221.
[85] A. F. Hattersley, *More Annals of Natal* (1936), p. 26.
[86] H. Akitt (1952), op. cit., pp. 63, 71; A. F. Hattersley, *Later Annals of Natal* (Longmans, London, 1938), p. 68.
[87] A. F. Hattersley, *Portrait of a Colony* (1940), pp. 14–15.
[88] A. F. Hattersley, *British Settlement in Natal* (1950), p. 286.
[89] Ibid., p. 314.
[90] A. F. Hattersley, *More Annals of Natal*, p. 108. The two are by no means unrelated as de Tocqueville found in American society of the 1830s: 'Each of them willingly acknowledges all his fellow-citizens as his equals, but will only receive a very limited number of them as his friends or his guests. This appears to me to be very natural. In proportion as the circle of public society is extended, it may be

public responsibility for classes of people unlikely to enjoy either in Britain;[91] and, from the earliest days, housing became an important symbol of social differentiation.[92] As is the case with present-day migration, there were many settlers who left the colony only to return again at some later date.[93]

On the question of race relations, Natal, the most exclusively British of the four provinces, shows a transition from a position of dependence on the powerful indigenous tribes to the traditional paternalism of a colonial society. In the early years, it was Shaka who held stereotypes of the white traders fully as much as the reverse, and Fynn discovered that the Zulu Chief 'well knew that for a black skin we would give all we were worth in the way of our arts and manufactures'.[94] Although Shepstone had advocated a policy of 'total apartheid', rather like Philip's proposals for the Eastern Frontier,[95] this was rejected by the majority of land-owning colonists who had no wish to lose their supplies of native labour. In short, 'the popular voice in Natal opposed Shepstone's policy when it was just and necessary, and supported it when it was obsolescent.'[96] The combination of British traditions with a 'preference for the Voortrekker rather than the official British "native policy"'[97] has been typical of Natal white sentiment from that time until the present. Most of the Natal settlers quickly acquired the racialist attitudes of the colonial situation,[98] but there were significant differences between the outlook of the officials, the settlers, and the missionaries.

These case studies of the first major British settlements in Southern Africa are not intended to be a comprehensive historical account, but rather a highly selective illustration of certain enduring elements in the contact between settlers and a particular racial and ethnic scene. That

---

anticipated that the sphere of private intercourse will be contracted . . .' *Democracy in America* (Mentor edn. 1956), pp. 247–8. See also the discussion of 'class consciousness' and 'social mobility' in the third section of the book.

[91] A. F. Hattersley, *British Settlement in Natal*, p. 334.

[92] Ibid., p. 216.

[93] Ibid., p. 219.

[94] J. Stuart and D. McK. Malcolm (eds.), *The Diary of Henry Francis Fynn* (1950), p. 81; S. A. Ritter, *Shaka Zulu* (1958), pp. 240–2.

[95] A. F. Hattersley, *British Settlement in Natal*, p. 300; J. Lewin, *Politics and Law in South Africa* (1963), p. 81.

[96] E. H. Brookes and C. de B. Webb, *A History of Natal*, p. 57.

[97] Ibid., p. 71.

[98] M. Wilson and L. Thompson (eds.), *The Oxford History of South Africa*. Vol. I (1969), p. 383.

the 1820 settlement scheme was an initial disaster with enduring disruptive consequences can be clearly seen in retrospect. Among the diverse occupational groups the artisans fared best, for the attempt to develop an agricultural rather than a pastoral settlement, and the frontier situation with no adequate policing to protect both sides from cattle plundering and territorial encroachment, led to a series of violent conflicts with their inevitable repercussions.

Several close parallels emerge between this state of affairs and later developments in immigration. Individual motives for migration were predominantly economic, while the Government's aim in supporting the scheme, reversing its traditional policy, was largely strategic although with strong economic undertones. The influence of the Fifth Frontier War may be seen as similar in its impact to the Sharpeville shootings, a shock event that persuaded the ruling circles, against more conservative opinion, that emigration might be a solution to their difficulties. The backgrounds of the settlers were mixed, and there can be no doubt that their expectations and hopes had been enormously inflated by current misconceptions and ignorance about the country and the nature of the settlement. On arrival, the majority of settlers developed an outlook and attitudes similar to those of the local Boers, a result of the unstable situation of frontier warfare.

The power situation at that time may be considered in terms of a triangle of forces in which the main axis of conflict was between black and white. Periodic military assistance to the settlers and the missionary-humanitarian lobby favouring the interests of the Africans were lesser forces operating on the over-all triangular structure. In later chapters I will show how this triangle changed shape with the defeat and destruction of the military power of the African tribal kingdoms, the axis of conflict swinging round to a battle between Briton and Boer for political control over the white élite. In more recent years there has been a reversal to the former pattern of white versus black, but with the Afrikaners rather than the British leading the white group. This has been a response to the rising sense of African nationalism accelerated by the forces of internal industrialization and external decolonization to the north of the Zambezi.

CHAPTER VII

The Uitlanders and Imperialism

WE LEFT the conditions on the Eastern Frontier at a time when the Albany settlers were becoming firmly established, 'the adventurers of 1820 had become the solid citizens of 1840'.[1] During the twenty years following their arrival, the additional immigrants joining the settlement were few and far between; in number they scarcely doubled the original total,[2] but this was not a result of a lack of enthusiasm on the part of the colonists themselves. At public meetings held in both Cape Town and Grahamstown in 1840, petitions were passed urging that money from the land revenues should be diverted towards assisted immigration.[3] However, neither the Governor nor the Secretary for Colonies was prepared to countenance such schemes. The scheme put forward by a Captain Van Reenen for promoting emigration from the Highlands and Islands of Scotland on an ambitious scale also failed to win acceptance.[4]

Four years later the appointment of a new Governor and Colonial Secretary brought a reversal of policy and a cautious introduction of assisted emigration through Maitland's bounty system.[5] Over seven hundred immigrants arrived under this scheme during 1846 and 1847, which coincided with a proposal by Sir Harry Smith to plant 'military villages' of discharged soldiers along the frontier after the most recent outbreak of warfare—a military echo of the 1820 settlement.[6] An increased appropriation in 1849, combined with the deteriorating economic conditions in Britain, led to a temporary accession of some three thousand new immigrants, but many of these moved on to Australia during the gold rushes of the fifties.[7]

In September 1849 the *Neptune* arrived in Simon's Bay with a group of convicts who were intended to start a new penal settlement in the

---

[1] D. E. Rivett-Carnac, *Thus Came the English* (1961), p. 113.
[2] J. C. Chase, *The Cape of Good Hope and the Eastern Province of Algoa Bay* (1967), p. 87.
[3] H. M. Robertson, 'The Cape of Good Hope and Systematic Colonization', *S.A.J.E.* 5, no. 4 (1937), p. 377.
[4] Ibid., p. 379.
[5] Ibid., pp. 381–2.
[6] Ibid., p. 383.   [7] Ibid., p. 390.

Colony. They met with a violently hostile reception from the local population and, not surprisingly, resistance to the plan was strongest in those areas where there was a substantial number of free immigrants.[8] The scheme had to be abandoned and the *Neptune* sailed away without discharging her prisoners; but the fear of convicts was to haunt the colonists for several years to come.[9] At the same time several parties of child immigrants were brought to the Cape by societies caring for the destitute and vagrant.[10] These schemes also came under censure from the colonists, who viewed them as backdoor methods of introducing transportation as a substitute for colonization.

The second half of the 1850s was a period in which the Governor, Sir George Grey, encouraged immigration with considerable enthusiasm.[11] A Select Committee reporting in April 1856 pointed to the following facts:

The present moment is favourable for making an effort to bring emigrants from England. If the war[12] be continued, the high price of provisions and other articles of consumption, the increased taxation, and the prospect of a conscription will lead many persons to desire to emigrate; and if the war be terminated, a large body of men, who have acquired a taste for a more active life than they will be able to enjoy in England, will turn towards a home in the colonies. These, too, will have acquired a training that may be useful in a frontier life.[13]

An Act of 1857 allowed sums of up to £50,000 to be set aside for the purpose of financing immigration either from the ordinary revenue of the Colony or, if this proved insufficient, by floating debenture loans. An Emigration Commissioner in the United Kingdom was charged with selecting immigrants, and Immigration Boards at Cape Town and Port Elizabeth were responsible for their settlement.[14] When, in

---

[8] A. F. Hattersley, *The Convict Crisis and the Growth of Unity* (1965), p. 104.

[9] The Lieutenant-Governor's opening speech to the Cape Parliament in 1860 mentioned a 'fear of pardoned convicts coming to South Africa from Western Australia' and suggested a bill to prevent this. A1'60 point 10, 27 Apr. 1860.

[10] A. F. Hattersley (1965), op. cit., pp. 18, 27, 98.

[11] For a useful guide to the official documents on immigration from 1854–1910, see *Cape of Good Hope: Index to the Annexures and Printed Papers of the House of Assembly* (1854–97), (Cape Town 1899); (1898–1903) (Cape Town 1903); (1904–10) (Cape Town 1910); For the years after 1910, see Department of Census and Statistics, *Official Yearbook of the Union* No. 1 (1910–16), and subsequent volumes.

[12] The Crimean War of 1854–6.

[13] *Report of the Select Committee of the House of Assembly* (1856), no. 7, p. 4.

[14] H. M. Robertson (1937), op. cit., p. 393.

August 1862, these Immigration Boards were closed down, almost ten thousand immigrants had arrived under the scheme, divided equally between Table Bay and Algoa Bay.[15] The motivation behind the policy was largely a question of relative numbers for, in the opinion of the colonial government, the demographic balance between both Englishmen and Afrikaners and between whites and blacks would be favourably influenced by increased British immigration. This has been a constantly recurring theme in relation to immigration to South Africa until the present day.[16] An official statement declared that the continuance of the present system 'until the proportions of the Europeans and native population shall have been more nearly equalized', especially on the frontier of the colony, 'appears to be an object of the highest importance.'[17]

It is possible to gain an insight into the experience of the colonists and their reception by various elements in the host society from an examination of a number of petitions published at that time. In 1860 the inhabitants of Worcester complained of 'the exorbitant rate of wages' demanded by the newcomers and, comparing them unfavourably with German, Swiss, and French settlers, pointed to the familiar fact that most British immigrants came with 'extravagant notions respecting the high rate of wages and other imaginary advantages supposed to be obtained here'.[18] On arrival they soon became 'disappointed, disgusted and discontented', left the colony as soon as possible and 'thus entail a severe loss upon this country at whose expense they were introduced'.[19] The reports of the Immigration Boards in Cape Town and Port Elizabeth, however, dismissed complaints of dissatisfaction as 'very insignificant' and claimed 'that as a body the immigrants have prospered even beyond their most sanguine wishes'.[20] The discrepancy in interpretation clearly reflects the interests of the parties concerned.

In general, there was a strong demand for immigrant labour in the Eastern Province as is witnessed by reports from local immigration

[15] Ibid. p. 397; & G39'63.

[16] Cf. 'Glanville calculated that it would take five years to swamp the Dutch in the Transvaal with 10,000 British born subjects even if a programme of assisted immigration, similar to the one suggested by Froude in 1875, were resorted to'. C. F. Goodfellow, *Great Britain and the South African Confederation* (1966), p. 141.

[17] A1'60 p. 3.   [18] A67'60.

[19] Loc. cit.; cf. Lady Duff Gordon's comments in 1861–2: 'wages are enormous and servants at famine price', *Letters from the Cape* (1921), p. 107.

[20] G29'61, p. 4. G35'61, p. 6.

boards in Grahamstown, Fort Beaufort, and Uitenhage,[21] but this was not the case among the landed proprietors, wine growers, and agriculturalists of the Western Cape. Petitions from both Wellington and Groot Drakenstein complained that British immigrants were 'wholly unsuitable for the agricultural wants of this colony' and urged the authorities to introduce a 'good supply of cheap labour' from 'India, China, the coast or interior of Africa, and other places where it can be procured',[22] and to put an end to the immigration from England.

After 1863 the flow of immigrants ceased and remained of negligible significance until the middle of 1873.[23] The discovery of diamonds at Hopetown in 1867, however, marks a crucial turning-point in both the economic and the immigration history of the country, for although mineral discoveries led initially to internal migration,[24] once the real value of the fields became known, Southern Africa experienced an influx of immigrants on an unprecedented scale. During this decade plans for the promotion of immigration were not lacking. Lord Newcastle, the Secretary of State, asked the Governor for a report on labour prospects in the colony in view of the 'distress which still prevails among the manufacturing population of the northern counties, and the apparent probability of its continuance'.[25] In 1864 the ever resourceful Scot, Alexander McCorkindale, proposed using Lourenço Marques as a base for a company that would settle immigrants in the Eastern Transvaal, but nothing had materialized from this venture at the time of his death in 1871.[26]

Immigration slowly gathered pace again in the latter half of 1873, but the colonial government's attitude towards it was cautious. John X. Merriman, at that time Commissioner of Crown Lands and Public Works, cited the problems of Canada and several other colonies where too many immigrants had arrived with 'high flown expectations of little work and excessive pay' which had led in many cases to

[21] A10'62; A32'62; A69'62.

[22] A39'62; A38'62.

[23] *Report of the Cape of Good Hope Government Emigration Office*, London, 8 Feb. 1877, mentions the reopening of the London Agency in August 1873. It was later expanded: *Report of the Emigration Office* G49'77, p. 23. From 1821 to 1870, one estimate suggested that 43,695 immigrants came from Britain to South Africa: I. Firenczi and W. F. Willcox, *International Migrations* (National Bureau of Economic Research, New York, 1929), vol. 1, pp. 627–30.

[24] O. Doughty, *Early Diamond Days* (1963), p. 4.

[25] *Newcastle to Wodehouse*, 11 Apr. 1863 (A38'63).

[26] E. A. Walker, *A History of Southern Africa*, p. 329.

disappointment and in not a few to great distress. The apprehension of the possibility of a similar disaster, he argued, justified the comparatively limited scale upon which the operations of the Government had been conducted, in addition to the peculiar circumstances of the Colony which afforded no grounds for 'brilliant but hazardous experiments in this direction'.[27] Despite official doubts and hesitation, the growth of railways and the sustained and increasing impact of mineral discoveries fostered immigration on an even greater scale, so that during the decade 1873–83 some 22,300 assisted immigrants came to South Africa at a total cost to the Colony of £224,000.[28]

A study of the various reports on immigration published during these years gives some idea of the occupational composition of these assisted immigrants.[29] They fell under two main categories: 'government immigrants', consisting of railway employees, agricultural settlers, and recruits for the Cape Mounted Rifles; and 'aided immigrants', a heterogeneous group of artisans—carpenters, joiners, plasterers, miners, tailors, and masons—in addition to considerable numbers of female domestic servants.

Immigration into Natal reached a peak in 1879–80,[30] while in the Cape the period 1884 to March 1889 was marked by a lull followed by a new era of unprecedented importance, not only in terms of numbers, but because of its vital political repercussions.[31] From the 1870s onwards the immigrants had become pawns in the power struggle between Briton and Boer. The military conquest of the Bantu had temporarily eliminated the majority of South Africans from the

[27] *Report on Cape Immigration for 1876*, p. 4.

[28] *Report of the Immigration Agents at London* (G58'84), Annexure No. 2: Comparative Statistics 1873–83.

[29] G49'77; G5'79; G19'81; G28'83; G58'84.

[30] E. A. Walker, op. cit., p. 391.

[31] *Memorandum of Government Immigration*, Government Agency, London (20 Feb. 1890) (G35'90); H. M. Robertson (1937), op. cit., p. 409. There are no direct data on the level of immigration during the 1890s. H. M. Robertson points to the high masculinity ratio of the 1890 Transvaal enumeration as a possible indication of substantial, though not necessarily foreign, immigration; secondly, to Rhodes's claim at the 1897 Jameson Raid Inquiry that Uitlanders outnumbered the original Transvalers 80,000 to 60,000, and were being supplemented at the rate of 25,000 per annum; and thirdly, to the *Guide Book of the Union Castle Line* which claimed that 20,000 and 30,000 immigrants left Britain for South Africa in 1895 and 1896. B. Thomas (ed.), *Economics of International Migration* (1958), pp. 173–84. For a careful discussion of the relative number of Boers and Uitlanders at this time, see J. S. Marais, *The Fall of Kruger's Republic* (1961), pp. 1–3.

chessboard of political conflict, leaving the ground clear for a direct confrontation between the two white cultural groups.

For most of the second half of the nineteenth century, British immigration into South Africa consisted of a varying flow of artisans, agricultural workers, and labourers, articulated to the demands of an economy that was based on an expanding railway network and developing extractive industries. Economic conditions in Britain kept available a ready supply of potential immigrants, and most of them made use of Government-assisted passages, bounties, or subsidies. Paradoxically, this later period has produced fewer diaries and other records of the experiences of individual settlers, and these lack, perhaps, some of the glamour of the pioneering frontier farmers of the 1820s. On the other hand, newspapers during the seventies and eighties were nearly always owned and edited by British settlers 'whether they appeared in English or Dutch, or both'.[32] Many features of immigration at this time are familiar, particularly the extravagant hopes that were further stimulated by the mystical lure of diamonds and gold. Once again, *The Times* warned its readers to beware of Cape diamond stories, advice that was not wasted on 'top people' for there were more than a few members of the middle and upper-middle classes among the diggers, and De Beers gained the reputation of being 'rather an aristocratic camp'.[33]

There was no lack of pamphlets offering 'guidance' to prospective emigrants who wished to try their luck at the diggings. One of these quoted a 'letter from the field' describing the situation at Pniel, in July 1870, in enthusiastic terms: 'the landscape . . . on both sides of the Vaal is one grand display of cheerful, eager and hearty labour'. It continued: 'if it were not for the fact that stern labour is the order of the day, one might fancy himself at a fair in England or a Methodist encampment in America'.[34] To the emigrant caught by the fever of the diamond rush, the proviso frequently passed unheeded.[35] Not all the pamphlets, even in the hey-day of the diamond and gold rushes, were quite so sanguine about the prospects concerning the journey to

[32] T. R. H. Davenport, *The Afrikaner Bond: the history of a South African political party, 1880–1911* (1966), p. 5.

[33] O. Doughty, *Early Diamond Days*, pp. 39, 65.

[34] J. G. Steytler, *The Emigrants' Guide to the Diamond Fields of South Africa* issued by Steytler & Steytler, Immigration and General Agents of Cape Town (1870), p. 8.

[35] However, many of the middle-class prospectors found the work far from arduous: J. H. and R. E. Simons, *Class and Colour in South Africa, 1850–1950*, p. 36.

the fields: 'as a pleasure excursion for healthy young fellows, it is not to be despised, but as an undertaking to bring in cash, it is, as a rule, a decided failure'.[36]

The attitude of the typical British immigrant towards the Africans working on the fields—'nude barbarians'[37] as the former pamphlet chose to describe them—was one of contempt tinged with fear of competition: a situation combining elements of both the 'paternalistic and 'competitive' poles of van den Berghe's ideal-types.[38] Such attitudes were not confined to the skilled manual class, and the English journalist Payton, after a short sojourn, soon adopted the stereotyped views that were familiar to the South African scene.[39] Another visitor at this time, the novelist Anthony Trollope, saw the economic forces acting at Kimberley as a means of 'civilizing the native', for he argued that the speed of 'simple philanthropy and religion' was 'terribly slow' whereas the 'love of money works very fast ... and here the natives are brought together not by the sporadic energy of the missionary or by the unalluring attraction of schools, but by the certainty of earning wages'.[40]

The motives for migration were largely economic: most Englishmen went to Johannesburg to 'make their pile and clear',[41] though many in the end decided to settle permanently. Controversy surrounding the uitlanders has so clouded the subject that it is difficult to obtain an unbiased picture of them from contemporary evidence.[42] However, certain facts are clear, notably that as a group they were very mixed, both in their nationality—many were not British, though

[36] Anon., *To the Transvaal Goldfields and Back* (1885), p. 107; those that did 'succeed' included many that provide classic illustration of Durkheim's concept of anomie as a two-way reaction, that sudden success can be as disrupting as sudden failure. 'The effect of sudden and unexpected wealth upon some was disastrous, leading only to drink, poverty and ruin ... but there were many with minds strong enough to bear sudden reverses or accessions of fortune with perfect equanimity' (O. Doughty, *Early Diamond Days* (1963), p. 108).

[37] J. G. Steytler, op. cit., p. 15.

[38] P. L. van den Berghe, 'The Dynamics of Racial Prejudice: an ideal-type dichotomy', *Social Forces*, 37 (1958), 138–41; 'The Dynamics of Race Relations: an ideal-type case study of South Africa', pp. 13–45; *Race & Racism*, pp. 27–34.

[39] G. V. Doxey, *The Industrial Colour Bar in South Africa*, p. 17.

[40] O. Doughty, *Early Diamond Days*, p. 181.

[41] A. W. Tilby, *South Africa, 1486–1913* (1914), p. 446.

[42] For general outlines of the uitlanders, see R. Crisp, *The Outlanders* (1964); A. P. Cartwright, *The Gold Miners* (Purnell, Cape Town–Johannesburg, 1962); the uitlanders' case is argued in J. P. FitzPatrick, *The Transvaal From Within* (1899); cf. also J. S. Marais, *The Fall of Kruger's Republic*; H. J. and R. E. Simons, op. cit., pp. 34–72.

most were English-speaking—and in their attitude towards Kruger and his Republic.[43] Even Lionel Phillips admitted that the majority of them 'didn't care a fig' for the franchise,[44] and their grievances, according to Bryce, 'did not prevent the Johannesburgers from enjoying life and acquiring wealth'.[45] This is not to deny the reality of their complaints but to emphasize their primary economic orientation.

In the bitter years leading to war, Smuts complained of the 'nightly meetings . . . held on the Witwatersrand, where Cornwall miners,[46] who send all their earnings "home"[47] every week and have no other thought than to go back "home" as soon as possible . . . shout for the franchise night after night with violent threats'.[48] Milner issued his famous dispatch bemoaning the plight of 'thousands of British subjects kept permanently in the position of helots'.[49] And yet, four years before, 'when the day of battle seemed to be at hand', many, including most of the Cornish miners, proved to be indifferent, and 'departed by train amid the jeers of their comrades'.[50]

In addition to their cosmopolitan background and their general lack of political involvement, the uitlanders possessed diverse skills and occupational experience. Bryce described them as:

miners, traders, financiers, engineers, keen, nimble-minded men, all more or less skilled in their respective crafts, all bent on gain, and most of them with that sense of irresponsibility and fondness for temporary pleasure which a chanceful and uncertain life, far from home, and relieved from the fear of public opinion, tends to produce.[51]

[43] G. A. Leyds, *A History of Johannesburg* (1964), pp. 69, 113.
[44] A. W. Tilby, op. cit., p. 452, n. 1; G. A. Leyds, op. cit., p. 82; and note the comment by R. Horwitz, op. cit., pp. 438–9, n. 3; cf. E. A. Walker, *A History of Southern Africa*, pp. 432, 436, 462.
[45] J. Bryce, *Impressions of South Africa*, p. xxiii.
[46] Many of the miners who came from Britain brought with them the traditions of militant trade unionism. These were soon modified to the South African environment and led in the extreme case to segregationalist communists. Such a glaring contrast between the universalism of an ideology and the particularism displayed in its interpretation, invites comparison with certain religious parallels. Cf. E. Q. Campbell and T. F. Pettigrew, 'Racial and Moral Crisis: The Role of Little Rock Ministers', 509–16; and *Christians in Racial Crisis: A Study of the Little Rock Ministry* (1959).
[47] In the sample survey, many immigrants mentioned that references to, or comparisons with, 'home' were not calculated to endear the newcomer to the native population.
[48] W. K. Hancock, *Smuts: The Sanguine Years, 1870–1919*, p. 88.
[49] Ibid., p. 90.   [50] J. Bryce, op. cit., p. 419.
[51] J. Bryce, op. cit., p. 408.

I

Perhaps it is this that led General Butler, British Commander in the Cape Colony, to describe Johannesburg as 'Monte Carlo super-imposed on Sodom and Gomorrah',[52] and John X. Merriman to refer to 'that sink of iniquity, Johannesburg'.[53] But these opinions have to be set against the experience of Cornelius Van Gogh, a brother of the painter Vincent, who found that because there was 'nothing to do on Saturdays and Sundays'[54] he was forced to stay in bed and read.

Socially, the English section of the uitlanders fell into three broad categories: the middle classes, traders, professional men, and engin-eers who were the main supporters of the National Union; the capitalist mine-owners; and, the most numerous of all, the working men. Although there were differences between these various classes in their desire for the franchise, there appears to have been little difference in their attitudes towards the African population of the Transvaal. James Bryce discovered that an 'attitude of contempt . . . may be noted in all classes', though it was strongest in those 'rough and thoughtless whites who plume themselves all the more upon their colour because they have little else to plume themselves upon'.[55] Under these circumstances it is not surprising that he found no socialist movement on the Rand, for the mass of workers 'to whom elsewhere socialism addresses itself, is mainly composed of black people, and no white would dream of collectivism for the benefit of blacks'.[56] In fact, such was the subordination of the Bantu at this time that they hardly entered the calculations of the disputing Boers and Britons. Though there were 700,000 'Kafirs in the Transvaal' during the war, 'no one reckoned them as possible factors in the con-test, any more than sheep or oxen'.[57]

[52] A. W. Tilby, *South Africa*, p. 446, n. 3.

[53] R. Horwitz, *The Political Economy of South Africa*, p. 439, n. 4.

[54] G. A. Leyds, *A History of Johannesburg*, p. 224, n. 10. Cornelius Van Gogh lived and worked in Johannesburg and on the Rand between 1889 and 1899. The capacity for self-entertainment is a valuable asset in adjusting to a new country according to both contemporary and earlier immigrants. Writing in July 1857, Harriet Rabone praised the new German immigrants 'who possess one great advantage—that of having resources of amusement *within themselves*— a very great blessing out here' (A. Rabone (ed.), *The Records of a Pioneer Family* (1966), p. 108).

[55] J. Bryce, op. cit., pp. 352–3.

[56] J. Bryce, op. cit., p. 396; for a discussion of the factors inhibiting the growth of trade unionism in early South Africa, see H. J. and R. E. Simons, *Class and Colour in South Africa, 1850–1950*, p. 25.

[57] Ibid., p. 419, n. 1.

Among the white community in the country at large, Bryce found that the general equality of conditions had produced 'a freedom from assumption on the one hand, and from servility on the other, and, indeed, a general absence of snobbishness, which is quite refreshing to the European visitor'.[58] However, in his observations about the Afrikaans language this normally perceptive writer came to some dubious conclusions. He was surprised that Dutch had held its ground so stubbornly in South Africa against the competition of his own language, particularly since it was not the 'cultivated Dutch of Holland', but a 'vulgarized . . . dialect called the Taal, which is almost incapable of expressing abstract thought or being a vehicle for any ideas beyond those of daily life . . .'. 'This defect might give English a great advantage', he continued, 'if the Boers wished to express abstract ideas. But they have no abstract ideas to express. They are a people who live in the concrete.'[59] If this was the considered opinion of a broadminded Liberal statesman, it is not difficult to imagine what the typical British immigrant thought of his Afrikaans-speaking neighbour.

The outbreak of war curbed the flow of immigrants, but the role of immigration in relation to the future balance of population within the Transvaal was never far from the thoughts of both politicians and generals. Kitchener even suggested the resettlement of the captured Boer population 'so that South Africa will be safe, and there will be room for the British to colonize'.[60] The war itself was almost entirely a 'white man's' war. There was an understanding that the 'native' should not be armed and when this occasionally happened it produced violent recriminations.[61]

It was Milner who was most clearly aware of the political consequences of immigration,[62] but he made two serious miscalculations, first, about the speed with which Boer resistance could be crushed,

[58] Ibid., p. 383.
[59] Ibid., p. 382; cf. C. Lévi-Strauss, *The Savage Mind* (1966), pp. 1–33, for a contemporary attempt to refute a similar argument.
[60] R. Kruger, *Goodbye Dolly Grey* (Mentor, London, 1967 edn.), p. 432.
[61] B. Gardner, *Mafeking: a Victorian Legend* (Cassell, London, 1966), p. 80; W. K. Hancock, *Smuts*, vol. 1, p. 143.
[62] C. Headlam (ed.), *The Milner Papers*, vol. 2, (Cassell, London, 1931–3, 2 vols.), pp. 279–80, 523–4; W. K. Hancock, *Smuts: The Sanguine Years*, vol. 1 (1962), p. 176 *Are There South Africans?*. It is interesting to note that 'Milner's team of college graduates and colonial officials took over the racial ideologies as well as the offices of their republican predecessors at Pretoria and Bloemfontein' (H. J. and R. E. Simons, *Class and Colour in South Africa, 1850–1950*, p. 66).

and secondly, about the automatic tide of immigration that he assumed would follow in its wake. He believed that the 'Augean stables' would soon be cleared and then the British immigrants would come swarming in, to swing the political balance of power against the Boers, 'rapidly, decisively and forever'.[63] For, he calculated, 'if, in ten years hence, there are three men of British race to two of Dutch, the country will be safe and prosperous, if there are three Dutch to two British we shall have perpetual difficulty. . . .'[64] This modified Micawber equation of happiness turned out, in the event, to be predictably precarious, and in 1904 the High Commissioner was lamenting the fact that 'the labour difficulty, and the consequent depression in trade and industry, have most seriously checked immigration.'[65]

Had the influx of new settlers proceeded at the rate which prevailed from the close of the war until the last quarter of 1903, the question of British predominance would have been settled, according to Milner's grand design, in a very few years. Although nearly 27,000 British subjects entered the Transvaal during the course of 1903, by March of the following year the flow was in the reverse direction. The post-war economic depression finally wrecked Milner's calculations and when immigration eventually revived again in 1910, the year of the Act of Union, the die had already been cast in favour of permanent Afrikaner hegemony in the Transvaal. Milner's final attempt to reverse the tide was, ironically, another immigration scheme—that of Chinese coolies to work the dislocated gold mines.[66]

It is not easy to gain a clear quantitative picture of the nature and type of British immigrants arriving during the first decade of the twentieth century.[67] An occupational breakdown of passenger arrivals from ports beyond South Africa, of which only 68 per cent were British nationals, was as follows:

Professional, business and leisured class	21·3 per cent
Tradesmen and Artisans	34·5 per cent
Agriculturalists	1·1 per cent
Undetermined (wives, minor children)	24·7 per cent
Not Stated	18·4 per cent
Total	100·0 per cent

[63] W. K. Hancock (1962), vol. 1, p. 171.   [64] Ibid., p. 174.

[65] C. Headlam (ed.), *The Milner Papers*, vol. 2, pp. 523–4.

[66] For the 'failure of Milnerism' see G. H. L. Le May, *British Supremacy in South Africa, 1899–1907* (1965), chap. 7.

[67] For such information that is available see *Report of the Working of the Immigration Act of 1902* (G63'04); *Report of the Officer in Charge of Immigration and Labour* (G4'06); *Report on Immigration and Labour* (G21'07); *Report of the Chief Immigration Officer* (G6'09).

In spite of the limited value of these figures one point is noteworthy, 'the exceedingly small proportion of immigrants of the agricultural class'.[68] Another interesting feature of this report is the evidence of the early seeds of anti-semitism—the Medical Officer of Health suggested the abolition of Yiddish as an educational test for entry[69] —which was to reach its full flowering in the Immigration Acts of the 1930s.

A sharp drop in passenger traffic during 1904–5 probably included a more than proportional fall in immigration, 'for the decrease has been most marked in the poorer classes, to which, in the main, the immigrant proper belongs'.[70] In July 1905 a Parliamentary vote made £1,000 available to subsidize certain classes of immigrants, particularly the wives of artisans, children, and domestic servants, at the rate of six pounds sterling per head, but the returns from the Customs Statistical Bureau suggested that 1906 was a year of net population loss.[71] Depression conditions persisted, and during the latter part of the year a government report announced that 'the issue of passages has . . . been altogether discontinued and the numerous applications are for the present refused in all cases'.[72] The net outflow appears to have continued until 1910,[73] when the Union was formed and Botha became the first Prime Minister. Among the clauses of the manifesto issued in June of that year was one approving of European immigration, while strongly rejecting immigrants from Asia.[74] However, Botha's talk of the need for white settlers at the Imperial Conference a year later caused alarm among certain Afrikaners,[75] a reaction that has persisted to the present day.

[68] G63'04, p. 7.
[69] Ibid., p. 23.
[70] G4'06, p. 3, 4.
[71] Ibid., p. 7; *Report on Immigration and Labour*, G21'07, p. 5.
[72] Ibid., p. 8.
[73] *Report of the Chief Immigration Officer*, G6'09, p. 2; and *Official Yearbook of the Union*, no. 7 (1924), p. 135, which contains a good summary of immigration from 1902 to 1924, at which date reliable and complete statistics for both immigration and emigration were finally recorded.
[74] T. R. H. Davenport, *The Afrikaner Bond*, p. 299.
[75] E. A. Walker, *A History of Southern Africa*, p. 545.

CHAPTER VIII

The Artisans and Apartheid

As a result of the First World War, British immigration fell from an annual total of nearly 10,000 to barely 1,500. It revived again in 1918, reaching a post-war peak in 1920, only to be checked by the economic depression which began in the following year.[1] This typical pattern of wartime diminution followed by an immediate, though temporary, post-war boom has repeated itself several times in South African history. In the year before the outbreak of war the Union Government passed an Immigration Act aimed largely at excluding Indians (the next two such acts, in 1930 and 1937, were directed against the Jews). It was in the same year, too, that Sir Percy Fitzpatrick established his Sundays River Settlement Company.[2]

Fitzpatrick's scheme was not unlike the attempt to promote settlement in the Eastern Province a hundred years earlier. Based on Botha's Land Settlement Act (1911), which authorized the acquisition of private lands suitable for settlement purposes,[3] it was advertised in a supplement of the *Farmers Weekly* during 1917 with a view to attracting settlers from the ranks of discharged soldiers.[4] The scheme soon encountered difficulties—the 1918 influenza epidemic, protracted drought, and even an outbreak of bubonic plague—but despite the warnings from the Union Government[5] many ex-servicemen were so anxious to go that they 'blindly bought their land and hoped for the best'.[6] The best, however, was not to materialize, and the disenchantment among the settlers when shown their farms, 'spots on a map which they had chosen in England, in reality, squares of dust in South Africa',[7] can only be imagined. Amid increasing

---

[1] *Official Yearbook of the Union* no. 7 (1924), p. 135.

[2] J. M. Meiring, *Sundays River Valley: its history and settlement* (1959); J. P. R. Wallis, *Fitz, the story of Sir Percy Fitzpatrick* (Macmillan, London, 1955).

[3] J. M. Meiring, op. cit., p. 62.

[4] Ibid., p. 71.

[5] *Morning Post* 27 Aug. 1919 in an article entitled 'South Africa—Misleading of Would-be Settler—Official Warning'.

[6] J. M. Meiring, *Sundays River Valley*, p. 81.

[7] Ibid., p. 85.

recriminations the Company went into voluntary liquidation in 1923, its assets being taken over by the Government two years later.[8] One Senator pointed to the detrimental effect of the scheme on the country's reputation, claiming that hundreds of settlers had been 'enticed to South Africa under false pretences, and that many of them had been reduced to the status of poor whites'.[9]

In South Africa, particularly during the interwar period, this was the ultimate damnation. The poor-white theme was of special relevance to both the question of immigration and the racial status system, for, like the 'educated native', it posed a threat to the established two-category hierarchy. Some illuminating comments on the situation were made in the Report of the Carnegie Commission, which was set up to investigate the poor white problem in South Africa.[10] The economic section of the Report stressed the role of such 'non-economic' factors as the prejudice against 'Kaffirs' work' and the general concern about status, and claimed that 'persons recently arrived from Europe are very often more particular about their status as white men than the older inhabitants'. It cited as further evidence from East Africa that young English artisans who had been but a few weeks in the country 'would not dream of carrying their own tool-bag but engaged a "personal boy"'.[11]

The psychological section of the Report contained similar cases relating to the status insecurity of those threatened by downward social mobility, observing that 'as this type of poor white finds himself sinking in the economic scale, he becomes more and more aware of the need of asserting his superiority over the native', and he tries to do so by 'refusing to demean himself and do Kaffir work'.[12] Thirty years earlier Bryce had noticed the growth of a class of people resembling the 'mean whites' of the Southern States of America, 'loafers and other lazy or shiftless fellows who hang about and will not take any regular work'. At that time they were a new social phenomenon and not numerous, but their appearance, he asserted, was the natural result of 'that contempt for hard unskilled labour which the existence of slavery inspired in the whites', and he predicted that they would constitute, as in the Southern States of America, the

[8] Ibid., pp. 127, 139.   [9] Ibid., p. 143.
[10] Report of the Carnegie Commission, The Poor White Problem in South Africa (1932).
[11] The Poor White Problem in South Africa (1932), pp. 1–175; cf. also Report of the Select Committee on the Poor White Question (A10'06).
[2] Ibid., pp. 11–56.

section of the population 'specially hostile to the Negro, and there-fore dangerous to the whole community'.[13]

Finally, in the education section of the Report, E. G. Malherbe made the vital point that the very fact that concern was being shown about 'poor *whiteism* and not with poverty as such'[14] proved the peculiarity of the South African situation. Had the pressure of immigration been towards South Africa during the 1920s and 1930s, which it was not, the political influence of the poor whites, clearly manifested in the labour legislation of the period, would have been exerted to exclude this influx of dangerously competitive rivals.

However, after 1923 immigration fell to the low level that was to persist throughout the interwar years, reaching its nadir during the depths of the Depression in 1932–3. The main focus of immigration conflict turned towards the growing flow of Jewish immigrants and both the Quota Act (1930) and the Aliens Act (1937) were aimed at checking the 'Israelitish invasion',[15] though they left British immi-gration unaffected. *The Annual Report on Statistics of Migration* warned that this type of immigration was introducing a feature into the 'racial composition of white South Africa' which was easily over-looked by those who were only concerned with the question of whether the country was gaining white population. In effect, it explained, 'we are losing Union-born citizens, chiefly to Rhodesia and South West Africa, and filling up the gaps largely with immi-grants from Eastern Europe.'[16]

In spite of its relative insignificance, British immigration was still a source of party political dispute during the interwar years. In May 1921 Malan accused Smuts of threatening the South African nation by bringing in immigrants from Britain.[17] In fact, 'the controlled immigration of Europeans of good quality and economic status'[18] was one of the three planks of Smuts's policy for economic development in the years leading up to his defeat in the general election of 1924. Five years later he was to return to this theme, against the wider background of British colonial Africa, in his Rhodes Memorial

[13] J. Bryce, *Impressions of South Africa*, p. 382; for a more general theoretical comment on the relation of such groups to class conflict and overall social strati-fication, see M. Weber, *The Theory of Social and Economic Organization* (1947), pp. 425–6.

[14] *The Poor White Problem in South Africa* (1932), pp. 111–22.

[15] E. A. Walker, *A History of Southern Africa*, p. 656.

[16] *Statistics of Migration, 1919–27* (UG38'29), p. v.

[17] W. K. Hancock, *Smuts: The Fields of Force, 1919–1950*, p. 44.

[18] Ibid., p. 157.

Lectures at Oxford, so much so that the Nationalist newspapers could then dub him an uitlander.[19]

The interwar years also saw the foundation and growth of the 1820 Memorial Settlers' Association.[20] Although in 1920 the Association's settlers represented only 5 per cent of the total flow of British migration to South Africa, this figure had reached 20 per cent by the outbreak of the Second World War. A study of the Association's work during these years clearly does not present us with a full picture of British immigration, but it can supply useful additional data to supplement the bald statistics, particularly with respect to the dominant attitudes, motives, and experiences of the settlers.

One hundred years after the first settler ships landed at Algoa Bay, the 1820 Memorial Settlers' Association was founded in Grahamstown and, four months later, on 6 August 1920, a London Committee was established. The aims of the Association, as defined in the constitution, were the encouragement of 'suitable settlers' to come to the Union of South Africa and Rhodesia 'in commemoration of the settlers of 1820', and to arrange 'their reception on landing, and the provision of such further aid as may be necessary to ensure their success'.[21] The Earl of Selbourne was the first Chairman of the London Committee, the Honorary Presidents included Milner and Smuts,[22] and among the many Vice-Presidents were Rudyard Kipling, Beit, Lionel Phillips, and Earl Grey.

For the first ten years of its life, the Association was dealing almost entirely with a socially exclusive section of British immigrants.[23] This was so apparent that Professor Wallace, who held the Chair in Agriculture and Rural Economy at Edinburgh University, wrote to the *Daily Telegraph* severely criticizing the 'middle-class emigration scheme for South Africa'.[24] It was not an inaccurate description, for

[19] Ibid., pp. 222–5.
[20] Much of the following information is based on, or supplemented by, the Association's files, records, minute books, and magazine.
[21] The Constitution (1920), Article (i).
[22] Minute Books (unpublished) 1820 Memorial Settlers' Association, London Committee (Aug. 1920–Oct. 1922).
It is interesting to note how soon Smuts's prediction, in his last letter to Milner some fifteen years earlier—'History writes the word "Reconciliation" over all her quarrels . . .'—seemed to be being fulfilled in so far as both men could support the same cause. However, in the wider context of the breach between Afrikaner and English-speaking South African 'reconciliation' has been the product of fear rather than time. Cf. W. K. Hancock, *Smuts: the Sanguine Years*, p. 198.
[23] Minute, 25 Oct. 1920. [24] *South Africa* (Journal), 16 Apr. 1926.

the early applicants were largely ex-officers who possessed some capital and were intent on farming, but the Association also co-operated with the 'Sons of England' by 'vetting certain teachers as prospective immigrants'.[25]

During the 1920s the Association's work gradually expanded to include a wider social basis of recruitment, and it is possible to gain some insight into current attitudes and expectations by considering the comments made by various officials and visitors to the Union at this time. Writing in 1926, one such visitor made the following obser-vations about the changing position of the Englishman at home and in Africa. He argued that only by travel in the colonies could the home Briton learn the true importance of maintaining 'in full vigour the sequence of Imperial aspirations and sentiments'. In this way alone contact could be made with the circumstances and incidents which govern the views of those who, although connected with home by many links, '*are compelled by their environment to look upon social and other problems from another standpoint* from those who live in the security and isolation of the British Isles'.[26] These 'social and other problems' referred primarily to the relations between different racial and ethnic groups.

In the same year, during a lecture at Aberdeen University about the Association's work, the Earl of Leven and Melville warned that though 'native labour' could be had at twenty-five shillings per month, 'no farmer could go out there and think that he could simply walk around and leave all the dirty work to be done by natives'. The native, he continued, 'was like a dog in that he would work well if well treated', but he was not of the same standard as a farm servant in Britain.[27] Later that year, it was stated explicitly that the aims of the Association were 'to ensure the future of the white races in South Africa by systematically introducing settlers of the right type', which meant, at that time, farmers, public-school boys, and men owning capital of at least £1,000, and among its most important functions was the 'tuition given by experts on how to handle native labourers'.[2]

These extracts reveal the restricted middle-class orientation of the Association's early policy. They suggest that the role of the 'native' was that of providing unskilled labour, while a stern 'paternalism' was

[25] Minute, 17 Nov. 1920.
[26] *Glasgow Herald*, 10 Apr. 1926, 'Impressions of South Africa', Article no. 2 (my italics).
[27] *The Scotsman*, 19 Feb. 1926.
[28] *The Scotsman*, 5 Oct. 1926.

still the main pattern of white race attitudes in the farming sector of the economy. Any competition between white and black workers was unthinkable as revealed in a statement by an ex-President of the National Farmers' Union which boldly asserted:

It must, however, be borne in mind that South Africa has no room for the man who does not come to her in the right spirit, determined to succeed despite setbacks. There is an ample supply of cheap native labour to do purely manual work, and she has no desire to add to the number of 'poor whites' which the country supports. The white man, however poor his type, cannot decently be allowed to compete in juxta-position with native labour, and so South Africa welcomes only those who have the character and the ability to make good as masters.[29]

The idea of baasskap was no Afrikaner monopoly.

The highly selective policy of the Association meant that of the several thousand settlers introduced by 1927, nearly 87 per cent remained to make South Africa their home.[30] But in March of that year, at a meeting of the Association in Durban, Sir Charles Crewe complained of the Union Government's lack of interest in its work. He argued that every settler was a recruit for that 'small band of Europeans who live in the Union, surrounded by several times their number of natives' and stressed that the only way to maintain white leadership was to encourage immigrants to join 'our all too small European garrison'.[31]

One reason for the apathy of the Government was suggested by Lionel Phillips who, while agreeing that 'the crying need of South Africa . . . is for more white population', mentioned the talks he had had many years earlier with 'the late General Botha on the subject of the poor whites'. Botha held the view, an erroneous one according to Phillips, that the poor whites should be placed on the land before immigration was encouraged. In rejecting the argument that immigrants took away jobs from the local population, one that was to be used extensively by the Nationalists in the post-war period, Phillips quoted a statement by Hofmeyr, 'if we had four times the population, we have four times the trade'.[32] This assertion, at least in the sense

[29] *South Africa* (Journal), 30 July 1926, p. 183.
[30] *African World*, 1 Jan. 1927.
[31] *Morning Post*, 7 Mar. 1927. In addition to the Association's complaint of Union Government's apathy, the London Committee complained of 'recent attacks made on the Association's work by the *Natal Witness*' (Minute Book: July 1925–Nov. 1931, for 31 Mar. 1927).
[32] *African World*, 21 May 1927.

implied by Phillips, is a revealing reflection of social attitudes at that time, for by multiplying the white population by four a figure approaching the actual population is reached. It was precisely this attitude that Smuts recognized and warned against in his 1942 lecture on 'The Basis of Trusteeship'.[33]

The years 1927–8 marked a fall in the number of immigrants, and the Report of the Chairman of the Association explained that 'the drought and the political controversies in the Union have had the effect of turning the thoughts of intending settlers to other parts of the Empire'.[34] In view of these figures, the Association became more concerned with publicity. A series of lectures on South Africa at the Regent Street Polytechnic, at which Smuts and John Galsworthy were invited to be chairmen, received the London Committee's support although they felt that 'the Polytechnic audience is not likely to be a rich recruiting field.'[35] Another proposal aimed at inducing boys from English and Scottish schools to pursue their higher education at the University of Cape Town with a view to permanent settlement in South Africa, 'on the lines of the scheme already in operation with McGill University, Canada'.[36]

Six months later the over-all situation showed little improvement and although advertising in Britain attracted a large number of inquiries, a low proportion of potential settlers actually sailed to South Africa. Association officials complained that 'the "snowball" effect has not come up to expectations' and attributed this to the fact that many men and women who had gone to South Africa during the previous few years were 'not inclined to encourage their friends at home to go out'.[37] Here is yet another example of the potent effect of 'personal influence' in the field of migration.

It was also during the 1930s that the Association began to assist settlers in the category that we later describe as 'ex-colonial'. These

[33] Smuts wrote: 'When people ask me what the population of South Africa is, I never say that it is two millions. I think it is an outrage to say it is two millions. This country has a population of over ten millions, and that outlook which treats the African and Native as not counting, is making the ghastliest mistake possible. If he is not much more, he is the beast of burden; he is the worker and you need him. He is carrying this country on his back.' J. C. Smuts, *The Basis of Trusteeship*, p. 14.

[34] *The Times*, 4 July 1928.

[35] Minute, 31 July 1929 565(b); the Committee's pessimism was later confirmed: Minute, 6 Nov. 1929, 601.

[36] Minute, 31 July 1929, 569.

[37] Minute, 1 Jan. 1930, 619(d); however, the return rate of those who did emigrate was only $7\frac{1}{2}$ per cent: *The 1820* magazine, Aug. 1930.

immigrants were drawn from 'the retired gentleman class, such as Army and Navy officers, Indian civil servants, and businessmen in the East' who did not wish to return to England, but preferred to go to South Africa and to bring up their children there as South Africans. The Association brought out 400 families belonging to this group and claimed that this facet of their work had 'extended enormously'.[38] Towards the end of the decade the Association could justly claim that it dealt with 'every class of settler which South Africa can absorb'.[39] The overwhelming majority of immigrants were going to employment in the non-agricultural sector, and the category of skilled artisan was becoming extremely important, foreshadowing post-war trends. In one month during 1938, to take an illustrative example, nearly all cases fell within this group and included joiners, bricklayers, plasterers, masons, carpenters, plumbers, fitters, mechanics, and coach builders.[40]

Immigration on the eve of the Second World War had begun to climb significantly, but with the outbreak of hostilities it fell again to a predictably low level.[41] The Association recognized that after the war opportunities would be greatest for the qualified artisan,[42] and inquiries for information steadily increased from 1942 to 1945.[43] By November 1945 applications from service- and ex-servicemen became proportionately greater, swelling into a flood of post-war interest that broke all previous records.[44] These inquiries were classified as follows: artisans = 75 per cent, professionals = 15 per cent, residential = 7 per cent, and farmers = 3 per cent.[45] The dominance of the artisan, the rising significance of the professionals, and the relative unimportance of farmers are all reflections of the changing social and economic structure of post-war Britain and South Africa. Shortage of transport created delays of up to twelve months, and the Association's London Office reported that 'people are desperately anxious' to proceed to the Union, and 'every possible and many impossible methods of transport have been discussed at interviews'.[46]

---

[38] *The 1820*, Aug. 1930, p. 13.   [39] *The 1820*, Sept. 1937.

[40] Minute, 1 Jan. 1938, and Minutes of Executive Committee, July 1939; contrast this with the more exclusive categories a few years before: The 1820, 1 Jan. 1931, and the Report of the Cape Area Executive: *Cape Times*, 12 Sept. 1925.

[41] Minute, July 1942.

[42] Minute of the Executive Committee, Mar. 1940.

[43] Minute, July 1945.   [44] Minute, 1 Nov. 1945.

[45] Minute, July 1946.   [46] Ibid.

This post-war emigration boom coincided with the crucial 1948 South African general election, crucial because Dr. Malan's National Party had very decided views about British immigrants. Before the end of the war the Nationalists had been pressing the Smuts Government for a clear statement about its post-war immigration policy, but the Minister of the Interior, while accepting the need for immigrants, assured the members of the Opposition that he was 'not going in for a huge wholesale scheme of immigration tomorrow'.[47] However, the scene was set for one of the major issues of the forthcoming election[48] for, although the United Party tried to deny it, immigration was becoming a critical element in the struggle for power. The Nationalists' policy was to accept the prior claim of 'our own people in our own country'[49] to the available housing and employment opportunities. While recognizing the value of increasing the white population, they argued that the real motive behind their opponents' enthusiasm for immigrants was to drown the aspirations of Afrikanerdom in a new flood of British uitlanders—the reincarnation of Milnerism at its very worst.[50]

The United Party's tactics were to stress the need to strengthen both the economy and the European population, that without immigration the white minority would inevitably 'go down in a sea of colour'.[51] Speaking in the House in March 1946, Smuts was less than enthusiastic; he described immigration as a 'difficult question', and claimed that he did not wish to 'bring these people to our country when they have no living to make and merely become a problem to us'.[52] Five months later he had completely changed his mind and announced to a party meeting in Pretoria:

[47] *House of Assembly Debates*, vol. 47 cols. 2200–1 (29 Feb. 1944).

[48] W. K. Hancock argues that the key issue of the campaign was that of 'native' policy and the two concepts of it embodied in the Fagan and Sauer Reports: 'the first document tried to explain how South Africans who differed from each other in race and colour could live together; the second document tried to explain how they could live apart.' *Smuts: the Fields of Force*, p. 491. My interpretation is somewhat different; it was more a question of the terms on which different 'races' would *work* together than live together. The Nationalists' policy did not represent a radical departure from established practice, so much as a change in official rhetoric.

[49] *House of Assembly Debates*, vol. 53, col. 5984, (24 Apr. 1945).

[50] Cf. J. G. Strydom's remarks: *House of Assembly Debates*, vol. 56, col. 3995 (21 Mar. 1946); however, by the time he was Prime Minister he was prepared to make assurances that he 'would seek skilled immigrants without any anti-British bias'. E. A. Walker, *A History of Southern Africa*, p. 924.

[51] *House of Assembly Debates*, vol. 56, cols. 3989–90 (21 Mar. 1946).

[52] Ibid., col. 4034.

If I have to put our problems in their proper order I would put first this matter of strengthening our European population. It is no use talking about the future unless you place first of all the paramount question . . . this task of immigration which lies before us . . . let us not be afraid we shall digest them. Let them come to industry which is clamouring for them. I look on this as a chance—a God given chance.[53]

Unfortunately for Smuts, the Nationalist Opposition also saw this as a chance, and the opening debate of the 1947 Parliament contained a motion, tabled by Malan, condemning the policy of 'large scale and state-aided immigration' as 'imprudent in concept and disastrous in its consequences'.[54] Malan was able to point to Smuts's volte-face on immigration policy, he could make capital out of the in-cautious and high-flown rhetoric of the speech of 14 August,[55] and he could raise up the spectre of a latter-day Milner to demand protection for the 'real South African nation'. He referred sarcastic-ally to the motives behind Smuts's new policy: 'I have no doubt that . . . it is good holism, but viewed from the national angle, it is false and rotten. . . . I say, Immigration and immigration are two different things.'[56]

The new policy also came under fire from Mrs. Ballinger, who saw in the scheme a harmful diversion away from the central problem of the co-operation between the 'races'.[57] She stressed the logical absurdity of discussing a 'shortage of labour' while simultaneously 'wasting not thousands but millions of labour hours a year in pass offices and gaols'. 'Labour', she concluded, 'as I intend labour to be understood . . . is obviously not short in South Africa.'[58] This plea for the majority of South Africans, though not quite the voice in the wilderness that Merriman's had been twenty years before,[59] was still quite unacceptable to members of the two major political parties:

[53] *Cape Times*, 15 Aug. 1946.

[54] *House of Assembly Debates*, vol. 60, col. 32–3.

[55] Cf. 'Let them come to South Africa in their thousands, their tens of thousands, their hundreds of thousands, and perhaps in their millions, the good and the bad, we can digest them all.'

[56] *House of Assembly Debates*, vol. 60, col. 39; The Nationalist policy called for stricter controls, particularly against 'unassimilable' elements. Louw defined 'assimilable' as: 'a type of immigrant who will identify himself not only with the people of South Africa, but will also conform to our customs and policy, particu-larly in regard to the Colour Question' . . . 'in the second place . . . we regard as unassimilable people . . . those who belong to the Jewish race.' (col. 67)

[57] Cf. M. Ballinger, *From Union to Apartheid: A Trek to Isolation* (1969).

[58] *House of Assembly Debates*, vol. 60, cols. 314–15.

[59] W. K. Hancock, *Smuts: The Fields of Force*, p. 77.

as yet the battle of culture had blinded its participants to the rising tide of African awareness.

In reply to the debate, Smuts claimed that the expansion of industry and the number of wartime visitors to the country had created a new situation that was particularly ripe for an extraordinary addition to the population. However, it was not too clear what had changed in the preceding five months to merit so drastic a reappraisal or to justify a complete reversal of policy. His reply to Mrs. Ballinger —he fully realized that her lone voice was the voice of the future— was both subtle and unconvincing:

Politics in South Africa on colour questions and racial questions are largely vitiated by this element of fear which I think we should remove, and one way to remedy it is to follow the policy now advocated. We can never redress the balance of numbers . . . but you can so strengthen the position of the minority that this fear that is gripping them . . . will be removed and you will be able to look at this gravest question in South Africa in a more sober and objective light.[60]

While maintaining this public position, Smuts was clearly worried by the political implications of his new immigration drive, for he wanted to avoid 'putting a handle in the hands of my opponents to use against us'. Later he was to claim 'they have used it and they have used it to some effect . . .'.[61] He refused, in spite of strong and repeated requests, to give any financial assistance to the 1820 Memorial Settlers' Association[62]—while Hofmeyr was sympathetic,[63] Smuts was adamant. In a letter to him, the Chairman of the Association argued:

You admitted the value of the services rendered and the only reason you did not wish to help financially was that you would have to defend it against the criticisms of the Opposition. With all due deference I would submit that nothing you can do will lessen their hostility to your immigration

[60] *House of Assembly Debates*, vol. 60, col. 322; for a sympathetic discussion of Smuts's views on Colour, see W. K. Hancock (1968), op. cit., pp. 473–91.

[61] *House of Assembly Debates*, vol. 64, col. 206 (16 Aug. 1948); the immigration issue was raised several other times before the election: ibid., vol. 61, col. 3512 (29 Apr. 1947), vol. 62, cols. 1690–1, 1734–8 (17 Feb. 1948).

[62] General Manager 1820 M.S.A. to London Secretary, letter, 18 Jan. 1947.

[63] General Manager to London Secretary, letters, 15 Feb. 1947, 24 Feb. 1947, and 20 Mar. 1947. Hofmeyr had long taken an interest in immigration and his maiden speech in Parliament had been on Malan's Immigration Quota Bill. This was not a success and it is possible that memories of it led him to take a stronger line than in the earlier debate. A Paton *Hofmeyr* (1964), pp. 169–70.

policy, and that by throwing our organization to the dogs you will not in anyway appease them.[64]

One month later, however, the General Manager felt that it would be 'wise to accept the (political) judgement of General Smuts', for there was evidence that the Government had plans for 'a big extension of our and their own work after the next General Election'.[65]

In spite of the political controversy, immigrants continued to arrive at an unprecedented rate: in 1947 there were nearly 25,000 new British settlers accounting for 87 per cent of the total. The austerity of post-war Britain was an important factor promoting this exodus, and the London Office of the Association reported that 'conditions here have been appalling . . . everywhere one goes one hears people discussing migration . . . our queues of applicants continue to litter the passages outside our office, and the mail gets heavier each morning'.[66] The English-language newspapers in South Africa referred to an 'avalanche of applications' and to the 'unqualified success' of the state-sponsored scheme, claiming that less than one per cent of the thousands of new arrivals had returned to Britain.[67] But they added that there were some immigrants who had 'come out under their own steam', had become embittered and disgruntled, and then wrote 'vituperative letters to the British Press, which were apt to give an entirely wrong impression.'[68]

The early post-war years also saw the continued arrival of the ex-colonial type of British immigrant; his numbers increased as decolonization in Africa followed the example set by India.[69] In the nine months before May 1947, the Association assisted some 500 settlers from India to come to Durban who, they felt, were 'good

---

[64] Chairman of 1820 M.S.A. to Smuts, letter, 12 Feb. 1947. This appeal met with no success and prompted the following remarks: 'You realize that the treatment of the Government here of this whole subject devolved into a political ramp. The action indeed of high authorities can only be described as immoral, but of course in political matters this counts for nothing.' General Manager to London Secretary, letter, 2 May 1947.

[65] General Manager to London Secretary, 19 Mar. 1947.

[66] London Office to Head Office, Cape Town, letter 18 Mar. 1947.

[67] *Cape Argus*, 26 Aug. 1947.

[68] Cape Times, 26 Aug. 1947.

[69] Ex-colonials, or rather their predecessors, had retired to South Africa for a very long time: 'Wynberg, a favourite retreat of Indian Army officers and servants of the Honourable Company,' A. F. Hattersley, *A Victorian Lady at the Cape*, p. 24. Modern ex-colonials were not simply retiring, many were seeking refuge there.

K

settlers, in spite of the view of General de Villiers on "Poona Colonels".[70] However, the deterioration of Indian–South African political relations at that time prevented the pursuit of a more active recruitment policy.[71]

The General Election of May 1948 resulted in the return to power of the National Party under the leadership of Dr. Malan, and with it came the expected reversal of immigration policy. By September the General Manager of the Association was convinced that the new government intended to reduce the number of British immigrants for 'though this may not be the "declared policy", it will be the result, however, of its adoption . . .'.[72] He noted that 'security measures' were going to be applied to immigrants, particularly from the background, character, political, and possibly Communistic angles.[73] Other features of the new policy included the closing down of much of the special immigration machinery set up by Smuts;[74] the termination of the contract with the Union Castle Line for the hire of three special immigrant ships;[75] and a 'tighter screening' system in London prior to departure.[76] In the House, Smuts demanded to know what the Government's policy was going to be, because 'judging from appearances it seems almost as if a curtain has descended on this country and as if there will be no further immigration.'[77] Other people, too, were anxious to know the full extent of Dr. Donges's 'drastic review'[78] of the immigration scheme and, with this in mind, Association officials had a meeting with the Minister on 7 September to 'clarify the situation', after the public statement entitled 'State Control of Immigration' had appeared in the *Cape Times* the week before.[79]

A succinct summary of government policy at this time can be found in a directive, *Immigration on a Selective Basis*, sent from Pretoria to the Immigration Selection committee in London. It recognized

[70] General Manager to London Secretary, letter 2 May 1947; (de Villiers was the head of South African immigration).

[71] Ibid., letter 6 Mar. 1946; cf. W. K. Hancock, *Smuts: The Fields of Force*, pp. 450–72.

[72] General Manager to Lord Elton of the Rhodes Trustees, Oxford, letter, 20 Sept. 1948.

[73] Loc. cit.

[74] *South Africa*, 18 Dec. 1948.

[75] *Daily Telegraph*, 19 Aug. 1948.

[76] *The Times*, 3 Sept. 1948; cf. Donges's statement: *House of Assembly Debates*, vol. 64, cols. 293–376 (16 Aug. 1948).

[77] *House of Assembly Debates*, vol. 64, col. 2534 (16 Sept. 1948).

[78] *The Times*, 17 Aug. 1948.

[79] 1820 M.S.A. Memorandum, 27 Sept. 1948.

the need to increase the population if 'the great experiment of creating an independent state under white supremacy' should succeed and 'Western Civilization be maintained in Africa in the centuries to come'. In its estimation, however, the absorptive capacity of the country was no more than a net increase of 14,000 whites a year. Even this figure was subject to a further constraint, that of the 'maintenance . . . of the existing composition of the European population and its way of life'. A further policy aim was the protection of the state against a 'World outlook' and an 'outlook on life foreign to that generally current in South Africa'. It was deemed obvious that people who did not share that outlook or who had other ideas about 'Christianity and democracy', would not be able to assist in maintaining the South African way of life. The practical implications of these aims were twofold: first, that whoever came to South Africa must proceed through the 'recognized funnel'; and second, that this funnel must have a 'filter' which would effectively prevent 'undesirables or less desirable immigrants from coming to the country'. Of these 'undesirables' the memorandum went on to state that the importation of people who, by reason of their ideological convictions, were bound to create difficulties, was not desired and, in this respect, 'Communism is regarded as a definite threat and danger to our way of life'.[80]

The impact of these measures, including the Citizenship Act (1949) discussed earlier, on the flow of British immigrants, was the subject of considerable controversy. On the surface, the figures are, perhaps, deceptively simple: 1948 was a year of record immigration with some 25,500 settlers from Britain; this fell precipitously to 9,650 in 1949, and dropped again to a little over 5,000 during 1950. The United Party and the English-language press[81] claimed that there was a direct and obvious causal link between the fall in immigration and the Government's new immigration policy. This was denied by Government spokesmen who retorted that it was the Opposition's propaganda that had scared potential immigrants from Britain; that the Government had not refused a single immigrant recommended by the 1820 Memorial Settlers' Association; and that the fall was attributable

---

[80] *Immigration on a Selective Basis* (1948), p. 3; This fear of a 'World outlook' and its equation with 'Communism' brings to mind certain parallels with the American 'Radical Right' of the 1950s. Communism becomes an essential symbol representing a fear of any change. Cf. D. Bell (ed.), *The Radical Right* (1964 edn.).

[81] *The Natal Mercury*, 6 Sept. 1950.

to other factors, principally 'the more attractive terms offered by other Commonwealth countries and to full employment in the United Kingdom.'[82]

A comparison with statistics of British migration to Australia[83] and Canada[84] shows a similar tendency for the level of immigration to fall off after 1948, although it had quickly recovered again by the early fifties. The real impact of Nationalist policy was to emphasize this initial drop and, having reduced immigration to a much lower level, prevent it from rising again throughout the whole of the following decade. At a time when the British economy was recovering from the post-war reconstruction, and when the other major receiving countries were competing for immigrants (Australia introduced an assisted-passage scheme in 1947,[85] Canada in 1951,[86] and Rhodesia started its pre-Federation immigration drive),[87] merely to follow a passive policy was enough to ensure a low level of immigration from Britain.

The proportion of British immigrants also fell from over 85 per cent of the total in the immediate post-war years to barely one third by the middle of the decade.[88] At the end of the decade British immigration reached its post-war nadir with net losses during 1960 and 1961. The Nationalist Government tried to increase immigration from the Netherlands and Germany,[89] for this was the only way in which to gain, simultaneously, skilled labour for the economy and additional white population without thereby weakening the Afrikaner's numerical superiority.

The fifties also marked fundamental changes in the balance of power, both within South Africa and on the African continent at large. With successive elections the Nationalists managed to entrench their Parliamentary position until it was virtually impregnable; the United Party split and dwindled into an ineffectual and irrelevant opposition; and the Liberals and Progressives failed to make any electoral impact. The axis of power was shifting dramatically so that

---

[82] *House of Assembly Debates*, vol. 74, cols. 1536–9 and 2981 (19 Feb. 1951).

[83] *International Migration*, vol. 1, no. 3 (1963).

[84] A. H. Richmond, *Post-War Immigrants in Canada*, p. 6.

[85] R. T. Appleyard, *British Emigration to Australia* (1964), pp. 36–7.

[86] A. H. Richmond (1967), op. cit., p. 11.

[87] P. Keatley, *The Politics of Partnership*, pp. 14, 215, 283; R. I. Rotberg, *The Rise of Nationalism in Central Africa* (1965), p. 229.

[88] E. A. Walker, *A History of Southern Africa*, pp. 815, 916.

[89] Ibid., pp. 842–3.

the politics of colour were once again superseding the politics of culture. Winds of change, sweeping colonial rule from the continent of Africa, released a hurricane of protest through the very institution that Smuts had helped to create—the United Nations. Apartheid became a symbol, an anathema to the Third World and an embarrassment to South Africa's Western trading partners. The decade ending in Sharpeville culminated, almost inevitably, in South Africa's departure from the Commonwealth and the establishment of a Republic.

British immigration, between the accession of the Nationalists and the foundation of the Republic, can only be understood against this wider sociological background. In contrast to the pre-war years, some immigrants were showing awareness and even mild apprehension about their probable reception in South Africa, both from an interracial and an intercultural standpoint. The London Secretary of the Association noted, at this time, that those prospective settlers who were worried about 'racial and political' problems had gained their impressions from 'exaggerated accounts given in the letters received from friends or relatives in Southern Africa'.[90]

The majority of British immigrants were skilled artisans who possessed little if any capital.[91] During the decade the conditions of entry for these types of workers gradually eased, although they were given no positive encouragement in the form of assisted passages advocated by the Opposition.[92] Such proposals were rejected by Dr. Donges on the not very plausible grounds that the 'financial implications made it a matter that could not be thought of'.[93] At the same time, he announced to the Natal Congress of the National Party that he would allow semi-skilled immigrants to come to South Africa as long as they could be assured of 'a European standard of living', and provided that 'certain sectors of industry were reserved for European workers'.[94] He argued that there must be an end to the

---

[90] Minute Book (17 July 1950–11 Dec. 1957), no. 8 (1 Feb. 1951). Note the distinction between 'racial' (i.e. black/white) and 'political' (i.e. Afrikaner/English-speaking) as a linguistic reflection of the shifting power structure. Before the war 'racial' problems referred essentially to Afrikaner-English friction, while the 'native question' (or 'problem', though it was not always elevated to that status) occupied a decidedly secondary position.

[91] Minute no. 3 (1 Feb. 1951); Minute no. 8 (19 Mar. 1952).

[92] Minute no. 7, (19 June 1951); *House of Assembly Debates*, vol. 87, col. 1187 (16 Feb. 1955) and vol. 88, cols. 3451–8 (29 Mar. 1955).

[93] *Cape Times*, 30 Mar. 1955.

[94] An implicit reference to the poor-white theme which confirms Doxey's

policy of economic integration after which it would be possible to consider bringing in 'even unskilled immigrants'.[95] The members of the Opposition were not impressed by such future visions, and Dr. Shearer, referring sarcastically to the filter analogy, claimed that the position had been reached 'when the filter is not even being asked to function because the stream is running the other way'.[96]

United Party motions on immigration emphasized both the economic and the security aspects of the situation but met with no success in altering Government policy. In reply, it was argued that the only way to safeguard 'Western Civilization' in South Africa was to 'ensure that the political power remains in the hands of the white man, then the ratio does not matter so much'.[97] This was hardly surprising in view of the conclusions of the Tomlinson Commission Report that estimated an annual need of 130,000 white immigrants in order to make any impact on the widening gap in the ratio of blacks to whites. When the Report was first published in 1956 the net total of white immigration was a mere 2,000.

A year later, in 1957, the Association reported that it was dealing almost entirely with skilled artisans 'of which South Africa seems to be more than short'. Commenting on the attitudes of these immigrants, the London Manager asserted that they were 'not interested in the native question'. He claimed that they merely wanted an opportunity to build a new life in a new country which they assumed would remain in allegiance to the British Crown. Completely over-estimating the average Englishman's fervour for the monarchy, he added that South Africa's chance of attracting white immigrants would 'hastily diminish' if a Republic were formed, particularly outside the Commonwealth.[98] Later events proved that this prediction was quite unfounded.[99] He attributed South Africa's failure

---

claim that 'even today the ghost of the poor white problem hovers on the fringe of South African thought', *The Industrial Colour Bar in South Africa* (1961), p. 78. *Cape Times*, ibid.

[95] *House of Assembly Debates*, vol. 88, cols. 3482–3 (29 Mar. 1955).

[96] Ibid., col. 3462.

[97] *House of Assembly Debates*, vol. 93, col. 2471 (8 Mar. 1957).

[98] *Daily Herald* (Port Elizabeth), 2 Sept. 1957.

[99] Cf. W. K. Hancock, *Are There South Africans?*, p. 17; other predictions have been wide of the mark: H. M. Robertson, 'South Africa' in B. Thomas (ed.) *Economics of International Migration*, p. 184; and Keppel-Jones, in his satire *When Smuts Goes* (1950), conjured up a Second 'Great Trek' for the years 1955–65 (pp. 93–114).

to attract large numbers of immigrants to four main factors: the lack of financial assistance to prospective migrants; the absence of a Government-sponsored publicity campaign; the unfavourable reaction to the Government's non-European policy which tended to 'discourage people who were otherwise interested in coming';[100] and the selective immigration regulations limited to skilled artisans at a time when conditions in Britain made it difficult 'to find enough people qualified to migrate to South Africa who want to migrate'.[101]

The Viljoen Commission, reporting in 1958, estimated an annual need for some 25,000 immigrants in order to maintain the pace of economic growth.[102] In reality net immigration rarely reached a third of that figure even at its highest peak. The influence of political instability and its resulting economic disruption had a powerful short-run impact. In 1960 the Association reported that the marked decline in immigration figures was due to specific events, 'the effects of an economic recession . . . and the Sharpeville incident . . . with all its repercussions'. While very few settlers committed to a passage cancelled their bookings, there was a marked disinclination on the part of applicants to 'finalize any future travel arrangements', and, out of several hundred inquiries in hand at the time, an 'overwhelming majority showed no further interest by the end of April'.[103] There can be little doubt that a combination of these forces, the growing internal unrest, and the increasing external hostility, caused the subsequent change in immigration policy.

By April 1960 Government spokesmen were propagating the idea of a positive immigration programme 'in the interests of our development and our civilization'.[104] The opening speech of the 1961 Parliament announced that a Department of Immigration would be established 'in the near future' and that 'special efforts' were to be made to bring suitable immigrants to the country.[105] The Department was set up in April of that year and in May details of the assisted-

---

[100] *Natal Mercury* 7 Sept. 1957; on the same theme he commented: 'The two events that have had the greatest adverse effect on overseas opinion are the packing of the Senate and the Mass Treason trial. The fact that people are being tried en masse gives . . . the impression that the Union is like Russia, and that South Africa is literally rotten with sedition.'

[101] *Daily Despatch* (East London), 3 Sept. 1957.

[102] *Report of the Commission of Enquiry into policy relating to the protection of industries* (U.G. 36'58), p. 33.

[103] London Manager's Annual Report (1960).

[104] *House of Assembly Debates*, vol. 104, cols. 5334–5 (11 Apr. 1960).

[105] Ibid., vol. 106, col. II (20 Jan. 1961) *Cape Times*, 18 Feb. 1961.

passage scheme and other related measures were explained to the House by Senator de Klerk.[106] It is interesting to note that the first Minister of Immigration was Senator Trollip, one of the rare English-speaking Nationalist Cabinet Ministers and an erstwhile member of the United Party. The announcement of the scheme was greeted by qualified approval from the Opposition, and the centre of resistance towards the new immigration policy reverted to the Government backbenches.

During the 1960s anti-Catholicism, associated with the growth of immigrants from Southern Europe, began to rival anti-British sentiments as an object on which to focus the xenophobia of the platteland.[107] These opponents were not unresourceful in devising alternatives to the Government's plan, as the *Cape Times* reported:

There is a certain comic desperation about the unofficial scheme, started in the Transvaal, to encourage the idea of attracting immigrants from the Deep South of the United States. But it is reported that Committees have actually been formed in Germiston and Pretoria . . . . [However] South Africa, assuming she wants immigrants, will have to cast the net wider, even at the risk of finding herself landed with settlers who have a less subtle appreciation of colour problems than the Whites of the Deep South.[108]

In 1962, British immigration reverted to its pre-crisis level of the 1950s. What accounted for the remarkable success of the new immigration policy so soon after the exodus following Sharpeville? Economic factors provide the most plausible explanation: a combination of South Africa's sustained economic prosperity, Britain's persistent deflationary crises, and the introduction of the assisted-passage scheme.[109] The first provided the opportunities and a greater

[106] Ibid., vol. 107, col. 5698 (17 May 1961); these measures included: (a) R60 (= £30 sterling at that time, i.e. R1 = 10s. Subsequent devaluations have altered this ratio, but this was the exchange rate in the early 1960s) subsidy per adult or child, plus a R60 loan (these loans were consolidated into a full grant of R120 in November 1962), (b) transport from the port of entry to the area of employment, (c) temporary hotel accommodation, (d) an expansion of the Immigration Selection Board, (e) financial support for two private immigration companies, Samorgan and Transa.

[107] The United Party in the Senate were quick to deplore the agitation 'against British and Catholic immigrants in the Afrikaans Press' (Transvaler and Dagbreek) and the attitude towards immigration of 'Mr. du Toit, Chairman of the Federal Council of Skakelkomitees'. *Senate Debates*, 20 Jan. 1967–3 Feb. 1967), cols. 504–7, 525.

[108] *Cape Times*, 21 Jan. 1961.

[109] Cf. 1820 United Kingdom Manager's Report (1962); General Manager's Report for 1964 (1964).

willingness on the part of the host society to accept the immigrants,[110] the second created the supply of potential immigrants, and the third diverted the direction of their flow away from alternative countries towards South Africa.

I will focus on these new British immigrants in the later chapters of the book. In addition to my own findings, it is worth noting the conclusions of a survey undertaken by the Association in 1965 on the subject of immigrant motivation. The survey consisted of a series of questions put to some 250 applicants concerning their reasons for wishing to settle in South Africa. These questions revealed that the primary factors were: 'greater opportunities; the expectation of a better standard of living and a brighter future for children in a vigorous young country . . . with climate and taxation as highly important secondary considerations'. But the Association discovered a 'surprising number' (7 per cent) who claimed that their main reason was related to various dissatisfactions such as 'politics and coloured immigration'.[111] The interpretation of such a survey, considering the circumstances under which it was conducted, should be cautious, but, in general, it seems to confirm the findings of our sample survey.

During 1965 there was a slight check to the growth in the number of immigrants, which had been rising steadily for the previous three years, and one of the factors mentioned by the Association to account for this was the 'Rhodesia crisis' which had 'an immediate and adverse impact' on recruiting.[112] The London Manager explained that the general public in Britain 'as a whole were rather vague as to the geography of Southern Africa' and as a consequence the Republic suffered by reason of being regarded as 'all of a piece with Rhodesia'.[113] It is important to recognize that even with contemporary standards of education and the indirect informative value of the mass media, the majority of immigrants lack detailed knowledge of South Africa and, without exaggeration, are probably no better informed about it than their early nineteenth-century predecessors.

The assassination of Dr. Verwoerd in September 1966, although it was followed by a fall in immigration, does not appear to have had

---

[110] Of course, attitudes towards immigration were still very mixed; see the debates: *Larger White Population for the Republic*, Senate Debates (18 Jan. 1963–28 June 1963); cols. 454–1020, and also *Motion on the Policy of the Minister of Immigration*, Senate Debates (20 Jan. 1967–3 Feb. 1967), cols. 290–610, 693–715.

[111] 1820 London Manager's Annual Report (1965).

[112] 1820 U.K. Manager's Annual Report (1966).

[113] Ibid.

much independent influence precisely because it lacked the economic repercussions of Sharpeville. In the following year more than 32,000 immigrants arrived in South Africa of whom nearly 13,000 came from Britain, and in 1968 the British component had risen to over 16,000. This trend continued until the end of the decade, when the annual flow of British immigrants reached the figure of 20,000.

CHAPTER IX

The Social Structure, Immigration, and Intergroup Relations

THE SURVEY of the development of British immigration to South Africa over the last 150 years, described in the previous three chapters, is necessarily incomplete and selective. I have attempted to set immigration against a background of changing social structures, to give some indication of the reactions of both the immigrants and the members of the host society, and to provide an essential depth to an understanding of the context of contemporary immigration. During the earliest phase of immigration in the first half of the nineteenth century, the power structure, conceived in terms of a triangle of forces, was such that the new settlers were either ranged against the African tribesmen on the Eastern Frontier or eased into the less turbulent society of the Cape. Under such conditions, the development of hostile patterns of race relations and negative racial stereotypes was almost inevitable, while the settlers' relationship with the neighbouring Boers, who were placed in a similar situation, was based on a sympathetic fellow-feeling.

With the breaking of the power of the African tribes, the emergence of the 'imperial factor', and the awakening of Afrikaner nationalism as a reaction to it, the structure of power relations within the society changed dramatically. The main axis of conflict was realigned so that immigration became a weapon in the struggle for hegemony between the two white groups. This situation prevailed from the time of the confederation plans in the 1870s, through the Anglo-Boer War and the post-war reconstruction, beyond the Act of Union and the interwar years, until the political entrenchment of the National Party in the 1950s. By this time the full impact of African nationalism, both inside and outside South Africa, had caused a reversion to the former lines of conflict, with the difference that the Afrikaner now held the reins of power within the white group.

Several recent analyses of South Africa have interpreted the situation not so much in terms of a triangular, three-group, conflict but rather as a dialectical battle between economic and political forces.[1] It is also possible to consider immigration in the light of the contrasting pressures of economy and polity. The trouble with this approach, however, is that the nominally 'economic' demand for skilled labour is a direct result of 'political' restrictions—job reservations and 'Bantu education'—which, in turn, are partly economically motivated. The intermeshing of economics and politics is immensely complicated and, as Max Weber emphasized, economic and political forces are merely different aspects of the over-all distribution of power in society.[2]

The importance of the underlying power structure can be seen if we consider Weber's basic distinction between the three vertical orders of class, status, and party.[3] It is then possible to trace the way that power has been transferred from one order to another: the economic power yet political impotence of the uitlanders inevitably led to conflict and to a more equitable distribution of political influence among the white group.[4] The more recent rise of Afrikaner finance and commerce has depended significantly on the backing of an Afrikaner Nationalist Government,[5] and the growth of African consumer and labour power will have important repercussions in both the political and status orders.[6] A sociological interpretation of immigration cannot be seen in isolation from such fundamental social developments.

The historical evidence also revealed important parallels with the findings reported in the remaining chapters of the book. Throughout the whole period, the dominant motives for migration, from the settlers' point of view, have been economic. Time and again immi-

[1] The 'economy-polity' approach is exemplified in the work of R. Horwitz, *The Political Economy of South Africa*, and A. Hepple *South Africa*; while the 'group approach' has been used by P. L. van den Berghe, *South Africa: a Study in Conflict*, and E. S. Munger, *Afrikaner and African Nationalism*. Perhaps the different authors' specialisms dictate their somewhat different, though by no means irreconcilable, perspectives.

[2] Cf. J. H. Goldthorpe and D. Lockwood, 'Affluence and the British Class Structure', *Sociological Review* II, no. 2 (1963), appendix.

[3] H. Gerth and C. W. Mills (eds.), *From Max Weber*, pp. 180–95. Cf. W. G. Runciman, 'Class, Status and Power' in J. A. Jackson (ed.), *Social Stratification* (1968), and Runciman, 'The Three Dimensions of Inequality' in A. Beteille (ed.), *Social Inequality* (1969), pp. 45–63.

[4] Cf. A. W. Tilby, *South Africa*, p. 448.

[5] Cf. N. Macrae, 'The Green Bay Tree', *The Economist* 29 June 1968, pp. ix–xlvi.

[6] Several examples can be cited from the sample survey, particularly in the case of shop assistants. In this situation the African's role as customer clearly modified the societal status hierarchy to a degree that was very apparent to the immigrants.

grants have arrived in the country, with inadequate knowledge and inflated expectations, have been temporarily disillusioned and, after having reverted to a former trade or profession, have gradually prospered. The assimilation of the race attitudes and stereotypes of the host society has been, in all but a minority of cases, rapid, and accomplished with apparent ease.

PART THREE

The Survey Evidence

'How can what an Englishman believes be heresy? It is a contradiction in terms.'

(SHAW, *St. Joan*)

CHAPTER X

The Basic Variables

THE THIRD section of this study consists of an analysis and inter-pretation of the data gathered from a sample survey of post-war British immigrants interviewed in South Africa during 1967 and 1968. This information will be viewed against the problems and hypotheses suggested in my theoretical discussion[1] and amplified in both the comparative and historical chapters of the book.

a: THE AREA OF RESIDENCE IN BRITAIN AND SOUTH AFRICA

The sample consisted of 514 adult British immigrants selected and interviewed in the manner described in Appendix A. Interviews were concentrated in the four major urban-industrial areas of South Africa—Johannesburg, Cape Town, Durban, and Port Elizabeth–East London—from the autumn of 1967 to the late summer of 1968.

The first basic variable to be considered was the immigrant's area of residence prior to emigrating from Britain, that is his last *permanent* address. Table 1 contains the geographical distribution of immigrants according to standard regions, compared with the 1961 census figures, and a rank ordering of regional unemployment and of coloured population of each area.

The distribution between the sample and the census figures shows certain differences: some regions, notably Scotland, London, and the Midlands,[2] contributed disproportionately to the number of migrants while others, particularly the Eastern, Northern, and North Midlands, were under-represented. This would suggest, at least at a superficial level, that neither unemployment nor concentrations of coloured immigrants were a primary factor in motivating migration to South

[1] For comparative purposes I shall refer to the following related studies: A. P. du Plessis, *Die Nederlandse Emigrasie na Suid-Afrika* (1956); J. F. Loedolff, *Nederlandse Immigrante 'n sosiologiese ondersoek van hul Inskakeling in die Gemeenskapslewe van Pretoria* (1960); R. T. Appleyard *British Emigration to Australia*; B. J. In den Bosch, *De Verschillende Aspecten van de Aanpassing der Nederlandse Immigranten in Zuid-Afrika* (1966); A. H. Richmond, *Post-war Immigrants in Canada*; P. H. W. Johnston, *British Emigration to South Africa: a study of their characteristics and a comparison with Australia* (1968).

[2] Cf. R. T. Appleyard, *British Emigration to Australia*, pp. 114–15.

L

TABLE 1

Regional Differences in Immigration (U.K.)[a]

Standard region	No.	%	1961 Census (1,000s)	%	Unemployment	Coloured population
Northern	11	2·1	3,252	6·2	5th	9th
E. & W. Ridings	40	7·7	4,172	7·9	4th	3rd
N. Midland	21	3·5	3,634	6·9	2nd	4th
Eastern	14	2·7	3,736	7·1	2nd	6th
London & S. E.	152	29·5	11,104	21·1	1st	1st
Southern	22	3·5	2,826	5·3	2nd	5th
South-West	20	3·5	3,411	6·5	3rd	8th
Wales	19	3·5	2,644	5·0	5th	10th
Midlands	58	11·2	4,757	9·0	4th	2nd
N. Western	64	12·5	6,567	12·5	6th	7th
Scotland	77	14·9	5,175	9·8	7th	11th
N. Ireland	16	3·1	1,425	2·7	8th	12th
TOTAL	514	100·0	52,653	100·0	—	—

[a] These figures show respectively the rank order of regional unemployment—adult unemployment compared with unfilled vacancies averaged for June 1956–61—and the rank order of coloured population based on the proportion of West Indian and Pakistani immigrants to the total regional population. They are based on Tables in G. C. K. Peach, *West Indian Migration to Britain*, pp. 65–8.

Africa. A sociologist should not be surprised that the relative deprivation of reduced overtime earnings can be just as potent a source of dissatisfaction as the more 'absolute' type of deprivation implied by unemployment.[3] Perhaps in a welfare state the very concept of absolute deprivation, for a majority of the *working* population, is misplaced. A very detailed regional sub-division would be necessary to see whether there was any statistical correlation between the inhabitants of Rex's 'twilight zones' and the propensity to emigrate to South Africa. But even if a significant association were found it need not imply a causal connection, for these areas are transitional zones of high mobility. Furthermore, the evidence concerning the motives for migration gives little support for this proposition.

The sample interviews were concentrated in South Africa's four main urban-industrial complexes approximately in proportion to their relative significance as immigrant catchment areas. There are no accurate statistics to show what proportion of British immigrants decide to settle in any one area of the country, but it seems reasonable to assume that the vast majority will go to these major urban centres which contain at least 40 per cent of the white population,

[3] Ibid., p. 116.

and a higher percentage of English-speaking whites. By concentrating on these centres, certain immigrants destined for mining areas in the Free State and South-West Africa, for the predominantly Afrikaans-speaking cities of Pretoria and Bloemfontein, and for more rural parts of the country, are excluded from the survey. While this may reduce the ability to generalize from the sample, other information suggests that some 84 per cent of the immigrants intended to settle in these major cities, and this may be an underestimation.[4]

TABLE 2

Provincial Distribution of Immigrants (S.A.)

Area of residence	Sample		White popn. Sample of urban-Industrial areas[a]		1820 Report[b] (1964)	Pre-test sample[c] (1963–6)
Johannesburg	243	47	504,000	44	50	29
Cape Town	159	31	305,000	27	25	26
Durban	54	11	178,000	16	15	19
Port Eliz.-E.L.	58	11	154,000	13	10	10
Other						16
TOTAL	514	100	1,141,000	100	100	100

[a] A. Gordon-Brown, *A Guide to Southern Africa* (1967).

[b] Percentages relate to relative 'after-care' services undertaken by the 1820 Memorial Settlers' Association at their various branches in South Africa during 1963. 'The General Manager's Report' (1964).

[c] 'Stated preferences' based on 447 questionnaires belonging to the London pre-test sample 1963–6. There is an undoubted bias against Johannesburg and a substantial 'Don't know' category. See Appendix C, p. 275.

This information enables us to consider the differences that arise between the various South African provinces,[5] whose diverse history, differing ethnic and racial balances, and separate cultural traditions might plausibly influence the process of integration. Cape Town is notable in South Africa for its tradition of a relatively 'liberal' attitude towards race relations: historically it was the home of a limited 'colour-blind' franchise; its atmosphere is more relaxed than in the Transvaal, without the ever-present burglar alarms and guard dogs of the Johannesburg suburbs; buses are not so rigidly segregated, and the beaches have only recently been subjected to Apartheid,[6] largely at the behest of Pretoria, and against persistent opposition

[4] Cf. A. H. Richmond, *Post-War Immigrants in Canada*, p. 38 and the London pre-test sample: Appendix C, p. 275.

[5] Loedolff's Pretoria study and In den Bosch's data for Cape Town revealed certain fairly marked differences: In den Bosch, op. cit., p. 72.

[6] *Cape Times*, 5 Feb. 1969.

from the local administration. The large Coloured population possesses an intermediate status between European and African, and,
until the early 1960s, had some indirect representation in the central
Parliament.[7] Among Afrikaners there is a tendency to produce politicians of a *verligte* as opposed to *verkrampte* persuasion; *Die*
Burger is less conservative than *Die Transvaler*; Stellenbosch
University is less reactionary than Potchefstroom or Pretoria. While
the greatest contrasts may be expected between Cape Town and
Johannesburg, differences could also arise in the other two regions,
the Eastern Province and Natal, where the immigrant is faced with an
atmosphere more strongly influenced by the traditions of British
colonialism.

The sixth hypothesis described in chapter five suggested that
regional differences were unlikely to be an important factor in determining the immigrant's integration, satisfaction, or attitude towards
Apartheid, while the length of his residence in South Africa almost
certainly would be critical in these respects. It was felt that the contrasts between Britain and South Africa outlined in chapter four
would be very much more salient than any internal differences
within the host society, particularly between the main urban centres.
The data did reveal some regional differences, though these were
essentially between Johannesburg and the other three areas.
Immigrants in the former had a tendency to be less well integrated
in the social and political-cultural dimensions,[8] but not in the economic dimension. The British immigrant in the Transvaal was more
likely to be dissatisfied with life in South Africa[9] and more prone to
wish to leave the country,[10] but he was not so very different in his
support for, or opposition to, the policy of Apartheid.[11]

[7] This was replaced by the 'Coloured Persons' Representative Council'. The
first elections in September 1969 produced a 26:14 majority for the anti-Apartheid
Coloured Labour Party, but the Government's nomination of 20 Apartheid supporters gave the pro-Apartheid Federal Party an actual majority of 34:26. *The
Observer*, 12 Oct. 1969.

[8] For a full discussion of the dimensions of integration, see chapters xii–xiv.

[9] 31 per cent in Johannesburg were either 'dissatisfied' or 'very dissatisfied',
compared with 18 per cent in Cape Town.

[10] 25 per cent in Johannesburg, 14 per cent in Cape Town.

[11] 87 per cent pro-Apartheid, 12 per cent anti-Apartheid (Johannesburg); 81
per cent: 9 per cent (Cape Town).

b: SEX AND MARITAL STATUS

The second basic variable to be considered is that of sex, to determine whether any major differences arise as a result of the varying roles and situations of the male and female in the processes of emigration and integration.[12] What were the important problem areas for each sex and how did they affect attitudes towards the various aspects of life in South Africa? Similarly, the marital status of the immigrant was recorded to assess its significance in the same processes.[13]

(i) men and women

The fourth hypothesis in chapter five postulated that sex would be a significant differentiating factor, particularly in the social, rather than the political-cultural, dimensions of integration. On *a priori* grounds it seemed reasonable to assume that women would be subjected to greater social and psychological strains than men: it was usually the the man who initiated the idea of emigrating; he was often its most enthusiastic early advocate; and the continuity of his work and familial roles would tend to act as a psychological shield against changes in the wider society. Furthermore, the disruption of kin ties and the more delicate and diffuse adjustments in neighbourhood relations and friendship patterns would seem to have a disproportionate effect on women.

In fact, my data do not support these hypotheses which form an example of migrants' 'conventional wisdom'. Women were only imperceptibly less well integrated on the social dimension, their mean social integration score[14] being $+0.608$ compared with the male figure of $+0.677$, in contrast to the political-cultural dimension which revealed a more marked divergence between the sexes. As a consequence, men were found to be better integrated than women from an over-all point of view, while the mean outgroup scores[15] rated women slightly more 'prejudiced' than men. This last fact is most

---

[12] Richmond found no significant difference between sex and the level of satisfaction with life in Canada. Op. cit., (1967), p. 168; In den Bosch found that Dutch women immigrants were less satisfied than men in South Africa. Op. cit., (1966) pp. 74–5.

[13] Somewhat over 75 per cent of the sample were married and there was a slight predominance of single males over single females.

Richmond (op. cit., 1967) found no association between marital status and satisfaction.

[14] See chapter xiii.

[15] See chapter xiv (ii).

interesting in view of Abrams's findings that British women tend to be more tolerant than men,[16] and Pettigrew's[17] and van den Berghe's[18] demonstration of the reverse relationship in South Africa. The evidence therefore suggests that the immigrant group is becoming acculturated towards the norms of Southern African society.

On particular sub-dimensions of integration sex discrepancies were not very pronounced, as might be anticipated from the mean scores, and there were no significant differences between men and women in their assessment of the ease of establishing friendships[19] or the comparative activity of their social lives.[20] On the other hand, women were significantly less prepared to become South African citizens.[21] In general, these findings are a warning against adopting the stereotype of women as poor migrants, even though many immigrants of both sexes held this view,[22] for while there is an element of truth in the assertion, it has been grossly exaggerated.

(ii) married and single

An immigrant's marital status, at the time of emigration, is another basic variable that is frequently considered to be a crucial factor in the process of integration. In this case the research findings are much more in accordance with conventional expectations. Appleyard found in his Australian study that many single emigrants used the opportunities provided by the assisted passage scheme to fulfil a desire for adventure and travel, or as a means of breaking loose from their family ties.[23] One would expect as a consequence that the motives, expectations, experiences, and attitudes of the single immigrant would differ sharply from those of the married migrant.

[16] M. Abrams, 'The Incidence of Race Prejudice in Britain' in E. J. B. Rose et al., Colour and Citizenship, p. 553.

[17] T. F. Pettigrew, 'Social Distance Attitudes of South African Students', 252.

[18] P. L. van den Berghe, 'Race Attitudes in Durban, South Africa', 55–72.

[19] chi-square = 3·655; p = n.s.; d.f. = 5.

[20] chi-square = 3·267; p = n.s.; d.f. = 5.

[21] chi-square = 12·71; p = ·01; d.f. = 2.

[22] One female immigrant explained: 'Its hardest for women to settle down, there's nothing to do—you've just got to go out to work. I've never written so many letters or read so many books in my life before.' (No. 438/96). One male immigrant declared: 'They [women] need to go back to England to realize that they have left nothing behind.' (No. 244/21). For scepticism about the Canadian version of this argument, the 'thousand dollar cure', see Richmond (1967), op. cit., p. 176.

For the Association's viewpoint, see 'Wives are the Weak Link', The Star (airmail edn.), 13 Mar. 1971.

[23] R. T. Appleyard, British Emigration to Australia, pp. 174–6.

While 47 per cent of the single immigrants mentioned economic factors as their primary source of motivation, 72 per cent of the married immigrants fell into this category; 33 per cent mentioned 'travel' as against 7 per cent for the married group; and social factors were almost twice as important for the single immigrant, none of them claiming that political or racial considerations were at all significant. Single immigrants confessed to slightly more ignorance about South Africa prior to emigrating, although married immigrants had a marginally lower mean score on the 'prior-knowledge' test.[24] (Does this indicate that celibacy is correlated with modesty, or that marriage promotes dishonesty?)

Single immigrants were slightly less favourably disposed towards the policy of Apartheid,[25] slightly more interested in politics in South Africa,[26] and somewhat less likely to support the National Party.[27] Mirroring the pattern of motives, the greatest differences were found in the social sub-dimensions of integration: 20 per cent of the single immigrants stated that economic factors constituted the greatest difficulty of life in South Africa compared with 35 per cent of the married group. The respective percentages for social factors were 35 per cent (single) and 13 per cent (married). The mean outgroup scores rated the single immigrant as considerably more tolerant,[28] and while over one half of the married group intended, at the time of the interview, to settle permanently in the country this was true of less than 30 per cent of the single group.

(iii) *intermarriage*[29]

In the sample, seventeen immigrants (3 per cent) were married to a South African and, predictably, were well integrated into South African society on all three basic dimensions.[30] Although the direction of causation is by no means clear-cut—for integration may promote intermarriage, the latter may promote the former, or both

[24] See chapter XI, pp. 173–5.

[25] 26 per cent as opposed to 41 per cent were 'strongly in favour' of Apartheid.

[26] 11 per cent as opposed to 6 per cent were 'fairly interested'.

[27] 15 per cent as against 25 per cent.   [28] -0.697 as against -1.764.

[29] The sample included 40 immigrants (8 per cent) who were partners in a mixed (Protestant–Catholic) religious marriage. Perhaps it is to be expected that those who are prepared to marry across traditional boundaries are also inclined to move across national boundaries. As a group, however, these immigrants were rather poorly integrated, particularly on the social and political dimensions, and, surprisingly, rather more prejudiced against outgroups than the sample mean. Cf. Appleyard (1964), op. cit., p. 139.

[30] Cf. A. H. Richmond, *Post-war Immigrants in Canada*, p. 238.

influences may be interacting simultaneously—there can be little doubt that the marriage bed was a potent source of immigrant satisfaction, more powerful even than the 'ex-colonial' nightmares of Uhuru.[31]

(iv) housewives

Another interesting basic distinction is that between housewives and 'working wives'. It raises the question of the differential impact of contact with the work environment as opposed to the home environment. Tentatively, the figures suggest that the working wife was less well integrated than the housewife[32] as well as being more hostile towards outgroups.[33] The lower integration was not a function of the economic or political dimensions, it was the social life of the working wife that was less satisfactory. Although an age and length of residence factor accounts for some of this difference, these results warn against incautious generalizations when considering the problems of the 'captive wife'.

C: AGE AND FAMILY SIZE

The age of the immigrant at the time of emigration is not related systematically to the three sub-dimensions of integration. Total integration scores increased slightly with each successive ten-year cohort up to a maximum age of fifty-two years, thereafter there was a drop attributable to the non-economic orientation of the oldest immigrants. For the main body of immigrants, the gradual increase in integration with age is related to social and political factors, and not to the economic position of the migrant which operates marginally in the reverse direction. However, there were no significant differences in these broad age categories with respect to Apartheid,[34] political interest,[35] or the desire to adopt South African citizenship.[36]

In general, the size of an immigrant's family on arrival in South Africa was not an important variable either. One interesting exception was the case of married couples without children who were considerably better integrated than any other group, including single

[31] The mean total integration score of the 'inter-married' group was 8·294 compared with the 'ex-colonial' score of 7·652. The latter were, however, more hostile to outgroups ($-3·0$ cf. $-1·4$).

[32] $+1·990$ cf. $+2·241$.   [33] $-2·157$ cf. $-1·778$.

[34] chi-square $= 13·835$; p $=$ n.s.; d.f. $= 10$.

[35] chi-square $= 9·365$; p $=$ n.s.; d.f. $= 8$. For a lack of generational factor in British politics, see P. Abrams and A. Little, 'The Young Voter in British Politics', *B.J.S.* 16, no. 2 (1965), 95–110.

[36] chi-square $= 4·385$; p $=$ n.s.; d.f. $= 4$.

immigrants. The difference is largely accounted for by the superior relative social integration of this group which manages to avoid the loneliness of the long-distance, single migrant, while escaping the home-centred isolation of the family with young children without near-by relatives to help shoulder the burden of looking after them.

d: LENGTH OF RESIDENCE IN SOUTH AFRICA

The sixth hypothesis stressed the importance of the length of residence as a factor in integration and attitude-change. This accords both with a commonsense evaluation and with the empirical studies of Loedolff,[37] Rogers and Frantz,[38] Franck,[39] In den Bosch,[40] Lever,[41] and Richmond.[42] The sample was stratified to include a random selection of immigrants in each of the seven residence categories and while the divisions are necessarily somewhat arbitrary, they do illustrate key stages in the immigrant's progress towards integration.

The first residence group, comprising those immigrants who had been in the country for less than seven days, was selected more for practical reasons than because it was ideal from a theoretical point of view. It was found to be easier to make contact with immigrants at their moment of arrival than to try to interview a representative sample in Britain. Every attempt was made to interview the immigrants at the earliest possible time to gain a clear picture of the 'expectations phase' before it was unduly influenced by the immigrants' initial contacts. There were two additional attractions of this procedure: first, any prospective immigrants who changed their minds at the eleventh hour were excluded from the sample and, secondly, it was easier to establish *rapport* with the immigrants at this time than in the last hectic weeks of preparation before emigrating.

The second stage, the 'period of initial contacts', includes immigrants who had been in the country from one week to three months,

[37] J. F. Loedolff, op. cit., p. 161.
[38] C. A. Rodgers and C. Frantz, 'Length of Residence and Race Attitudes of Europeans in Southern Africa', 46–54.
[39] T. Franck, *Race and Nationalism* (1960), pp. 245–6.
[40] B. J. In den Bosch, op. cit., p. 75.
[41] H. Lever, 'Ethnic Preferences of Immigrants', *Journal For Social Research*, 17, no. 2 (1968), 11–13.
[42] A. H. Richmond (1967), op. cit., pp. 155–6, who found that education was more important than length of residence in determining acculturation. However, this was based on a sample of immigrants including many non-English-speaking Southern Europeans.

and represents the generally chaotic first encounter with the new economic, social, and political environment. It was frequently a time of anticlimax in which the stark reality of settling into a new country superseded the excitement and expectations of earlier days. Many of the interviews took place in 'immigrant' hotels, often ghettos of discontent containing a hard-core of bitterly disappointed migrants. Several well-integrated immigrants referred to this initial period of hotel life as their most unpleasant experience in South Africa.

We have called the next stage, from three months' to twelve months' residence, the 'period of initial adjustment'. Although the majority of immigrants in this group had secured employment and accommodation, and had begun to settle into a routine pattern of life, this was still a time of disorganization and dissatisfaction, so much so that the figures in Table 3 suggest that this period marks the nadir of social and political-cultural integration.

TABLE 3

Integration and Outgroup Scores by Length of Residence in South Africa

Residence up to:	7 days	3 mo.	12 mo.	2 yrs.	4 yrs.	8 yrs.	8+	Total
Mean outgroup score	−0·045	−0·924	−1·579	−1·766	−1·909	−2·726	−2·118	−1·617
Mean econ. integ.	1·955	1·303	1·487	2·065	2·670	2·575	3·824	2·276
Mean soc. integ.	1·576	0·485	−0·671	0·229	0·750	0·301	2·000	0·646
Mean pol. integ.	−0·621	−0·788	−1·500	−0·909	−1·170	−0·096	−1·176	0·597
Mean total integ.	3·227	1·606	−0·421	1·481	2·409	2·904	7·000	2·531

The 'early', 'middle', and 'later' years which comprise the next three periods are successively characterized by a comparative assessment of life in the host and the home society, a crystallization of the decision to settle permanently or to leave, and the development of a distinct, new way of life indicating a further progression towards full integration. By far the most successfully integrated immigrants on all three dimensions were those who had been in the country for more than eight years.

A comparison between immigrants of short residence (less than one year) and those of longer residence, revealed strongly significant differences on each sub-dimension of integration. This was also true of their changed attitudes towards the African[43] and towards Apartheid,[44] as we would expect from an inspection of the mean outgroup

[43] chi-square = 15·507; p = ·01; d.f. = 4.
[44] chi-square = 24·687; p = ·01; d.f. = 10.

scores in Table 3. One respondent described the changes in his attitudes in the following way:

You pass through three phases: first, you feel sorry for the native, which lasts for a few weeks and is a result of British feelings about equal rights; then, for about six months when you begin to know and work with them, you dislike them *more* than South Africans do; finally, things even up and fit into the picture and you accept them for what they are. (No. 453/37)[45]

'What they are' in the opinion of an integrated British immigrant is by no means complimentary, but this will be considered in more detail later.

A longitudinal study of one particular group of immigrants would have been the optimum research strategy to test the hypothesis in this section, but considerations of time, money, and the necessary official co-operation made this impossible. As a second-best substitute the data from this survey confirmed the hypothesis linking integration and race attitudes to the length of residence in South Africa.

e: SOCIAL CLASS AND EDUCATION

The two final basic variables to be considered—social class[46] and education—are closely related, yet analytically distinct. Sociologists and social critics have often pointed to the considerable prestige and influence enjoyed by the educated élites of societies, from the *literati* of the Chinese empires[47] to the 'New Mandarins'[48] of modern America. In this study, I have recognized the analytical distinction by using occupation as the basis of my 'class' categories and considering education as a separate variable. The sample was divided into three basic class groups—'professional-managerial', 'intermediate', and 'skilled manual'—largely to facilitate comparison with related studies. Marginal occupations were assigned according to the Hall-Jones

[45] To ensure anonymity, serial numbers, rather than the basic characteristics of the immigrant, have been used in most of the following quotations. The second figure relates to the number of the question on the interview schedule.

[46] For a basic discussion of class and élite in relation to modern society, see T. B. Bottomore, *Classes in Modern Society* (1965); *Elites and Society* (1964).

[47] As Max Weber wrote: 'For twelve centuries social rank in China has been determined more by qualification for office than by wealth. This qualification, in turn, has been determined by education and especially by examinations. China has made literary education the yardstick of social prestige in the most exclusive fashion. . . .' in Gerth and Mills (eds.) *From Max Weber: Essays in Sociology* (1948), p. 416.

[48] Cf. N. Chomsky, *American Power and the New Mandarins* (1969).

scale,[49] and problems arising out of international comparisons of occupational prestige were ignored on the basis of Inkeles's and Rossi's findings.[50] This section is concerned with class as a static concept, while dynamic considerations involving social mobility will be discussed in a later chapter.[51]

In the sample, 6 per cent of the immigrants were classified as 'professional', 25 per cent as 'intermediate', and 68 per cent as 'manual'. All three classes were approximately equal in their degree of economic integration. The intermediate class, followed by the professionals, was the best integrated socially, while the professional class was slightly less well integrated politically than the manual class, with the intermediate class leading the field. Thus, as far as integration is concerned, South Africa would appear to be a 'black-coated worker's' paradise with the professional immigrant being only marginally better integrated than the artisan, the difference being a social one.

According to the mean outgroup scores, 'intolerance' was inversely related to social class. The experience of migration caused attitudes to change among the professional classes towards greater intolerance and stronger support for the policy of Apartheid. But the *relative* change was significantly less marked in this class than in the other two, so that while the divergence in the support for Apartheid was not significantly different when the immigrants were in Britain,[52] it was significant at the time of the interview in South Africa.[53] This would support the proposition in my seventh hypothesis, that attitude-change is greater among the 'working class' immigrants than among the 'middle classes'.

The sample was also divided into five basic educational groups[54]

[49] Cf. A. N. Oppenheim, *Questionnaire Design and Attitude Measurement* (1966), pp. 276–84.

[50] A. Inkeles and P. H. Rossi, 'National Comparisons of Occupational Prestige', *A.J.S.* 61 (1956), 329–39, reprinted in P. I. Rose, *The Study of Society*, pp. 587–602.

[51] Cf. chapter XVI, pp. 238–9.   [52] chi-square $= 6\cdot380$; p $=$ n.s.; d.f. $= 5$.

[53] chi-square $= 13\cdot210$; p $= \cdot05$; d.f. $= 5$.

[54] The educational profile of the sample is similar to that of the British population as a whole: elementary $= 2$ per cent; secondary modern $= 67$ per cent; grammar $= 24$ per cent; public $= 3$ per cent; university $= 4$ per cent; cf. the per cent distribution of 14-year-olds in Britain: s.m. $= 66$ per cent; grammar $= 24$ per cent; public $= 6$ per cent. R. Miller, *The New Classes* (Longmans, London, 1966), p. 107. Immigrants to South Africa were better educated than those going to Australia, a fact that is related to the restriction on unskilled workers. R. T. Appleyard (1964), pp. 139–40.

which reflected differences in both the amount and the type of academic training. As suggested in hypothesis 11, prejudice was inversely related to the immigrant's level of education, and public school immigrants were slightly less tolerant than their grammar school peers. This supports the second proposition, that the *type* of education may be an important variable, which is further reflected in the mean integration scores shown in Table 4.

TABLE 4

Education, Integration, and Intolerance

	Elem.	S.M.	Gram.	Pub.	Univ.	Total
Mean outgroup score	−3·6	−1·7	−1·4	−1·5	−1·1	−1·6
Econ. integ. score	2·5	2·2	2·5	2·8	1·8	2·3
Soc. integ. score	0·1	0·5	0·8	2·4	1·0	2·3
Pol. integ. score	−0·4	−0·7	0·5	0·6	−1·0	−0·6
Total integ. score	2·3	2·2	3·1	5·8	1·6	2·5

The fact that those immigrants with a university education are the least well integrated, while those with a public school education alone are the most highly integrated, indicates that the relationships are complex. Clearly there is something about the ethos of the public school that accords well with life in South Africa, and something about the university that does not. There is also evidence to show that the university-educated immigrant is the least likely to support Apartheid and the most likely to condemn it, but this finding must be kept in a Southern African perspective, for 75 per cent of this group were in favour of the policy and only 20 per cent were against it. Mannheim's *freischwebend* intellectual does seem to be *slightly* less prone to intolerance and attitude-change but he is by no means immune from the strain towards racist consistency.

CHAPTER XI

The First Stage of Migration

WE WILL follow the analysis of these fundamental variables with a closer consideration of the processes of migration in the home society. The 'value-added' framework discussed in the second chapter involved six stages: 'means', 'incentive', 'awareness', 'precipitating factors', 'mobilization', and 'social controls'. Each stage will be considered in turn, bearing in mind that they are not rigid categories and, in practice, need not follow chronologically in the order in which they are discussed.

a: THE 'MEANS' TO MIGRATE

The means to migrate, social, psychological, physical, and financial, form what Smelser has termed the 'structural conduciveness', a necessary condition without which a particular type of collective behaviour could not arise, even in its incipient form. Modern Britain, like most industrial societies, is characterized by a high incidence of both social and geographical mobility.[1] The relative ease of travel and its customary nature, combined with the various assisted-passage schemes organized by the Australian, Canadian, and New Zealand governments, all support a conducive structural base for migration to a broad cross-section of the British population. After the war-time and immediate post-war shipping shortages had been overcome, there were few physical limitations placed in the path of potential migrants. The role of government political restrictions will be considered at the 'social controls' stage.

The idea of migration is firmly rooted in British culture: both immigration and emigration have been of continuous significance for several centuries and have created networks of kin, friendship, and acquaintances in many parts of the world. The nature of 'personal influence'[2] and the development of 'chain migration'[3] will be stressed

[1] This is particularly true of international mobility. A recent Gallup International Survey placed Britain at the head of a list of countries in terms of the percentage of its population who expressed a wish to emigrate 'if they were free to do so'— a figure of 41 per cent compared, for example, with 16 per cent for the Netherlands —(*New York Times*, 21 Mar. 1971).

[2] Cf. E. Katz and P. F. Lazarsfeld, *Personal Influence: the part played by people in the flow of mass communications*.

[3] C. A. Price, 'Immigration and Group Settlement' in W. D. Borrie, *The Cultural Integration of Immigrants* (1959), p. 270.

TABLE 5

The Use and Influence of the Assisted Passage Scheme

(i) *Use*			(ii) *Influence*		
	per cent			per cent	
Yes	84	(N = 431)	Yes, crucial to decision	42	(N = 214)
No, N/A.	16	(N = 83)	No significance	42	(N = 219)
			Emigrate elsewhere	16	(N = 81)
TOTAL	100	(N = 514)	TOTAL	100	(N = 514)

at a later stage. Such contacts, combined with the increasing frequency of travel, both civilian and military, form continuous forces breaking down inertia and the psychological impediments to international mobility. Richmond's 'transilients'[4] also suggest that something of the ethos of the international 'jet set' has been slowly percolating through to the middle classes.

The financial means to migrate were significantly increased by the introduction of the South African Government's assisted-passage scheme in 1961. After its extension two years later, from a mixed loan and grant to an outright grant of R120 per head, it probably ranked as the most generous scheme available to a British migrant. It enabled selected immigrants to travel to South Africa at virtually no cost, provided free hotel accommodation until employment was secured, and contained no commitment to a minimum period of residence in the country. The impact of the scheme can be gauged both by the sharp rise in immigration statistics after 1961, and by the survey data shown in Table 5. Nearly all those who were eligible to make use of the free passage did so, and some 58 per cent of the sample stated that without such assistance they would not have emigrated at all or would have chosen another country. The remaining 42 per cent, who claimed that financial assistance was not a factor in their decision, probably exaggerates the true figure. One respondent reflected the attitude of the majority with an illuminating analogy: 'Yes, indeed, like Aladdin's lamp it made the difference between the possible and the impossible.' (No. 408/25).

b: THE 'INCENTIVE' TO MIGRATE[5]

Once the underlying means to migrate are available, the next stage in the value-added framework is an analysis of the 'incentive',

---

[4] Defined by Richmond as migrants for whom 'the return to their former country did not imply any failure on their part to adjust either economically or socially', *Post-War Immigrants in Canada*, p. 252.

[5] I have discussed this topic in a more popular version elsewhere. Cf. J. Stone, 'Migrants to Apartheid', *New Society*, 29 May 1969, 836–7.

or the fundamental motives for migration. The incentive roughly corresponds with Smelser's 'structural strain' or with what Eisenstadt terms the 'inability to adapt'. This stage forms a central part in any analysis of emigration and the results are interesting to compare with related studies of British immigrants in Australia and Canada, as well as with non-British immigrants in South Africa.

All studies of post-war British emigration agree on one central point: that economic factors are the fundamental determinant and key motivating influence behind such movements.[6] My results are no exception to this rule as is shown by the statistics in Table 6, and expressed more vividly in the open-ended replies to the interview questions. Most immigrants mentioned several reasons for their decision:

The Labour government had just been voted in and I was afraid that this would mean a period of austerity. I liked South Africa when we called in there while I was in the Merchant Navy. I was a bit fed up with racial mixing in Britain . . . but that wasn't really very important. Then there's the weather, high taxes, and I couldn't stand my mother-in-law (No. 410/ 10-12).

The immigrant was then asked to clarify the situation by stating the *specific* reasons that made him decide to emigrate and to rank them

TABLE 6

(a) *The motives for migration* (First choice)[a]	N.	%	(b) *Reasons for choosing South Africa*	N.	%
Econ. push	192	37	Job offer	89	17
Econ. pull	153	30	Recommendation	88	17
Pol. push			Opportunities (econ.)	63	12
(i) colour/Africanization	9	2	Elimination	61	12
(ii) Labour Govt.	12	2	Relatives	49	10
Soc. push	36	7	Propaganda	42	8
Soc. pull	34	7	Proximity	33	6
Other push (climate)	16	3	Contact	33	6
Other pull (i) travel	53	10	Way of life	28	6
(ii) climate	4	1	Climate	20	4
(iii) misc.	5	1	Other	9	2
TOTAL	514	100	TOTAL	514	100

[a] Subsequent choices do not modify this picture.

[6] P. H. W. Johnston (1968), op. cit., p. 22; R. T. Appleyard (1964), op. cit., p. 163; A. H. Richmond (1967), op. cit. p. 29; J. Isaac *British Post-War Migration* (1954) p. 298; A. Richardson 'Some Psycho-Social Aspects of British Emigration to Australia', p. 333; this also applies to non-British immigrants to South Africa: J. E. Loedolff, op. cit., p. 44; B. J. In den Bosch (1966), op. cit., p. 71.

in their order of importance. In the case cited above the foremost incentive for migration was 'the economic opportunities in a new country that's not overdeveloped', while the precipitating factor was the 'advent of the Labour government' (410/13). This example, which is not completely typical, illustrates some of the problems involved. Whenever there were ambiguities in the replies, supplementary questions were asked to clarify the issue: if it were not immediately obvious whether economic factors should be classified under the heading of 'pull' or 'push',[7] then the respondents were asked to state what they considered was the direction of the forces involved.

Economic 'push' factors were expressed in a variety of ways: some found that 'work was getting tight at home' or that they were actually unemployed; others complained of 'high taxes', 'the cost of living', 'the freeze and squeeze', 'finding it hard to make ends meet', or that they were 'struggling—living from hand to mouth'. Yet others stressed the 'lack of economic opportunities' or the feeling that they were stranded 'in an economic rut with no future prospects at all'. Frequently, economic, social, and political factors were closely interwoven into a matrix of discontent: hybrid complaints about a lack of both economic and social status, or the economic consequences of manifestly political events:

I'm a mechanical engineer. In England you've got no status, people think you work under a car. In South Africa both the pay and the status are much better (No. 318/10-12).

It's easier for me to see now: Britain is a good old Socialist State, which means that the 20% 'who do' are sacrificed to the 80% 'who don't'. You understand what I mean? The 'get-up-and-go' types are taxed out of existence so there's no incentive to work (No. 303/10-12).

Being a 'colonial', I'm more English than the English . . . but England for me was the England of 1940. I could forsee the impending economic, political and even social decline of the country and the entry into a twilight world of grey tones. You have only to travel between Putney and Charing Cross on the tubes to know what I mean: those balding, harassed, middle-aged men with no other prospect than a gold watch and a pension on retirement (No. 256/10-12).

I went to evening classes rather than taking a degree at University and so my social standing with regard to education was not up to British society's requirements. I could go so far and then the doors closed . . . several times this happened . . . I hoped for better in South Africa (No. 451/10-12).

[7] For a further discussion of the 'push-pull' dichotomy, see O. Gish and C. Peach in *Race*, 10, no. 4 (1969), pp. 515–17.

M

We couldn't get anywhere to live . . . we had waited three years for a flat while three hundred Coloureds moved to new flats in Paddington (No. 216/10-12).

The economic forces attracting immigrants to South Africa were described in simple, clear-cut terms: 'better opportunities for myself and my family', 'the general prospects and pay', 'to get a better financial position', and similar statements. A few saw South Africa as an economic El Dorado—perhaps Monomatapa would be a geographically more apt analogy—while the majority expected a more modest improvement in their standard of living.

Political factors, within which category we include Coloured immigration, the politics of Britain's ex-colonies, and domestic political events, were of little significance as motives for migration. A very few saw themselves as refugees from a flood of black immigrants: 'It was particularly the rising number of Coloureds . . . I'm not prejudiced, but I've no wish for Coloured grandchildren' (No. 317/10–12). Others mentioned this factor at a later stage of the interview but frequently perceived a logical contradiction in their attitudes: 'Some parts of Britain *are* black . . . I was concerned . . . [pause] . . . and yet I've come out here . . . it had no real effect on my decision to emigrate' (No. 171/38). Among British ex-colonials there were those who had 'moved South with Uhuru' (No. 320/10–12), but the majority of immigrants motivated by politics had an aversion to the Labour Government, though it was usually the economic consequences of Mr. Wilson's actions that underpinned an overtly political rejection. No one stated that he had been attracted to South Africa first and foremost by the politics of Apartheid.

Social motives for emigrating were important in a number of cases but they were of far less significance than the economic factors. Many aspects of the British way of life were severely censured, and the criticism ranged from the general to the specific, from the impersonal to the highly personal. Some complained of a 'poor social life', 'too much bureaucracy', 'class barriers', 'television', 'the Welfare State', or 'just plain boredom'; others mentioned 'divorce', 'a broken engagement', or the need to 'get away from relatives'. Still others explained:

There was a take-over bid by some large combine: we became as important as a computer number (No. 41/10-12).

If a Henry Higgins opens his mouth he's shoved in a pigeon hole—I've no dreary exile's view of Britain, you can see it in sharp relief from six thousand miles (No. 268/10–12).

Many immigrants come for personal reasons like our former neighbours here. Their marriage was on the rocks so they decided to emigrate, but it didn't work out of course. You can change your country but you cannot change your personality (No. 198/100).

To get away from relatives; you can choose your friends but relations are chosen for you (No. 186/10–12).

Religion. We just got married . . . my wife's a Protestant and I'm a Catholic and we come from Northern Ireland (No. 112/10–12).

Social factors encouraging immigrants to South Africa fell into three main groups: those attracted by 'the South African way of life', many having visited the country during the war or on business; those who had come to join relatives or family already domiciled in South Africa, or had come in order to avoid the family being broken up; and those 'ex-colonials' drawn by the 'pull of Africa', an almost mystical attachment to their adopted continent and its peculiar 'colonial' style of social life.

Of the remaining factors which constitute the 'incentive', only climate and travel were of real significance. A few immigrants were attracted by the African sun, Lady Duff Gordon's 'weather of paradise'; others had earthly reasons for desiring a warm climate, principally health and the economics of the building industry. This last point was mentioned several times by immigrants as a reason for rejecting Canada. The wish to travel—expressed as 'adventure', 'experience', 'a working holiday', 'a challenge', and similar terms— was the most important non-economic motive, and applied particularly to the young and unmarried. Some replies revealed a certain amount of romanticism, others had decidedly mixed motives:

Africa sounded exotic, although we intended to stay only for two years and then move on to Australia . . . I wrote to the Embassy—can't really remember why—it was the exotic thing to do, everybody was going to New Zealand and Australia, that was the petty bourgeois thing to do . . . so we thought 'let's go to the jungle' (No. 110/10–12).

I had an urge to travel . . . read about it for one and a half years, and went only because my father did not want me to go (No. 218/10–12).

After the Army I was restless and footloose . . . it wasn't that I was discontented with the U.K., just that I wanted to see the World. So I planned a two-year working holiday starting in South Africa . . . then I put down roots and stayed. It was 'itchy feet' I suppose (No. 401/10–12).

In order to complete the discussion of the incentive factor, it is necessary to consider the reasons for the specific selection of South Africa as well as the more general motives for migration. Table 6(b) re-emphasizes the stress placed on economic factors, the most important single reason for choosing the country being an offer of employment:

It was the job and not the country. I had no real intention of emigrating at all. I'd applied for six or seven other jobs at home but the pay was low . . . then I saw an advert in a trade journal at double the money and a significant step up. It just happened to be in Johannesburg . . . (No. 138/15).

I never even considered South Africa, it was a Company transfer (No. 363/15).

We came to South Africa quite by chance. I happened to get an offer of a job and went to the interview thinking it was for Nepal. I only discovered the mistake when we started to talk about the effect of altitude on turbines—Johannesburg's high, but they must have thought I was mad . . . (No. 77/15).

Others mentioned the greater economic opportunities in a country with a 'smaller white population' and a more selective immigration policy than Australia which 'let's just anyone go who can raise £10' (No. 186/15); or more bluntly:

So long as the black man is as stupid as he is, people like me are going to have a hell of a good time . . . it doesn't matter whether it's a white or black government. In South Africa you have to have the brains for twenty people, in Britain only for two others (No. 342/15).

A further 27 per cent were influenced by the presence or recommendation of relatives, friends, or acquaintances:

Quite simply it was the easiest. I have a sister in Kenya who knew several South Africans. She said that Kenya was no good for an artisan because the Indians do all that type of work. Therefore she recommended South Africa (No. 212/15).

Originally we had written to Australia and New Zealand House, but there was a lack of technical openings. Then, quite out of the blue, a friend suggested 'why not try South Africa?'—her brother-in-law had come out here in 1947 and done very well. That was in the tea room of Waterloo Station if you want a bit of local colour! He wrote us a . . . down-to-earth resumé of prices and work, and so we came' (No. 297/15).

The sample also revealed, as Johnston discovered in his study of immigrants in Durban, that a considerable number of immigrants selected South Africa in a negative way by a process or eliminating originally more popular alternatives:

South Africa was an afterthought, we got here by elimination (No. 132/15).

We rejected Australia because once you're out of town you are in the desert; New Zealand was good but we couldn't get in—you need a sponsor and plenty of money; Canada had stopped taking tradesmen, and so that left South Africa (No. 214/15).

The remaining third of the replies reflected a diverse mixture of reasons. Some found the immigration scheme relatively attractive: 'the free passage was very important with three kids, its completely free and there's no two year limit' (No. 432/15); others viewed South Africa in its traditional role of 'half-way house', 'in between Britain and Australia so you can either go on, go back, or stay' (No. 375/15); and yet others stressed their previous contact with the country. 'For seventeen years I kept telling the family stories about my wartime adventures; about naked Zulu women and life on the tobacco farms . . .' (No. 252/15).

Finally, I quote two interesting reactions to the political and race relations image of South Africa—the one illustrating an awareness of the situation stressed in the theoretical section, the other showing the possible 'boomerang effect' or 'adverse' publicity.

We realized that South African whites had troubles and expected to be accepted into the white community easier than in Australia where immigrants are looked down on (No. 459/15).

It started over Sharpeville. The Bishop of Johannesburg's book brought South Africa to my attention. I began to feel that the British reaction was biased, particularly when a few friends sent back glowing reports about the work and the weather (No. 472/15).

In sum, my exploration of the motives for migration and the reasons for the selection of South Africa underlines the economic interpretation of similar studies and lends little support to the hypothesis of substantial and systematic self-selection on political–racial grounds.

C: THE 'AWARENESS' OF OPPORTUNITIES TO MIGRATE

Dissatisfaction at home, or good prospects abroad, do not of their own accord lead to migration. The potential emigrant must first be aware of the opportunities for emigration and so define his situation that it is seen as a legitimate and attractive solution to his present predicament. What stimulates an individual towards 'emigration-mindedness'? How significant are 'personal influence' and 'chain migration'—the role of friends, relatives, and acquaintances in supplying information, persuasion, and acting as informal ambassadors? What is the importance of 'personal contact' as a factor in the emigration decision? Under the general heading of 'awareness' I shall consider several related topics: the degree to which inquiries were made about other countries, the extent and importance of contacts with South Africa, the principal sources of information, and the level of prior knowledge about the country.

(i) *inquiries*

Nearly two thirds of the sample claimed that they had made 'inquiries' about the possibility of emigrating to other countries apart from South Africa, the most important of these being Australia.

TABLE 7

Inquiries and Alternative Choices

Yes, inquiries	331	65	Australia	225	44
No, inquiries	181	35	New Zealand	132	26
			Canada	110	21
			U.S.A.	23	4
			Other	26	5
TOTAL	512	100		516	100

This is in contrast to Appleyard's study which found that 72 per cent of assisted British immigrants had considered Australia alone.[8] The difference may be explained partly by the 'elimination' factor mentioned above, and partly by the definition of 'inquiries'.

We had no need to make enquiries as so many people emigrate from Northern Ireland . . . we *know* people everywhere (No. 475/14).

We had friends all over the world and they all wanted us to go to their country . . . its so hard to get 'honest' facts (No. 403/14).

Much of the discussion on the extent to which the typical migrant diverges from the classical model of economic man is misconceived. Few migrants appeared to be in avid pursuit of 'perfect knowledge'— 'We'd decided to go no matter what it was like' (No. 219/14)—

---

[8] R. T. Appleyard, *British Emigration to Australia*, pp. 158–60. Only 25 per cent of a Dutch sample had considered any alternative to South Africa. Cf. A. P du Plessis, op. cit., p. 242.

but this may be less a reflection of economic irrationality than of the irrationality of the assumptions of classical economics. Frequently, the personal reports of friends, family, and fellow-workers are a more reliable source of information and a more valid interpretation of prospects than Embassy pamphlets, or any elaborate attempts at calculating international comparative costs, prices, and incomes.

(ii) *contacts and visits*

Some 17 per cent of the sample had visited South Africa before emigrating, and just over one third had family, more distant kin, or friends living there before they left Britain. When the characteristics of the sample are considered, particularly the skewed

TABLE 8
Prior Contacts and Visits

Contacts	178	35	Family	64	12
No contacts	336	65	Kin	27	6
			Friends	87	17
			None	336	65
TOTAL	514	100	TOTAL	514	100
Yes visits	88	17	War	32	36
No visits	426	83	Navy	11	13
TOTAL	514	100	Business	8	9
			Holiday	15	17
One visit	62	70	Transit	15	17
Many visits	26	30	Other	7	8
TOTAL	88	100	TOTAL	88	100

distribution with respect to length of residence which would tend to reduce the significance of war-time contact, then the importance of 'personal contact' with the country can be assessed. For some, contact was brief but decisive: 'I just jumped ship and squared it with the Immigration Authorities later' (No. 140/7); for others the war-time experience was passed from one generation to another: 'After the Navy my father wanted to come out but mother wouldn't leave. He gave me the idea' (No. 3/7). Personal contacts with people living in South Africa were important in a minority of cases, but of the 35 per cent of the sample with such connections almost 22 per cent claimed that they had told them 'little or nothing' about the country.[9]

[9] A. H. Richmond, *Post-War Immigrants in Canada*, p. 128.

In both respects—contact and contacts—the 'ex-colonials' were over-represented, often visiting South Africa while 'in transit' to England or on 'holiday' from colonial Africa and, as a result, having a greater opportunity of meeting and making friends with South Africans: 'I knew several South Africans in Kenya—in fact, I even witnessed the "Great Trek" from the White Highlands' (No. 92/7). However, for the majority, migration seemed to be confined within the nuclear family—there is little evidence of extensive 'chain migration'—but personal influence did play a part as a source of information.

(iii) *information*

A third aspect of 'awareness' includes the source from which the immigrant receives most of his information about the country before emigrating. In this the Embassy and the two immigrant organiza-

TABLE 9

Sources of Information[a]

South African Embassy	146	28
Personal influence (U.K.)	117	23
1820–Samorgan	67	13
Personal influence (S.A.)	62	12
Personal contact	49	10
Mass media–books	46	9
South African Company	26	5
Other	1	0
TOTAL	514	100

[a] Cf. R. T. Appleyard, *British Emigration to Australia*, p. 155.

tions, the 1820 Memorial Settlers' Association and Samorgan, shared the dominant position with the role of personal influence and contact. It is in this respect that the part played by *people* in mediating the message of mass communications, emphasized by Katz and Lazarsfeld, can be seen to be of considerable importance as opposed to the more formal sources of information and propaganda. Some immigrants complained of a lack of suitable information: 'it's so hard to get factual books on South Africa in Britain as Apartheid seems to prevent publishers from printing balanced accounts—it's all opinion and no facts' (No. 124/17). Many, though by no means all, approached the Embassy publications with caution: 'I read the newspapers in South Africa House, the glossy handouts leave out all the depressing stuff' (No. 232/17). Others discovered the value of 'just talking to people . . . it's surprising how many have been to South Africa' (No. 287/17). The last quotation illustrates the importance of 'personal influence' operating within the home society which was almost twice as significant as that emanating from the host society.

(iv) *knowledge*

Finally, while considering the 'awareness' of opportunities for emigration, it is important to have some estimate of the typical immigrant's knowledge of South Africa before he leaves Britain. Because of the research design of the study, test questions asked in

TABLE 10
Extent of Prior Ignorance[a]

(a) Amount of knowledge: (self-assessment)			(b) Knowledge on specific questions: (retrospective answers)						
				Population		*Prime Minister*		*Afrikaner's History*	
Much	29	6	Yes	325	63	364	71	90	17
Fair	140	27	No	92	18	87	17	296	58
Little	248	48	Unsure	97	19	63	12	128	25
None	97	19							
TOTAL	514	100	TOTAL	514	100	514	100	514	100

[a] Cf. R. T. Appleyard, *British Emigration to Australia*, pp. 194–206.

an *ex post facto* situation would obviously be unsatisfactory, but it is possible to gain some idea of *minimum ignorance*. This will tend to underestimate the true situation, but because the measure is remarkably high it is most revealing. On the basis of a self-rated assessment, two-thirds of the sample admitted that they knew 'little or nothing' in the way of general knowledge about the country (Table 10(a)). Over one third stated that they had no clear idea of the proportion of whites to blacks in the population before emigrating; nearly one-third were unsure of the Prime Minister's name at that time; and over 80 per cent expressed ignorance of the most basic events in the Afrikaner's history and, one suspects in many cases, of his existence in South Africa at all. A few, not untypical, quotations may help to substantiate this statistical portrait.

The general knowledge question was sometimes greeted with the wry comment: 'not enough' (No. 27/19), or with the assertion that:

'you can't know before you come' (No. 205/19). One lady assessed her prior knowledge succinctly: 'to me "Africa" was Tarzan and the Apes' (No. 368/19), and another declared in a similar vein: 'I knew very little, in fact my mother kept on talking about stewpots and black men' (No. 231/19). Several of the men, suffering under similar though less colourful illusions, explained:

I was surprised by the 'with-it' commercialism of Jo'burg . . . almost on an American level. It was far too frantic so I came to Cape Town (No. 225/19).

We didn't realize Johannesburg would be so sophisticated . . . *this* is not Africa (No. 66/19).

Some expected to witness Apartheid in literally monochrome terms:

I expected black buses to be painted black, and white buses to be painted white (No. 220/19).

In reply to the population question, one immigrant remarked:

I didn't expect to see so many of *them* [i.e. Africans] . . . strange really since it is their country (No. 383/20a).

While 71 per cent claimed that they knew the Prime Minister's name before coming, some of these explained that this was: 'only because he was shot [Dr. Verwoerd]' (No. 195/20b). Another, while not being sure of his name, at least knew that: 'He was a German [*sic*] . . . yes, a German government, many of them ex-Nazis' (No. 72/20b).

The question about the Afrikaner's history revealed the greatest amount of prior ignorance:

Afrikaners? . . . Aren't they the same as Africans? (No. 3/20c).

We knew nothing about the 'Dutch' side apart from the Boer War: we certainly didn't realize the Afrikaner exists as he does (No. 212/20c).

I thought the Afrikaner was a tribe, a mixture of Coloured and Bantu . . . I'd have known if they had said Boer (No. 461/20c).

I must say I was puzzled by the person on the coins [Van Riebeeck] . . . the long hair had me fooled (No. 223/20c).

A few tried to duck the question with what is, in the South African context, a remarkable confession of ignorance: 'We are looking towards the future; we are not bothered by the past' (No. 391/20c).

In general, most immigrants were more concerned with obtaining information about the 'bread and butter' issues—employment, housing, and the cost of living—than facts about the ethnic, racial, and political situation. The extent of the ignorance about these latter issues is highly significant: these were not the delusions of an eccentric minority, but the views of a quite typical cross-section of British immigrants before they left for South Africa.

d: FACTORS 'PRECIPITATING' EMIGRATION

In this sub-section I consider two related aspects of the next stage of migration: the length of time the immigrant had been thinking about emigrating—the gestation period—and the factors that finally crystallized his decision and precipitated action. Table 11

TABLE 11

Gestation Period and Precipitants

10 years or more	55	11	Personal influence	131	25
5–9 years	43	8	Impersonal influence	101	20
2–4 years	110	21	Discontinuities	79	15
12–23 months	72	14	Disturbances: econ.	95	19
3–11 months	147	29	Disturbances: pol.	35	7
Under 3 months	39	8	Disturbances: soc.-pers.	23	5
Spontaneous	32	6	Disturbances: climate/travel	38	7
Other	16	3	Other/none.	12	2
TOTAL	514	100		514	100

shows that unlike Appleyard's sample of immigrants to Australia, of whom only 21 per cent had considered emigrating for less than a year,[10] immigrants to South Africa took a much shorter period, on average, to arrive at a decision—43 per cent falling into this 'quick-decision' category. Some claimed that they had made:

A spot decision . . . about three days . . . we gave it no prior thought, there was no prelude (No. 234/9).

It took about five minutes. We were in London and feeling a bit fed up when we happened to walk through Trafalgar Square, so we called at the first Embassy (No. 92/9).

At the other extreme, the prospect of emigration had been seriously considered: 'all my life' (No. 34/9), but in general it took a much shorter period for the seeds of discontent to germinate into action.

With the potential immigrant poised on the threshold of decision, aware of his opportunities, pushed and pulled by the contending incentives, and supplied with the means to migrate, it remains to

---

[10] R. T. Appleyard, *British Emigration to Australia*, p. 212. P. H. W. Johnston's Durban study placed the figure at 50 per cent, (1968), op. cit., chap. 8.

analyse the factors that finally precipitated his action. This raises the same problems as those associated with the 'incentive': problems of defective memory and recall, particularly among those emigrants who had lived in South Africa for several years; and, secondly, the extent to which respondents were capable of assessing, or prepared to divulge, their 'true' motives.[11] These limitations must never be forgotten when considering the survey evidence, and the interpretation should be accepted with due caution.

The precipitating factors proved to be very diverse but it was possible to classify them into three broad categories which I have termed 'influence', 'discontinuities', and 'disturbances'. The most important single set of precipitating factors consisted of the advice, persuasion, and demonstration effects of individuals received at the face-to-face level. Many of the migrants stepped over the threshold after they had seen, and subsequently heard from, workmates and colleagues, friends and acquaintances who had preceded them. Others crystallized their decision on seeing a relative emigrate, or after having heard from relatives already domiciled in South Africa. The largest single group in this category decided to emigrate with their families, fiancés, or fellow-workers, although they themselves had not originated the decision. They emigrated, in fact, at one remove. There were also cases where South Africans and former immigrants, either on holiday or temporarily resident in Britain, had acted in the capacity of private ambassadors.

The 'impersonal' influence category includes those immigrants who reached their final decision as a result of the mass media or other less direct forms of communication and propaganda. These consisted of advertisements for specific occupations in trade journals and newspapers, often sponsored by the various bodies trying to promote immigration, and occasional press articles about South Africa, notably in *The Daily Express*—'in the final analysis you can blame Lord Beaverbrook' (No. 476/13) was how one man summed it up. Another explained:

We saw a programme on T.V. about the cotton mill workers who had gone to East London. 'Lucky devils', we thought and wished that we were going too. They were just ordinary artisans . . . so we wrote to the Embassy (No. 188/13).[12]

The second set of factors—'discontinuities'—occurred when the

[11] Cf. R. T. Appleyard, op. cit., pp. 146–7.
[12] Cf. Appendix C.

decision to emigrate coincided with some natural break in the individual's life history. The end of an apprenticeship, the completion of education, retirement, and marriage are all instances where the changing of a social role either released an individual to follow a course which had previously been difficult, or had sufficiently unsettled him to push him across the immigration threshold.

The 'disturbance' category consisted of all those events—economic, political, social, climatic, etc.—whose chance occurrence launched the potential immigrant into actual migration. Economic disturbances were again the most important single causes: 'Quite simply, the factory closed down' (No. 380/13). Seven per cent of the sample claimed that political factors were the final determining influence on their decision. Once again, probing behind the initial responses suggested that it was the economic consequences of Harold Wilson's actions that were the real roots underlying a manifestly political rejection. Social disturbance factors included the important 'freedom from family commitments' which often acted as a break on the potential emigrant:

It was my wife's mother's death . . . apart from that we would still be in the U.K. now (No. 242/13).

Our opportunity came when our only son went to the Army College then we were free to come (No. 148/13).

A few emigrants said that migration had followed immediately in the wake of a divorce, had been the means of escaping from an awkward affair, or the result of other disturbing personal experiences:

We had just lost a baby—we were unsettled (No. 497/13).

The divorce decree held things up . . . I left soon afterwards (No. 30/13).

Climate and travel, sometimes acting together, constitute the last of the major disturbance factors. Exceptionally bad weather or a holiday in a sunny climate could equally supply the final catalyst:

We came back from a holiday in Capri . . . that really started us off (No. 481/13).

I know it sounds ridiculous but we went to North Wales for a holiday . . . we became thoroughly fed up with the weather . . . the rain came through the tent and so we came home early. Then we both said together, 'let's emigrate' (No. 181/13).

A few immigrants found it impossible to remember the reasons why they had come to a decision at all. While it was possible in many of these cases to infer[13] the major precipitating factors from the replies to other questions, it remains true that for some immigrants the transition across the threshold was so gradual, or was the result of so many interacting variables, that it was subjectively impossible to isolate after the event. Although it is important not to subscribe to an 'over-rationalized concept of man in sociological theory', nevertheless it was possible to reduce this residual category to a relatively insignificant 2 per cent. The over-all pattern of precipitating factors and the comparatively short gestation period, while being tied a little less closely to economic forces than the basic motives for migration, give no grounds for altering my fundamental interpretation of the mechanics of British migration to South Africa. A quick decision triggered off by a great variety of motives seems to provide little evidence of systematic self-selection.

e: AGENCIES FOR THE 'MOBILIZATION' OF IMMIGRANTS

The completion of this discussion of the value-added scheme requires consideration of certain mobilizing agencies of a non-individual type. There is, of course, no clear distinction between 'awareness' and 'mobilization'; the former leads to the latter, the latter promotes the former. However, apart from the personal influence exercised by friends and relatives, there is also a considerable amount of similar work undertaken by the Immigration Section of South Africa House, the 1820 Memorial Settlers' Association, and the South African Immigration Company (Samorgan), a private firm undertaking the promotion of immigration for profit. Table 12 shows the proportion of the sample who came in contact with the non-Government agencies. It is at this point that a selective factor may begin to operate—though it is at the 'social controls' stage that this takes its most open form—but the selection is negative rather than positive, the action of a filter not that of a magnet, and one with an economic rather than a political mesh.

TABLE 12

Contacts with Mobilizing Agencies

1820 M.S.A. in U.K. and S.A.	124	24
1820 M.S.A. in S.A. only	183	36
Samorgan	60	12
Neither	147	28
TOTAL	514	100

[13] For the importance of the 'editing' stage of social surveys, see C. A. Moser, *Survey Methods in Social Investigation* (1958), pp. 269–72.

f: 'SOCIAL CONTROLS' ON IMMIGRATION

The social controls stage, the last in the value-added sequence, consists of the rules and regulations, restrictions and conditions that can prevent the potential immigrant from fulfilling his plans even when all the other five stages are in operation. In practice, these are the criteria laid down by the host society and incorporated in the immigration selection procedure. For an immigrant to be 'suitable' from the South African point of view he must be of 'pure white' ('European') parentage; have a definite job offer from an employer in South Africa, or be a member of a trade or profession in short supply (i.e. not an unskilled worker), or have other proved means of financial support. In addition he must not admit to, or be found to possess, certain 'undesirable' characteristics or affiliations: notably he must not be a member of the Communist Party or a professed atheist. Thus for the majority of potential British immigrants the key restrictions were economic and not political.

CHAPTER XII

The Process of Integration:
(1) The Economic Dimension

IN THE previous chapter the overwhelming significance of economic factors in the genesis of the decision to emigrate suggests, logically, that we should turn to this sphere of integration first in order to assess the over-all pattern of settlement in South Africa. Three major facets of integration will be isolated—the economic, social, and political-cultural—and combined at a later stage in an assessment of 'total' integration among the sample of British immigrants. The various sub-dimensions of economic integration will be approached from a perspective of subjective perception rather than objective reality for the sociological reasons presented in the theoretical section.

a: HOUSING

We found in the comparative discussion that housing was a crucial sphere in the development of race relations. It also plays a vital role in the economic integration of immigrants. No attempt has been made to tackle this question in a sophisticated manner; what was required for the purposes of this study was a simple subjective assessment of relative well-being. The over-all trends suggested in Table 13 need very careful interpretation, particularly with the low median length of residence. Thus a slight fall in the ratio of owned-

TABLE 13

Accommodation in U.K. and S.A. with comparative Assessment

U.K.			S.A.					
Detached	26	5	Detached	36	7	Much better	67	13
Semi-detached	193	38	Bungalow	175	34	Better	50	10
Terraced	83	16	Terraced	10	2	Same	64	12
Flat/Rooms	114	22	Flats	184	36	Worse	151	29
Other (with parents)	98	19	Other (hotel)	109	21	Much worse	133	26
						No comparison, etc.	49	10
TOTAL	514	100		514	100		514	100

to-rented accommodation, from 50:50 to 41:59 (discounting the 'other' category), probably signifies a long-run *rise* in the propensity towards owner-occupation. The other two features of note were the relative insignificance of terraced housing in South Africa and the increased use of rented flats. While a little less than a quarter of the sample felt that their housing was superior to that which they had enjoyed in Britain, some 55 per cent thought that it was worse, or much worse.

It was the price of accommodation, particularly for the artisan who had been living in subsidized council housing in Britain, that was the greatest source of complaint:

In Britain we had a two-bedroom council flat at £1/16/- a week; in South Africa a one-bedroom bachelor flat at R68 a month. The rent is four times as much for a smaller flat (No. 27/26–7).

Flats are four times what we paid at home for a mortgage (No. 51/26–7).

For the average immigrant this is the biggest obstacle: rent is exorbitant. A typical tradesman earning R200 a month has an average rent of R75 . . . that is 40% of his income which is ridiculously high and the deposit to buy a house is just hopeless (No. 271/26–7; a builder).

Rents are very expensive, it's the equivalent of income tax in England (No. 298/26–7).

They paint a rosy picture of large houses and huge lawns, but they forget to mention that Bank Rate is 8% (No. 316/26–7).

Another unpleasant surprise was the paradoxical situation that many immigrants found themselves in, being forced to live in central city flat areas[1] in a country of wide open spaces:

Jo'burg is terrible . . . we were determined not to live in a concrete postage stamp in the centre of town so we found this place 28 miles out of town (No. 134/26–7).

Hillbrow is a dungeon for immigrants (No. 98/26–7).

Other immigrants, who had taken the precaution of checking the prices of houses and flats in South African newspapers before arrival,

[1] The effect of flat life on social integration should be interpreted with caution. For a study challenging ecological determinism in Johannesburg, see H. Lever, L. Schlemmer and O. J. M. Wagner, 'Some Patterns and Correlates of Informal Social Participation in a Highly Urbanized Flat-Dwelling Community in South Africa,' paper presented to the 'Focus on Cities' conference, Institute for Social Research, University of Natal (Durban), 9 July 1968; for a more general argument in the same vein, see H. J. Gans, 'Urbanism and Suburbanism as Ways of Life: A Re-evaluation of Definitions', reprinted in P. I. Rose, op. cit., pp. 306–22.

N

found that suburbs like 'Mayfair' had very different connotations in Johannesburg from London. It would be misleading, however, to paint the picture in purely negative terms, for some of the dissatisfaction was probably a short-lived reaction to a totally different structure of incomes, prices, and costs. The factors of time and space were important in shaping attitudes:

I come from the Sheffield slums where houses have outside toilets and there is nowhere for the kids to play (No. 32/26–7).

Flats are not so expensive compared to London and they are very good value (No. 67/26–7).

It was incredibly easy in 1962, immediately in the aftermath of Sharpeville; there were so many South Africans in Hampstead that you could walk into any block of flats in Hillbrow and virtually make your own terms (No. 267/26–7).

Indeed, some immigrants were extremely satisfied:

Its like a palace compared with home (No. 115/26–7).

After South Africa, I always feel the British live in boxes (No. 343/26–7).

Often, the conditions of the South African housing market persuaded many working-class immigrants into a home ownership which they would not have considered in Britain:

I'm buying a bungalow . . . now what working man could do that in Scotland? (No. 13/26–7).

An ordinary working man's house in South Africa is equivalent to executive-type accommodation in Britain (No. 147/26–7).

An interesting reflection on this last comment took place at the end of one interview, showing that changed material standards need not have much influence on class norms. Just before I left a friendly Lancastrian couple—the husband was a skilled manual worker—they took me on a tour of their house. The prize exhibit was their lounge, the door of which they specially unlocked to show me a very large, beautifully decorated room. 'Where would you find one that size in Britain?', they proudly demanded, 'do you think we would go back and leave this?' The interview, which lasted over three hours, took place in the kitchen.[2]

[2] Thus care must be taken with the 'embourgeoisement' thesis in Africa as well as in Britain. Cf. J. H. Goodthorpe and D. Lockwood, 'Affluence and the British Class Structure' 113–63; 'The Affluent Worker and the Thesis of Embourgeoisement: some preliminary research findings', *Sociology*, 1, no. 1 (1967), 11–31; *The Affluent Worker in the Class Structure* (1969).

There was only one case in which the human implications of the Group Area Acts made a forceful impression on an immigrant:

It really hit us first when a Coloured onion seller came around and told us that he had been living in our suburb for forty-five years but had just been forced to move. You can imagine what we felt like having been in the country for less than three months . . . that was over six years ago . . . I still often feel that we *ought* to go back . . . (No. 253/26–7).

The reaction of immigrants to housing in South Africa has been emphasized because of its crucial role in the process of integration. In general, at least during the early stages of adjustment, it tends to have a negative influence.

b: TRANSPORT

Closely allied to the question of accommodation is that of the ownership of, or access to, a private car.[3] There are several reasons why a car can be regarded as more essential in South Africa than in Britain: distances are greater, public transport tends to be less frequent, and, in many parts of the country, it is considered unsafe to

TABLE 14

Ownership of/Access to Private Car in U.K. and S.A.

	U.K.			S.A.	
Yes	369	72	Yes	403	79
No	145	28	No	83	16
			Intend	28	5
TOTAL	514	100		514	100

walk around the streets after dark, particularly for women. Table 14 reflects this increase in car ownership even at the crudest level of comparison.

c: OCCUPATIONAL CHANGE

A third aspect of economic integration is that of occupational mobility. Table 15 shows a net upward shift of 11 per cent out of manual into non-manual occupations. Once again, this is an extremely rough estimate of occupational mobility, but an accurate comparative assessment would be incredibly complex, if not impossible, to calculate. It may be compared with the immigrants' subjective assessment of their own social mobility in which 29 per

[3] Cf. A. H. Richmond, *Post-War Immigrants in Canada*, p. 86; B. J. In den Bosch, op. cit., p. 71.

TABLE 15

Occupational Class in U.K. and S.A.

U.K.			S.A.		
Professional	31	6	Professional	44	9
Intermediate	129	25	Intermediate	170	33
Manual	349	68	Manual	295	57
Other	5	1	Other	5	1
TOTAL	514	100		514	100

cent thought that they had risen, and 5 per cent thought that they had fallen in relation to their social position in Britain. As an index of integration we may assume that upward occupational mobility will usually signify greater economic integration, and downward mobility the reverse.

d: WORKING CONDITIONS

The fourth dimension of economic integration involves differences in the working conditions associated with employment in the two countries. Housewives were also asked about their working conditions and about the use of servants.

TABLE 16

Comparative Working Conditions and the Employment of Servants

Much better	60	12	Full-time servants	247	48
Better	61	12	Part-time servant	80	16
Same	160	31	No servant	76	15
Worse	103	20	Too early, etc.	111	22
Much worse	57	11			
N/A, etc.	73	14			
TOTAL	514	100		514	101

Considering the tendency towards upward occupational mobility, and the widespread employment of servants shown in Table 16, it is interesting that more immigrants claimed a deterioration than claimed an improvement in their working conditions. Many disliked the relative insecurity of South African industry, the smaller-scale firms, the versatility required of a tradesman, or the less formal atmosphere of industrial relations.

You can get sacked in one day ... it happened to me ... it's like England in the sixteenth century (No. 223/74).

It's not so good. You have to stand up for yourself as there's no Trade Union (No. 30/74).

It's the union factor: they are too strong in Britain, too weak in South Africa—it's very different (No. 480/74).

They don't have the facilities here as the firms are smaller (No. 359/74).

It's less specialized . . . you're a Jack-of-all-trades here (No. 49/74).

They're more 'pro-boss' in South Africa. In the U.K. people are Bolshie, here people creep . . . like after a depression. In South Africa the boss is king; in Britain the boss is the enemy (No. 410/74).

Others viewed the same situation from a different perspective:

The management approach is far better here and relations are very good. In the U.K. it's 'us' and 'them', in South Africa they are prepared to listen to you (No. 376/74).

Wonderful. It's so airy and clean compared to the filth of the industrial North (No. 369/74).

There's a big difference as labour is so much easier to get here. *Son:* What he *really* means is that the nig-nogs carry the bricks for him (No. 126/74).

Domestic working conditions were clearly influenced by the rapid adoption of the white South African norm of employing servants. Some three-fifths of those immigrants who had been in the country for more than a few weeks employed at least one full-time servant, and a further one-fifth had part-time assistance.

Servants are just great . . . you just can't beat it. At first you get a servant because everyone else does, but then they become a necessity . . . it's just laziness I suppose (No. 438/74).

It's marvellous . . . I've got a 'girl' . . . I love it . . . *I'm a lady* out here (No. 426/74).

It's wonderful to have a girl, particularly with three kids. In fact it's quite a lady's life, but it saps your incentive and you seem to do far less (No. 454/74).

The employment of servants may account for some of the increase in the number of working wives—from 44 per cent to 49 per cent—but there was evidence that some potential women workers were being frustrated by the restrictions of the industrial colour bar: 'I can't get a job because the natives do it here' (No. 91/74), and 'there's nothing I can do here' (No. 213/74) were typical complaints. However, not all the white victims of Apartheid were perturbed by the situation: 'No work: that's one of the benefits of the country' (No. 127/74).[4]

---

[4] Thus, for some, servants proved to be the liberators of the 'captive wife,' for others the source of mental imprisonment and boredom. Cf. H. Gavron, *The Captive Wife: conflicts of household mothers* (1966).

e: STANDARD OF LIVING[5]

TABLE 17

Comparative Standard of Living, Income, and Cost of Living

Much higher	191	37	Much higher	181	35	Much higher	7	1
Higher	178	35	Higher	181	35	Higher	56	11
Same	88	17	Same	110	21	Same	344	67
Lower	44	9	Lower	23	4	Lower	93	18
Much lower	9	2	Much lower	7	1	Much lower	2	0
Don't know	4	1	Don't know	12	2	Don't know	12	2
TOTAL	514	101		514	98		514	99

We established earlier that the chief motive for emigration was economic so that the figures in Table 17, whether measured in terms of the 'standard of living', 'relative income', or the 'cost of living', suggest that a majority of the sample was achieving this aim at the time of the interview.

It's much better in South Africa, we have a middle-class income and standard of living (No. 252/75).

I can easily compare as I recently spent three months with a friend in England who was in exactly the same job—he exists and I live (No. 280/75).

You can earn £14–15 a week in England, but if you earn that in South Africa you're mad . . . you can get £25 a week driving a bus . . . I used to get £15 a week and now I'm on £3,000 a year, and I landed with £20 in my pocket four years ago (No. 307/75).

It's not so much a question of wealth as the fringe benefits like servants (No. 416/75).

Some, however, qualified this picture of relative affluence:

It depends on your line of business . . . no good for a joiner because the Coloured people do it. Thus it varies, for some it is the land of milk and honey, while for others it's quite hard (No. 212/75).

If you take a gamble there's more chance in South Africa; but if you go broke it's a lot harder here (No. 212/75).

f: PROSPECTS AND OPPORTUNITIES

The final aspect of economic integration to be considered is that of prospects and opportunities, a dynamic perspective on the standard of living. Many immigrants came to the country with a view to long-run economic gains, rather than immediate returns, both for themselves and for their children.

---

[5] Richmond found that 75 per cent of his sample felt that their standard of living had improved, 9 per cent that it had fallen (*Post-War Immigrants in Canada*, p. 92).

TABLE 18

Comparative Prospects, Education, and Children's Opportunities

Prospects			Education			Child's opportunities[a]		
Much better	273	53	Much better	9	2	Much better	78	15
Better	116	23	Better	37	7	Better	103	20
Same	75	15	Same	86	17	Same	49	10
Worse	24	5	Worse	101	19	Worse	21	4
Much worse	8	2	Much worse	40	8	Much worse	7	1
Don't know, etc.	18	4	N/A., etc.	241	47	N/A., etc.	256	50
TOTAL	514	102		514	100		514	100

[a] In den Bosch found that two-thirds of his sample of Dutch immigrants were 'satisfied' with their children's education in South Africa. *De Verschillende Aspecten van de Aanpassing der Nederlandse Immigranten in Zuid-Afrika*, p. 72.

The immigrants' assessment of comparative economic prospects between the two countries echoes the improvement in the standard of living:

Wonderful . . . there's no real limit here, there's much more scope. In Britain you must be in the 'charmed circle'. I was, so I should know, but here anyone who is determined can succeed (No. 92/78).

Quite superb in South Africa: you don't stagnate, ability counts, there are less restrictive practices and you don't have to shout you want more money (No. 98/78).

It's fantastic . . . equivalent to America a hundred years ago (No. 397/78).

I've come as far in three years here as it took me thirty years in Britain (No. 506/78).

Once again, there were some qualifications to this over-all picture of enthusiastic optimism:

You can get on better in British industry, there's the language barrier to promotion here (No. 130/78).

There are definite opportunities but it's more insecure: you make steady progress in Britain compared with violent fluctuations over here (No. 472/78).

Much better opportunities . . . that's why so many shouldn't be here, they are living a lie (No. 110/78).

The majority of immigrants with children thought that their opportunities had improved alongside their parents', and, in some cases, in contrast to their parents':

Personally, my firm has grown so much in England that there's less scope here, but for my son the world really is his oyster—this is a salesman's paradise (No. 296/78).

There was a mixed reaction to South African education. Many immigrants claimed that the standard was lower, but that the opportunities and the emphasis placed on academic achievement more than offset any disadvantages:

Everyone aims at matric or even University education . . . matric's a dire necessity here (No. 85/39).

The standard is lower, but there is more scope and opportunity (No. 401/39).

They seem to be 'matric-mad' over here . . . South Africa is very qualification-conscious and parents show much more interest (No. 508/39).

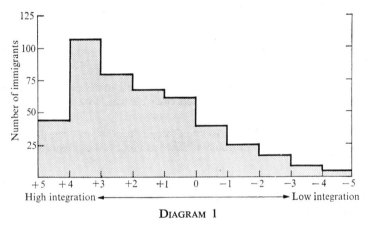

DIAGRAM 1

Frequency Distribution of Economic Integration Scores

Finally, an index based on three of the sub-dimensions[6] of economic integration was calculated as a means of comparing relative degrees of integration between different sub-groups of the sample. The mean integration score of the sample, based on a +5 to −5 scale, was +2·276, and the frequency distribution is shown in Diagram 1. The over-all picture of the economic dimension of integration is one of substantial improvement and general satisfaction. While housing and work conditions gave some cause for complaint, the overwhelming majority had significantly improved their standard of living and regarded the future economic prospects, both for them-

[6] 'Standard of living', 'prospects and opportunities', and 'occupational mobility'. The first two were scored on a +2/−2 scale, the last on a +1/−1 scale. 'Don't know' replies were given a score of zero.

selves and their children, as incomparably better than they had been in Britain.

TABLE 19

Congruence of Economic Expectations and Realities

Much better	117	23
Better or equal	236	46
Slightly below	94	18
Much below	45	9
None, etc.	22	4
TOTAL	514	100

This interpretation mirrors the findings of other studies of immigrants in South Africa, and is also reflected in the replies to the interview question concerning the degree of congruence between economic expectations and economic realities (see Table 19).

CHAPTER XIII

The Process of Integration: (2) The Social Dimension

SOCIAL INTEGRATION is the second major dimension to be considered, and though social factors were less important than economic factors in motivating migration, they were relatively much more important at the stage of integration. The following analysis contains six basic sub-divisions of social integration.

a: PATTERNS OF FRIENDSHIP

The development, or the non-development, of friendship patterns with members of the host society is a crucial element of social integration. In the theoretical discussion I pointed to the attenuation and breaking down of the ties of kin and friendship which may be regarded as an inevitable result of the act of migration. The re-establishment of new friendship patterns as a substitute for old ones left behind—a functional alternative when friends replace kin—must be considered in more detail.

TABLE 20

Comparative Ease of Friendship and Ethnic Differences

Much harder	49	10	Ethnic diff. Yes	274	53	E.S.A. more	248	48
Harder	89	17	Ethnic diff. No	179	35	A.S.A. more	25	5
Same	129	25	Don't know	61	12	The same	241	47
Easier	141	27						
Much easier	103	20						
Don't know	3	1						
TOTAL	514	100		514	100		514	100

Immigrants were asked to assess the comparative ease of establishing friendships in the two countries, first with 'South Africans'—deliberately left undefined to see whether immigrants would differentiate between the various language and colour groups—and, secondly, to compare English-speaking and Afrikaans-speaking (white) South Africans in this respect. The majority interpreted the question as referring to white South Africans alone, and to many the title 'South African' was even more narrowly defined as being synonymous with English-speaking South Africans:

The South Africans are not bad, but the Dutchmen are difficult (No. 44/30).

South Africans are friendly enough but Afrikaners are more dubious. There is a definite anti-British feeling which is a hangover from the Boer War . . . they tolerate you but resent you, and claim that the country does not need immigrants (No. 49/30).

A majority of two to one found it easier to make friends in South Africa. There was talk of 'fantastic hospitality' (No. 6/30) and some even complained that it was:

Overfriendly . . . people come round *every* night. That's how we lost most of our South African friends (No. 461/30).

But most immigrants kept their new friends and clearly enjoyed the company of:

A nation of uninhibited extroverts, they will talk to you on buses and things like that . . . (No. 453/30).

They are much more friendly than the British . . . there I often felt like an outcast in my own country, a complete lack of comradeship and *esprit de corps* that you find here (No. 419/30—an ex-colonial).

Of course, there were qualifications, and not a few outright dissenters from this dominant impression:

Pretty easy . . . it's a nation that lives on the surface; easy people to know socially but it's a comparatively shallow friendship (No. 371/30).

They are not as friendly as they like to pretend they are (No. 101/30).

Some immigrants were clearly surprised at the group structure of South African society:[1]

We certainly didn't expect the 'Apartheid', to use the word very loosely, among the whites: Afrikaners, Jews and English . . . all little nations on their own and to hell with the rest, all pulling against each other rather than together—the Union of South Africa [*sic*] is a complete misnomer . . (No. 234/33).

Others displayed the confusion about the Afrikaner mentioned earlier:

[1] For the influence of ethnic hostility on the integration of immigrants in Canada, see A. H. Richmond, *Post-War Immigrants in Canada*, p. 257.

I don't know much about the Afrikaan [*sic*] . . . don't they all live in the Free State? (No. 1/33).

I think the English Afrikaners are all right. *Husband:* [patronizingly] Who are they? Your friend is a South African Jewess—the Afrikaners are descendants of the Boers (No. 78/33).

Those who had a clear conception of the ethnic divisions of South African society were divided between those who found the English-speaking members of the host society easier to befriend, and those who had experienced no appreciable difference at all.

The English are O.K., the Afrikaners hate us (No. 8/33).

It depends: the *ignorant* Afrikaner is very bad, the educated Afrikaner is very nice (No. 116/33).

A few diehard Boers are suspicious . . . I can understand them easily as I'm an Irishman. They live in their history just as so many Irishmen live in 1916 (No. 198/33).

Afrikaners don't go out of their way to be friendly . . . I don't like their mentality . . . but I don't like the English-speaking South Africans either. I call them all Afrikaners because they all think the bloody same (No. 110/33).

It's particularly with the older generation of Afrikaners, like Anglo-German relations . . . we are wary and keep to ourselves (No. 177/33).

There's a tremendous difference. Afrikaners have a terrible inferiority complex which makes them arrogant, antagonistic and awful liars. I get on fine with them (No. 108/33).

Many, however, challenged this interpretation and some found the Afrikaner to be a more 'genuine' friend. An interesting minority found the Afrikaner to be more friendly:

I've not met that mythical person hating the guts of the British, only the very occasional dyed-in-the-wool Afrikaner from up country . . . but generally that crowd has died off and the majority like the British (No. 248/33).

The majority are very friendly. You hear all the Piet van der Merwe jokes, but that's a load of rubbish (No. 405/33).

There's the language of course and it depends on the area, but if you start by saying a few words in Afrikaans there's no difficulty. No worse than getting on with Scots or for that matter Jewish people (No. 179/33).

Afrikaners are even more friendly: they go out of their way to speak English and have never tried to inflict their language on us. We even met some at the Sons of England Dramatic Society (No. 296/33).

English-speaking South Africans are very ready at first, but as soon as they find that you have nothing to give them they are off—they *want* the Joneses living next door to them. It's a very superficial and irresponsible type of friendship, while Afrikaners are more friendly and genuine, more responsible and have more dignity about them (No. 235/33).

Thus the re-establishment of friendships with the host society did not pose any insuperable barriers for the majority of British immigrants. Contacts were soon established, particularly with English-speaking South Africans, and were confined within the white community. The Africans, indeed all non-whites, following the dictates of Apartheid, were considered to be outside the pale of friendship at the social level.

b: LEISURE-TIME ADJUSTMENT AND COMPARATIVE SOCIAL LIFE

The adjustment to a different pattern of leisure-time activity and to a new style of social life forms another important aspect of social integration. Some three-quarters of the sample recognized that there had been a significant change in their leisure-time activities: 47 per cent considered their new social life to be more active, and 25 per

TABLE 21

Leisure-time Change and Comparative Social Life

Significant change	388	75	Much more active	78	15
No significant change	105	20	More active	161	32
Don't know, etc.	21	5	Same	135	26
			Less active	60	12
			Much less active	68	13
			Don't know, etc.	12	2
TOTAL	514	100		514	100

cent thought that it was less active than in Britain. The nature of these changes is illustrated better by the open-ended replies to the interview questions than by tables based on the often misleading closure imposed by the fixed-choice type of question. Immigrants were also asked comparative questions about the mass media, television, radio, and the newspapers, partly to balance some 'neutral-sounding' items among the rather more personal and politically probing ones, and partly to spark off lines of thought on controversial matters by means of a more indirect attack.

From the typical characteristics of both migration and social mobility, acting in conjunction with other differences like climate, one might expect certain basic changes in leisure patterns. An increase in the home entertainment of friends, rather than relatives, is a likely result of both geographical and social mobility; a reduction in the segregation of leisure activities between husbands and wives might be expected as a consequence of social mobility.[2] These familiar class differences would lead us to anticipate bigger changes and problems of adjustment for artisans than for middle-class immigrants.

The range of opinions about South African social life varied enormously, from the ecstatic to the scornful:

In Britain we looked forward to the August, Easter and Christmas holidays, but here every weekend is a holiday (No. 236/43–4).

You don't just watch sport as in the U.K., you *participate*. You go riding and at the races you can see in comfort as if you were one of the well-to-do. My ten year old son plays golf which is unthinkable in Britain . . . you have a billiard table in your own home and a swimming pool in the garden. It's a vast change (No. 457/43–4).

The South African idea of fun is sitting on their silly stoeps, drinking sundowners, and making facile conversation (No. 111/43–4).

They boast about their great outdoor life but its so dark by six o'clock they can't even see outdoors (No. 470/43–4).

The majority seemed to have adjusted to the new conditions with varying degrees of alacrity, and the predicted changes in the patterns of social life could be seen to emerge clearly in many cases:

At home our social life was centred on the family, now it's based on friends (No. 192/51).

In England the husband leads a more separate life (No. 393/43–4).
It's more taking the wife to a nightclub rather than going to the pub with the boys (No. 400/43–4).

Thus, by British standards, a more 'middle-class type' of social life appeared to be developing side by side with increased social mobility:

It's a completely different way of life: no television and more social life . . . it's a more social type of life, more entertaining . . . (No. 55/43–4).

Football, pubs and T.V. in Britain; picnics, drive-ins and shows here. That's the difference (No. 143/43–44).

[2] Cf. E. Bott, *Family and Social Network* (1957), for a recent comment. J. Platt 'Some Problems in Measuring the Jointness of Conjugal-role relationships', *Sociology*, 3, no. 3 (1969), 287–97.

It's an outdoor, active type of life . . . *Wife:* . . . but you can't go out at night . . . I miss the long summer evenings, there's the natives and the transport problem (No. 79–80/43–4).

A considerable number did find significant problems of adjustment:

It's changed a lot. Hotels are not like pubs . . . I'd rather drink at home. *Wife:* I'm scared to go out in the evenings, there's no bingo, no television . . . social life for working people is just hopeless, we're tied to the home as a consequence (No. 96–7/43–4).

I'm bored on the whole, I really miss that goggle-box (No. 127/51).
The evenings and the loneliness shattered me and I had a nervous break-down (No. 146/43–4).

We don't drink here . . . pubs are not like they are in Britain . . . they get all obstropulous [*sic*] here (No. 253/43–4).

The degree of satisfaction depended, in general, on the degree of adaptability: the positive gains of climate, outdoor life, sporting facilities, and socializing with friends had to be set against the lack of television, the relatively sober atmosphere of the English pub, and the comfort and support of relatives. One immigrant, and immigrants were often their own most severe critics, summarized the situation with the following advice:

If you're a pub-crawler, don't come; if you're always with your relatives, bring 'em out too, or don't come; and if you're glued to the 'tele', don't come. And don't expect the best of both worlds because you won't get it (No. 188/100).

The questions about the mass media provoked a number of interesting reflections on South African society: 'a country curiously wrapped up in itself' (No. 474/49). Direct replies revealed that 50 per cent of the sample regretted the lack of television, and over 80 per cent were in favour of its introduction in South Africa. Most immigrants had a fairly poor opinion of the standard of South African radio programmes; and the assessment of South African newspapers, though mixed, was inclined to be critical. The indirect information provoked by the questions suggested several areas of concern, variously related to the three types of media.

Two principal sets of explanations were offered to account for the surprising lack of television in South Africa,[3] the one cultural-linguistic, and the other racial. This reflects an appreciation of the

[3] For a critical assessment of the official stated reasons on the subject, see S. Uys in *Sunday Times* (S.A.), 31 Dec. 1967 and 10 Mar. 1968.

triangular power structure mentioned in earlier chapters. Nearly 45 per cent of the sample related it to tensions between the English-speaking and the Afrikaans-speaking white communities about language and cultural influence, and particularly to the political power of the Dutch Reformed Church.

I really miss the news . . . you felt in the middle of things with an immediacy and involvement in World activities. They won't have television here because canned programmes from the U.S.A. and Britain don't go down too well with a Calvinist Culture . . . international coverage might dissolve the image of a parochial utopia cocooned from the outside world (No. 267/45c).

It's a Church-state over here . . . the N.G.K. are against it because they are afraid of too much cosmopolitan influence (No. 58/45c).

Hertzog runs this country, if you object you just disappear for 180 days. (No. 126/45c).

The other major explanatory theme stressed the possible revolutionary impact of television on the African majority:

It *shows* the illiterate what they are missing while the radio doesn't, that's the huge difference between hearing and seeing (No. 342/45c).

Mainly because the backward natives would come forward too quickly (No. 77/45c).

It would make the natives too intelligent, you would have T.V. aerials on all the rondavels (No. 74/45c).

A few immigrants accepted that expense was the critical factor—one of the less idiotic, though rather implausible official explanations—and one lady announced that the real reason was 'thunderstorms in the Transvaal', meant (I think) in a literal rather than a metaphorical sense.

Unstructured comments about South African radio revealed a certain irritation at what was defined as blatant political bias and anti-British sentiments:

The S.A.B.C. is very anti-British, at times I could strangle that announcer . . . we believe in live and let live (No. 202/47).

That dreadful 'Current Affairs' programme is just Nationalist viewpoint . . . it's sheer propaganda (No. 294/47).

The radio is very biased . . . you listen to Lord Haw Haw for five minutes every morning . . . there's no attempt at impartiality (No. 453/47).

'Current Affairs'—something a mature man can laugh at (No. 377/47).

South African newspapers, the third type of mass media, did not meet with such severe censure. Many immigrants were surprised at the forthright political criticism of the English-language press:

I expected greater censorship but they are quite prepared to run the Government down on the colour problem. I was quite surprised (No. 403/49).

C: ASSOCIATIONAL ACTIVITY—SECULAR

Apart from primary group social interaction, the secondary group serves an important contributory function in strengthening the ties between immigrant and host society. Some 38 per cent of the sample were members of at least one club or association in South Africa, excluding those linked to religion, the trade unions, or the 1820 Memorial Settlers' Association. The majority of these clubs were social or recreational and there was evidence that many manual workers were participating in them in a way in which they had never done before:

It's quite different . . . I'm a member of the Moths here. I'd *heard* of them in the U.K., but I'd never considered *joining* them (No. 506/50).

I belong to a yacht club and I'm just a toolmaker. I mix with judges, lawyers and doctors, and if they tried to snub me here *they* would be regarded as in the wrong (No. 269/50).

This last comment raises the problems of class-consciousness, social mobility, and social acceptance which will be considered later.

Trade unions are one of the most important types of voluntary association in most industrial societies. It is convenient to consider them at this stage, for, though they do not play a major part in social integration, they are related to several interesting aspects of society in both Britain and South Africa. Trade union membership fell significantly within the sample after emigration, from 39 per cent to 17 per cent. This was not just a temporary result of dislocation, but reflects a real change in attitudes—some 40 per cent stated that they were in favour of British trade unions, while only 8 per cent shared these sentiments about their South African counterparts. Over two-thirds of the sample recognized important differences between the power and influence of unions in the two countries; 34 per cent were in favour of encouraging non-whites to join trade unions,[4] 19 per

---

[4] Both British trade union members (39 per cent:33 per cent) and South African trade union members (40 per cent:34 per cent) were more inclined to

O

cent gave qualified approval (separate unions or the proviso that they be severely controlled), while 38 per cent were totally opposed to such a move.

The immigrants characterized the differences between trade unionism in the two countries in a number of ways:

They speak the same fire and water but in a police-state it's different. This is a management country (No. 44/86b).

Trade unions here have an additional function: to safeguard the white man against the encroachment of coloured labour at all levels . . . equal pay for blacks is just not practical (No. 77/86b).

Totally different . . . they are friendly societies not trade unions . . . dealing with pensions, medical aid, etc (No. 359/86b).

It's way back in the Dark Ages of trade unionism. They are not politically-minded, and so long as the black man is working for them they are quite satisfied (No. 421/86b—a former U.K. branch secretary).

Attitudes towards African participation in trade unions were mixed, reflecting similar divisions of opinion within the white South African labour movement:

I don't see why they shouldn't join unions, colour is irrelevant (No. 24/87). I'm wary of this . . . it's a form of power and they haven't got the intelligence to use it . . . (No. 32/87).

In the short run it would increase resentment against them, but in the long run it might be a good thing . . . like the Tolpuddle Martyrs . . . it's like the nineteenth century in our factory, they would benefit from a bit of security (No. 132/87).

No, they would rebel at the slightest opportunity (No. 65/87).

Several replies revealed an awareness of a moral dilemma between white exclusivism and the universalistic creed of the trade union movement:

From a selfish white point of view, no; from the black point of view, yes. Like the nineteenth century British worker, they are fighting for their rights (No. 179/87).

Politically it would be a disaster, morally I should say yes (No. 415/87).

While the position of the trade unionist in South Africa epitomizes

---

give unqualified support to non-white membership of trade unions than non-unionists in either country. This casts doubt on hypothesis 14 and implies that there is little difference between the trade unionist in Britain and the trade unionist subject to the norms of the South African labour movement.

those dilemmas which we anticipated in the general case of the British immigrant, trade union members as a group were not significantly more inclined to support or to oppose the policy of Apartheid,[5] though they were noticeably more ethnocentric than non-members (see Table 22).

TABLE 22

Mean Outgroup Scores among Unionists and Non-Unionists

T.U. members	Non-members
U.K.—1·891	U.K.—1·494
S.A.—1·841	S.A.—1·679

d: ASSOCIATIONAL ACTIVITY—RELIGIOUS

For the majority of immigrants, as for the majority of British people, organized religion played a minimal part in their daily lives, but for a minority quite the reverse was true. Religion may even have motivated their initial decision to emigrate, and a satisfactory adjustment in the religious sphere was quite crucial to their over-all integration. Some 62 per cent of the sample stated that they were Church members in Britain, but only 21 per cent claimed to have attended church regularly (i.e. at least once a week). For 14 per cent of the sample religion was 'very important', a further 22 per cent found it 'quite important', while the remaining 64 per cent claimed that it had little or no importance in their daily lives. As with trade union membership, migration led to a fall in interest,[6] as measured by attendance, but in this case it may well have been a temporary phenomenon.

TABLE 23

Comparative Religious Attendance

U.K.			S.A.		
Regular	109	21	Regular	63	12
Occasional	77	15	Occasional	57	11
Infrequent	122	24	Infrequent	90	18
Never	206	40	Never	266	52
			Don't know, etc.	38	7
TOTAL	514	100		514	100

[5] U.K. members: chi-square = 4·747; p = n.s.; d.f. = 10.
   S.A. members: chi-square = 14·517; p = n.s.; d.f. = 10.
[6] For similar findings among Dutch immigrants, see In den Bosch (1966), op. cit., p. 73.

This religious profile of the immigrant may be explored in greater detail by reference to the open-ended replies to the interview questions. The extent to which religion had ceased to be an important, or indeed a controversial issue, can be judged by the facetious remarks that the questions about attendance and belief provoked:

No, I've had no contact with 'celestial bodies' at all (No. 147/68).

You mean, do I invest in the Church of England Building Society at $2\frac{1}{2}\%$?[7] (No. 248/67).

No, I gave up the choir for the pub at fifteen (No. 250/68).

Rarely, mind you I'm the local vicar's favourite atheist (No. 397/68).

You mean belief in an all-seeing Father Christmas? No—but it's good for the children (No. 408/67).

Perhaps the consensus was best summarized by the immigrant who declared:

I believe but I'm not a *fanatic*, I don't practise it (No. 136/67).

However, there was a significant minority of devoutly religious immigrants, one of whom pointed to the contrast in the religious life of the two countries:

I'm a Christian, not a professed Christian, and South Africa is a religious country. Every church and chapel is full on Sundays, morning, noon, and night. In Britain if you see six people outside a church on Sundays you knows it's C. of E.; if there's twenty people it's Methodist; and if it's two hundred it's Roman Catholic (No. 377/69).

While the salience of religion, measured in terms of attendance or expressed belief, was not high, this does not imply that the social and political influence of religion was a matter of no concern. Several church-goers found that their clergy were surprisingly 'liberal'—too liberal in some cases—with respect to inter-racial worship and the social implications of Apartheid:

We went to a church in Sea Point for a few weeks and found that there were Coloureds in the congregation. They were very well dressed, mind you, but we were quite surprised (No. 201/68).

Actually we had a row with our priest: he was all for the Coloureds and none for the Europeans, so we changed our church (No. 192/68).

Once again, the Dutch Reformed Church came under severe criticism from many immigrants:

The Dutch Reformed Church is outrageously Calvanistic (No. 318/68).

[7] A devalued echo of 'philanthropy and five per cent'?

The Dutch Reformed Church is like the Roman Catholic Church in Eire, its aim is to keep the Afrikaner in the fold (No. 473/69).

All the sexual assaults seem to be by Dutch ministers and they always seem to be finding them in bed with native girls (No. 74/69).

Some 41 per cent of the sample felt that the Church had a right to criticize South African society:

Yes, a right and a duty to comment on social situations . . . both Joost de Blank and the Dutch Reformed Church (No. 301/70).

Everyone has a right . . . but I don't think they have any *cause* to (No. 85/70).

As was the case with trade union members, so with many Christians there was an awareness of a contradiction between the tenets of the religion and the social practices of the society:

Apartheid makes a farce out of Christianity which teaches that everyone is equal . . . it's just a mockery (No. 83/70).

Certainly a religious person can't argue for Apartheid, although some Afrikaners claim it's based on the Bible . . . Old Kruger and his Sons of Ham (No. 228/70).

More hypocritical? Or perhaps it's just that they are more tested in South Africa (No. 267/70).

The blacks are more sincere about religion here than the whites (No. 507/70).

It's not the Church but the people: they are South Africans first and Christians afterwards. A sincere Christian friend of ours refused to take the sacrament after some Indians—you see what I mean? (No. 362/70).

Some professed Christians found ways of reconciling the claims of God and those of Caesar, for others it remained an unresolved enigma:

In England people at Church used to ask us what we would do about Apartheid as it is against the scriptures . . . but the scriptures also say that you must not abuse your hosts. I think we understand it more now (No. 65/70).

I know it's against our Christian principles but I look at our African maid and ask myself whether I could sit down and eat lunch with her. I couldn't really. I know they will ask us about Apartheid in England when we go back next year . . . I don't really know what to say (No. 80/70).

Most immigrants were not seriously influenced by religious participation or affiliations in the process of social integration, though for a minority of perhaps 10–20 per cent the Church did provide a source of friendship and social links with the host society. Church membership,[8] attendance,[9] denomination,[10] and the intensity of religious belief[11] were not found to be significantly associated with the degree of support for, or opposition to, the policy of Apartheid. Members of sects were less prejudiced[12] than Anglicans, Roman Catholics, and Nonconformists, which leads me to reject hypothesis 13 of chapter four. As in the case of political party affiliations, a more subtle breakdown of categories may be necessary to reveal the true complexity of the situation,[13] an exercise which the size of my sample did not allow.

e: SOCIAL RELATIONS AT WORK

The attitude of fellow-workers and colleagues, as perceived by the immigrant himself, forms another important and interesting index of social integration.

TABLE 24

Attitudes of Fellow-workers to British Immigrants

Very friendly	26	5
Friendly	129	25
Neutral	221	43
Hostile	98	19
Very hostile	13	3
Don't know, etc.	27	5
TOTAL	514	100

The over-all pattern of social relations at work shown in Table 24 resembles the one for friendships (Table 20), with the friendly reactions outweighing the hostile. Most immigrants found their colleagues:

Very friendly on the whole (No. 68/79).

[8] chi-square $= 10 \cdot 656$; p $=$ n.s.; d.f. $=$ 5.
[9] chi-square $= 16 \cdot 940$; p $=$ n.s.; d.f. $=$ 15.
[10] chi-square $= 25 \cdot 833$; p $=$ n.s.; d.f. $=$ 25.
[11] chi-square $= 19 \cdot 388$; p $=$ n.s.; d.f. $=$ 15.
[12] sectarian $= -0 \cdot 6$; Anglicans $= -1 \cdot 6$; Catholic $= -1 \cdot 6$; Non-Conformist $= -1 \cdot 9$.
[13] We may expect differences between 'adventist', 'conversionist', 'intro-versionist', and 'gnostic' sects in their reaction to race relations. B. R. Wilson, 'An Analysis of Sect Development', *A.S.R.* 24 (1959), 3–15; and the development of the 'response to the world' classification in 'A Typology of Sects in a Dynamic and Comparative Perspective' in R. Robertson (ed.), *Sociology of Religion: selected readings* (1969), pp. 361–83.

There's no 'immigrants-pinching-our-jobs-whilst-we're-unemployed' attitude as in Britain, its a fairly neutral reaction (No. 179/79).

Considering we are foreigners, much better than foreigners in Britain (No. 223/79).

This was qualified in a number of cases, and there were some immigrants who faced outright hostility:

It all depends: whether they are professional or artisan, English-speaking or Afrikaner (No. 181/79).

Foreigners are a little inferior anywhere (No. 305/79).

We are respected but, by God, they don't like us (No. 155/79).

An intruder (No. 96/79).

Rooineks . . . an unjustified feeling that any immigrant is taking over a 'South African' job (No. 119/79).

The majority, however, had made a satisfactory adjustment at the work level and, if not greeted with open arms, were at least tolerated by the host work force.

f: CLASS CONSCIOUSNESS AND SOCIAL MOBILITY

I will complete the discussion of the social dimension of integration by considering two aspects of social stratification: the immigrant's perception of comparative class consciousness, and his subjective assessment of social mobility. At this stage, it is the importance of class consciousness and social mobility in the process of integration, rather than their impact on attitudes and beliefs, that will be discussed. This involves an assessment of the whole social structure of South African society as seen through the eyes of the immigrant.

TABLE 25
Class Consciousness and Social Mobility

Much more (in S.A.)	49	10	Much higher (in S.A.)	49	10
More	74	14	Higher	97	19
Same	88	17	Same	311	61
Less	174	34	Lower	22	4
Much less	98	19	Much lower	4	1
Don't know, etc.	31	6	Don't know, etc.	31	5
TOTAL	514	100	TOTAL	514	100

As a rule, it is safe to assume that the greater the degree of social mobility, the greater the degree of social integration;[14] the lower the

[14] Upward mobility and satisfaction were strongly related among British immigrants in Canada. A. H. Richmond, *Post-War Immigrants in Canada*, p. 184.

perceived level of class consciousness, the greater the feeling of acceptance and identification. The two are clearly related, for the likely consequence of social mobility unaccompanied by social acceptance would be a sense of relative deprivation leading to negative social integration. There were a few cases where adjustment to *less* class consciousness posed problems; some individuals felt more comfortable in a firmly stratified society—an argument analogous to those immigrants who claimed that the African in South Africa was better off than the black man in Britain because 'at least he knows his place'—though this hardly seemed a significant cause of dissatisfaction:

There's virtually none, disconcertingly so at times from an English point of view. I'm a member of a classless community—both kings and dustmen (No. 248/89).

You've got to be socially equal to people who would not be your social equal in Britain and sometimes that's hard (No. 371/89).

Two major aspects of the problem are particularly interesting: the frame of reference in which the immigrant perceives society, and the exact nature of the class consciousness in the two countries. While many immigrants viewed their class position purely in relation to the white community, or even confined it within the English-speaking sub-community, others were aware of the interrelationship of class and colour.

Yes, because of the Coloureds we start half way up (No. 3/89).

I feel a bit higher up . . . you've got more power, I know it's wrong but there it is (No. 19/89).

There's only one class here, first class . . . and last, for the wogs (No. 188/89).

Slightly higher, perhaps it's unreal but it feels that way because so many non-Europeans are supposed to be below you (No. 359/89).

You are a little tin God to the natives of course (No. 383/89).

Most immigrants have never been called 'master' before and they lap it up (No. 472/88).

In recognizing the crucial importance of the racial hierarchy, many immigrants pointed to it as the key source of social differentiation:

It's caste rather than class consciousness (No. 74/89).

It's on the basis of different racial groups as opposed to different social groups in Britain. In South Africa it's not what job you do, you are accepted into any community of your own colour (No. 223/88).

They've got race consciousness so there's no need to bother with any other type of consciousness (No. 329/88).

Within the frame of reference of the white community there were two major types of response to the question of comparative class consciousness. Some emphasized the 'general absence of snobbishness'[15] discovered by James Bryce at the turn of the century, while others were acutely aware of a type of 'status consciousness' found in 'young' countries lacking historically sanctioned estates or ranks, as described by de Tocqueville in *Democracy in America*.[16] It was to this latter situation that many immigrants were referring when they talked of 'money consciousness' in South Africa, as distinct from British class consciousness. Over half the sample stressed the relative lack of social barriers—'we are all middle class now'—while nearly a quarter pointed to increased status consciousness. Keeping up with the van der Merwe's was clearly different from keeping up with the Joneses.

Not in white European society . . . you are readily welcome in the company of millionaires. There's not that 'middle-class' type of attitude, the pin-striped trousered character who lives in a semi-detached in Surbiton (No. 121/88).

There's no class here, just one middle-class (No. 55/88).

One and all are alike: no class distinction, no snobs (No. 4/88).

There's no class here . . . you don't refuse to drink with van der Merwe because he calls a napkin a serviette. The status symbol is not the family tree but money, and money alone (No. 372/88).

People here have as much respect for the job of a worker as a pen-pusher. Why? Perhaps its Christianity, or perhaps its because they fought together in the Kaffir Wars—a bullet doesn't ask you where you went to school (No. 377/88).

In the evening you mix with the idle rich, with the boss and the boss's wife. You're encouraged to feel that all are one happy band (No. 506/88).

Yes, but they don't know how to justify it of course . . . no blue blood and none of them want to look too far back in their ancestry in case they find a Coloured Granny (No. 116/88).

[15] J. Bryce, *Impressions of South Africa*, p. 383.
[16] A. de Tocqueville, *Democracy in America* (Mentor edn., New York, 1956), pp. 247–52. Cf. J. Bryce, *The American Commonwealth*, vol. 2 (1928 edn.), p. 813.

South Africans are more dress-conscious, you must keep up appearances at all costs and working class people run for bigger cars than they can afford . . . I feel higher up, I'm a bus driver and I own a car, a house on half an acre, a servant and a swimming pool (No. 496/88).

Yes, but in different ways—if your car is two years old you qualify as a poor white (No. 299/88).

Housewives get dolled up to the eyeballs to go to the pictures, it's like Church, a real fashion display . . . women really live it up here. *Husband:* It's the lower income groups who do it here, whereas in Britain it is only the rich (No. 212-3/88).

Tremendously class conscious, full of social climbers, only money matters here. It's a Capitalist society like America, within two minutes of meeting someone they will be telling you their salary, while in the colonial service no one talked about money—'it just wasn't done, old boy' (No. 92/88).

We are working class people forced to be middle class. Some English immigrants like to pretend that they have always been middle class but they haven't. Everyone's middle class here (No. 252/88).

'Not class conscious in a social sense, but in a materialistic sense. In Jo'burg it's the amount of money on display. In Durban, what counts is how you made the money, and in Cape Town how long you've had it. At the top class distinctions are equally as sharp as Britain, it's just that the bases of judgement are different (No. 267/88).

The general situation for British immigrants with respect to social stratification was one of significant social mobility combined with widespread social acceptance, which corresponds with the picture presented in the theoretical discussion. For those immigrants who found South African society more 'class conscious' than society in Britain, it was, nevertheless, an 'open' type of differentiation based on money or acquirable status symbols.

TABLE 26

The Congruence of Social Expectations and Experience

Much better	89	17
Better or equal	232	45
Slightly below	102	20
Much below	65	13
None, etc.	26	3
TOTAL	514	100

The over-all picture of the social dimension of integration was slightly less satisfactory, from the immigrants' point of view, than in the case of economic integration. Nearly two-thirds of the sample felt that their social experience in South Africa had equalled or exceeded their expectations, a third felt that it had not. A social integration index was calculated in a similar way to that of the economic index[17] giving a mean integration score for the whole sample of +0·646, and the frequency distribution of these scores is shown in Diagram 2.

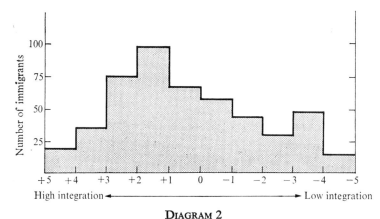

DIAGRAM 2
Frequency Distributon of Social Integration Scores

[17] The sub-dimensions scaled were: 'friendship', 'relations at work', and 'comparative social life'.

CHAPTER XIV

The Process of Integration: (3) The Political-Cultural Dimension

THE THIRD major dimension of integration consists of six rather heterogeneous sub-dimensions: the Afrikaans language, group stereotypes, citizenship, republicanism and national identification, political orientations and affiliations, and attitudes towards Apartheid.

a: THE AFRIKAANS LANGUAGE

South Africa is a multi-lingual country, but it has only two official languages, Afrikaans and English. Although Afrikaans is now a compulsory subject in all (white) schools up to the matriculation standard, many English-speaking South Africans have a far from perfect command of the language. Many more Afrikaners approach the ideal of bilingualism. In many fields, particularly in commerce and industry, it is possible to 'get by' with English alone, so for an immigrant to become reasonably fluent in Afrikaans—not merely to buy a book and allow it to collect dust on the bookshelf—is a good indication of a serious attempt to adjust and integrate into South African society.

Seventy-eight per cent of the sample stated that they had either no intention of learning, or only the vaguest wish to learn, Afrikaans.[1] Of the remainder, 7 per cent claimed to be 'fairly fluent', 9 per cent were making a 'serious attempt', while a further 6 per cent were merely 'making a gesture'. Most immigrants were apathetic:

I always mean to but I always put it off . . . I can hardly speak a word of Afrikaans after twenty-three years (No. 118/41).

I've tried but its very difficult . . . young people should: they are an interesting race and you are in their country (No. 158/41).

No, but we did buy the records (No. 189/41).

I can speak a kind of pidgin Afrikaans (No. 349/41).

---

[1] 74 per cent of a sample of Dutch immigrants claimed that they spoke good English: In den Bosch, op. cit., p. 72; cf. A. P. du Plessis, op. cit., p. 243.

I'm prepared to spend about an hour a week and try a bit at work, but not if it will require too much effort. In sum, I'm making an 'unserious' attempt to learn Afrikaans (No. 248/41).

Those who were against learning the language gave several reasons:

No, Afrikaans is an isolating language (No. 98/41).

I'm a linguist and I can read it although I can't pronounce it. I won't learn it partly because it's forced down your throat, but particularly because it's an ugly language and should die a natural death (No. 133/41).

We put it off at first until we were settled and now we've missed the free classes. *Wife:* Incidentally the sauce bottles are no good, they don't translate at all literally (No. 147–8/41).

No, not in Durban, it's better to learn Zulu . . . after all they are bound to become rulers eventually (No. 405/41).

Other immigrants showed a greater sensitivity towards bilingualism:

I can see the reason why the Afrikaner's bigoted about his language—you'd expect him to talk English in England (No. 153/41).

One immigrant related a not untypical encounter illustrating some of the initial tensions that may occur over the language question:

At first I had some problems with an Afrikaner foreman. He came up to me and spoke Afrikaans, so I asked him to speak in English. 'Can't you speak Afrikaans?' he said, 'even the bloody Kaffirs can.' So I replied to him in Gaelic. 'What language is that?', he enquired. 'Gaelic', I replied, 'even the bloody gypsies can speak it at home.' I've had little trouble since (No. 195/41).

However, in spite of such incidents, only a small minority of immigrants made a sustained effort to master South Africa's other official language.

b: GROUP STEREOTYPES

The extent to which the immigrant tends to accept or adopt the ethnic attitudes and group stereotypes prevailing in the host society is another aspect of cultural integration. Most of the studies in South Africa, following from MacCrone's pioneering work,[2] have shown how attitudes are firmly rooted in group membership. To what group standards, then, do we expect the British immigrant to conform? The ethnic attitudes of the English-speaking South Africans are the obvious basis for such a comparison.

[2] I. D. MacCrone, *Race Attitudes in South Africa.*

TABLE 27

Group Stereotypes

	Afrikaners		Jews		Africans		Coloureds		Indians	
Very favourable	30	6	4	1	3	0	2	0	2	0
Positive stereotype	53	10	63	12	20	4	12	2	13	2
Neutral-mixed	178	35	166	32	122	23	122	24	120	24
Negative stereotype	118	23	96	19	226	44	132	26	104	21
Very hostile	36	7	17	3	54	10	51	10	52	10
Don't know, etc.	99	19	168	33	99	19	195	38	223	43
TOTAL	514	100	514	100	514	100	514	100	514	100

The problem of attitude measurement under the particular research circumstances was a key consideration. It would have been interesting to have used a modified Bogardus-type social-distance test to make comparisons with the findings of the MacCrone-Lever school, but because of a number of crucial factors—the need to maintain 'rapport', the fact that the sample did not consist of a 'captive' student audience, and the sensitive situation of the British immigrant in South Africa—it was decided to employ a looser, quasi-projective method of questioning. Immigrants were simply asked to describe a 'typical' (i.e. 'not the best nor the worst you have known') member of five major South African ethnic groups—Afrikaners, Jews, Africans, Coloureds, and Indians—to an imaginary friend in Britain who knew nothing about the country. These open-ended replies were then rated by the interviewer on a crude friendliness-hostility scale and independently cross-checked by a second judge. In spite of the obvious shortcomings of this approach, it remains true that more formal tests would have certainly meant a significantly higher refusal rate and would not have guaranteed more valid results.

It must also be noted that the immigrant was deliberately invited to generalize and stereotype; many were fully aware of this,[3] and some even refused to do it:

You can't judge off a few, they vary (No. 157/80).
I accept people for what they are, all are so different it's hard to say (No. 147/80).

Therefore the replies shown in Table 27 must be interpreted with the utmost caution. Like a conjurer producing a white rabbit out of his top hat, the sociologist can all too easily produce a white racialist out of his questionnaire—the trick being, of course, that he was there all the time. (The reverse of this is also true as I argued in relation to the 'tolerance bias' of Abrams's U.K. survey.)[4]

[3] For a discussion of Eysenck's attack on the Katz and Braly Princeton study of 1932, cf. M. Banton, *Race Relations*.
[4] Above, pp. 78–80.

Some 81 per cent of the sample expressed classifiable views about the Afrikaner. The remaining 19 per cent, mainly comprising those immigrants who had been in the country for only a few days or even hours, were naturally reluctant (though not in all cases) to express views about people whom they had not even met. The most common description was neither unduly laudatory nor excessively pejorative; praise and insults, compliments and criticism, approximately balancing in number and intensity. Nearly one third of the sample gave critical or outrightly hostile replies, while about a half that number were well disposed towards the Afrikaner:

Some are very bigoted and narrow but they are very decent and upright. My son married an Afrikaans girl, as straight-laced as the Highlanders (No. 200/80a).

Don't believe everything you hear about them, only some live up to the 'bullneck farmer' image. They are the backbone of South Africa, up-and-coming, a great untapped resource (No. 304/80a).

Very big, very basic, very friendly, and very biased (No. 407/80a).

They are the same as us . . . there's the farmer type and the intellectual, but if people can say *what* they are like, then they are biased either for or against (No. 413/80a).

Not unintelligent, but a limited outlook . . . one might say boorish. *Wife:* Ignorant farmers, but don't quote me (No. 298–9/80a).

A robust man of the land; has a terrible inferiority complex; touchy about criticism; convinced that his country and people are the leaders of the World; treats the native as a child but is only harsh when he gets in a crowd (No. 472/80a).

Afrikaners are very arrogant, stubborn, loud-mouthed and coarse, they know it all and many of them have never left Jo'burg in their lives (No. 71/80a).

Arrogant: there's more Apartheid between Afrikaners and South Africans than between Europeans and the Bantu (No. 380/80).

Pig-headed devils, a load of stupid farmers . . . (No. 451/80a).

The attitude profile of immigrants towards the Jewish South African[5] is similar to that for the Afrikaner, slightly less hostile and

---

[5] The position of the Jews in South Africa might be explored as a case study in 'cross-pressures'. See: R. G. Weisbrod, 'The Dilemma of South African Jewry', *Journal of Modern African Studies*, 5 (1967), 233–41; E. Feit, 'Community in a Quandary: The South African Jewish Community and Apartheid', *Race*, 8, no. 4 (1967), 395–408; E. S. Munger, *The Jews and the Nationalist Party* (1961); D. M. Krikler, 'The Jews of Rhodesia', *I.R.R.* (U.K.) *Newsletter*, 3, no. 1 (1969), 33–7. There are similar problems in the relations between Israel and South African Jewry. Cf. *Rand Daily Mail*, 9 Nov. 1967, and *The Star*, 24 Nov. 1967.

favourable at either extreme (the latter may be due to the absence of intermarriage, which did occur with Afrikaners), and a significantly larger proportion had not come into meaningful contact with this particular section of South African society. Once again, the illustrative quotations are arranged in an approximately ascending order of abusiveness or, in social-psychological parlance, with increasing social distance.

If I wasn't a Scotsman, I wouldn't mind being a Jew (No. 194/80b).

Totally different from any other Jewish people elsewhere. Here you know them as friends, not like the East End of London and I've lived there (No. 363/80b).

Very nice . . . they vary like all other people . . . I don't think of them as Jews, I'm against anti-Semitism . . . [pause] . . . Why do I support Apartheid then? (No. 377/80b).

Very good and warm-hearted, but in business so like Shylock that it's unbelievable (No. 430/80b).

They are a little bit more understanding about the non-Europeans than other groups (No. 314/80b).

Not as tolerant of the African as you would expect from a people who had suffered themselves (No. 475/80b).

I worked for a Jewish firm . . . they would side with the kaffirs against me for a few cents (No. 439/80b).

Jo'burg shuts down on Jewish holidays. I suppose it's jealousy because they own so much . . . you're brought up as a kid to say: 'Oh, he's a Jew' . . . Why on earth do we hate them? I can't think why, but we do (No. 83/80b)·

Bloody Jews, they are a miserable crowd . . . very tight . . . some live opposite (No. 76/80b).

The attitude of the British immigrant to the African, the majority group of the host society, revealed the familiar rise in the 'tolerance–intolerance' threshold associated with the officially defined 'non-white' groups. I have already cited examples of those who refused to generalize, but there were others who found it difficult to particularize, especially about the non-white groups:

They are just 'there'—you are conscious of *them* as a group, never as individuals (No. 329/80c).

This is a classic illustration of 'race' as a social category. There were also many examples of 'paternalistic' attitudes towards the African that were noticeably lacking in the case of the Coloured and the Indian.

We feel very sorry for them, they are *not* happy. On the surface they are obsequious but with the more intelligent there is a lot of hatred. When they see our homes . . . one day they will rise (No. 111/80c).

Very meek, very poor, very proud, and very underprivileged (No. 407/80c).

I've worked in Langa . . . it would do them good to be under Communism . . . they do wish to better themselves but they've no sense of responsibility (No. 244/80c).

I came during the Durban riots of 1948 [*sic*] when well-dressed Africans ran amuck, broke windows, raped, became like savages . . . but still, so have Europeans—it's a question of culture I suppose (No. 423/80c).

Stupid, noisy, smelly, and crafty . . . but most of them can speak three languages so they can't be *that* stupid (No. 476/80c).

I will treat them as others do; not as underdogs or slaves, but as a child, they have a child's mentality (No. 37/80c).

They are not the 'true' Bantu in the towns, sophisticated and worldly wise, more like West Indians at home (No. 67/80c.—this is an example of missionary paternalism: a search for the poor benighted (black?) heathen, not unlike the quest of certain anthropologists for tribes untainted by outside contacts).

They are solid from the shoulders upward, but there are exceptions which raises problems. If educated, they feel they shouldn't do anything, if not, they don't know how to do anything (No. 451/80c).

Treat them like a dog—fair and firm. I told them that in the U.K. and they nearly had a fit (No. 348/80c).

Bloody kaffirs, very cheeky which I didn't expect . . . horrible, I can't stand them (No. 97/80c).

The marginal status of South Africa's Coloured population has always led to a certain ambiguity in feeling towards them among both Afrikaners and English-speaking South Africans. However, the over-all pattern of feeling is similar to that for the African, although, because of the geographical concentration of Coloured people in the Cape, a larger proportion of immigrants did not feel able to venture an opinion about them.

Quite intelligent and less cheerful than the Bantu because they realize how much they have been discriminated against (No. 116/80d).

Apartheid is unfair to these people (No. 88/80d).

A very disappointed people and they feel it. If given more scope they could easily be assimilated in two or three generations . . . the rough element is a cry against unfairness . . . they are not their own fault—they didn't create themselves, they only procreate themselves (No. 366/80d).

P

I wish the African could help himself; I wish the Coloured would help himself (No. 354/80d).

You can accept him as nearly equal in Cape Town . . . We saw some lovely Coloured 'crumpet' on the beach (No. 365/80d).[6]

All the white man's vices and none of his virtues (No. 360/80d).

Irresponsible and immoral, like the dregs from the U.K. slums (No. 343/ 80d).

South African Indians are the last ethnic group to be considered. At the turn of the century, Bryce commented: 'In Natal both races [i.e. English and Afrikaner] are equally anti-Indian.'[7] Fifty years later, Pettigrew found that 'the most striking feature of the responses concerning Indians is the intense antipathy shown by many of the subjects'.[8] The general attitude profile was similar to that of the Coloureds, with a slightly higher 'no comment' rate and a tendency for adverse opinions to be very hostile indeed.

There are some Indians at work with degrees and they are doing jobs that lower them. They are very nice . . . I could accept them as equals, they are cleverer than I am (No. 88/80e).

I'm not too keen, I've a vague feeling that they are climbing on my back —they always want to sell you something. *Wife:* Maybe that's because they are shopkeepers (No. 98–9/80e).

They work too hard, they're greedy. *Son:* Don't be ridiculous (No. 123/ 80e).

The biggest rogues, I'm always being done by them. But they are very nice and pleasant and not aggressive (No. 201/80e).

Brown Jews: none of this 'master' and 'boss' stuff, they are independent and they know it (No. 472/80e).

Vermin on the face of the Earth (No. 430/80e).

A greasy race of spivs, they twist you, the Coloureds and the Bantu into the bargain (No. 348/80e).

Indians stink, I'd shoot them all . . . I've never met a decent one except in a box . . . Gandhi was a fool, he started all this rot . . . (No. 188/80e).

[6] A study of the effects of 'race education' on a large group of London printing apprentices attending day release courses showed an *increase* in prejudice as a result. The researcher found that: 'the one positive tactic that seemed to create more favourable attitudes to coloured people involving discussing pictures of attractive Negresses' (*The Guardian*, 1 Nov. 1969).

[7] J. Bryce (1900), op. cit., pp. 398–9; P. L. van den Berghe, *Caneville: The Social Structure of a South African Town* (1964).

[8] T. F. Pettigrew, 'Social Distance Attitudes of South African Students' (1960), 248.

These quotations concerning attitudes towards the five ethnic groups do not purport to show 'average' views so much as illustrate the range of the immigrants' opinions with some of the qualifications they made. The over-all pattern of group stereotypes is basically similar to the results of the social distance studies of MacCrone, Pettigrew, van den Berghe, and Lever, which suggests that there is a definite movement towards the acculturation of the immigrant into the race attitudes of English-speaking South Africans. A crude index of outgroup rejection (prejudice) was calculated by assigning numerical values to the responses on a $+/-10$ scale[9]—both ethnocentrism and polycentrism tended to generalize across all groups—and the index was used to compare sub-groups within the sample.

C: CITIZENSHIP[10]

Citizenship may be seen as the seventh veil of political integration, exposing the immigrant's naked intentions and revealing his hidden fears and underlying loyalties. Almost three-quarters of the sample stated categorically that they would not become South African citizens, 19 per cent were undecided, while the remaining 10 per cent had either become citizens or claimed that they would as soon as they were eligible. Those in favour declared:

Yes I will: if it's good enough to live in, it's good enough to be a citizen of (No. 485/52).

Yes, I'm earning my living here and I'm not just an Englishman sponging . . . I'm not afraid to settle, there's nowhere to run (No. 377/52).

Those who were undecided or against becoming citizens explained:

I'm on the fence, only if I'm forced (No. 437/52).

I've not the slightest intention, at the moment the Government is on a collision course . . . there are many similarities between the language problem and Ireland (No. 93/52).

Never, I want to keep my British passport and they can keep their vote (No. 201/52).

I don't know, if trouble broke out I'd do my bit. *Wife:* I wouldn't, I'd nip back to England (No. 219–20/52).

[9] Ibid., p. 252; my data tend to confirm the generalization of outgroup rejection to all groups, although the relationship is complex.
[10] Cf. In den Bosch, op. cit., p. 74: who found that 29 per cent of his Cape Town sample were in favour of adopting South African citizenship.

No, it's a matter of expediency. In the back of your mind there's that feeling of eventual trouble—this year, next year, sometime or never. Anyway a British passport is acceptable anywhere, while a South African one is restricted (No. 232/52).

It's too early yet, it requires much heart-searching. I've been an Englishman for fifty years . . . at least it wouldn't be a cold-blooded business arrangement (No. 248/52).

No, there's no advantage at the moment . . . purely a technicality and it costs £5 into the bargain. So long as it does not harm my career or job I won't (No. 342/52).

A real problem, I'm quite worried about it. My firm keeps digging me about it . . . I just want to be an Englishman in South Africa but they won't let me (No. 252/52).

I try to be an international citizen, see everywhere and everyone but become involved in none (No. 267/52).

I'm wary, I prefer British . . . it's really putting you're head on the block to take out citizenship: the black situation could explode in two hundred years—or tomorrow (No. 463/52).

The adoption of citizenship[11] is a giant step in the direction of full integration and it is not surprising that many immigrants hesitated to take it in the early years of settlement. It is essentially a symbolic act, for there are few material benefits reserved exclusively for the South African citizen apart from the right to vote. Historically the National Party[12] has been very suspicious about the political consequences of immigration and has never placed any pressure on the British immigrant to change his citizenship and thereby acquire the vote. On present evidence this appears to be a misconceived fear, for the Nationalists have many more immigrant supporters than opponents, although they do not seem to be aware of the fact. My data also revealed a highly significant association between citizenship intention and the length of residence in South Africa,[13] confirming Loedolff's findings among his sample of Dutch immigrants.[14]

---

[11] T. H. Marshall's influential discussion of 'citizenship' as an added dimension of social stratification in modern societies is most interesting when considering the position of the non-white citizens of South Africa: 'Citizenship and Social Class' reprinted in S. M. Lipset (ed.), *Class, Citizenship and Social Development* (1964); cf. also W. K. Hancock: 'Are There South Africans?' (1966).

[12] The exclusive orientation of the National Party has much the same connotations as Louis XIV's maxim 'L'État c'est moi'. For a related discussion in political sociology see R. Michels, *Political Parties* (1962), pp. 220–3.

[13] chi-square = 29·090; p = ·001; d.f. = 4.

[14] J. F. Loedolff, op. cit., p. 242.

However, no one could claim that the typical British immigrant was adopting South African citizenship with alacrity. The 'Uitlander' jibe of the anti-immigration lobby had at least that much truth in it.

d: REPUBLICANISM AND NATIONAL IDENTIFICATION

The Republican Declaration of 1961 and South Africa's subsequent departure from the Commonwealth brought the question of citizenship into sharp perspective: after a period of five years the immigrant must choose between renouncing his British citizenship or remaining an 'alien' in the land of his residence.

TABLE 28

Identification and Republicanism[a]

British	393	76	Good	279	54
South African	46	9	Bad	25	5
Equally both	64	12	Irrelevant	77	15
Other, don't know	11	2	Don't know	133	26
TOTAL	514	99	TOTAL	514	100

[a] In 1958, 54 per cent of a sample of Dutch immigrants were in favour of a Republic (In den Bosch, op. cit., p. 73).

Two other aspects of political-cultural integration are closely related to citizenship, though they do not raise the dilemma of divided loyalties in quite such an acute form. Immigrants were asked about their primary sense of national identification and their attitude towards South Africa's Republican status. The overwhelming majority regarded themselves as British, though some were a little apologetic about it:

British, I'm afraid so (No. 194/53).

We are still very British: home is not where your feet are but where your heart is, and mine's not in South Africa (No. 227/53).

Others found themselves in an intermediate position:

In between, I vacillate between extremes (No. 415/53).

Both, South Africans are fully responsible for what goes on here just as the Germans were for Buchenwald—not that I'm making a comparison—I'm responsible too (No. 377/53).

Nine per cent of the sample considered themselves to be exclusively South Africans:

I must be a South African as I never refer to Britain as home and never want to return. I must be successfully integrated (No. 70/53).

More South African than anything else; certainly not British when you see what Britain has done to Africa from Kenya downwards (No. 85/53—an ex-colonial).

Very much pro-South Africa and anti-Britain; we tend to ally with South Africa against Britain, our thinking is very acid towards anti-South African Britishers living here (No. 297/53).

South African of course, I don't think like an Englishman any more (No. 342/53).

The status of South Africa in relation to Britain has long been a bone of contention between English-speaking South Africans and Afrikaners, and between Afrikaners of different persuasions. When the Republic was declared in 1961 it marked the final outcome of a long struggle: the symbolic recognition of Afrikaner political supremacy, the renaissance of Kruger's Republic on an incomparably larger scale. The consequences of the Anglo-Boer War had followed the predictions of Bryce rather than those of Milner, the 'crop of dragon's teeth' had indeed produced a harvest of 'permanent hatred and disaffection', but it was the Afrikaner and not the Englishman who inherited the earth.

When questioned about the Republic several immigrants were honest enough to admit their ignorance: 'I didn't even know South Africa was a Republic' (No. 123/56). Others emphasized the relevant perspective:

For the white population good, for the black population bad: it depends on which side of the line you are on (No. 24/56).

From our point of view or the Natives'? From theirs, definitely bad (No. 157/56).

A common pattern for those immigrants who were living in the country at the time of the transition, was that of a hostile reaction followed by a gradual conversion:

I thought it was awful at the time . . . but it's not so bad now, possibly better. South Africa seems to get on better with Britain now that the 'tie' —we British never regarded it as such—has gone, she feels more independent (No. 200/56).

At the time it seemed a disaster, but it turned out extraordinarily well for South Africa. She kept all the economic advantages of Imperial preference, access to the London money markets, etc., but none of the political obligations (No. 267/56).

I was sorry at the time but I can appreciate Verwoerd's position: in the Commonwealth the tail is wagging the dog (No. 359/56).

The ex-colonial element was particularly vociferous in its anti-British sentiments (which may surprise those who normally associate the retired denizens of Tunbridge Wells and Cheltenham with 'super-patriotism'):

It was better than going down with a sinking ship . . . Britain's only interested in poor states like Tanzania (No. 188/56).

South Africa's not doing badly . . . the Commonwealth is just a bunch of Coloured Chiefs. England spends money on something for nothing, it would have been better if we had kept the Empire (No. 83/56).

In one case the question provoked a verbal rampage through the decline and fall of the British Empire:

I'll never go back. I remember when half the World was coloured red on the map, the Union Jack was everywhere. Now what's left? We should never have got out of India. They seem to be afraid of Jomo Kenyatta—a bloody murderer—while with Ian Smith, whose got a well organized country, they apply sanctions on him. It's all wrong . . . the thinking is haywire, it must be a masterplan from the Kremlin. The Common Market is a plot. . . . They give Zambia £5½ millions in aid and they go and spend it on Japanese goods . . . and then there's Nasser. South Africans still prefer British but for how much longer if we don't recognize who are our friends? So much for the Commonwealth, it ends at bloody Buckingham Palace railings . . . what we need is a bit of Nationalism in Britain . . . it's the greatest bloody place on earth. The Indian monsoons would get down foreigners, but not the British . . . I want to return to Britain eventually, but not just yet . . . (No. 77/56).

The most usual justification for favouring the Republic was to point to the value of independence; the most common criticism, to stress the dangers of isolation:

It means a lot to South Africans, they now feel they can stand on their own feet (No. 36/56).

It's bad really, now Britain and South Africa have drawn apart we are more alone and even English-speaking South Africans run Britain down—it's a big change (No. 464/56).

e: POLITICAL ORIENTATIONS AND AFFILIATIONS

The last two sub-dimensions of political-cultural integration consist of the most controversial topics of the interview. A marked decline in political interest and involvement, as hypothesized in the theoretical discussion, is clearly shown in Table 29. This is much more than a random lack of interest resulting from the temporary dislocation of migration, rather it is a deliberate and sustained characteristic of the British immigrant in South Africa.[15]

TABLE 29

Comparative Political Interest and Allegiance

U.K. interest			S.A. interest		
Active	19	4	Active	0	0
Fair	186	36	Fair	34	7
Slight	194	38	Slight	120	23
None	95	18	None	225	44
Anti	20	4	Deliberate ignorance	135	26
TOTAL	514	100		514	100
U.K. Party			S.A. Party		
Cons.	251	49	Nat.	123	24
Lab.	167	32	U.P.	30	6
Lib.	35	7	Prog.	13	3
Nat.	10	2	Lib.	2	0
None	51	10	None	346	67
TOTAL	514	100		514	100

The reasons for this are best illustrated by reference to the immigrant's perception of South African politics. Many expressed a wariness that could not be interpreted simply as political apathy.

I'm not interested at the moment, we were warned not to become involved (No. 16/59).

Daren't (No. 27/59).

We were advised to keep out, otherwise you get chucked out (No. 65/59).

On one occasion the interviewer was greeted with the utmost suspicion:

Is it about Communism? I'm not talking politics, it's too dangerous . . . nor my views on the Africans (No. 63/59).

Though this immigrant relented after much persuasion, it does illustrate underlying fears that were by no means uncommon:

I suppose it's a Police-State. One evening four men from the Department of Bantu Affairs called to check up on the girl's pass, I thought they had come to arrest *me* (No. 83/59).

I thought that if three people spoke politics together it was illegal . . . they are so security-minded (No. 145/59).

[15] 40 per cent of In den Bosch's Dutch sample refused to comment on politics (Op. cit. p. 73).

Keep well out. If you're a Nat. it's O.K., but anything else gets you into trouble, particularly if you're an immigrant . . . I don't want ninety days (No. 232/59).

You can't be. I used to be a police reservist in the U.K. so I joined here too. I saw lots of things at the local station, how they treated the Coloureds and the like . . . so I soon became an embarrassment to them. I even asked where they kept the torture chamber and then I was fired. They even tried to get me sacked from my job for an 'un-South African' attitude—I nearly went crazy . . . they kept asking me about the Labour Ward Chairmanship as if it was Communism, but eventually they cleared me thank God. I've learnt to hold my tongue (No. 252/59).

No, it's a dictatorship (No. 273/59).

Most immigrants appeared to be conscious of a significant difference in the political atmosphere and style of politics between the two countries.

It's funny nobody talks about it here, it's never mentioned at work while in Britain everybody used to argue about politics (No. 261/59).

It's so hard to talk about politics in South Africa, with both South Africans and immigrants; the former are just not interested and the latter are afraid to discuss it (No. 327/59).

Some immigrants considered the difference lay not so much in a lack of political discussion but rather in an absence of 'politics' itself:[16]

No, there isn't any politics, just the Afrikaner Government and the rest (No. 55/59).

No, you're not allowed to be, there is no politics here . . . the opposition United Party has only one seat [sic] . . . it's really a ruling body (No. 116/59).

There's no politics under the present set up . . . I'm interested but somewhat apprehensive . . . there is an equation here: Liberal equals Communist equals goal (No. 179/59).

South Africa's almost a one-party state and so politics are not so stimulating (No. 301/59).

As a result of this interpretation, the decision to remain apolitical[17]

[16] Cf. B. Crick, *In Defence of Politics* (1964).

[17] Although there is a natural tendency for first-generation immigrants to be apolitical, this is not always the case. The American example of the social role of 'ward bosses' and 'precinct captains', particularly among the Irish in the nineteenth century, is a clear case of how immigrants may be drawn into politics. For the latent functions of the political machine, see R. K. Merton, *Social Theory and Social Structure*, pp. 72–82.

was not confined to immigrants who had just arrived in the country:

As an Englishman with no South African passport, I have no views (No. 346/59—11 years residence).
I don't begin to understand it, it's all Greek to me (No. 466/59—5 years residence).

The political party affiliation of the immigrants, both in Britain and in South Africa, is another interesting aspect of the sub-dimension which has been strangely ignored in related studies. A political sociology of migration lacks sufficient comparative data to make it anything more than exploratory. Figures in Table 29 might suggest, at first sight, the possibility of Conservative self-selection, though this may not be the case when a number of factors are taken into consideration. There was an absence of unskilled manual workers in the sample; the time span and distribution of the immigrants, concentrated in the early and middle 1960s but stretching back to the late 1940s, might be a deceptive influence, the effects of defective memory and recall combined with a tendency towards conservatism engendered by long residence in Southern Africa, and the impact of the ex-colonials, who comprised 5 per cent of the sample, unmistakably biased it towards Conservatism.

Nevertheless, a breakdown of skilled manual immigrants by party affiliation does suggest an over-representation of the working-class Tory[18]—Disraeli's 'angels in marble' or Tressell's 'ragged-trousered philanthropists', depending from which perspective they are viewed —though whether they were 'deferentials', 'pragmatists', 'seculars', or classifiable under any other of the plethora of terms devised to label sub-species of this fashionable political animal cannot be determined from my data. Nor is there any simple relationship between conservatism and racialism as recent studies have shown;[19] just as Shils, Robb, Eysenck, Lipset, and others[20] have demonstrated that authoritarianism may be found among the 'Left', the 'Right', and the 'Centre'.

The replies to the question about South African political affiliations revealed considerable ignorance. One immigrant, after he had been

[18] Cf. E. A. Nordlinger, *The Working Class Tories*; R. T. McKenzie and A. Silver, *Angels in Marble: working class Conservatives in Urban England* (1968).
[19] E. J. B. Rose, *et al.*, *Colour and Citizenship*, pp. 557–9.
[20] E. A. Shils in R. Christie and M. Jahoda, *Studies in the Scope and Method of the Authoritarian Personality*; J. H. Robb, *Working Class Anti-Semite* (1954); S. M. Lipset, 'Fascism—Left, Right and Center' in *Political Man* (Doubleday, New York, 1960), pp. 131–76.

resident in the country for over eighteen months, referred to the two major parties as: 'Republicans and Democrats' (No. 250/60); another admitted:

I don't know the difference between the verkrampte and the vigilantes [sic] . . . (No. 258/60).

While the majority expressed no political commitment, the largest politically minded minority explained their support for the National Party in the following terms.

I was keen on politics in the U.K. and used to support the Labour Party. Now I'd vote Nat., it's the only party with a definite policy, the others are mere shadows (No. 377/60).

Probably the Nats. Before coming out we decided to keep our noses clean and we have. Anyway the Progs. are all for letting the intelligent natives have the vote and I don't think that's right (No. 81/60).

I used to vote Conservative being a Capitalist as are the present Government [Nationalists] although they won't admit it. They are well entrenched and discourage opposition to their basic principles, not de Villiers Graaff, he doesn't concern them, but those who aim to undermine the pillars of society (No. 342/60).

We should support the United Party but it's the wrong policy . . . the Nats. are best (No. 461/60).

I'm telling you that if the British had been in charge rather than the Afrikaners we wouldn't be here now—there would be a lot of bloody black men in power (No. 184/60—ex-colonial).

Many immigrants saw little difference between the policy of the two major parties and could summon scant enthusiasm for the United Party—'Graaff's washed-out party, what's it called?' Another explained:

There's no effective opposition . . . the reason for this is *not* ruthless suppression, as people in England believe, but because South Africa is faced with an overwhelming problem and the United Party cannot devise an alternative to the Nats. (No. 268/60).

The Progressive Party received a little support, but it was often qualified:

The Progs. are the only ones and even they are ten years ahead of the times —economics is the answer to politics. Mind you the Nats. are no fools: they placate one side by what they say, and placate the other by what they do (No. 280/60).

In one case the political impact of South Africa was a movement away from Conservatism:

> We came as black Conservatives, but now having seen *real* conservatism working we are returning as red-hot Socialists. Seriously, it helps to produce a more balanced view—there are certain advantages in community responsibility (No. 290/60).

Support for either of the major British political parties was not significantly associated with support for the Nationalists,[21] the United Party, or withdrawal from the political arena. In general, the last response was the most typical for most immigrants, including those who had been in the country for several years, many of whom felt that it was:

> ... too early for us to tell them how to run their bloody country ... after all we are only immigrants (No. 230/60).

f: ATTITUDES TO APARTHEID

To many outside observers Apartheid and South Africa are synonymous, and no discussion of integration would be complete without consideration of the attitudes of immigrants towards this critical feature of their host society.

TABLE 30

Attitudes to Apartheid in Britain and South Africa

U.K.			S.A.			
Very favourable	23	4	Very favourable	200	39	(−2·7)
Favourable	85	17	Favourable	191	37	(−1·4)
Mixed	98	19	Mixed	70	14	(−0·6)
Hostile	112	22	Hostile	35	7	(−0·1)
Very hostile	55	11	Very hostile	15	3	(+1·0)
Don't know, etc.	141	27	Don't know, etc.	3	1	
TOTAL	514	100		514	101	(−1·6)

In theory, there is no necessary relationship between support for Apartheid and anti-African feelings, although in practice the two seem to be related. Lever and Wagner's study of Hillbrow found a significant correlation between two scales of 'anti-African prejudice' and 'pro-Apartheid ideology',[22] while the mean outgroup scores

---

[21] chi-square = 0·975; p = n.s.; d.f. = 2.

[22] H. Lever and O. J. M. Wagner, 'Urbanization and the Afrikaner', *Race*, 11, no. 2 (1969), 183–8.

from my investigation (shown in brackets in Table 30) indicate a similar progression.

Many of the replies suggested that the immigrants were fully aware of the change in their attitudes towards Apartheid from the time when they were living in Britain to the time of the interview. In some cases the crucial change in attitudes seemed to have started just before emigration, an example of anticipatory socialization.

In Britain I was against Apartheid, here you just have to agree with it—whites and blacks will never mix, it's like oil and water (No. 4/62ab).

Morally, ethically, from a Christian point of view, it's wrong. But you can't run an outfit on these principles entirely, it's simply a practical solution to a problem . . . but I haven't any anti-black feelings personally, at least not yet. Before I came I was anti-Apartheid until I read an article by Dr. Verwoerd and I believed him . . . look at the U.S.A. where the Negroes are more mature and only 10% of the population—the riots proved that it doesn't work (No. 32/62ab).

It seemed sort of bad, so I read it up in the Samorgan leaflet and then it seemed quite reasonable. Experience confirms this (No. 46/62ab).

I was against Apartheid before based on my knowledge of British Coloured people. In principle I'm against it still, but in practice it's essential, for if there were equality, everything would be over-run . . . Afrikaners resent British attitudes as being pro-Coloured, but that's because British Coloureds are a completely different kettle of fish from the Africans out here (No. 57/62ab),

I vowed that I would never do to the African what I thought was being done to him from reports on T.V. and in the Press. After a year and a half, I feel it is quite suitable and the best possible solution at the moment. I've had a very definite change in attitude (No. 112/62ab).

I used to feel it was pretty cruel, now I know these people aren't human beings but you can't tell them that in England—they steal, rape and kill; without it it would be the jungle . . . (No. 376/62ab).

While a third of the sample claimed that they were opposed to Apartheid when they were living in Britain, a further 27 per cent said that they had no views about the subject prior to emigrating. Once again, the ignorance factor was by no means uncommon:

In Britain, I didn't really know what the word meant and rather than confess my ignorance I was against it, like many others I think (No. 248/62ab).

I didn't know anything about it really and Sharpeville had no bearing on my feelings. People asked about 'all the fighting out there'. Where? I used to wonder, I didn't even know Sharpeville was in South Africa (No. 453/62ab).

What does the average British working man know, or for that matter care, about South Africa? Just tin huts in the jungle and beating the wogs about, if they know where Africa is at all. What does he care?—so long as his pay packet, tax and glass of beer is all right (No. 232/62ab).

Some support for Apartheid could be clearly related to a conscious wish to conform:

At first I was a little worried but I will become one of the sheep . . . (No. 25/62ab).

When in Rome . . . to me personally colour makes no difference . . . I don't agree or disagree, anyway it doesn't affect us really (No. 147/62ab).

If one's anti-Apartheid it's stupid to come, the majority of artisans say 'to hell with politics' and good luck to them (No. 228/62ab).

We came to conform: you must accept it (No. 476/62ab).

Many immigrants gave qualified, or, in some cases resigned, support for the policy. This was not surprising since 78 per cent of the sample could think of no practical alternative to it as a basis for South African society, and only 9 per cent were specific in their proposals for a non-Apartheid community.

I'm against Apartheid in sport but segregation is essential in living conditions (No. 55/62ab).

The idea of separation is wrong . . . things must change, but not at this stage—I don't think it's escapism either, just a practical solution (No. 98/62b).

I don't worry like I did at first when you see the police shoving them around, but it's a pity the innocent have to suffer with the bad (No.230/62b).

Job reservation is un-Christian but it's good at this stage, to save my own skin. After all if they [the Africans] were all about to become doctors of sociology you'd feel the same way yourself—you've got to be practical (No. 362/62b).

Anyway, it's not as simple as seen 5,000 miles away as a purely moral issue (No. 415/62b).

Those immigrants who were whole-heartedly in favour of Apartheid, comprising some 40 per cent of the sample, justified their convictions in three major ways: first, by reference to 'experience':

You mustn't judge South Africa until you have come out and worked here a while, you must live and work with them. Judging from a distance as far as Britain is as if you were to look at a field from an aeroplane: it looks like a carpet, you just don't see the thorns—you see the river, but you don't see the crocodiles until you try and swim in it (No. 137/62).

Secondly, by variations on a *tu quoque* theme: some demanded rhetorically: 'What bigger Apartheid is there than the Apartheid of money?' (No. 441/62b), and others launched into a lecture on comparative stratification—both legitimate reminders that racial differentiation is merely one branch of a broader sociological phenomenon.[23]

In the U.K. we have Apartheid between the upper and the lower classes; a dockworker would get thrown out of Claridges . . . we tend to forget that—*class distinction*. In Devon, farm workers still tug at their caps to the 'Lord of the Manor' and get tied cottages at 3/6d. a week . . . until that's rectified . . . (No. 225/62).

There's Apartheid in England, the Dorchester and the Ritz; in America you are never allowed to forget it on buses and trains; India has Apartheid in the caste system; and in Japan it's on a social basis—'snob Apartheid'; only in New Zealand are the Maoris accepted as normal people . . . (No. 356/62b).

Apartheid was taught to me in the British Army: in Aden in 1940 we were shown how to treat the natives; throw money on the floor and let them grovel for it . . . a real miniature British Raj and I, being a Socialist, didn't agree with it. But I do believe in Apartheid, Kipling's 'East is East, and West is West' . . . Apartheid is an experiment and the Transkei is no worse than Bechuanaland and Basutoland (No. 377/62b).

The third type of 'argument' used to justify Apartheid revealed a hard core of arrant racist thinking:

They lack the basic intelligence: the whites supply the brains and they do the manual work, there's no starvation and it's a damn sight better than the bloody Congo. They're happy so long as they can get their drink (No. 30/62b).

It's the only way; yes, the only bloody way: fishes don't cohabit with cats, zebras with lions . . . it's better for both. If God had intended all one type, he would have made all one type (No. 77/62b).

They are a bit sub-human, they lack the ability to concentrate . . . part of their brain seems to have been left out . . . (No. 449/62b).

Essential, if you gave them a new house they would only put coal in the bath and urinate in the sink (No. 506/62b).

A 10 per cent minority of the sample was opposed to Apartheid, though this was often based on the discrepancy between practice and theory, rather than an objection to the theory itself.

---

[23] Cf. the main thrust of the argument in P. Mason, *Patterns of Dominance*; and the wide selection of articles in a recent reader on stratification, A. Beteille (ed.), *Social Inequality*.

I agree with 'separate development' but not as it's administered here, for in South Africa there is only one class of person and that is the white. *Real* separate development means equality for all, they must make their own rules even though it would upset a few white people (No. 103/62b).

I'm not race conscious, I just like to pick my friends—it's the Kenya answer again: if you feel comfortable then you can let the African in. There were multi-racial clubs in Nairobi, but it must be left to the individual. I'm against legislative Apartheid because that breeds resentment (No. 92/62b).

I know it sounds trite, but here I find a lack of the 'dignity of Man'. All this 'yes mam', 'no baas'—a man who might be the head of a family having to bow and scrape to tuppenny ha'penny kids. . . . that's bad. It's not as cruel as people overseas think, but the kindness is always patronizing, it's always charity—I'd hate it if I were on the receiving end. My daughter and son-in-law say I just don't understand the African, they are probably right, the trouble is I regard him as a human being (No. 101/62b).

We didn't expect 'petty Apartheid', we despise and detest Apartheid (No. 110/62b).

Before, we had only the propaganda from the Embassy; that all the natives live in little 'semis' with free medical care and education. I don't think they do, do you? The theory's good, but not how it's put into practice (No. 130/62b).

I don't know whether they were real feelings or just reflections from the conditioning of press and T.V., I was indignant then. Now I feel it's the source of the greatest damage done to this country . . . it's a wanton waste of manpower, not petty, 'bus', Apartheid but the real thing that leads to the chronic lack of tradesmen and skilled operatives. Yes I'm still indignant but it's a change from a 'protection-of-the-underdog' indignity to an indignity based on sympathy for the country as a whole (No. 271/62b).

We understood Apartheid to be an equal opportunity but social barriers. We could accept this, but in fact it is just exploitation—the recent steel pay award is less than the poverty datum line (No. 326/62b).

I still think it stinks, particularly the way the educated ones are kept down by the masses—a blanket condemnation just because they have a black skin (No. 459/62b).

In spite of the deviant minority opposed to Apartheid, most immigrants had been converted to accept, and many positively to support, the policy by the time of the interview.[24] As this also represents the consensus of opinion among white South Africans, it is clear that

[24] Among a sample of Dutch immigrants, support for Apartheid increased from 32 per cent in the first year of residence, to 75 per cent after five years of residence. J. F. Loedolff, op. cit., p. 161.

on this sub-dimension most immigrants were exceptionally well integrated.

TABLE 31

The Congruence of Political Expectations and Experience

Much better	58	11
Better and equal	331	64
Slightly below	65	13
Much below	21	4
None, etc.	39	8
TOTAL	514	100

The over-all picture of political-cultural integration is more complex than either of the other dimensions, partly because of the heterogeneity of the components that have been assigned to the sub-dimension. This also accounts for the apparent discrepancy between the figures in Table 31, which resemble the findings from the economic and social dimensions, and the frequency distribution (and mean political integration score of -0.597)[25] which do not. The very different reaction of immigrants to the questions of the Afrikaans language or citizenship, compared with that of Apartheid, suggest that the assessments shown in Table 31 are based on the latter.

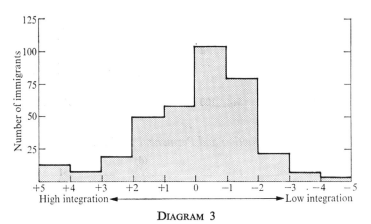

DIAGRAM 3

Frequency Distribution of Political-Cultural Integration Scores

---

[25] The sub-dimensions scaled were: 'Afrikaans', 'citizenship', 'identification', and 'Apartheid'.

Q

CHAPTER XV

Total Integration

NOW THAT I have discussed the three major dimensions of integration, it remains for me to make an over-all appraisal of integration for the sample as a whole. This may be done by comparing the the information classified under the eighteen sub-dimensions with the replies to the six final questions on the interview schedule. These questions were all related to the immigrant's own assessment of his over-all integration. As the scoring and the selection of components for each dimension was somewhat arbitrary, their relative significance in the total pattern can only be related through the immigrant's self-assessment.

TABLE 32

South African Difficulties and British Dislikes

(a)			(b)		
Economic	171	33	Economic	122	24
Social-pers.	191	37	Social	43	8
Political	14	3	Political	66	13
Other	12	2	Climate	207	40
None	126	25	None	39	8
			Everything	28	5
			Other	9	2
TOTAL	514	100		514	100

Satisfaction and Permanent Residence

(c)			(d)		
Very satisfied	183	36	Yes	251	49
Quite satisfied	115	22	No	105	20
Satisfied	90	18	Unsure	158	31
Fairly dissatisfied	81	16			
Very dissatisfied	40	8			
Don't know	5	1			
TOTAL	514	100		514	100

All three dimensions of integration were closely interrelated: those immigrants who were well integrated economically tended to score highly on the social and political indexes too.[1] The tables comparing 'expectations' with 'experience' suggest that the greatest dissatisfaction is to be found on the social dimension (33 per cent), followed by the economic (27 per cent), with the amount of political dissatisfaction (17 per cent) trailing some way behind. This pattern corresponds with the immigrants' assessment of the greatest difficulties that they had to overcome in order to settle in South Africa (see Table 32(a)).

In all, 83 per cent of the sample stated that they would still emigrate to South Africa if they could have their choice over again, 12 per cent claimed that they would not, while 5 per cent were undecided.[2] Just over half the sample were prepared to give an unqualified recommendation of South Africa to a 'friend in Britain thinking of emigrating', a further 30 per cent signified qualified approval, while 13 per cent stated that they would warn prospective migrants not to come. There were many zealous advocates of 'spreading the gospel' (No. 242/95), balanced by a few warnings that South Africa was '*not* a land flowing with milk and honey' (No. 107/95). Three-quarters of the immigrants were 'satisfied' with their life in South Africa,[3] the remaining quarter were not. One half had firmly resolved to settle in the country, one fifth were equally determined to leave, leaving nearly one third undecided.

A slightly different perspective was sought by asking the immigrants to state those factors that they would most dislike about Britain if, or when, they returned to live there[4] (Table 32(b)). These may be compared with the problems faced in South Africa cited in Table 32(a). Forty per cent mentioned climate, contrasting the 'pastel shades' of Southern Africa with the 'dull, grey, drab buildings of the industrial north' (No. 428/97). Nearly a quarter claimed that a reduction in their standard of living would be the most salient contrast, while the political category was divided between those who objected to the (Labour) Government, and those who were repelled by some aspect of coloured immigration or race relations in Britain (6 per

---

[1] The correlation coefficient for political and economic integration, $r = 0.3732$ ($p = .001$); for social and economic integration, $r = 0.4292$ ($p = .001$); and for social and political integration, $r = 0.4141$ ($p = .001$).

[2] Cf. In den Bosch, op. cit., p. 75: 88 per cent of his sample stated that they would emigrate again if given a second choice.

[3] Richmond found that 84 per cent of his Canadian sample were 'satisfied' (1967) op. cit., p. 164.

[4] Cf. J. F. Loedolff, op. cit., p. 186.

cent). A few enthusiastic settlers replied that they would object to 'everything', or at least to the 'Three "W's": the weather, Wilson, and the Welfare State' (No. 141/97).

Two characteristics of the sample dictate caution when attempts are made to generalize, from these findings, on the nature of British immigration as a whole. The relatively short mean length of residence of the sample tends to exaggerate the level of dissatisfaction, for I have already shown how the two are related, thus confirming Loedolff's conclusion from his sample of Dutch immigrants. On the other hand, the selection of immigrants of longer standing tends to overlook those immigrants who return to Britain dissatisfied, consequently biasing the sample in the reverse direction. The extent to which these two factors cancel each other out is hard to determine, though some estimate of the rate of return migration will be considered later.[5]

Nevertheless, most immigrants seemed to be satisfactorily integrated into South African society *according to their own definition of the situation*. It was the economic and social adjustments that the typical immigrant deemed crucial, and although we may consider that he was far from well integrated on certain aspects of the political-cultural dimension, it does not seem that this fact unduly disturbed him.

[5] Cf. chapter XVI, pp. 241-42.

Testing the Hypotheses

IN THIS final chapter in which I focus directly on the data derived from the survey, I shall consider some of the outstanding basic problems posed by the hypotheses of my earlier theoretical discussion. These will be reviewed against the background of the research findings so far, and in conjunction with additional evidence from the interview schedule. The 'testing' of the hypotheses, as in the previous chapters, depends on the availability of suitable evidence and may be quantitative or qualitative in nature. This is in accordance with the over-all research strategy chosen to suit the special circumstances of the study, and consequently the results must be treated as tentative and exploratory.

a: ATTITUDE-CHANGE OR SELF-SELECTION?

The first three hypotheses were all related to one of the fundamental premises of the study: that there is a rapid and significant change in the race attitudes and in the degree of support for the policy of Apartheid among British immigrants once they arrive in South Africa. It was postulated that the majority of immigrants were motivated by economic forces and did not choose to emigrate to South Africa as a result of racial or political self-selection. The analysis of the social structure of the immigrant situation, in the specific context of South African society, was regarded as a sufficient explanation of the phenomenon in question.

I have already considered the motives for migration which lend little support to the selective process suggested as a possibility by Kuper. Evidence concerning the 'precipitating factors' and the motives for the selection of South Africa are equally free from the biases of racial selection. There were other questions on the interview schedule dealing both directly and indirectly with these problems. As was demonstrated in the analysis of attitudes towards Apartheid, there was a marked change after emigration, and this change was also found in attitudes towards the African. Many of the immigrants were aware of, and readily admitted to, a dramatic shift in their views tantamount to a socio-political conversion (see Table 33).

In the sample as a whole, some 38 per cent of the respondents admitted to a significant change in their attitudes towards the African, and a further 22 per cent were unsure at the time of the interview— substantial percentages considering that these were retrospective judgements.

TABLE 33

Attitudes towards the African before and after Emigration

	U.K.		S.A.	
Very favourable	7	1	5	1
Positive stereotype	25	5	20	4
Neutral (mixed)	234	46	139	27
Negative stereotype	96	19	295	57
Antagonistic	18	4	48	9
Don't know, etc.	134	26	7	1
TOTAL	514	101	514	99

Another perspective on the problem was sought by asking the immigrants for their reaction towards coloured immigration into Britain. While the salience of this issue was much lower for British immigrants who emigrated before the late 1950s, this did not affect the vast majority of the sample. Slightly less than two-thirds of the replies were either unfavourable or very hostile (28 per cent), while exactly one third were prepared to mention both positive and negative aspects of the question. This may be compared, for example, with the Gallup Poll held in May 1968, during the later part of the interviewing in South Africa, which suggested that 75 per cent of a national sample supported Mr. Enoch Powell's anti-immigration speeches, 15 per cent were opposed to them, while 11 per cent remained undecided.[1] While not exactly comparable, these figures do provide further supporting evidence in favour of the third hypothesis rejecting self-selection.

The qualitative evidence obtained from the interviews also suggests that many of those opposed to coloured immigration held qualified stereotypes, rather than being uncompromising supporters of bigoted racialism:

I'm not fanatical about coloured immigration but it does seem a little foolish to import unskilled workers when there's unemployment at home (No. 32/38).

[1] Reported in *The Eastern Province Herald*, 8 May 1968; see also: 'Powell, Polls and People', in *I.R.R. Newsletter* (U.K.) 2, no. 5 (1968), 212–14.

Yes, it's bloody awful: it wasn't the *Coloureds* so much as the Pakistanis, there's a place in Scotland called the Khyber Pass (No. 219/38).

I'd ban all foreigners, the Irish as well . . . they hate our guts but take our charity. *Son:* The Irish are in exactly the same position as we are in South Africa (No. 126/38).

Of the two exceptions mentioned in hypothesis 3, the 'ex-colonial' immigrant was clearly visible. There were 23 (4·4 per cent) such immigrants in the sample, who, having been brought up and educated in Britain, had spent some time living in former colonies, particularly in East and Central Africa and India. Some had migrated directly to South Africa, while others had returned temporarily to Britain and had subsequently re-emigrated. Many of these immigrants had selected South Africa as the nearest substitute for their former colonial environment and a 'self-selection' influence on their attitudes was undeniable. As a group the ex-colonials were characterized by exceptionally high integration on all three dimensions,[2] with the greatest relative difference from the sample mean scores on the political, and then the social dimensions. They were also much more intolerant of outgroups[3] than the general run of immigrants. Without a doubt, the experience of colonial service in the twilight of the Empire was the best finishing school for those wishing to launch themselves into South African society.

On the basis of the motives for migration, less than 5 per cent of the sample mentioned politics or race relations as a primary influence on their decision. If we take all those immigrants who claimed that race factors played some part in the process, at no matter what level of priority, a sub-group of 29 (5·6 per cent) immigrants is obtained which may be described as 'racially-propelled'. These were even more hostile towards outgroups than the ex-colonial category ($-3·310$ cf. $-3·000$), but significantly less well integrated than their ex-colonial cousins.[4] Nevertheless, they had a considerably higher total integration score than the sample mean which was almost entirely a function of superior political integration.

It has already been shown that only six per cent of the sample

---

[2] Economic score $= 3·043$; social score $= 2·391$; political score $= 2·087$; total integration score $= 7·652$.

[3] $-3·0$ cf. sample mean of $-1·6$.

[4] Total integration score $= 3·207$. This is higher than the sample mean of 2·531. The outgroup score of the 'racially-propelled' ($-3·3$) was higher than that of the 'ex-colonials' ($-3·0$).

claimed that 'coloured immigration' would be the aspect of life in Britain that they would most object to if they were to return and live there. This is a very small percentage seen against the background of Southern African socialization, and at the end of an interview dealing extensively with questions of race attitudes, race stereotypes, and race relations. In conclusion, it would seem that a maximum of 10 per cent of the sample could be regarded as self-selected on political-racial grounds, and that the relative intolerance and the degree of support for Apartheid found among the British immigrants in South Africa must be a result of changed attitudes induced by social structural forces.

b: THE IMMIGRANT SITUATION: (1) CONFORMITY AND IGNORANCE

The fact that conformity to group norms would be one of the natural tendencies resulting from the structure of the immigrant situation played an important part in our explanation of attitude change. Pettigrew has also shown how conformity and social distance are associated in the South African context.[5] In the interview, immigrants were asked to assess the importance that they attached to conforming to the 'South African way of life': 63 per cent claimed that it was 'very important', 21 per cent 'fairly important', 10 per cent of 'little importance', and only 2 per cent felt that it was of 'no importance' at all. This is in marked contrast to Gans's study of suburban America in which he found that: 'enough of the sub-urban critique had seeped into the reading matter of the Levittowners to make conformity a pejorative term.'[6] To the typical immigrant, conformity was: '. . . vital, you must adapt to the country, you cannot expect it to adapt to you' (No. 30/35).

There were many instances in the interviews that revealed the immigrants' early uncertainty and confusion, and their strong desire to adopt the 'correct' form of South African behaviour:

In Jo'burg the ladies shout at them [the Africans]. I'm not used to it, but everyone says you do it like that and so you have to—after all they live with them don't they? (No. 368/35).

I just don't know how to treat the Kaffirs, I don't know whether I'm doing right or wrong (No. 46/35).

[5] T. F. Pettigrew (1960), op. cit., pp. 246–53.
[6] H. Gans, *The Levittowners: ways of life and politics in a new suburban community* (1967), p. 175.

The situation is an illustration of Edward Shils's contention that:

Man is much more concerned with what is near at hand, with what is present and concrete than with what is remote and abstract. He is more responsive on the whole to persons, to the status of those who surround him and the justice he sees in his own situation than he is with the symbols of remote persons, with the total status system in the society and with the global system of justice. Immediately present authorities engage his mind more than remote ones.[7]

Thus the average immigrant recognizes the importance of 'conformity', but by conformity he does not mean becoming a South African citizen, learning Afrikaans, or taking an interest in South African politics: it is a passive, not active, conformity suggesting an integration into the ethos and pattern of life of English-speaking (white) South Africans.

A second characteristic of the immigrant situation suggested in hypothesis 9 is what I have termed 'deliberate ignorance'. This is not the same as ignorance, pure and simple, many examples of which have been already cited in the survey evidence and in the historical account of British immigration to South Africa. By 'deliberate ignorance' I mean a conscious (though sometimes possibly subconscious) attempt on the part of the immigrant to isolate himself from the conflicts and dilemmas posed by life in South Africa; to surround himself, so to speak, with a cloud of unknowing. The very nature of the phenomenon defies direct examination, though many comments made in the course of the interviews lend support to the hypothesis. Not all the immigrants were as frank as the man who openly declared: 'If there's going to be trouble here I'd rather not know. I don't know whether my attitude is typical but I'd rather be an ostrich and bury my head in the sand' (No. 500/100).

Related to this phenomenon is the theme of apoliticality stressed earlier during the examination of the first part of hypothesis 15 concerning the degree of political interest and participation. Although this may be partly explained in terms of conformity to group norms —English-speaking South Africans, as a group, could hardly be described as political fanatics—it may also be seen as an extension of the concept of deliberate ignorance. While this situation clearly predominates in a large section of the immigrant community, it would be wrong to give the impression that all British immigrants were

---

[7] E. A. Shils, 'Primordial, Personal, Sacred and Civil Ties', *B.J.S.* 8 (1957), 130.

political eunuchs, a few were well versed in the art of political provocation:

> I often ask Afrikaners, 'where was Vorster during the war when your Dutch ancestors were being mangled up by the Nazis?' Some take it, but most don't (No. 116/100).

C: THE IMMIGRANT SITUATION: (2) SOCIAL MOBILITY AND ACCEPTANCE

In this sub-section, class will be considered in its dynamic aspect to assess the two related hypotheses, 8 and 10, which link social mobility, social acceptance, and support for the *status quo*. Although some may regard Apartheid as a utopian policy for change, I will interpret it as an ideology supporting the political and social *status quo*.

It has already been argued that social mobility in the South African context is as much a function of the structure of the racial hierarchy as it is of the movement from one occupational class to another. Thus it is quite possible for an immigrant who has not experienced 'objective' mobility, with reference to my basic class groupings, to feel that he has experienced 'subjective' social mobility—an impression that is rooted in fact, not a figment of his social imagination.[8] The data from the sample confirm the hypothesis that those immigrants with the greatest feelings of social elevation are also the strongest advocates of Apartheid (see Table 34).

TABLE 34
Social Mobility and Support for Apartheid (the status quo)

SOC. MOB.	Much Higher		Higher		Same		Lower		Much Lower	
APARTHEID	N	%	N	%	N	%	N	%	N	%
Strongly pro	25	51	51	53	123	36	1	5	0	0
Pro	18	37	31	32	133	39	7	32	2	50
Mixed	6	12	9	9	45	13	10	45	0	0
Anti	0	0	4	4	28	8	2	9	1	25
Strongly anti	0	0	2	2	10	3	2	9	1	25
Other	0	0	0	0	3	1	0	0	0	0

There is another aspect of social mobility which is particularly important: the degree to which immigrants felt that they were

---

[8] Cf. Goldthorpe and Lockwood's warning concerning: 'the all too easy exercise of discovering how many manual workers are willing to "upgrade" themselves by uttering three syllables', 'Affluence and the British Class Structure', 133–63.

accepted into their new social status by members of the host society. The reason why the majority of immigrants seemed likely to meet with a friendly reception from English-speaking South Africans has been outlined in the theoretical section, and their actual experience has been described as a sub-dimension of social integration. Whether 'acceptance' is measured in terms of perceived 'friendliness', either from South Africans in general[9] or from workmates and colleagues,[10] or in terms of an absence of class consciousness,[11] there appears to be a strong association between it and support for the existing order of South African society implicit in the acceptance of the policy of Apartheid.

d: INTEGRATION: APARTHEID, IDEOLOGY, AND THE RETURNING MIGRANT

In order to complete the analysis of the empirical evidence, I shall consider the three remaining hypotheses which deal respectively with those immigrants who reject Apartheid, with ideological variations within the sample, and with those immigrants who return to Britain.

The twelfth hypothesis, which is closely related to those in the last section, states that the fiercest critics of Apartheid will be the immigrants who are also the least well integrated on the economic and social dimensions. This raises a problem of cause and effect: is the main line of causation from economic or social dissatisfaction towards political uneasiness and disapproval, is it the reverse, or are the two forces interacting? Several reasons suggest that the first alternative is the most plausible, for it is unlikely that the minority of Britons who are strongly aroused and upset by Apartheid in principle would select South Africa as a suitable country to migrate to in the first place. My earlier contention that racialist self-selection is not a primary influence on the composition of immigrants does not preclude the possibility of a negative selective factor deterring immigrants of a strongly egalitarian or non-racialist outlook. On the other hand, fear of the consequences of the 'race situation' in South Africa could equally deter a racialist immigrant, who logically should prefer 'white' Australia[12] to a minority position in a predominantly black

[9] chi-square = 76·368; p = ·001; d.f. = 25.
[10] chi-square = 49·280; p = ·001; d.f. = 25.
[11] chi-square = 103·869; p = ·001; d.f. = 25.
[12] Cf. R. T. Appleyard's comments on 'the other side of the coin' in *British Emigration to Australia*, p. 160.

South Africa—if colour *per se* were the real objection. The fact that most immigrants were driven by economic forces makes it seem most likely that satisfactory integration in the economic dimension would tend to generalize into the other major dimensions, while dissatisfaction would spread in the reverse direction.

A certain number of the immigrants seemed to be fully aware of this relationship: that 'moral' man is rarely divorced from 'economic' man.

There's piles of scope to make money here, the only ones who are happy with the political set up are those with the good jobs (No. 365/62).

I feel a general disappointment with the lower standard of living and the political future. *Wife:* . . . if we had more money and were able to live in luxury, I wonder what our political views would have been then . . . even so, the future here is not for our children (No. 326–7/96).

The data from the survey gave quantitative support to the hypothesis with economic and social integration scores varying positively with the degree of support for Apartheid (see Table 35).

TABLE 35

Apartheid and the Economic and Social Dimensions of Integration

APARTHEID	+ +	+	0	−	− −	Don't know
Economic integration score	2·6	2·3	2·0	1·5	0·1	2·3
Social integration score	0·9	1·0	0·2	−0·6	−2·3	0·3
Outgroup score	−2·7	−1·4	−0·6	−0·1	1·0	—

Immigrants were also asked to speculate about the development of South African society during the next twenty years. Hypothesis 16 was based on the strong evidence that Mannheim's stress on the social determination of belief systems[13] applied in the South African situation. Danziger found that the 'views of the future' held by a sample of school children, as measured by a content analysis of their essays, were determined largely by their ethnic group membership.[14] In Mannheim's terminology, the whites subscribed to conservative ideologies, the blacks adhered to radical utopias. In an analogous manner, I anticipated that the 'views of the future' held by immigrants would conform to a similar pattern. Those immigrants who were

[13] K. Mannheim, *Ideology and Utopia: an introduction to the sociology of knowledge* (1936).
[14] K. Danziger, 'Ideology and Utopia in South Africa: A Methodological contribution to the sociology of knowledge', *B.J.S.* 14 (1963), 59–76.

well integrated on the economic and social dimensions would tend to see the future development of South African society in conservative or evolutionary terms; those who were poorly integrated or positively alienated would contemplate, or even relish, the thought of impending revolution. For the former, 'optimism' coincided with self-interest while 'pessimism' was pushed to the back of the mind (deliberate ignorance again?). Psychologically there was too much to lose.

Many immigrants clearly enjoyed the role of Cassandra, though one woman had the frankness to admit: 'I haven't a clue, I just don't think that far ahead' (No. 388/92). Opinions seemed to differ very much in accordance with the immigrant's level of satisfaction and ranged from one end of the spectrum to the other:

I think that we are on the edge of a precipice, a Hitlerian Age . . . (No. 234/92).

South Africa will become an example to the world: it's the most peaceful country in the world, and I've lived in four (No. 243/92).

The over-all statistics further support the impression gained during the interviews. Table 36 shows that the mean total integration scores and each of the sub-dimension scores fit into the expected pattern. The ability to contemplate radical change was also strongly associated with the immigrant's level of satisfaction,[15] standard of living,[16] and desire to settle permanently in the country.[17] The Mannheim thesis, if not the pure Marxist thesis, was fully vindicated by the British immigrant in South Africa.

TABLE 36

Future Change and Integration

	Yes change	No change	Don't know change
Mean outgroup score	−1·059	−1·938	−0·873
Mean economic score	1·304	2·622	2·014
Mean social score	−0·569	1·044	0·479
Mean political score	−1·422	−0·302	−0·831
Total integ. score	−0·588	3·604	1·859

To complete this exploratory study some mention is required of those immigrants who do not settle permanently but return to

[15] chi-square = 61·163; p = ·001; d.f. = 10.
[16] chi-square = 62·089; p = ·001; d.f. = 10.
[17] chi-square = 53·384; p = ·001; d.f. = 4.

Britain.[18] By its very nature, the sample survey can only shed light on this interesting topic from an oblique angle. Official estimates of the proportion of returning migrants are implausibly low, the product of wishful thinking rather than careful enumeration. To the bureaucratic mind a returning immigrant is a measure of failure— Richmond's 'transilients' make this a premature generalization— and as a consequence the subject is consigned to statistical conjecture.

According to an official estimate 'the number of assisted immigrants leaving South Africa is less than 2 per cent';[19] according to the 1820 Memorial Settlers' Association, a reasonable estimate is 5 per cent;[20] according to a plausible calculation based on the 1961–6 immigration statistics, a figure of 12·5 per cent has been suggested;[21] according to my factory case study (see Appendix C), 25 per cent is the relevant figure; and according to a recent assertion by a South African sociologist, the true proportion is 50 per cent.[22] From my sample survey 20 per cent of the respondents stated that they would definitely return, 49 per cent said that they would settle permanently, while 31 per cent were undecided. This contains biases in both directions; the high proportion of relatively short-residence immigrants will exaggerate dissatisfaction, the selection of immigrants of longer standing will overlook those who have already returned. Even if all the undecided immigrants actually stayed, we are still left with a return rate of ten times the official estimate. This is much more in accordance with the return rates from the other countries that attract large-scale British immigration.

The last hypothesis in the theoretical section suggested that those immigrants who return are driven primarily by non-political rather than political forces. In order to examine this suggestion further we must first of all paint a less impressionistic portrait of the returning immigrant. Is he a dissatisfied refugee from disappointment, or an international citizen leaping over the boundaries of individual countries in his quest for adventure, travel, and occupational mobility? The figures in Table 37 would place 70 per cent in the

[18] Richmond estimated a return rate for Canada of 30 per cent (1946–61) (1967) op. cit., p. 229; Appleyard has suggested a figure of 14·8 per cent for Australia (1955–60), 'The Return Movement of U.K. Migrants from Australia', *Population Studies*, 15, no. 3 (1962), 214–25.
[19] Personal communication, Immigration Section, S.A. House (London), 28 Apr. 1969.
[20] *The Star*, 30 Aug. 1967.
[21] Ibid.
[22] *The Star* (overseas edn.), 13 Feb. 1971.

former category, while 27 per cent may be classed as 'transilients'—to use Richmond's terminology.[23]

TABLE 37

Residence Intention and Satisfaction

	Settle		Return		Unsure	
Very satisfied	165	66	5	5	13	8
Quite satisfied	57	23	12	11	46	29
Satisfied	26	10	12	11	52	33
Slightly dissatisfied	3	1	37	35	41	26
Very dissatisfied	0	0	37	35	3	2
Don't know	0	0	2	2	3	2
TOTAL	251	100	105	99	158	100

A cross-tabulation (Table 38) reveals that the returning immigrants are more critical of Apartheid than those who intend to settle, a fact that is hardly surprising in the light of my previous conclusions concerning the relationship between satisfaction, integration, and support for the *status quo*. It is particularly noteworthy that while 28 per cent of the returning immigrants disapproved of Apartheid, 71 per cent were by no means critical. Therefore, under the strictest assumptions, over half the returning (non-transilient) immigrants were not opponents of Apartheid, which does not imply that the remainder were *motivated* by this factor. In fact, of those intending to return, only 9 per cent mentioned political-racial factors as the greatest obstacle to their satisfactory integration into South African society, while 48 per cent claimed social-personal problems, and 34 per cent referred to economics.

This impression of a symmetrical pattern of economically motivated and orientated immigrants with economically and socially dissatisfied returning immigrants, was given added confirmation by interviews with a small sample of the latter, travelling back to Britain on the *Edinburgh Castle* during September 1968 (see Appendix C). This would seem to support the claim of one immigrant:

People say they leave because of Apartheid but believe me that's only an excuse. The truth is that they are not prepared to work and give it a try (No. 506/100).

Therefore, while returning migrants are more opposed to Apartheid than those who remain, it is more interesting to note that few, if any,

[23] Richmond found: 'with the exception of some males in manual occupations, the returning British migrants were more economically successful and more satisfied than those who had not returned' ((1967), op. cit., p. 266).

TABLE 38

Residence Intention, Apartheid, and Integration

Apartheid	Settle		Return		Unsure	
Very favourable	120	48	20	19	60	38
Favourable	90	36	36	34	65	41
Mixed	33	13	19	18	18	11
Hostile	8	3	16	15	11	7
Very hostile	0	0	14	13	1	11
Don't know, etc.	0	0	0	0	3	2
TOTAL	251	100	105	99	158	100
Mean outgroup score	−1·944		−1·486		−1·184	
Econ. integ. score	3·155		0·943		1·766	
Soc. integ. score	1·729		−1·657		0·456	
Pol. integ. score	0·291		−2·362		−0·835	
Total integ. score:	5·327		−2·733		1·589	

of those who are satisfied with the economic and social aspects of life in South Africa also strongly reject Apartheid. The rejection of Apartheid is invariably part of a total rejection, which suggests that if it is not merely an epiphenomenon—a rationalization for 'failure' or dissatisfaction—it is an altogether secondary influence. The typical immigrant is not a fervent idealist,[24] nor a bigoted racialist, but a normal human being with social and material aspirations. Return from South Africa does not mark a flight of the politically disenchanted, it is much more an escape from social and economic disillusionment.

[24] Few were quite as honest (cynical?) as the following immigrant who candidly admitted to a simple equation: 'You must balance economic gains, opportunities and climate against freedom of expression. To me, on balance, the former outweighs the latter' (No. 37/100).

PART FOUR

Summary and Conclusions

'Caelum non animum mutant qui
trans mare currunt.'
(HORACE, *Epistles*, I. xi. 27)

CHAPTER XVII

Colonist or Uitlander?—Towards a Reassessment

a: A SUMMARY OF THE ARGUMENT

FOR THE past hundred and fifty years British immigration has been an important, and at times a crucial, element affecting the complex interaction of ethnic and racial groups in South African society. The historical section of this study described the manner in which the 'immigration factor' has changed and developed over time in relation to internal variations in the power structure.[1] The implications of the arrival of a British immigrant in the 1820s were very different from the repercussions of those who came during the 1890s, while after a further seventy years, in the 1960s, the situation had changed yet again. An appreciation of the forces underlying these dynamic changes in the 'immigration factor' can be best gained by viewing history from a sociological perspective,[2] with the stress on relationships rather than events.

An attempt was also made to link the situation of the British immigrant to more general aspects of sociological theory. This involved combining the insights and generalizations of two streams of sociological thought: those concerned with migration, following in the tradition of Thomas and Znaniecki, and those focusing attention on the conflict between values and actions exemplified by Gunnar Myrdal's *An American Dilemma*. The latter had been clearly anticipated, with respect to South African conditions, by James Bryce when he argued in his Romanes Lecture of 1902:

If political privileges are refused to the backward race, the contrast between principle and practice, between a theoretical recognition of the rights of man as man and the denial of them to a section of the population, will be palpable and indefensible.[3]

[1] Cf. H. M. Blalock, 'A Power Analysis of Racial Discrimination', *Social Forces*, 39 (1960), 53–9.
[2] For important studies combining history with sociology, see E. E. Evans-Pritchard, *The Sanusi of Cyrenaica* (1949) and N. J. Smelser, *Social Change in the Industrial Revolution* (1959).
[3] J. Bryce, 'The Relations of the Advanced and the Backward Races of Mankind', Romanes Lecture (1902), p. 31.

Though Bryce, like Myrdal, underestimated the ease with which people can be morally schizophrenic, this is a predicament that faces the British immigrant in South Africa.

From the theoretical analysis, five key factors were isolated to form the basis of a set of more specific hypotheses around which the empirical section was organized. These factors were: conformity to group norms during the insecurity of the adjustment to the host society; the peculiar effects of the South African social structure on the reception of the immigrant; the tendency for social acceptance to encourage social conservatism; and the quest for both personal and societal legitimacy. The specific practical implications of these factors were translated into a set of seventeen hypotheses.

One further, yet fundamental, problem had to be considered before exploring the hypotheses in relation to the survey evidence. This was the exact nature of the differences between British and South African society, with particular respect to comparative race relations. It was argued that there were substantial and significant differences in the historical genesis of race relations patterns, in etiquette and tradition, in demographic balances, and in the fundamental legal and social structure, and that these would necessitate a specific 'race relations adjustment' within the overarching processes of integration into South African society.

The third section of the study comprised the evidence from the sample survey and was both descriptive and analytical in content. Among the basic variables considered, it was found that there was no systematic regional recruitment of immigrants to suggest a simple causal process of motivation. In South Africa, there was some evidence to show that the immigrant in Johannesburg (Transvaal) was slightly less well integrated socially and politically, though not in the economic dimension, than his fellow migrant in the Cape or in Natal. Sex was not a crucial factor in most aspects of integration, although women were significantly less prepared to adopt South African citizenship and were marginally more prejudiced than men. The single immigrants were less well integrated and much more tolerant than the married, while age, *per se*, and family size were not particularly crucial. Length of residence, social class, and education all exerted a vitally important influence on both attitudes and integration.

The first stage of migration—the forces at work in the 'home' society—was seen from a modified version of Smelser's 'value-added' perspective, and the importance of the economic interpretation of migration was constantly reiterated. Of the three dimensions of integration, the economic adjustment of the immigrant was the most satisfactory, followed by the social and then by the political-cultural.

In the final interpretation of the survey evidence, the racial self-selection hypothesis was rejected, while the influence of conformity and the prevalence of 'deliberate ignorance' was stressed. The socially mobile immigrants, being generally accepted into their group of orientation, were the strongest advocates of Apartheid, as were those immigrants who were best integrated on the economic and social dimensions. The migrants' vision of the future development of South African society was closely structured by the degree of their integration: those well-integrated were the most conservative, those least integrated the most revolutionary. About 70 per cent of the immigrants who wished to return to Britain were dissatisfied with aspects of South African life, but this dissatisfaction was a product of social or economic disillusionment.

b: A TYPOLOGY OF MIGRANT INTEGRATION

Before making a final assessment of the British immigrant in South Africa it is worth considering some broader implications of the study for the sociology of migration. By employing Max Weber's concept of the 'ideal type',[4] it is possible to develop a dichotomous typology based on the immigrant's (immigrant group's) *orientation towards the host society*. At one extreme there is the 'colonist' (or settler) type, at the other the 'uitlander' (or international-commuter) type. In certain respects this is Merton's distinction between the 'local' and the 'cosmopolitan'[5] rendered dynamic and writ large.

Few, if any, of our migrants will exactly fit these ideal types—to expect that they must would be an example of the 'fallacy of mis-placed concreteness'—for they represent the poles of a continuum. The 'colonist' is an immigrant who is motivated by a wish to settle permanently in the host society; who identifies totally with that society, and, if necessary, is prepared to align with it in opposition to his home society. He is one who quickly becomes acculturated into the norms and values of the host society, and is prepared to

---

[4] For a methodological critique of Weber's formulation of the concept, see T. Parsons, *The Structure of Social Action* (1937), pp. 601–10.
[5] R. K. Merton, *Social Theory and Social Structure*, pp. 387–420.

remain there in the face of temporary or even permanent setbacks. The 'uitlander' is the migrant whose orientations are overwhelmingly economic;[6] who has no wish to settle permanently; who has no affective ties with the host society; who has a desire to preserve his own culture and way of life with a minimum of conformity to that of the host community; and who does not scruple to leave the sinking ship if his treasure is likely to be drowned with it. The extreme positions are epitomized by the following two responses to the interview question concerning residence intention:

I often tell South Africans that we are here just for the money and as soon as we've made it we will be back off home (No. 81/99).

We are never going back: I would rather fight or be chopped up than crawl back to Britain (No. 237/99).

Clearly the 'uitlander' disposition can change over time; the longer the immigrant stays in the country the further he moves towards the 'colonist' pole of the continuum. This makes a generalization from my sample difficult, but if we take those immigrants who have been in South Africa for the longest length of time—for a minimum period of eight years—and consider their reaction to citizenship, identification, and residence intention, this will provide a basis for a preliminary classification. While an overwhelming majority (88 per cent) of this critical group intended to remain in the country, as far as the key factors of identification[7] and citizenship[8] were concerned, more than a hint of the uitlander mentality hovered at the back of the mind of most immigrants. Perhaps in our case the shadow of a uitlander is walking closely in step with the body of a colonist.

Such a typology may have a wider application outside the South African context—though it may be necessary to extend it beyond the first generation of immigrants—as a means of classifying the relations of different immigrant communities to their respective host societies. But immigrant-host relations are the result of a two-way process of mutual interaction, so in order to complete the picture the study of the *orientation of the host society towards the immigrant*

---

[6] As Bryce noted, 'most of them [i.e. the Uitlanders] had come not to stay, and to identify themselves with the old citizens, but to depart after amassing gain' (*Impressions of South Africa*, p. 426).

[7] 41 per cent of the sample immigrants considered themselves to be South Africans, 28 per cent British, and 25 per cent equally both.

[8] 32 per cent of the sample immigrants were either citizens or definitely intended to become citizens, 22 per cent were not, while 46 per cent were undecided.

must also be included. Parallel with the colonist-uitlander continuum is a second axis, an 'integrationalist-segregationalist' continuum, representing the extent to which the host society is prepared to accept the newcomer or insists on his conformity. This provides a four-celled diagram (Diagram 4) in which different types of situation may be classified.[9]

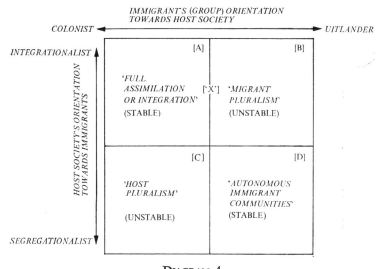

IMMIGRANT'S (GROUP) ORIENTATION
TOWARDS HOST SOCIETY

COLONIST ←————————————————→ UITLANDER

INTEGRATIONALIST ↑

HOST SOCIETY'S ORIENTATION
TOWARDS IMMIGRANTS

	[A]	[B]
	'FULL ASSIMILATION ['X'] OR INTEGRATION' (STABLE)	'MIGRANT PLURALISM' (UNSTABLE)
	[C]	[D]
	'HOST PLURALISM' (UNSTABLE)	'AUTONOMOUS IMMIGRANT COMMUNITIES' (STABLE)

SEGREGATIONALIST ↓

DIAGRAM 4

Cells (A) and (D) represent stable situations of compatible orientations, accompanied by low conflict and a low salience of immigration as a political-social issue. The cells (B) and (C) are different examples of conflicting orientations, unstable positions associated with controversy and social friction. A few examples may help to elucidate the situations represented in the diagram.

The migration of West Indians to Britain during the post-war years can be seen as an example of 'unstable host pluralism' (C). In spite of their links with the home society, most West Indians were orientated towards full acceptance into the society of the 'mother country'. The comparative chapter provides many examples

[9] The essential crudity of the diagram, with its stress on the cultural rather than the structural side of the process, is fully recognized. In the South African case, a pluralistic structure gives rise to a fairly strong integrationalist orientation towards the British immigrant. The immigrant's mixed orientations would, therefore, place him around point 'X' on Diagram 4.

of the 'segregationalist' orientation of the host society. There are three possible future developments: there may be a change in the attitude of the host community leading to a gradual movement towards 'full assimilation' (A); the West Indians may change their frame of reference to form 'autonomous immigrant communities' (D); or a persistence in the present balance of orientations will lead to increasing conflict—to the self-fulfilling vindication of the Powellite prophecy.

A very different situation is represented by the Indian communities in East Africa, or the Chinese in Indonesia.[10] Starting from a position of stability in cell (D), a combination of uitlander attitudes and the segregationalist policies of colonial administrations, there has been a movement in the post-colonial era towards 'unstable migrant pluralism' (B). The mobilization systems of the new nationalisms have produced an integrationalist ideology, leading in the first case to the exodus of Indians from East Africa, and in the second to the massacre of the Chinese in Indonesia.

Many other examples could be cited to illustrate some other uses of the typology.[11] Its merit, however, is the stress placed on the reciprocal orientations of migrant and host community which avoids the indiscriminate use of terms like pluralism[12] for situations varying greatly in their nature and potential stability.

C: CONCLUSIONS

The final picture that emerges from this study of the British immigrant in South Africa is that of a group of men who, both in the past and today, are very little different from their fellow countrymen who chose to emigrate to Australia,[13] Canada, or New Zealand. They may

[10] For brief summaries see M. Freedman and W. E. Willmott, 'South-East Asia, with special reference to the Chinese' in *Research on Racial Relations* U.N.E.S.C.O. (1966), pp. 159–77; G. Delf, *Asians in East Africa* (1963). There are clear links between the uitlander and J. S. Furnivall's idea of a plural society in *Colonial Policy and Practice* (1948).

[11] Richmond's 'transilients' are a special type of uitlander.

[12] The most recent way of justifying discrimination and prejudice is through the concept of 'pluralism'. What was previously a measure of prejudice has now become an index of tolerance. Used indiscriminately this term is simply apartheid dressed up in liberal clothing, for it would be quite wrong to use the same criteria to judge the successful integration of immigrants from the West Indies as immigrants from Pakistan. For a related discussion see T. F. Pettigrew, 'Racially Separate or Together?' *Journal of Social Issues*, 25, no. 1 (1969), 43–69.

[13] Appleyard has captured the modest ambitions of the British immigrant in Australia in his phrase: 'these were not people who planned to build empires in the antipodes', (1964), op. cit., p. 213.

differ from a random cross-section of the British population—it would be surprising if they did not—but this is the result of their being immigrants, not a result of their being immigrants to South Africa. As far as the racial-political dimension is concerned, the situation is one of ignorance rather than one of calculation. This is not to claim that there is no selective factor in operation, but that the selection is a negative and not a positive one, and that in the racial sphere it is of entirely secondary importance, being confined mainly to the ex-colonial category. We are not witnessing the mass attraction of bigoted racialists to a segregationalist's dream, rather we are observing how ordinary people, confronted by a particular social structure, will tend to conform to the attitudes, values, and norms implicit in it.[14] As James Bryce perceptively observed:

Impunity corrupts the ordinary man . . . it needs something more than the virtue of a philosopher—it needs the tenderness of a saint, to preserve the same courtesy and respect towards the members of a backward race as are naturally extended to equals.[15]

The image held by some—one might call it the 'Hampstead image'[16] —of a group of jack-booted fascists marching off to their paradise under the sun, could not be further from the truth. The most distinctive feature of these immigrants is their *lack* of distinctiveness.

[14] While some may find this a depressing omen for the future, it does contain at least one ray of hope: if attitudes are flexible in one direction, they may be equally flexible in the other. What is required is the 'right' social structure, though how to achieve it is an altogether different question. However, perhaps we should heed Bryce's warning: 'You cannot argue with a fatalist any more than with a prophet . . . phrases such as "it was bound to happen" are the last refuge of despairing incompetence' (*Impressions of South Africa*, p. xxxviii).

[15] *Romanes Lecture* (1902) p. 40; I have considered Bryce's analysis of race relations in more detail in my paper, 'James Bryce and the Comparative Sociology of Race Relations in *Race*, 13, no. 2 (Jan. 1972) 315–28.

[16] For a recent portrait of the 'unromantic exiles' see *New Society*, 24 July 1969.

PART FIVE

Appendices

A Note on Methods, Terms, and Values

EVERY SOCIAL investigation poses its own unique problems of research design.[1] A study of immigrants raises all the difficulties of locating minority populations,[2] compounded with any special problems peculiar to social research in South Africa. The sample consisted of 514 adult British immigrants interviewed in the four major urban industrial areas of South Africa between September 1967 and August 1968. It was stratified according to seven 'length of residence' categories[3] which were selected partly to facilitate crucial comparisons, and partly because of the great difficulty in securing an unbiased, random sample of immigrants of several years' standing.

The files of the 1820 Memorial Settlers' Association were used as a basic sampling frame; for the most recent immigrants the Department of Immigration's records provided a full coverage, while the Association comes into contact with some 70 per cent[4] of total British immigration. The longest residence categories were supplemented by a number of immigrants randomly selected from the personnel lists of several firms, both large and small, and British- and South African-owned.

Great care was taken to minimize non-response; only three immigrants refused to be interviewed while 7 per cent were unable to be contacted owing to changed addresses. Repeated calls were made where necessary and some forwarding addresses were followed up in different areas of the country. Over 20,000 miles were covered in the course of the investigation.

It is difficult to estimate what biases these procedures inevitably involve: the Association's files probably include immigrants who are well integrated and 'problem' cases who are badly integrated. The representativeness of the sample almost certainly decreases with the length of residence, so that Taft's conclusion that assimilation studies 'under-represent both the highly assimilated and the completely unassimilated'[5] applies equally to this survey.

[1] For some good basic texts on research methods, see C. A. Moser, *Survey Methods in Social Investigation* (1958); A. N. Oppenheim, *Questionnaire Design and Attitude Measurement* (1966); J. Madge, *The Tools of Social Science* (1953); C. Sellitz, M. Jahoda, M. Deutsch, and L. S. Cook, *Research Methods in Social Relations* (1962); R. K. Merton, M. Fiske, and P. L. Kendall, *The Focused Interview* (1956).

[2] Cf. E. Krausz, 'Locating Minority Populations: a research problem', *Race*, 10, no. 3 (1969), 361–8.

[3] Above, pp. 157–9.

[4] At least to record their names and addresses.

[5] R. Taft, *From Stranger to Citizen* (1966), p. 27.

As far as the interview schedule is concerned, I have chosen a middle course which seemed most appropriate for an exploratory study of this nature. An attempt was made to steer between the two extremes: not to get lost in a maze of detailed case-study material,[6] while equally avoiding being drowned in a sea of statistics—'quantophrenia', to use Sorokin's evocative phrase.[7] In other words, I have employed a bastardized technique combining both anthropological insight and sociological rigour.[8] This immediately exposes one to the accusation, by devotees of both techniques,[9] of falling between two methodological stools. In fact, the two extremes form a continuum of research methodology, and it is for the researcher to fit the methodology to the problem, not to fit the problem to the methodology—no matter how much wrath one is likely to provoke from those who have spent a lifetime in developing techniques and ignoring problems.

Faced with a choice between a trivial methodological masterpiece—Durkheim's *Suicide* shows that the two are not synonymous—or a less rigorous, though intrinsically more interesting exploratory study, I have, decided to adopt the latter: to suggest new problems rather than provide definitive answers to all the old ones.

The extensive use of quotations in the empirical section is not equivalent to 'letting the immigrants speak for themselves'. It represents the author's subjective perception of their views. All that can be hoped is that sufficient insight and open-mindedness have been exercised in the selection and interpretation so as not to distort the picture out of all recognition—that it will be distorted in some measure is inevitable.

The interview itself is a social situation[10] and the interview style is all important. Sharing the same nationality,[11] and being placed in a temporary

[6] The *reductio ad absurdum* being Oscar Lewis's recent work, about which Dr. John Beattie has perceptively remarked: 'it is the art of photography rather than that of painting' (the camera, or rather the tape-recorder, may not lie, but what about the photographer?). Cf. also Zweig's casual, non-random approach ('dropping into the pub and chatting with the barmaid') which has similar pitfalls, being a somewhat cavalier dismissal of the tenets of probability sampling.

[7] P. Sorokin, *Fads and Foibles in Modern Sociology and Related Sciences* (1956).

[8] Cf. M. Banton, *Anthropological Perspectives in Sociology* (1964); for a balanced discussion of the use of quantitative methods in anthropology, see J. C. Mitchell, 'On Quantification in Social Anthropology' in A. L. Epstein (ed.), *The Craft of Social Anthropology* (1967), pp. 17–47.

[9] 'Methodocentrism' would form an interesting topic in the sociology of knowledge.

[10] G. E. Simpson and J. M. Yinger, 'The Sociology of Race and Ethnic Relations' in R. K. Merton, *et al.*, *Sociology Today* (1959), p. 383.

[11] Taft found that Dutch immigrants were more critical to a Dutch interviewer than to an Australian interviewer, (1966) op. cit., pp. 27–9. See also S. Biesheuvel, 'Methodology in the Study of Attitudes of Africans', *Journal of Social Psychology*, 47 (1958), 168–84.

immigrant situation myself allowed me to establish good 'rapport' without resort to quasi-theatrical subterfuge.[12] The atmosphere of the interview was one of 'friendly permissiveness',[13] suitable for a non-captive audience, and every encouragement was given to the qualification and expansion of replies. All the interviews were undertaken by me, which should produce consistency, though it may exaggerate any personal biases.

The coded data were analysed on the Science Research Council's Atlas computer at Chilton, using multiple variate counter (M.V.C.) compiler language. Most of the calculations—chi-squares and correlations—were computed mechanically according to standard formulae.[14]

The techniques adopted place heavy stress on my own personal biases, though there seems little point in a Myrdal confessional,[15] which is a psychologically naïve claim to self-insight—the ability to disengage oneself from Mannheim's paradox. Dollard has written perceptively about the researcher's motivation[16] (as one would expect of a social-psychologist), and Dahrendorf has discussed more general questions related to the classical problem of 'values and social science'.[17]

Certain terms used in the sociology of migration and race relations[18] have not been defined precisely, or have been used in different ways by different writers. In this study *assimilation* is taken as a general term to describe the process by which an immigrant merges both culturally and structurally into the host society—changes may take place in one direction or in both (i.e. the host society may change too). *Amalgamation* applies to the biological process of intermixing between immigrant and host society. *Acculturation* refers to the value or normative level, while *integration*, the term most applicable in the present case, denotes the fitting of an immigrant group into one section of the existing host society; it is the more appropriate, the more pluralistic the structure of the host society.[19]

Race is strictly speaking a biological concept (abstraction), though its use as a *social* category causes many experts to be very cautious in the

[12] e.g. Robb's pose as a barman (*Working Class Anti-Semite* (1954)).

[13] Moser (1958), pp. 204–5.

[14] G. Singh, *A Manual of the Multiple Variate Counter* (1968), p. 97. Cf. also, A. E. Maxwell, *Analysing Qualitative Data* (1961); H. C. Selvin, 'A Critique of Tests of Significance in Survey Research', *A.S.R.* 21 (1957) 519–27.

[15] *An American Dilemma* (1944), pp. 1035–64; P. Streeten (ed.), *Values in Social Theory* (1958); cf. J. Madge, *The Origins of Scientific Sociology* (1963) pp. 277–84.

[16] J. Dollard, *Caste and Class in a Southern Town* (1949), pp. 33–40.

[17] R. Dahrendorf, *Essays in Sociological Theory* (1968), pp. 1–18.

[18] For basic terms in the social sciences, see D. L. Sills (ed.), *International Encyclopedia of the Social Sciences* (1969), vols. 1–17; J. Gould and W. L. Kolb (eds.), *A Dictionary of the Social Sciences* (1964); and G. D. Mitchell (ed.), *A Dictionary of Sociology* (1968).

[19] See the various uses in: S. Patterson, *Dark Strangers: a study of West Indians in London* (1965), pp. 16–35; R. Taft, *From Stranger to Citizen* (1966), pp. 6–10; E. K. Rose *et al.*, *Colour and Citizenship* (1969), pp. 23–5.

manner in which it is employed. *Ethnicity* is probably a better generic term to include 'racial', cultural, national, linguistic, and religious differences which are frequently (and erroneously) ascribed to biological 'race'. *Prejudiced* attitudes and *discriminatory* behaviour, as well as the concept of *caste* in a non-Indian environment, have already been briefly discussed in the text.[20]

[20] Above, pp. 7–10 and 20, n. 36.

The Interview Schedule[1]

INTRODUCTORY REMARKS

I WOULD like to ask you a few questions about your experiences as an immigrant in South Africa. This is part of a study I am making of British immigrants in this country for the purposes of a degree at Oxford University. It is a purely academic study and all your answers will be treated in the strictest confidence, so please feel free to tell me whatever *you* feel with complete frankness. There are no 'correct' answers to the following questions, I just want to find out your opinions (or less formal paraphrase).

1. *Area of Residence in South Africa at time of interview.*

JOHANNESBURG	
CAPE TOWN	
PORT ELIZ./E.L.	
DURBAN	

2. *Sex of Adults.*

MALE	
FEMALE	

3. *When you emigrated, were you married, single, widowed, or divorced?*

MARRIED	
SINGLE	
WIDOWED	
DIVORCED	

[1] The question numbers missing were eliminated during the pre-test of the interview schedule.

S

4. *How old were you at that time?*

0 – 21	
22 – 31	
32 – 41	
42 – 51	
52 – 61	
62 +	

5. *How many dependent children did you have when you emigrated?*
6. *How long have you been living in South Africa since emigrating?*

LESS THAN 7 DAYS	
3 MONTHS	
12 MONTHS	
2 YEARS	
4 YEARS	
8 YEARS	
8 YEARS OR MORE	

7. *When you emigrated, was this your first visit to South Africa?*

YES	
NO	

    (b) **If NO**: *How many visits had you made to South Africa before emigrating?*
    (c) *What was the purpose of these visits?*
8. *What part of Britain were you living in before you emigrated?*
    (N.B. that is your last *permanent* address)
9. *For about how long were you seriously thinking about emigrating before you came to a firm decision?*
10. *Can you tell me how you arrived at your decision to emigrate and some of the factors which influenced you?*
11. *What reasons, then, made you decide to emigrate?*

	(H.) PUSH	PULL		(W.) PUSH	PULL
ECONOMIC					
SOCIAL					
POLITICAL (i)					
POLITICAL (ii)					
PERSONAL					
CLIMATIC					
TRAVEL					
OTHER					

12. *Which of these reasons was the most important?*
    (b) *Can you list the others in their order of importance?*
        (mark 1, 2, 3 . . . in boxes above)
13. *Was there any one particular event that finally made you take a firm decision?*

YES	
NO	

(b) If YES: *What was it?*

INFLUENCE (i)	
INFLUENCE (ii)	
DISCONTINUITIES	
DISTURBANCES (i)	
(ii)	
(iii)	
(iv)	
OTHER	

14. *Did you make inquiries about emigrating to any other countries apart from South Africa?*

YES	
NO	

(b) If YES: *Which countries?*

15. *Why did you choose to emigrate to South Africa in particular?*
16. *Did you have any relatives and/or friends living in South Africa before you emigrated?*

YES	
NO	

(b) If YES: *Were they:*

CLOSE FAMILY	
WIDER KIN (uncle, cousin etc)	
FRIENDS	

(c) *How much did they tell you about South Africa?*

A GREAT DEAL	
FAIR AMOUNT	
ONLY A LITTLE	
NOTHING	

17. *From what sources did you receive most of your information about South Africa before you emigrated?*

EMBASSY	
1820's	
SAMORGAN	
S. A. COMPANY	
VISIT	
BOOKS	
NEWSPAPERS	
RADIO/T.V.	
RELATIVES/FRIENDS IN U.K.	
RELATIVES/FRIENDS IN S. A.	

18. *Can you list these sources in their order of importance?*
(mark 1, 2, 3 . . . in boxes above)

19. *Before you emigrated how much would you say you knew about South Africa as a country?*

A GREAT DEAL	
FAIR AMOUNT	
ONLY A LITTLE	
VIRTUALLY NOTHING	

20. For example: (a) *Did you know the exact proportion of whites to non-whites in the population?*

YES	
NO	
UNSURE	

(b) *Could you name the Prime Minister at that time?*

YES	
NO	
UNSURE	

(c) *Did names like 'Van Riebeeck' or events like 'The Great Trek' mean anything specific to you at that time?*

YES	
NO	
UNSURE	

21. *In the light of your experience in South Africa so far, how near to your expectations have the following proved to be:*
    (a) *Your Economic situation?*
    (b) *Your Social Life?*
    (c) *The Political Situation?*

MUCH BETTER			
BETTER OR EQUAL			
SLIGHTLY BELOW			
MUCH BELOW			
NO EXPECTATIONS			

24. *Did you make use of the 1820 Settlers' Association or Samorgan when you emigrated?*

1820 (U.K. & S.A.)	
1820 (S.A. only)	
SAMORGAN	
NEITHER	

25. *Did you come on the South African government's assisted passage scheme?*

YES	
NO	
FIRM PAID	
N/A.	

    (b) **If YES:** *Would you have still come to South Africa at that time if you had had to pay all your own fares?*

YES	
NO	
EMIGRATED ELSEWHERE ·	
D. K.	

26. *What type of housing did you live in in Britain before emigrating?*

DETACHED	
SEMI	
TERRACED	
FLATS/ROOMS	
WITH PARENTS	
OTHER	

27. *What type of housing are you living in now?*

DETACHED	
BUNGALOW	
TERRACED	
FLAT / ROOMS	
HOTEL	
OTHER	

27. (b) *How does your present housing compare with what you were used to in Britain?*

MUCH BETTER	
BETTER	
SAME	
WORSE	
MUCH WORSE	

28. *Did you run a car in Britain?*

YES	
NO	
COMPANY CAR	
ACCESS TO CAR	

29. *Do you have a car now?*

30. *How easy have you found it (expect to find it) to make friends with South Africans compared with making friends in Britain?*

MUCH HARDER	
HARDER	
SAME	
EASIER	
MUCH EASIER	
D.K. etc.	

33. *In your own experience have you found any noticeable differences in this respect between English-speaking and Afrikaans-speaking South Africans?*

YES	
NO	
D.K.	

(b) If YES: *specify:*

E–S. MORE FRIENDLY	
A–S. MORE FRIENDLY	

35. *How much importance, if any, do you attach to conforming to the 'South African way of life?'*

VERY IMPORTANT	
FAIRLY IMPORTANT	
LITTLE IMPORTANCE	
NO WISH TO AT ALL	
OTHER	

36. *Can you tell me what you expected the Africans (Bantu/Native) to be like before you came to South Africa?*
37. *Have those views changed at all since you have been living in South Africa?*

YES	
NO	

(b) If YES: *In what ways?*

38. *What, if anything, did you feel about Coloured Immigration into Britain before you emigrated?*

VERY GOOD	
GOOD	
IRRELEVANT	
BAD	
VERY BAD	
OTHER	

39. *How do you feel the standard of South African education, as it affects your children, compares with education in Britain?*

MUCH BETTER	
BETTER	
SAME	
WORSE	
MUCH WORSE	
D. K. etc.	

41. *Have you (do you intend) made a serious attempt to learn Afrikaans?*
    (b) If YES: *specify:*

43. *What were your main leisure activities in Britain—the sort of things you used to do in the evenings and at week-ends?*
44. *Have these changed much as a result of living in South*
    (b) If YES: *In what sort of ways?*
45. *Do you miss television?*
    (b) *Would you like South Africa to have television?*
    (c) *In your opinion, why do you think South Africa does not have it?*

47. *How does South African radio compare with British radio?*
48. *What newspaper(s), if any, did you read in Britain?*
49. *How do South African newspapers compare with them?*
50. *Are you a member of any clubs or associations in South Africa?* (excluding trade unions, churches, or the 1820s)
    (b) If YES: *specify:*

51. *How active is your present social life compared to what it was like in Britain?*

MUCH MORE	
MORE	
SAME	
LESS	
MUCH LESS	
D. K.	

52. *Do you intend to become a South African citizen?*

YES I AM	
DEFINITELY INTEND	
UNSURE	
DEFINITELY NOT	

53. *What do you think of yourself now as primarily:*

BRITISH	
SOUTH AFRICAN	
EQUALLY BOTH	
OTHER	

56. *In 1961 South Africa became a Republic and left the Commonwealth. In your opinion was this a good, bad, or irrelevant event as far as South Africa was concerned?*

57. *How interested, if at all, were you in politics in Britain?*

ACTIVELY INTERESTED	
FAIRLY INTERESTED	
SLIGHTLY INTERESTED	
NOT INTERESTED AT ALL	
(ANTI–POLITICAL)	

58. *Before you emigrated, which British political party most nearly represented your views?*

59. *How interested, if at all are you in South African politics?*

ACTIVELY INTERESTED	
FAIRLY INTERESTED	
SLIGHTLY INTERESTED	
NOT INTERESTED AT ALL	
DELIBERATELY AVOID	

60. *Which South African political party most nearly represents your present views? (or, what are the names of the major South African political parties?)*

62. *What were your views about the policy of Apartheid before you emigrated? Would you say you were:*

STRONGLY IN FAVOUR	
FAVOURABLE	
INDIFFERENT	
UNFAVOURABLE	
STRONGLY AGAINST	
OTHER	

(b) *What are your present views?*

(c) *Do you see any alternative to Apartheid as a policy for South Africa in the near future?*

(d) If YES: *specify.*

65. *Were you a Church member in Britain?*

(b) *How often, if at all, did you attend church?*

REGULAR (once a week)	
OCCASIONAL (once a month)	
INFREQUENT	
NEVER	

66. *What is your religious denomination?*
67. *Of how much importance, if any, is religion in your life?*

VERY IMPORTANT	
QUITE IMPORTANT	
OF LITTLE IMPORTANCE	
NO IMPORTANCE AT ALL	

68. *How often, if at all, do you attend church in South Africa?*
69. *Are there any important differences between the churches in South Africa and the churches in Britain?*
    (b) If YES: *specify:*

70. *Some South African religious leaders have expressed strong views about South African society. Do you feel they have a right to do this?*
71. *What was your last* (full-time) *job before emigrating?*
72. *What is your present job?*
73. *What type of school did you go to?*

ELEMENTARY ONLY	
SECONDARY MODERN	
GRAMMAR	
PUBLIC	
UNIVERSITY	

   (b) *And any qualifications you may have?* (apprenticeship etc.)
74. *How do your working conditions compare with Britain?*

MUCH BETTER	
BETTER	
SAME	
WORSE	
MUCH WORSE	
OTHER	

   (b) (to housewife) *How does the housework compare with Britain?*
   (c) *Do you employ a servant?*
75. *Taking all things into consideration* (e.g. tax, overtime, fringe benefits, etc.) *how does your present standard of living compare with Britain?*

MUCH HIGHER	
HIGHER	
SAME	
LOWER	
MUCH LOWER	
D. K. etc.	

76. *How do your current earnings compare with what you were earning just before you emigrated?* (can you give a rough %?)
77. *How do overall prices, the cost of living, compare with Britain just before you emigrated?*
78. *How do you feel your own prospects and opportunities compare between the two countries?*

MUCH BETTER	
BETTER	
SAME	
WORSE	
MUCH WORSE	

79. *From your own experience, what do you feel the 'typical' South African fellow-worker/colleague thinks of British immigrants generally?*

VERY FRIENDLY	
FRIENDLY	
INDIFFERENT	
UNFRIENDLY	
VERY UNFRIENDLY	
OTHER	

80. *If you had to describe the main characteristics of 'typical'* (i.e. not the best nor the worst you have known) *members of the following groups, what sort of things would you mention?*
    (a) *Afrikaners?*
    (b) *Jewish South Africans?*
    (c) *Africans* (Bantu)*?*
    (d) *Coloureds?*
    (e) *Indian South Africans?*
84. *Were you a member of a trade union in Britain?*
    (b) *What did you think of trade unions in Britain?*

VERY GOOD THING	
GOOD	
IRRELEVANT	
BAD	
VERY BAD	

85. *Are you a member of a trade union in South Africa?*
   (b) *What do you think of South African trade unions?*
86. *Do you think there are any important differences between trade unions in the two countries?*
   (b) *If YES: specify:*
87. *Do you think non-Europeans should be encouraged to join trade unions in South Africa?*
88. *In your own experience, how class-conscious have you found South Africa to be compared with Britain?*

MUCH MORE	
MORE	
SAME	
LESS	
MUCH LESS	
OTHER	

   (b) *Can you mention any examples of this?*
89. *Do you feel your own class position has changed from what it was in Britain?*
   (b) *If YES: in what direction?*

MUCH HIGHER	
HIGHER	

LOWER	
MUCH LOWER	

90. *Has moving to South Africa affected your children's opportunities?*
   (b) *If YES: specify:*

MUCH BETTER	
BETTER	
WORSE	
MUCH WORSE	

92. *Do you think South Africa will change radically in the next 20 years?*
   (b) *If YES: in what sort of ways?*

94. *If you could have your choice over again, with your present knowledge, would you still come to South Africa?*

95. *Would you recommend South Africa to a friend in Britain thinking of emigrating?*

96. *What has been your greatest single problem in trying to settle down?*

97. *If you had to return to Britain, what would you most dislike about it now?*

98. *How would you assess your present attitude to life in South Africa?*

99. *Do you intend to stay in South Africa permanently?*
    (b) If not: *what are your future plans?*

100. *Is there anything else you would like to tell me about your experiences in South Africa?*

Case Studies and Samples

a A FACTORY CASE STUDY

THE PHYSICAL contrasts between the 'dark satanic mills' of industrial Lancashire and a bright new factory in the rolling countryside of the Eastern Cape Province are sharp indeed; so are the social contrasts. In 1963, as one factory closed down in Britain another, using the same capital equipment, opened up in South Africa. Under the scheme eighty-seven artisan families emigrated, and although the majority did not come from the original factory, most came from Lancashire.

This situation presented an interesting case study of the British migrant in South Africa but there were too many special features for it to be confidently regarded as typical. The factory was visited nearly five years after its opening and a small number of the employees were interviewed. On all the basic characteristics they did not seem to differ markedly from the immigrants in the main sample. Some 24 per cent of the original immigrants had returned to Britain within the first five years—the firm did not hold the five-year contracts as binding—and, according to the personnel manager, most of these had been motivated by problems of a social-personal nature. Some of the artisans, however, expressed dissatisfaction over cash and working hours. All immigrants appeared to have found no trouble in adjusting to the political and race relations situation.

b A CASE STUDY OF RETURNING MIGRANTS

The problem of estimating the number of immigrants who return to Britain has already been considered, and I have ventured a range of between 10 per cent and 20 per cent as a probable level.[1] It is very difficult to secure a random sample of returnees,[2] but the opportunity of interviewing a small

[1] Calculating on the Australian figures for 1959–68, an average return rate of 10 per cent is found. *Australian Immigration: consolidated statistics* No. 2., Dept. of Immigration, Canberra (1968). This is fractionally lower than earlier estimates (Taft (1966), op. cit., p. 26). Neither Canada nor New Zealand records the number of returning immigrants. The South African return rate is probably somewhat higher than the Australian rate because of the relative ease of returning (it is cheaper and there are no two-year contracts) but, by the same token, the re-return rate is probably higher too.

[2] Cf. Appleyard's technique of contacting re-registrants for National Insurance in *Determinants of Return Migration—A Socio-economic Study of United Kingdom Migrants who Returned from Australia, Economic Record*, vol. 38 no. 83 (1962) pp. 352–68; 'The Return Movement of United Kingdom Migrants from Australia', *Population Studies*, XV, no. 3 (1962), 214–25; A. H. Richmond, *Post-war Immigrants in Canada* (1967), pp. 229–52.

sample of such immigrants travelling back to Britain on the *Edinburgh Castle* in September 1968 threw a little extra light on the subject. To select one boat, on one particular route, at one particular time, involves many biases, as does the small size of the sample—twenty-eight adults—but for lack of other evidence it is worth quoting as additional exploratory data on the problem.

The greatest stress was on social discontent—inability to settle, lack of entertainment, and homesickness—and the language problem. There was also considerable economic dissatisfaction, and while a few were strongly anti-Apartheid this was never found to be the sole reason for leaving. The average length of residence in South Africa was three and a half years.

C THE LONDON PRE-TEST SAMPLE

A sample of 447 British immigrants (heads of households, representing 1,226 individuals) was randomly selected from the files of the London Office of the 1820 Memorial Settlers' Association for the years 1963-6. Because of the paucity of official statistics and their unhelpful aggregation for my purposes, this pre-test sample was of great value in providing the initial orientation of the study. It supplied basic information about a group of immigrants, all of whom had sailed for South Africa, although the sampling frame was somewhat less representative than that based on the Association's South African files which cover a much larger percentage of total immigration.

As was the case with the main sample, there was no evidence of systematic recruitment from certain types of regions in Britain, while the destinations shown in Table 2 (p. 151) reveal a bias towards the coastal locations of Cape Town and Durban, underestimating the numbers that finally go to Johannesburg. 71 per cent of these immigrants were married at the time of filling in the application forms; 64 per cent were concentrated between the ages of 21–41; one third had no children accompanying them, 20 per cent had three or more children. Almost half (49 per cent) had incomes in the £10–20 per week range; a further 27 per cent were in the £20–40 bracket. Similarly, capital was bunched into two groups: 34 per cent had less than £500, 33 per cent possessed between £500 and £5,000 (a few had considerable sums of up to £25,000 but there was a large gap in the information—27 per cent). 60 per cent of the sample could be classified as artisans, 41 per cent had served apprenticeships, and 37 per cent were trade union members. 63 per cent had attended secondary modern schools or their equivalent, 3 per cent elementary schools, 15 per cent grammar schools, and 4 per cent public schools.

Migrant Statistics

U.K. Immigrants to South Africa and Emigrants for the years 1924–70

Year	Total immigrants	Total emigrants	Immigrants from U.K.	Emigrants to U.K.	Net gain from U.K.	Net total gain
1924	5,265	5,857	3,755	2,770	+985	−592
1925	5,428	4,483	3,704	1,997	+1,707	+945
1926	6,575	3,799	3,817	1,455	+2,362	+2,776
1927	6,598	3,988	3,324	963	+2,361	+2,610
1928	7,050	4,127	3,263	802	+2,461	+2,923
1929	7,895	3,597	3,093	674	+2,419	+4,298
1930	5,904	4,623	2,477	932	+1,545	+1,281
1931	4,140	2,697	1,976	952	+1,024	+1,443
1932	3,098	2,339	1,169	1,264	−95	+759
1933	3,031	1,829	1,235	777	+458	+1,202
1934	4,702	1,767	2,052	696	+1,356	+2,935
1935	6,500	1,865	2,954	681	+2,273	+4,635
1936	10,840	2,716	3,119	887	+2,232	+8,124
1937	7,927	3,716	3,767	832	+2,935	+4,211
1938	7,435	4,022	4,035	869	+3,166	+3,413
1939	6,304	3,650	3,224	710	+2,514	+2,654
1940	3,021	2,284	1,968	160	+1,808	+737
1941	1,509	1,702	882	77	+805	−193
1942	1,665	1,839	643	178	+465	−174
1943	896	2,153	370	147	+223	−1,257
1944	953	2,441	312	335	−23	−1,488
1945	2,329	4,818	1,265	1,518	−253	−2,489
1946	11,256	9,045	7,470	2,396	+5,074	+2,211
1947	28,839	7,917	20,596	1,386	+19,210	+20,922
1948	35,631	7,534	25,502	739	+24,763	+28,097
1949	14,780	9,206	9,655	1,057	+8,598	+5,572
1950	12,803	14,644	5,097	1,906	+3,191	−1,841
1951	15,243	15,382	5,903	1,259	+4,644	−139
1952	18,473	9,775	6,942	1,033	+5,909	+8,698
1953	16,257	10,220	5,416	1,617	+3,799	+6,037
1954	16,416	11,336	4,629	1,715	+2,914	+5,080
1955	16,199	12,515	4,444	1,763	+2,681	+3,684
1956	14,917	12,879	4,474	1,515	+2,959	+2,038
1957	14,615	10,943	4,723	1,242	+3,481	+3,672
1958	14,673	8,807	4,450	1,481	+2,969	+5,866
1959	12,563	9,378	3,782	2,119	+1,663	+3,185
1960	9,789	12,612	2,292	4,166	−1,874	−2,823
1961	16,309	14,903	2,323	5,073	−2,750	+1,406
1962	20,916	8,945	4,968	2,783	+2,185	+11,971

Year	Total immigrants	Total emigrants	Immigrants from U.K.	Emigrants to U.K.	Net gain (1963–'50) from U.K.	Net total gain
1963	37,964	7,156	10,135	1,860	+8,275	+30,808
1964	40,865	8,092	12,807	2,385	+10,422	+32,773
1965	38,326	9,206	12,012	2,535	+9,477	+29,120
1966	41,920	9,888	13,130	3,338	+9,792	+32,032
1967	32,487	10,737	12,993	3,232	+9,661	+21,750
1968	40,548	10,589	16,044	3,144	+12,900	+29,959
1969	41,446	9,018	19,000	3,100	+15,900	+32,428
1970	41,523	9,154	21,323	3,041	+18,282	+32,369

(Sources: Annual Reports on Statistics of Migration (1927–48) (UG38–'29 to UG19–'50); Official Year Books of the Union; State of South Africa Year Books; Bulletins of Statistics, Bureau of Statistics, Pretoria, vol. 1, no. 1 +; Immigration Attaché, South Africa House, London.)

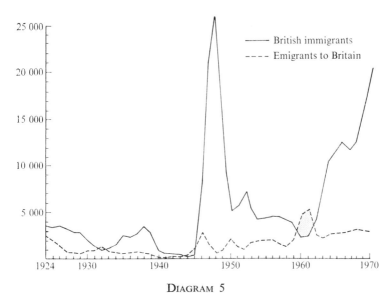

DIAGRAM 5

U.K.–South Africa Immigrants and Emigrants: 1924–70

T

Chronology of Dates particularly relevant to British Immigration to South Africa

1579	Thomas Stevens rounds the 'evill shore' of Cape 'Das Agulias'.
1580	Sir Francis Drake passes the 'fairest Cape' in the whole circumference of the Earth.
1615	Captain Crosse's band of convicts land in Table Bay.
1620	Shillinge and Fitzherbert claim the Cape for the British Crown.
1652	Van Riebeeck establishes a Dutch settlement at the Cape.
1690–1700	Captain Rogers finds the natives of Natal 'extraordinary civil to strangers'.
1795–1803	First British occupation of the Cape.
1806	Second British occupation of the Cape.
1808	Colonel Collins proposes immigrant settlement on west bank of the Great Fish river.
1813	Lt.-Col. John Graham's scheme for settling Highlanders in the Eastern Province is refused official permission.
1817	Benjamin Moodie and his apprentices sail from Leith.
1819	Fifth 'Kaffir' War; Parliament grants £50,000 for Albany settlement.
1820	Arrival of the 1820 Settlers.
1824	Farewell and Fynn establish first permanent settlement in Natal.
1832	More settlers arrive in Natal.
1836	The Great Trek
1840	Public petitions in Cape Town and Grahamstown urging the encouragement of immigration.
1843	Natal proclaimed a British Colony.
1846–7	Sir Harry Smith proposes 'military villages'.
1847	East London founded.
1849–52	Byrne Settlers in Natal.
1849	*Neptune* convict ship meets hostile reception.
1857	Sir George Grey encourages immigration.
1863–73	British immigration virtually ceases.
1867	Diamonds discovered at Hopetown.
1869	Diamonds discovered near Kimberley.
1872	Responsible Government granted to the Cape Colony.

1873–83	Arrival of over 22,000 assisted immigrants attracted by the railways and the mineral discoveries.
1877	British annex the Transvaal.
1879–80	Immigration reaches a peak in Natal.
1880	The First Anglo-Boer War.
1884	Good discovered on the Witwatersrand.
1886	Foundation of Johannesburg.
1890–8	Heavy migration to the goldfields; conflicts between the Uitlanders and the Afrikaners of Kruger's Republic.
1899–1902	Second Anglo-Boer War.
1905	Milner introduces Chinese coolies to work the Rand goldmines.
1906–10	Slump in immigration figures associated with the post-war economic depression.
1909	The South Africa Act passed by the Imperial Parliament.
1914–18	First World War: immigration falls from an annual flow of 10,000 to barely 1,500.
1917–23	Sir Percy FitzPatrick's Sundays River Valley Settlement scheme.
1920	Post-war immigration peak. Foundation of the 1820 Memorial Settlers' Association.
1922	The Rand Revolt.
1924	Hertzog–Creswell Pact Government.
1930	Quota Act of Dr. Malan aimed at Jewish immigration.
1932–3	Lowest immigration point during the depths of the Great Depression.
1936	The Representation of Natives Act.
1937	Aliens Act aimed largely at the Jews.
1939–45	Second World War.
1946–8	Post-war rise in immigration to record levels.
1947	India achieves Independence.
1948	Election victory of Dr. Malan's Nationalist Party pledged to the policy of Apartheid.
1949	Dr. Donges's 'Citizenship' Act; sharp drop in British immigration figures.
1950–60	Consistently low level of British immigration.
1955	Senate Act passed.
1957	Ghana becomes first independent 'black' African State in the Commonwealth.
1960	Sharpeville shootings. Net loss of immigrants to Britain.
1961	South Africa becomes a Republic outside the Commonwealth. Introduction of an assisted-passage scheme, establishment of Department of Immigration.
1963	Mixed loan and grant converted into an outright grant. Total net immigration exceeds post-war records.
1965	Rhodesia declares U.D.I.

1968   British immigration reaches highest peak since 1948.
1969   Completion of first major study of British immigrants in South
            Africa.
1970   150th Anniversary of the first major British settlement in South
            Africa. Immigration remains at record levels. Arrival of the
            100,000th British immigrant under the auspices of the 1820
            Memorial Settlers' Association.

Select Bibliography

Since this book is concerned with several different fields of study, including sociology, South African history, and race relations, any bibliography must necessarily be selective. Only those works that are particularly relevant or useful have been included.

UNPUBLISHED SOURCES:

The unpublished memoranda, files, minute books, and letters of the 1820 Memorial Settlers' Association are referred to in the footnotes of the historical section. They have not been classified systematically.

Many pamphlets and other relevant historical material may be found in: The South African Public Library, Cape Town; The Jagger Library, University of Cape Town; Port Elizabeth Public Library; The Public and University Libraries in Durban; The Strange Library, Johannesburg; Witwatersrand University Library; and the Rhodes House Library, Oxford.

BOOKS, ARTICLES AND THESES:

ABRAMS, P., AND LITTLE, A., 'The Young Voter in British Politics, *B.J.S.* 16, no. 2 (1965), 95–110.

ADAM, H., AND K. (eds.), *South Africa; sociological perspectives*, essays on aspects of the basic racial situation (Oxford University Press, London, 1971).

ADORNO, T. W., FRENKEL-BRUNSWICK, E., LEVINSON, D. J., AND SANFORD, R. N., *The Authoritarian Personality* (Harper, New York, 1950).

AGAR-HAMILTON, J. A. I., *The Native Policy of the Voortrekkers* (Maskew Miller, Cape Town, 1928).

AKITT, H., 'Government Assisted Immigration into Natal: 1857–62' (unpublished M.A. Thesis, University of Natal, P.M.B., 1952).

ALLPORT, G. W., 'Prejudice: A Problem in Psychological and Social Causation' in Parsons, T., and Shils, E. (eds.), *Towards a General Theory of Action* (Harper & Row, New York, 1962), pp. 365–87.

—— *The Nature of Prejudice* (Doubleday Anchor, New York, 1958).

—— *Personality and Social Encounter* (Beacon, Boston, 1960).

ALMOND, G. A., AND COLEMAN, J. S., *The Politics of Developing Areas* (Princeton University Press, Princeton, 1960).

—— AND VERBA, S., *The Civic Culture: Political Attitudes and Democracy in Five Nations* (Princeton University Press, Princeton, 1963).

ANDERSON, P. AND BLACKBURN, R., *Towards Socialism* (Fontana, London, 1965).

T 2

ANDRESKI, S., *Elements of Comparative Sociology* (Weidenfeld & Nicolson, London, 1964).

ANONYMOUS, *An Account of the Colony of the Cape of Good Hope with a view to the information of emigrants* (pamphlet in Port Elizabeth Public Library).

—— *Consideration of the means of affording profitable employment to the redundant population of Great Britain and Ireland* (London, 1818. Pamphlet in Rhodes House Library, Oxford).

—— *To the Transvaal Goldfields and Back: being a four months tour in South Africa* (Townshend & Son, Cape Town, 1885).

ANTONOVSKY, A., 'The Social Meaning of Discrimination' in Rosenberg, B., Gerver, I., and Howton, F. W., *Mass Society in Crisis* (Macmillan, New York, 1964), pp. 408–25.

APPLEYARD, R. T., 'Determinants of Return Migration', *Economic Record*, 38, no. 83 (1962), 352–68.

—— 'The Return Movement of U.K. Migrants from Australia', *Population Studies*, 15, no. 3 (1962), 214–25.

—— *British Emigration to Australia* (Weidenfeld & Nicolson, London, 1964).

APTER, D. E., *Ideology and Discontent* (Free Press, New York, 1964).

—— *The Politics of Modernization* (University Press, Chicago, 1967).

AUSTIN, D., *Britain and South Africa* (Oxford University Press, London, 1966).

—— 'White Power?', *Journal of Commonwealth Political Studies*, VI, no. 2 (July 1968), 95–106.

BAGLEY, C., 'Relative Deprivation and the Working Class Racialist', *I.R.R. Newsletter*, 2, no. 5 (1968), 223–7.

BALL, H. V., SIMPSON, G. E., AND IKEDA, K., 'Law and Social Change: Summer Reconsidered', *A.J.S.* (1962), 532–40.

BALLINGER, M., *From Union to Apartheid, A Trek to Isolation* (Bailey Brothers & Swinfen, Folkestone, 1969).

BANTON, M., *The Coloured Quarter* (Cape, London, 1955).

—— *White and Coloured: the behaviour of British people towards coloured immigrants* (Cape, London, 1959).

—— 'Sociology and Race Relations', *Race*, 1, no. 1 (1959), 3–15.

—— 'Anthropological Perspectives in Sociology', *B.J.S.*, 15, no. 2 (1964), 95–112.

—— 'Race as a Social Category', *Race*, 8, no. 1 (1966), 7–14.

—— *Race Relations* (Tavistock, London, 1967).

—— 'Integration into what Society?', *New Society* (9 Nov. 1967).

—— 'What do we Mean by Racism?', *New Society* (10 Apr. 1969). Based on 'Racism and Racialism', paper delivered to the British Sociological Association, 28 Mar. 1969.

BARNARD, LADY ANNE, *South Africa a Century Ago* (Maskew Miller, Cape Town, 2nd edn. 1924).

BEATTIE, J., *Other Cultures* (Routledge, London, 1966).

BELL, D. (ed.), *The Radical Right* (Doubleday Anchor, New York, 1964 edn.).

BENDIX, R., *Work and Authority in Industry: ideologies of management in the course of industrialization* (Harper & Row, New York, 1963).

—— *Max Weber: An Intellectual Portrait* (Methuen, London, 1966).

—— 'Concepts and Generalizations in Comparative Sociological Studies', *A.S.R.* 28, no. 4 (1963), 532–9.

—— *Nation Building and Citizenship*, (Wiley, New York, 1964).

—— AND LIPSET, S. M., *Class, Status and Power* (Free Press, New York, 1953; 2nd. edn. Routledge, London, 1967).

BENNETT, G., *The Concept of Empire, from Burke to Attlee* (A. & C. Black, London, 1953; 2nd edn. 1962).

BENSON, M., *The African Patriots* (Faber, London, 1963).

BERLIN, I., *Karl Marx* (Oxford University Press, London, 1963).

—— 'Historical Inevitability', reprinted in *Four Essays on Liberty* (Oxford University Press, London, 1969), pp. 41–117.

BETEILLE, A. (ed.), *Social Inequality: selected readings* (Penguin, Harmondsworth, 1969).

BETTELHEIM, B., AND JANOWITZ, M., *Social Change and Prejudice* (Free Press, New York, 1964).

BIERSTEDT, R., 'Toynbee and Sociology', *B.J.S.* (1959), 95–104.

BIESANZ, J., 'Race Relations in the Canal Zone', *Phylon*, 2 (1950), 23–30.

—— AND SMITH, L. M., 'Race Relations in Panama and the Canal Zone', *A.J.S.*, 62 (1951), 7–14.

BIESHEUVEL, S., 'Methodology in the study of Attitudes of Africans', *Journal of Social Psychology*, 47 (1958), 168–84.

BIRD, J., *The Annals of Natal* (Struik, Cape Town, 1888), vol. I (2 vols.).

BIRD, W. W., *The State of the Cape of Good Hope in 1822* (Struik, Cape Town, 1966).

BIRLEY, R., 'African Education in South Africa', *African Affairs*, 67, no. 267 (1968), 152–8.

BLALOCK, H. M., 'A Power Analysis of Racial Discrimination', *Social Forces*, 39 (1960), 53–9.

—— *Toward a Theory of Minority Group Relations* (Wiley, New York, 1967).

BLUMER, H., 'Industrialization and Race Relations' in Hunter, G. (ed.), *Industrialization and Race Relations* (Oxford University Press, London, 1965), pp. 220–53.

BOGARDUS, E. S., *Immigration and Race Attitudes* (D. C. Heath, Boston, 1928).

BOND, J., *They were South Africans* (Oxford University Press, Cape Town, 1956).

BORRIE, W. D., *The Cultural Integration of Immigrants* (U.N.E.S.C.O., Paris, 1959).

BOTT, E., *Family and Social Network* (Tavistock, London, 1957).

284 SELECT BIBLIOGRAPHY

BOTTOMORE, T. B., *Elites and Society* (C. A. Watts, London, 1964).
—— *Classes in Modern Society* (Allen & Unwin, London, 1965).
BOWKER, J. M., *Speeches, letters and selections* (Godlonton & Richards, Grahamstown, 1864).
BOXER, C. R., *Race Relations in the Portuguese Colonial Empire, 1415–1825* (Clarendon Press, Oxford, 1963).
BRETT, E. A., *African Attitudes: A Study of the Social, Racial, and Political Attitudes of Some Middle-Class Africans* (S.A.I.R.R., Johannesburg, 1963).
BRINTON, C., *The Anatomy of Revolution* (Vintage Books, New York, 1958).
BROGAN, H. (ed.), introduction to de Tocqueville's *The Ancien Regime and the French Revolution* (Collins, London, 1966), pp. 7–22.
BROOKES, E. H., *The History of Native Policy in South Africa* (Nasionale Pers, Cape Town, 1927).
—— *Apartheid: a documentary study of modern South Africa* (Routledge, London, 1968).
—— AND MACAULAY, J. B., *Civil Liberties in South Africa* (Oxford University Press, Cape Town, 1958).
—— AND WEBB, C. DE B., *A History of Natal* (Natal University Press, Pietermaritzburg, 1965).
BROWN, D., *Against the World: a study of White South African Attitudes* (Collins, London, 1966).
BROWN, W. O., *Race Relations in the American South and in South Africa* (University Press, Boston, 1959).
—— 'Race consciousness among South African Natives', *A.J.S.* 40 (1935), 569–81.
BRYCE, J., *Impressions of South Africa* (Macmillan, London, 1900 edn.).
—— *The American Commonwealth* (Macmillan, New York, 1928 edn.).
—— 'The Relations of the Advanced and the Backward Races of Mankind' (Romanes Lecture, Clarendon Press, Oxford, 1902).
BURGIN, T., AND EDSON, P., *Spring Grove: the Education of Immigrant Children* (I.R.R., Oxford University Press, London, 1967).
BURNEY, E., *Housing on Trial* (I.R.R., Oxford University Press, 1967).
BURNS, T., AND SAUL, S. B. (eds.), *Social Theory and Economic Change* (Tavistock, London, 1967).
BURROWS, H. E., *The Moodies of Melsetter* (A. A. Balkema, Cape Town/Amsterdam, 1954).
BUTLER, D. E., AND KING, A., *The British General Election of 1964* (Macmillan, London, 1965).
—— *The British General Election of 1966* (Macmillan, London, 1966).
BUTLER, G., *A Book of South African Verse* (Oxford University Press, London, 1959).
—— 'The Cultural and Political Future of English-speaking South Africa', *New Nation* (Feb. 1968).

BUTTERWORTH, E., 'The Presence of Immigrant Schoolchildren: a study of Leeds', *Race*, 8, no. 3 (1967), 247–62.

CAHNMAN, W. J., AND BOSKOFF, A. (eds.), *Sociology and History* (Free Press, New York, 1964).

CALLEY, M. J. C., *God's People* (I.R.R., Oxford University Press, London, 1965).

CALPIN, G. H., *There are no South Africans* (Nelson, London, 1946).

Campaign Against Racial Discrimination, Memorandum of Evidence presented to the Royal Commission on Trade Unions and Employers' Association (1967).

CAMPBELL, A., CONVERSE, P. E., MILLER, W. E., AND STOKES, D. E., *The American Voter* (Wiley, New York, 1960).

CAMPBELL, E. Q., 'Moral Discomfort and Racial Segregation: an Example of the Myrdal Hypothesis', *Social Forces*, 39, no. 3 (1961), 228–34.

—— AND PETTIGREW, T. F., 'Racial and Moral Crisis: The Role of Little Rock Ministers', *A.J.S.* 64, no. 5 (1959), 509–16.

—— AND PETTIGREW, T. F., *Christians in Racial Crisis: a Study of Little Rock's Ministry* (Public Affairs Press, Washington, 1959).

CAREY, A. T., *Colonial Students* (Secker & Warburg, London, 1956).

CARMICHAEL, S., AND HAMILTON, C. V., *Black Power: The Politics of Liberation in America* (Penguin, Harmondsworth, 1969).

Carnegie Commission on the Poor White Problem in South Africa (Pro Ecclesia Drukkery, Stellenbosch, 1932).

CARR, E. H., *What is History?* (Penguin, Harmondsworth, 1964).

CARTER, G. M., *The Politics of Inequality: South Africa since 1948* (Praeger, New York, 1958).

—— KARIS, T., AND STULTZ, N. W., *South Africa's Transkei: the Politics of Domestic Colonialism* (Heinemann, London, 1967).

CHASE, J. C., *The Cape of Good Hope and the Eastern Province of Algoa Bay* (1843. Facsimile copy, Struik, Cape Town, 1967).

CHOMSKY, N., *American Power and the New Mandarins* (Penguin, Harmondsworth, 1969).

CHRISTIE, R., AND JAHODA, M. (eds.), *Studies in the Scope and Method of the 'Authoritarian Personality'* (Free Press, New York, 1954).

COHEN, B., AND JENNER, P., 'The Employment of Immigrants: a case study within the wool industry', *Race*, 10, no. 1 (1968), 41–55.

COHEN, P. S., 'Social Attitudes and Sociological Enquiry', *B.J.S.* 17, no. 4 (1966), 341–52.

—— *Modern Social Theory* (Heinemann, London, 1968).

CONVERSE, P. E., 'The Nature of Belief Systems in Mass Publics' in Apter, D. E., *Ideology and Discontent* (Free Press, New York, 1964).

COPE, J., *King of the Hottentots* (Howard Timmins, Cape Town, 1967).

CORY, G. E., *The Rise of South Africa* (Longmans, London 1913), vol. 2 (6 vols).

CORTIS, L. E., 'A Comparative Study in Attitudes of Bantu and European Workers', *Psychologia Africana*, 9 (1962), 148–67.

COSER, L. A., AND ROSENBERG, B., *Sociological Theory: a book of readings* (Collier-Macmillan, New York, 1964).

COTGROVE, S., *The Science of Society* (Allen & Unwin, London, 1967).

COX, O. C., *Caste, Class and Race: a study in social dynamics* (Doubleday, New York, 1948).

CRICK, B., *In Defence of Politics*, (Penguin, Harmondsworth, 1964).

CRIJNS, A. G. J., *Race Relations and Race Attitudes in South Africa* (Janssen, Nymegen, 1959).

CRISP, R., *The Outlanders: the men who made Johannesburg* (Peter Davies, London, 1964).

CROWDER, M., *Senegal: a study in French assimilation policy* (Methuen London, rev. edn. 1967).

DAHL, R. A., 'A Critique of the Ruling Elite Model', *American Political Science Review*, LII (1958), 463–9.

—— *Who Governs? Democracy and Power in an American City* (Yale University Press, New Haven, 1961).

DAHRENDORF, R., 'Out of Utopia: Toward a Re-orientation of Sociological Analysis', *A.J.S.* 64 (1958), 115–27.

—— *Class and Class Conflict in Industrial Society* (Routledge, London, 1959).

—— *Essays in Sociological Theory* (Routledge, London, 1968).

DANIEL, W. W., *Racial Discrimination in England* (Penguin, Harmondsworth, 1968).

DANZIGER, K., 'Ideology and Utopia in South Africa: A Methodological contribution to the sociology of knowledge', *B.J.S.* 14 (1963), 59–76.

DAVENPORT, T. R. H., *The Afrikaner Bond: The History of a South African Political Party 1880–1911* (Oxford University Press, Cape Town, 1966).

—— 'African Townsmen? South African Natives (Urban Areas) legislation through the years', *African Affairs*, 68, no. 271 (1969), 95–109.

DAVIES, I., *African Trade Unions* (Penguin, Harmondsworth, 1966).

DAVIES, J. C., 'Towards a Theory of Revolution', *A.S.R.* 6, no. 1 (1962), 5–19.

DAVISON, R. B., *Commonwealth Immigrants* (I.R.R., Oxford University Press, London, 1964).

—— *Black British: Immigrants to England* (I.R.R., Oxford University Press, London, 1966).

DEAKIN, N. (ed.), *Colour and the British Electorate 1964* (Pall Mall, London, 1965).

—— 'Race, the Politicians and Public Opinion: a preliminary study' (mimeo paper to B.S.A. conference, Mar. 1969).

—— LAWRENCE, D., SILVEY, J., AND LELOHE, M. J., 'Colour and the 1966 General Election', *Race*, 8, no. 1 (1966), 17–42.

DEIGHTON, H. S., 'History and the Study of Race Relations', *Race*, 1, no. 1 (1959), 16–25.

DE KIEWET, C. W., *A History of South Africa: Social and Economic* (Clarendon Press, Oxford, 1941).

DELF, G., *Asians in East Africa* (I.R.R., Oxford University Press, London, 1963).

DEMERATH, N. J., AND PETERSON, R. A., *System, Change and Conflict* (Free Press, New York, 1967).

DESAI, R., *Indian Immigrants in Britain* (I.R.R., Oxford University Press, London, 1963).

DEUTSCH, M., AND COLLINS, M. E., *Interracial Housing* (University of Minnesota Press, Minneapolis, 1951).

DICKIE-CLARKE, H. F., *The Marginal Situation: a Sociological Study of a Coloured Group* (Routledge, London, 1966).

DOLLARD, J., *Caste and Class in a Southern Town* (Yale University Press, New Haven, 1937).

DONALDSON, G., *The Scots Overseas* (Hale, London, 1966).

DOUGHTY, O., *Early Diamond Days* (Longmans, London, 1963).

DOUGLAS, J. W. B., *The Home and The School* (MacGibbon & Kee, London, 1964).

DOXEY, G. V., *The Industrial Colour Bar in South Africa* (Oxford University Press, Cape Town, 1961).

DUFF GORDON, LADY, *Letters from the Cape* (Humphrey Milford, London, 1921).

DUGMORE, H. H., *The Reminiscences of an Albany Settler* (Richards, Glanville & Co., Grahamstown, 1871).

DU PLESSIS, A. P., *Die Nederlandse Emigrasie na Suid-Afrika* (Teerhuis & Klinkenberg, Amsterdam, 1956).

DURKHEIM, E., *The Rules of Sociological Method* (Free Press, New York, 1950).

—— *Suicide: a Study in Sociology* (Free Press, New York, 1951).

EASTON, D., 'An Approach to the Analysis of Political Systems', *World Politics*, 9, no. 3 (1957), 383–400.

EDWARDS, I. E., *The 1820 Settlers in South Africa* (Longmans, London, 1934).

ESSIEN-UDOM, E. U., *Black Nationalism: the rise of the Black Muslims in the U.S.A.* (Penguin, Harmondsworth, 1966).

EISENSTADT, S. N., *The Absorption of Immigrants* (Routledge, London, 1954).

—— *The Political Systems of Empires* (Free Press, New York, 1963).

—— *Modernization, Protest and Change* (Prentice-Hall, New Jersey, 1966).

EVANS-PRITCHARD, E. E., *The Sanusi of Cyrenaica* (Clarendon Press, Oxford, 1949).

—— *Essays in Social Anthropology* (Faber, London, 1962).

EYBERS, G. W., *Select Constitutional Documents illustrating South African History 1795–1910* (Routledge, London, 1918).

FAIRBRIDGE, D., *Lady Anne Barnard at the Cape of Good Hope 1797–1802* (Oxford University Press, London, 1924).

FEIT, E., *South Africa—The Dynamics of the African National Congress* (I.R.R., Oxford University Press, London, 1962).

—— 'Community in a Quandary: the South African Jewish Community and Apartheid', *Race*, 8, no. 4 (1967), 395–408.

FIGUEROA, P. M. E., 'West Indian School Leavers in London—Prospects and Prejudice' (mimeo paper to B.S.A. education group, 29 Mar. 1969).

FIRENCZI, I., AND WILLCOX, W. F., *International Migrations* (National Bureau of Economic Research, New York, 1929).

FISHER, *The importance of the Cape of Good Hope independently of the advantages it possesses as a naval and military station* (London, 1816).

FITZHUGH, G., 'Sociology for the South' and 'Cannibals All', reprinted in Wish, H. (ed.), *Ante-Bellum* (G.P. Putnams, New York, 1960).

FITZPATRICK, J. P., *The Transvaal from Within* (Heinemann, London, 1899).

FOOT, P., *Immigration and Race in British Politics* (Penguin, Harmondsworth, 1965).

FRANCK, T., *Race and Nationalism* (Allen & Unwin, London, 1960).

FRAZIER, E. F., 'Sociological Theory and Race Relations', *A.S.R.* 12, no. 3 (1947), 265–71.

FREEDMAN, M., 'Some Recent Work on Race Relations: A Critique', *B.J.S.* (1954), 342–50.

—— *A Minority in Britain* (Vallentine Mitchell, London, 1955).

—— AND WILLMOTT, W. E., 'South East Asia, with special reference to the Chinese' in *Research on Racial Relations* (U.N.E.S.C.O., Paris, 1966), pp. 159–77.

FRIEDMAN, M., *Capitalism and Freedom* (University of Chicago Press, Chicago, 1962).

FURNIVALL, J. S., *Colonial Policy and Practice* (Cambridge University Press, Cambridge, 1948).

GALBRAITH, J. S., *Reluctant Empire: British policy on the South African Frontier, 1834–54* (University of California Press, Berkeley, 1963).

GANS, H. J., 'Urbanism and Suburbanism as Ways of Life: a Re-evaluation of Definitions' in Rose, P. I., *The Study of Society* (Random House, New York, 1967), pp. 306–22.

GANS, H. J., *The Levittowners: ways of life and politics in a new suburban community* (Allen Lane, London, 1967).

GAVRON, H., *The Captive Wife: conflicts of housebound mothers* (Routledge, London, 1966).

GERTH, H., AND MILLS, C. W., *From Max Weber: Essays in Sociology* (Routledge, London, 1948).

GHAI, D. P., *Portrait of a Minority: Asians in East Africa* (Oxford University Press, 1965).

GILLESPIE, J. M., AND ALLPORT, G. W., *Youths Outlook on the Future* (Doubleday, New York, 1955).

GINSBERG, M., *On the Diversity of Morals* (Heinemann, London, 1962).

GLAZER, N., AND MOYNIHAN, D. P., *Beyond the Melting Pot* (Harvard-M.I.T. Press, Cambridge, Mass., 1964).

GLOCK, C. Y., 'The role of deprivation in the origin and evolution of religious groups' in Lee, R., and Marty, M. E., *Religion and Social Conflict* (Oxford University Press, New York, 1964), pp. 24–36.

GLUCKMAN, M., *Custom and Conflict in Africa* (Blackwell, Oxford, 1955).

GODLONTON, R., *Memorials of the British Settlers of South Africa* (R. Godlonton, Grahamstown, 1844).

GOLDTHORPE, J. H., 'Social Stratification in Industrial Society', *The Sociological Review, Monograph no. 8* (1964), 97–122.

—— AND LOCKWOOD, D., 'Affluence and the British Class Structure', *The Sociological Review*, 11, no. 2 (1963), 133–63.

—— AND LOCKWOOD, D., 'The Affluent Worker and the Thesis of Embourgeoisement: some preliminary research findings', *Sociology*, 1, no. 1 (1967), 11–31.

—— LOCKWOOD, D., BECHOFER, F., AND PLATT, J., *The Affluent Worker: Industrial Attitudes and Behaviour* (Cambridge University Press, Cambridge, 1968); *The Affluent Worker: Political Attitudes and Behaviour* (C.U.P., 1969); *The Affluent Worker in the Class Structure* (C.U.P., 1969).

GOLIGHTLY, C. L., 'Race, Values and Guilt', *Social Forces*, 26 (1947), 125–39.

GOODFELLOW, C. F., *Great Britain and South African Confederation 1870–1881* (Oxford University Press, Cape Town, 1966).

GOODY, J., *Comparative Studies in Kinship* (Routledge, London, 1969).

GORDON, M. M., *Assimilation in American Life* (Oxford University Press, New York, 1964).

GORDON-BROWN, A., introduction to Burchell, W. J., *Travels in the Interior of Southern Africa* (Struik, Cape Town, 1967).

GOULD, J., *Penguin Survey of the Social Sciences* (Penguin, Harmondsworth, 1965).

—— AND KOLB, W. L. (eds.), *A Dictionary of the Social Sciences* (Tavistock, London, 1964).

GREENBLUM, J., AND PEARLIN, L. I., 'Vertical Mobility and Prejudice: A Social-psychological Analysis' in Bendix, R., and Lipset, S. M. (eds.), *Class, Status and Power* (Free Press, New York, 1953) 480–91.

HAHLO, K. G., 'A European-African worker relationship in South Africa', *Race*, 11, no. 1 (1969), 13–35.

HAKLUYT, R., *Principal Navigations . . . of the English Nation* (Hakluyt Society, London, 1903–5).

HALE, J. (ed.), *Settlers—extracts from journals and letters of early colonists* (Faber, London, 1950), pp. 210–99.

HALSEY, A. H., FLOUD, J., AND ANDERSON, C. A., *Education, Economy and Society* (Free Press, New York, 1961).

HAMMOND, E., 'The Settlement of Byrne Immigrants in Natal, 1849–52', *S.A.J.S.* (1927), 599–606.

HANCOCK, W. K., 'Evolution of a Settler's Frontier in Southern Africa' in *Survey of British Commonwealth Affairs* (Oxford University Press, London, 1942), pp. 1–128.

—— *Smuts: Vol. I The Sanguine Years, 1870–1919* (Cambridge University Press, Cambridge, 1962); *Smuts: Vol. II The Fields of Force, 1919–50* (C.U.P., 1968).

—— 'Are There South Africans?' Hoernlé Memorial Lecture, 1966.

HANDLIN, O., *The Uprooted* (Little Brown & Co., Boston, 1952).

HARTZ, L., *The Founding of New Societies* (Harcourt-Brace, New York, 1964).

HATTERSLEY, A. F., *More Annals of Natal* (Warne, London, 1936).

—— *The Natalians* (Shuter & Shooter, Pietersmaritzburg, 1940).

—— *Portrait of a Colony* (Cambridge University Press, Cambridge, 1940).

—— *British Settlement in Natal* (Cambridge University Press, Cambridge, 1950).

—— *A Victorian Lady at the Cape* (Maskew Miller, Cape Town, n.d.).

—— *The Convict Crisis and the Growth of Unity* (University of Natal Press, Pietermaritzburg, 1965).

HELLMANN, E., 'The Application of the Concept of Separate Development to the Urban Areas in the Union of South Africa' in Kirkwood, K. (ed.), *St. Antony's Papers* (Chatto & Windus, London, no. 10 1961), pp. 120–46.

—— AND ABRAHAMS, L., *Handbook of Race Relations in South Africa* (Oxford University Press, Cape Town, 1949).

HELPER, H. R., 'The Impending Crisis of the South' in Wish, H. (ed.), *Ante-Bellum* (G.P. Putnam's, New York, 1960), pp. 157–256.

HENDERSON, J., *Coloured Immigrants in Britain* (I.R.R., Oxford University Press, London, 1960).

HENRIQUES, F., 'The Sociology of Immigration' in Wolstenholm, G. E., and O'Connor, M., *Immigration: Medical and Social Aspects* (J. & A. Churchill, London, 1966), p. 18–30.

HEPPLE, A., *South Africa: a political and economic history* (Praeger, New York, 1966).

—— *Verwoerd* (Penguin, Harmondsworth, 1967).

HEPPLE, B., *Race, Jobs and the Law* (Allen Lane, London, 1968).

HERD, N., *1922, The Revolt on the Rand* (Blue Crane Books, Johannesburg, 1966).

HILL, C. R., *Bantustans: the Fragmentation of South Africa* (I.R.R., Oxford University Press, London, 1964).

HILL, C. S., *West Indian Migrants and the London Churches* (I.R.R., Oxford University Press, London, 1963).

—— *How Colour Prejudiced is Britain?* (Gollancz, London, 1965).

HOCKLY, H. E., *The Story of the British Settlers of 1820 in South Africa* (Juta, Cape Town, 1957).

HOFMEYR, J. H., 'Christian Principles and the Race Problem', Hoernlé Memorial Lecture, 1945.

HOLLEMAN, J. F., MANN, J. W., AND VAN DEN BERGHE, P. L., 'A Rhodesian White Minority Under Threat', *Journal of Social Psychology*, 57 (1962), 315–38.

HOMANS, G. C., 'Bringing Men Back In', *A.S.R.* 29 (1964), 809–18.

HOPPER, E. I., 'A Typology for the Classification of Educational Systems', *Sociology*, 2, no. 1 (1968), 29–45.

HORRELL, M., *Racialism and the Trade Unions* (S.A.I.R.R., Johannesburg, 1959).

—— *Legislation and Race Relations* (S.A.I.R.R., Johannesburg, 1963).

—— *Bantu Education* (S.A.I.R.R., Johannesburg, 1964).

—— *Group Area Acts* (S.A.I.R.R., Johannesburg, 1966).

—— *A Survey of Race Relations in South Africa* (S.A.I.R.R., Johannesburg, 1951).

HORTON, J., 'Order and Conflict Theories of Social Problems as Competing Ideologies', *A.J.S.* 71, no. 6 (1966), 701–13.

HORWITZ, R., *The Political Economy of South Africa* (Weidenfeld & Nicolson, London, 1967).

HUGHES, E. C., *French Canada in Transition* (Routledge, London, 1943).

—— 'Race Relations and the Sociological Imagination', *A.S.R.* 28, no. 6 (1963), 879–90.

—— AND HUGHES, H. M., *Where Peoples Meet: racial and ethnic frontiers* (Free Press, New York, 1952).

HUNTER, G., *Industrialization and Race Relations* (I.R.R., Oxford University Press, London, 1965).

HUTT, W. H., *The Economics of the Colour Bar* (André Deutsch, London, 1964).

INDEN BOSCH, B. J., 'De Verschillende Aspecten van de Aanpassing der Nederlandse Immigranten in Zuid-Afrika', *Journal for Social Research*, 15, no. 1 (1966), 69–76.

INKELES, A., *What is Sociology?* (Prentice-Hall, New Jersey, 1964).

—— AND ROSSI, P. H., 'National Comparisons of Occupational Prestige', *A.J.S.* 61 (1956), 329–39.

ISAAC, J., *British Post-War Migration* (Cambridge University Press, Cambridge, N.I.E.S.R., 1954).

JACKSON, B., *Streaming: an education system in miniature* (Routledge, London, 1964).

—— AND MARSDEN, D., *Education and the Working Class* (Routledge, London, 1962).

JACKSON, J. A., *The Irish in Britain* (Routledge, London, 1963).

—— (ed.), *Social Stratification* (Cambridge University Press, Cambridge, 1968).

—— (ed.), *Migration* (Cambridge University Press, Cambridge, 1969).

JAHODA, M., AND WARREN, N., *Attitudes* (Penguin, Harmondsworth, 1966).

JOHN, DEWITT, *Indian Workers' Associations in Britain* (I.R.R., Oxford University Press, London, 1969).

JOHNS, S. W., III, 'The Birth of Non-White Trade Unionism in South Africa', *Race*, 9, no. 2 (1967), 173–91.

JOHNSTON, P. H. W., 'The Kenyan Immigrant: a study of social adaptation', B.A. Hons. thesis, University of Natal, 1966.

—— 'British Emigration to South Africa: a study of their characteristics and a comparison with Australia', unpublished M.A. thesis, University of Natal, 1968.

JOHNSTONE, F., 'White Prosperity and White Supremacy in South Africa Today', *African Affairs*, 69, no. 275 (1970), 124–40.

JOOSTE, C. J., 'Immigrasie- Enkele demografiese en sosio-ekonomiese aspekte', *Journal of Racial Affairs*, 18, no. 3 (1967), 132–43.

KARN, V., 'A Note on "Race, Community and Conflict"', *Race*, 20, no. 1 (1967), 101–4.

—— 'Property values among Indians and Pakistanis in a Yorkshire Town', *Race*, 10, no. 3 (1969), 269–84.

KATZ, E., AND LAZARSFELD, P. F., *Personal Influence: the part played by people in the flow of mass communications* (Free Press, New York, 1955).

KAWWA, T., 'Three Sociometric Studies of Ethnic Relations in London Schools', *Race*, 10, no. 2 (1968), 173–80.

KEATLEY, P., *The Politics of Partnership* (Penguin, Harmondsworth, 1963).

KEET, B. B., *Whither South Africa?* (Stellenbosch and Grahamstown University Press, 1956).

KEPPEL-JONES, A., *When Smuts Goes* (Shuter & Shooter, Pietermaritzburg, 1950).

—— *Philipps, 1820 Settler* (Shuter & Shooter, Pietermaritzburg, 1960).

—— *South Africa: a short history* (Hutchinson, London, 1963).

KERR, C., *Marshall, Marx and Modern Times: The Multi-Dimensional Society*. The Marshall Lectures, 1967–8 (Cambridge University Press, Cambridge, 1969).

—— DUNLOP, J. T., HARBISON, F. H., AND MYERS, C. A., *Industrialism and Industrial Man* (Heinemann, London, 1962).

KILLIAN, L. M., 'The Effects of Southern White Workers on Race Relations in Northern Plants', *A.S.R.* 17, no. 3 (1952), 328–30.

KIRKWOOD, K., *The Group Areas Act* (S.A.I.R.R., Johannesburg, 1951).

—— (ed.) *St. Antony's Papers*, no. 10 (Chatto & Windus, London, 1961).

KIRKWOOD, K., *Britain and Africa* (Chatto & Windus, London, 1965).
—— *Report on the meaning of racial discrimination* (U.N., New York, 1966).

KRAUSE, E., 'Locating Minority Populations', *Race*, 10, no. 3 (1969), 361–8.

KRIKLER, D. M., 'The Jews of Rhodesia', *I.R.R. Newsletter*, 3, no. 1 (1969), 33–7.

KRUGER, D. W., *South African Parties and Politics*, 1910–1960 (Bowes & Bowes, Cambridge, 1960).

KUPER, H., 'The Colonial Situation in South Africa', *Journal of Modern African Studies*, 2, no. 2 (1964), 149–64.

KUPER, L., *Passive Resistance in South Africa* (Yale University Press, New Haven, 1957).
—— 'The Heightening of Racial Tension', *Race*, 2, no. 1 (1960), 24–32.
—— *An African Bourgeoisie: Race, Class and Politics in South Africa* (Yale University Press, New Haven, 1965).
—— WATTS, H., AND DAVIES, R., *Durban: a study in racial ecology* (Cape, London, 1958).

LAMBERT, J., *Crime, Police and Race Relations: a study in Birmingham* (I.R.R., Oxford University Press, London, 1970).

LANDES, R. A., 'Preliminary Statement of a survey of Negro-white relationships in Britain', *Man* (Sept. 1952).

LANE, R. E., *Political Life* (Free Press, New York, 1959).
—— *Political Ideology* (Free Press, New York, 1962).

LAPIERE, R. T., 'Race Prejudice: France and England', *Social Forces*, 7 (1928), 102–11.

LEACH, E., 'Caste, Class and Slavery: the Taxonomic Problem' in Reuck, A. de, and Knight, J., *Caste and Race: comparative approaches* (C.I.B.A., J. & A. Churchill, London, 1967).

LEGUM, C., and M., *South Africa: Crisis for the West* (Pall Mall, London, 1964).

LELOHE, M. J., AND GOLDMAN, A. R., 'Race in Local Politics', *Race*, 10, no. 4 (1969), 435–7.

LE MAY, G. H. L., *British Supremacy in South Africa, 1899–1907* (Clarendon Press, Oxford, 1965).

LERNER, D., *The Passing of Traditional Society* (Free Press, New York, 1958).

LEVER, H., *Ethnic Attitudes of Johannesburg Youth* (Witwatersrand University Press, Johannesburg, 1968).
—— 'Ethnic Preferences of White Residents in Johannesburg', *Sociology and Social Research*, 152 (1968), 157–73.
—— 'Ethnic Preferences of Immigrants', *Journal for Social Research*, 17, no. 2 (1968), 11–13.

LEVER, H., 'The Johannesburg Station Explosion and Ethnic Attitudes' *Public Opinion Quarterly*, XXXIII, no. 2 (1969), 180–9.

LEVER, H., 'Urbanization and the Afrikaner', *Race*, 11, no. 2 (1969), 183–8.

—— AND WAGNER, O. M., 'Father's education as a factor affecting social distance', *Journal for Social Research*, 14 (1965), 21–30.

—— WAGNER, O. J. M., AND SCHLEMMER, L., 'Some Patterns and Correlates of Informal Social Participation in a Highly Urbanized Flat-Dwelling Community in South Africa', paper to 'Focus on Cities' Conference, University of Natal, 9 July 1968.

LEVI-STRAUSS, C., *The Scope of Anthropology* (Cape, London, 1967).

—— *The Savage Mind* (Weidenfeld & Nicolson, London, 1966).

LEWIN, J., *Politics and Law in South Africa* (Merlin Press, London, 1963).

LEYDS, G. A., *A History of Johannesburg* (Nasionale Boekhandel, Cape Town, 1964).

LEYS, S., 'The theory and practice of social anthropologists working in urban or literate societies', unpublished B. Litt. thesis, Oxford, 1967.

LIEBERSON, S., 'A Societal Theory of Race and Ethnic Relations', *A.S.R.* 26, no. 6 (1961), 902–10.

—— 'Suburbs and Ethnic Residential Patterns', *A.J.S.* (1962), 673–81.

LINCOLN, C. E., 'The Black Muslim Movement', *Journal of Social Issues*, 19 (1963), 73–88.

LIPSET, S. M., 'A Sociologist Looks at History', *Pacific Soc. Rev.* 1, no. 1 (1958).

—— *Political Man* (Heinemann, London, 1960).

—— *The First New Nation* (Basic Books, New York, 1963).

—— (ed.), *Class, Citizenship and Social Development* (Doubleday, New York, 1964).

—— *Revolution and Counter-revolution: change and persistence in social structures* (Basic Books, New York, 1969).

—— TROW, M., AND COLEMAN, J. S., *Union Democracy* (Free Press, New York, 1956).

—— AND BENDIX, R., *Social Mobility in Industrial Society* (University of California Press, Berkeley, 1959).

LITTLE, A., AND WESTERGAARD, J. H., 'The trend of class differentials in educational opportunity in England and Wales', *B.J.S.* 15, no. 4 (1964).

LITTLE, K. L., *Negroes in Britain* (Routledge & Kegan Paul, London, 1947).

LOCKWOOD, D., 'Some Remarks on "The Social System"', *B.J.S.* 7, no. 2 (1956), 134–46.

—— *The Blackcoated Worker* (Allen & Unwin, London, 1958).

—— 'Some Notes on the Concepts of Race and Plural Society', paper delivered to British Sociological Association, 26 Mar. 1969.

LOEDOLFF, J. F., *Nederlandse Immigrante n' sosiologiese ondersoek van hul Inskakeling in die Gemeenskapslewe van Pretoria* (Haum, Kaapstad, 1960).

LOHMAN, J. D., AND REITZES, D. C., 'Notes on Race Relations in Mass Society', *A.J.S.* 63, no. 3 (1952), 240–6.

LONG, U. (ed.), *The Chronicle of Jeremiah Goldswain* (Van Riebeeck Society, Cape Town, 2 vols., 1946, 1948).

LUGARD, F., *The Dual Mandate in British Tropical Africa* (W. Blackwood, Edinburgh, 1922).

MACKEURTAN, G., *The Cradle Days of Natal*, 1497–1845 (Longmans, London, 1930).

MACCRONE, I. D., *Race Attitudes in South Africa: historical, experimental and psychological studies* (Oxford University Press, Oxford, 1937).

—— 'Group Conflicts and Race Prejudice', Hoernlé Memorial Lecture, 1947.

——'Reaction to domination in a colour-caste society', *Journal of Social Psychology*, 26 (1947).

—— 'Race Attitudes: An Analysis and Interpretation', in Hellmann, E., *Handbook of Race Relations in South Africa* (Oxford University Press, London, 1949), pp. 670 ff.

—— 'Parental Origins and Popular Prejudice', *Proceedings of the South African Psychological Association*, 5 (1954), 10–12.

MACMILLAN, W. M., *The Cape Colour Question* (Faber, London, 1927).

—— *Bantu, Boer, and Briton* (Clarendon Press, Oxford, rev. edn. 1963).

MACRAE, D., 'Karl Marx' in Raison, T. (ed.), *The Founding Fathers of Social Science* (Penguin, Harmondsworth, 1969), pp. 59–67.

MACRAE, N., 'The Green Bay Tree', *The Economist*, 29 June 1968.

MADGE, J., *The Tools of Social Science* (Longmans, London, 1953).

—— *The Origins of Scientific Sociology* (Free Press, New York, 1963).

MALHERBE, E. G., *Education in South Africa, 1652–1922* (Juta, Cape Town, 1925).

—— 'Race Attitudes and Education', Hoernlé Memorial Lecture, 1946.

—— 'The Nemesis of Docility', Presidential Address to the South African Institute of Race Relations, 30 Jan. 1968. (1968).

MANNHEIM, K., *Ideology and Utopia: an introduction to the sociology of knowledge* (Routledge, London, 1946).

MANNONI, O., *Prospero and Caliban: the Psychology of Colonization* (Praeger, New York (2nd edn. 1964)).

MANSERGH, N., *South Africa, 1906–61: the price of magnanimity* (Allen & Unwin, London, 1962).

MARAIS, B. J., *The Colour Crisis and the West* (van Schaik, Pretoria, 1953).

MARAIS, J. S., *The Fall of Kruger's Republic* (Clarendon Press, Oxford, 1961).

MARQUARD, L., *The Peoples and Policies of South Africa* (Oxford University Press, London, 1962).

MARSH, P., *The Anatomy of a Strike* (I.R.R., Oxford University Press, London, 1967).

MARSHALL, T. H., *Sociology at the Crossroads* (Heinemann, London, 1947).

MARX, G. T., 'Religion: Opiate or Inspiration of Civil Rights militancy among Negroes', *A.S.R.* 32, no. 1 (1967), 64–72.

—— *Protest and Prejudice: a study of belief in the Black Community* (Harper & Row, New York, 1967).

MAXWELL, A. E., *Analysing Qualitative Data* (Methuen, London, 1961).

MAYER, P., *Townsmen and Tribesmen* (Oxford University Press, Cape Town, 1961).

—— 'Migrancy and the Study of Africans in Towns', reprinted in Pahl, R. E., *Readings in Urban Sociology* (Pergamon, Oxford, 1968), pp. 306–30.

MCKENZIE, R. T., AND SILVER, A., *Angels in Marble: working class Conservatives in Urban England* (Heinemann, London, 1968).

MEDALIA, N. Z., 'Myrdal's assumptions on Race Relations', *Social Forces*, 40 (1962), 223–7.

MEIRING, J. M., *Sundays River Valley: its history and settlement* (A. A. Balkema, Cape Town, 1959).

MERTON, R. K., 'Discrimination and the American Creed' in MacIver, R. M. (ed.), *Discrimination and National Welfare* (Harper & Row, New York, 1949).

—— *Social Theory and Social Structure* (Free Press, New York, 1957).

—— FISKE, M., AND KENDALL, P. L., *The Focused Interview* (Free Press, New York, 1956).

MICHELS, R., *Political Parties: a sociological study of the oligarchical tendencies of Modern Democracy* (Collier, New York, 1962).

MILLS, C. W., *The Sociological Imagination* (Oxford University Press, New York, 1959).

MINARD, R. D., 'Race Relations in the Pocahontas Coal Field', *Journal of Social Issues*, 8, no. 1 (1952), 29, 44.

MITCHELL, G. D., *A Dictionary of Sociology* (Routledge, London, 1968).

MITCHELL, J. C., 'On Quantification in Social Anthropology' in Epstein, A. L. (ed.), *The Craft of Social Anthropology* (Tavistock, London, 1967), pp. 17–47.

MOODIE, J. W. D., *Ten Years in South Africa* (Richard Bentley, London, 1835).

MOORE, W. E., AND TUMIN, M. M., 'The Social Functions of Ignorance', *A.S.R.* 14 (1949), 787–95.

MOSER, C. A., *Survey Methods in Social Investigation* (Heinemann, London, 1958).

MULLER, C. F. J., Van JAARSVELD, F. A., AND VAN WIJK, T., *A Select Bibliography of South African History* (University of South Africa, Pretoria, 1966).

MUNGER, E. S., *The Jews and the Nationalist Party* (S.A.I.R.R., Johannesburg, 1961).

MUNGER, E. S., *Afrikaner and African Nationalism: South African Parallels and Parameters* (I.R.R., Oxford University Press, London, 1967).

MYRDAL, G., *An American Dilemma: The Negro Problem and Modern Democracy* (Harper & Row, New York, 1944), 2 vols.

NAPIER, E. LT.-COL., *The Book of the Cape, or past and future emigration* (T. C. Newby, London, 1851).

NICHOLSON, G., *The Cape and its Colonists with hints to Settlers* (J. & D. A. Darling, London, 1849).

NIEBUHR, H. R., *The Social Sources of Denominationalism* (Holt, New York, 1929).

NISBET, R. A. (ed.), *Emile Durkheim* (Prentice-Hall, New Jersey, 1965).

NOLUTSHUNGU, S. C., 'Before the Election: Issues of the South African "Enlightenment"', unpublished paper delivered at St. Antony's College, Oxford, 14 May 1970.

NORDLINGER, E. A., *The Working Class Tories* (MacGibbon & Kee, London, 1967).

OPPENHEIM, A. N., *Questionnaire Design and Attitude Measurement* (Heinemann, London, 1966).

PAHL, R. E., *Readings in Urban Sociology* (Pergamon, Oxford, 1968).

PARK, R. E., *Race and Culture* (Free Press, New York, 1950).

PARSONS, T., *The Structure of Social Action* (McGraw-Hill, New York, 1937).

—— *The Social System* (Routledge, London, 1951).

—— 'The School Class as a Social System', *Harvard Educational Review*, 29 (1959), 297–318.

—— 'Evolutionary Universals in Society', *A.S.R.* 29, no. 3 (1964), 338–57.

—— AND SHILS, E., *Toward a General Theory of Action* (Harper, New York, 1962).

—— AND CLARK, K. B., *The Negro American* (Houghton Mifflin, Boston, 1966).

PATON, A., *Hofmeyr* (Oxford University Press, Cape Town, 1965).

PATTERSON, S., *The Last Trek* (Routledge, London, 1957).

—— *Dark Strangers* (Tavistock, London, 1963; Penguin, Harmondsworth, 1965).

—— *Immigrants in Industry* (I.R.R., Oxford University Press, London, 1968).

—— *Immigration and Race Relations in Britain, 1960–1967* (I.R.R., Oxford University Press, London, 1969).

PAUW, B. A., *The Second Generation: A Study of the Family Among Urbanized Bantu in East London* (Oxford University Press, Cape Town, 1963).

PEACH, C., *West Indian Migration to Britain* (I.R.R., Oxford University Press, London, 1968).

PEEL, J. D. Y., 'Spencer and the Neo-Evolutionists', *Sociology*, 3, no. 2 (1969), 173–91.

PENDLE, G., *A History of Latin America* (Penguin, Harmondsworth, 1963).

P.E.P., *Racial Discrimination* (P.E.P., London, 1967).

PETERSEN, W., 'A General Typology of Migration', *A.S.R.* 23, no. 3 (1958), 256–66.

PETTIGREW, T. F., 'Personality and Socio-cultural Factors in inter-Group Attitudes', *Journal of Conflict Resolution*, 2, no. 1 (1958), 29–42.

—— 'Regional differences in Anti-Negro Prejudice', *J. Abnormal and Soc. Psych.* 59 (1959), 28–36.

—— 'Racial and Moral Crisis: the Role of Little Rock Ministers', *A.J.S.* 64, no. 5 (1959), 509–16.

—— 'Social Distance Attitudes of South African Students', *Social Forces*, 38 (1960), 246–53.

—— 'Racially Separate or Together?', *Journal of Social Issues*, 25, no. 1 (1969), 43–69.

—— AND CAMPBELL, E. Q., *Christians in Racial Crisis: a Study of Little Rock's Ministry* (Public Affairs Press, Washington, 1959).

PIENAAR, S., AND SAMPSON, A., *South Africa. Two Views of Separate Development* (I.R.R., Oxford University Press, London, 1960).

PLATT, J., 'Some Problems in Measuring the Jointness of Conjugal-Role relationships', *Sociology*, 3, 3 (1969), 287–97.

PORTER, J., *The Vertical Mosaic* (University of Toronto Press, Toronto, 1965).

POPPER, K. R., *The Poverty of Historicism* (Routledge, London, 1961).

—— *The Open Society and its Enemies* (Routledge, London, 1966) (2 vols.).

PRICE, C. A., 'Immigration and Group Settlement' in Borrie, W. D., *The Cultural Integration of Immigrants* (U.N.E.S.C.O., 1959).

PRINGLE, T., *Narrative of a Residence in South Africa* (Struik, Cape Town, 1966).

—— *Some Account of the present state of the English Settlers in Albany, South Africa* (T. & G. Underwood, London, 1824).

PYRAH, G. B., *Imperial Policy and South Africa, 1902–10* (Clarendon Press, Oxford, 1955).

RABONE, A., *The Records of a Pioneer Family* (Struik, Cape Town, 1966).

RADIN, B., 'Coloured Workers and British Trade Unions', *Race*, 8, no. 2 (1966).

RAISON, T. (ed.), *The Founding Fathers of Social Science* (Penguin, Harmondsworth, 1969).

RALLS, R. E., 'Early Immigration Schemes in Natal, 1846–53', unpublished M.A. thesis, University of Natal (P.M.B.) (1934).

RAVEN-HART, R., *Before Van Riebeeck*, (Struik, Cape Town, 1967).

REID, J., 'Employment of Negroes in Manchester', *The Sociological Review*, 4, no. 2 (1956).

Report of the National Advisory Commission on Civil Disorders, (Bantam, New York, 1968).

REUCK, A. DE, AND KNIGHT, J., *Caste and Race: comparative approaches* (Churchill, London, 1967).

REX, J., 'The Plural Society in Sociological Theory', *B.J.S.* 10 (1959), 114–24.

—— *Key Problems of Sociological Theory* (Routledge, London, 1961).

—— *Labour's Last Chance* (Penguin, Harmondsworth, 1968).

—— 'The Concept of Race in Sociological Theory', paper delivered to the British Sociological Association, 26 Mar. 1969.

—— *Race Relations in Sociological Theory* (Weidenfeld & Nicholson, London, 1970).

—— 'The Plural Society: The South African Case', *Race*, 12, no. 4 (1971), 401–13.

—— AND MOORE, R., *Race, Community and Conflict* (I.R.R., Oxford University Press, London, 1967).

RICHARDSON, A., 'Some Psycho-Social Aspects of British Emigration to Australia', *B.J.S.* 10 (1959), 328–9.

RICHMOND, A. H., *Colour Prejudice in Britain: a study of West Indian workers in Liverpool, 1942–51* (Routledge, London, 1954).

—— 'Immigration as a Social Process: the case of Coloured Colonials in the United Kingdom', *Social and Economic Studies*, 5, no. 2 (1956).

—— 'Sociological and Psychological Explanations of Racial Prejudice', *Pacific Soc. Rev.* 4, no. 2 (1961), 63–8.

—— *Post-war Immigrants in Canada* (Toronto University Press, Toronto, 1967).

RIDDER, J. C. DE, *The Personality of the Urban African in South Africa* (Routledge, London, 1961).

RIESMAN, D., *Individualism Reconsidered* (Free Press, New York, 1954).

RITTER, E. A., *Shaka Zulu* (Longmans, London, 1955).

RIVETT-CARNAC, D. E., *Thus Came the English* (Howard Timmins, Cape Town, 1961).

—— *Hawk's Eye* (Howard Timmins, Cape Town, 1966).

ROBB, J. H., *Working Class Anti-Semite* (Tavistock, London, 1954).

ROBERTSON, H. M., 'The Cape of Good Hope and Systematic Colonization', *S.A.J.E.* 15, no. 4 (1937).

—— 'The 1849 Settlers in Natal', *S.A.J.E.* 17, no. 2 (1949), 274–88; 416–42.

—— *South Africa, Economic and Political Aspects* (Cambridge University Press, London, 1957).

—— 'South Africa' in Thomas, B. (ed.), *Economics of International Migration* (I.E.A., London, 1958), pp. 173–84.

ROBERTSON, R. (ed.), *Sociology of Religion: selected readings* (Penguin, Harmondsworth, 1969).

ROGERS, C. A., AND FRANTZ, C., 'Length of Residence and Race Attitudes of Europeans in Southern Africa', *Race*, 3, no. 2 (1962), 46–54.

—— *Racial Themes in Southern Rhodesia* (Yale University Press, New Haven, 1962).

ROSE, E. J. B. *et al.*, *Colour and Citizenship* (I.R.R., Oxford University Press, London, 1969).

ROSE, P. I., *The Study of Society: an integrated anthology* (Random House, New York, 1967).

ROSENBERG, B., GERVER, I., AND HOWTON, F. W. (eds.), *Mass Society in Crisis* (Macmillan, New York, 1964).

ROSENTHAL, E., *Southern African Dictionary of National Biography* (Warne, London, 1966).

ROTBERG, R. I., *The Rise of Nationalism in Central Africa* (Harvard University Press, Cambridge, Mass., 1965).

ROUTH, G., *Industrial and Race Relations* (S.A.I.R.R., Johannesburg, 1952).

RUNCIMAN, W. G., *Social Science and Political Theory* (Cambridge University Press, Cambridge, 1963).

—— *Relative Deprivation and Social Justice* (Routledge, London, 1966).

—— 'Class, Status and Power?' in Jackson, J. A. (ed.), *Social Stratification* (Cambridge University Press, Cambridge, 1968), pp. 25–61.

—— AND BAGLEY, C., 'Status Consistency, Deprivation and Attitudes to Immigrants', *Sociology*, 3, no. 3 (1969), 359–75.

SACHS, E. S., *Rebel Daughters* (MacGibbon & Kee, London, 1957).

SCHREUDER, D. M., *Gladstone and Kruger: Liberal Government and Colonial Home Rule 1880–85* (Routledge, London, 1969).

—— 'History on the Veld: towards a new dawn?', *African Affairs*, 68, no. 271 (1969), 149–59.

SELLITZ, C., JAHODA, M., DEUTSCH, M., AND COOK, S., *Research Methods in Social Relations* (Methuen, London, 1962).

SELVIN, H., 'A Critique of tests of significance in Survey research', *A.S.R.* 21 (1957), 519–27.

SHERIF, M., AND SHERIF, C. W., *Groups in Harmony and Tension* (Harper, New York, 1953).

SHERWOOD, S., 'The Bantu Clerk: a study of role expectations', *Journal of Social Psychology*, 47 (1958), 285–316.

SHILS, E., 'Primordial, Personal, Sacred and Civil Ties', *B.J.S.* 8 (1957), 130–45.

—— *Political Development in the New States* (Mouton, The Hague, 1962).

SHUVAL, J. T., 'Emerging Patterns of Ethnic Strain in Israel', *Social Forces*, 40, no. 4 (1962), 323–30.

SICHEL, F. H., *From Refugee to Citizen* (A. A. Balkema, Cape Town, 1966).

SILBERMAN, C. E., *Crisis in Black and White* (Random House, New York, 1964).

SILLS, D. L. (ed.), *International Encyclopedia of Social Sciences* (Macmillan–Free Press, New York 1969), vols 1–17 (17 vols).

SIMONS, H. J., AND R. E., *Class and Colour in South Africa, 1850–1950* (Penguin, Harmondsworth, 1969).

SIMPSON, G. E., AND YINGER, J. M., 'The Sociology of Race and Ethnic Relations' in Merton, R. K., Broom, L., and Cottrell, L. S., *Sociology Today* (Basic Books, New York, 1959), pp. 376–99.

—— *Racial and Cultural Minorities* (Harper & Row, London, 3rd. edn., 1965).

SIMS, V. M., AND PATRICK, J. R., 'Attitude towards the Negro of Northern and Southern College Students', *Journal of Social Psychology*, 7, no. 2 (1936), 192–209.

SINGH, G., *A Manual of the Multiple Variate Counter* (Atlas Computing Service, University of London, 1968).

SINGHAM, A. W., 'Immigration and the Election' in Butler, D. E., and King, A., *The British General Election of 1964* (Macmillan, London, 1965), pp. 360–8.

SIVERTSEN, D., *When Caste Barriers Fall: a Study of Social and Economic Change in a South Indian Village* (Humanities Press, New York, 1963).

SMELSER, N. J., *Social Change in the Industrial Revolution* (Routledge, London, 1959).

—— *Theory of Collective Behaviour* (Free Press, London, 1963).

—— *Sociology: an Introduction* (Wiley, New York, 1967).

—— AND SMELSER, W. T., *Personality and Social Systems* (Wiley, New York, 1963).

SMITHIES, B., AND FIDDICK, P., *Enoch Powell on Immigration* (Sphere, London, 1969).

SMUTS, J. C., *The Basis of Trusteeship in African Native Policy* (S.A.I.R.R., Cape Town, 1942).

SOROKIN, P., *Fads and Foibles in Modern Sociology* (Regnery, Chicago, 1959).

STEPHENS, L., 'The Employment of Coloured Workers in the Birmingham Area', Institute of Personnel Management, Occasional Paper, 1956.

STEYTLER, J. G., *The Emigrants' Guide to the Diamond Fields of South Africa* (Saul Solomon & Co., Cape Town, 1870).

STINCHCOMBE, A. L., MCDILL, M. S., AND WALKER, D., 'Is there a racial tipping point in changing schools?', *Journal of Social Issues*, 25, no. 1 (1969), 127–36.

STONE, J., 'Migrants to Apartheid', *New Society* (29 May 1969).

—— 'Some Sociological Aspects of the integration of British Immigrants in South Africa' (unpublished D.Phil Thesis, Oxford, 1969).

—— 'James Bryce and the Comparative Sociology of Race Relations', *Race*, 13, no. 2 (Jan. 1972).

U

STOUFFER, S. A., *et al.*, *The American Soldier* (Princeton University Press, Princeton, 1949), 2 vols.

STREETEN, P. (ed.), *Values in Social Theory* (Routledge, London, 1958).

STUART, J., AND MALCOLM, D. McK. (eds.), *The Diary of Henry Francis Fynn* (Shuter & Shooter, Pietermaritzburg, 1950).

STULTZ, N. W., 'The Politics of Security: South Africa under Verwoerd, 1961–66', *Journal of Modern African Studies*, 7, no. 1 (1969), 6–20.

SUNDKLER, B. G. M., *Bantu Prophets in South Africa* (Oxford University Press, London, 2nd edn., 1964).

SWANSON, M. W., 'Urban Origins of Separate Development', *Race*, 10, no. 1 (1968), 31–40.

TABATA, I. B., *Education for Barbarism* (Prometheus, Durban, 1960).

TAEUBER, K. E., AND A. F., *Negroes in the Cities: residential segregation and neighbouring change* (Aldine, Chicago, 1965).

TAFT, R., *From Stranger to Citizen: a survey of studies of immigrant assimilation in Western Australia* (Tavistock, London, 1966).

THAYER, G., *The British Political Fringe* (Blond, London, 1965).

THEAL, G. M., *History of South Africa, 1486–1691* (Allen & Unwin, London, 1888).

THOMAS, B. (ed.), *Economics of International Migration* (I.E.A., London, 1958).

THOMAS, W. I., AND ZNANIECKI, F., *The Polish Peasant in Europe and America* (Richard G. Badger, Chicago, Boston, 1919) 5 vols.

THOMPSON, E. T., AND HUGHES, E. C., *Race: Individual and Collective Behavior* (Free Press, New York, 1958).

THOMPSON, L. M., *The Unification of South Africa 1902–1910* (Clarendon Press, Oxford, 1960).

—— 'The South African Dilemma' in Hartz, L., *The Founding of New Societies* (Harcourt-Brace, New York, 1964).

THOMSON, D., *Europe Since Napoleon* (Penguin, Harmondsworth, 1966).

TILBY, A. W., *South Africa, 1486–1913* (Constable & Co., London, 1914).

TOTEMEYER, G., *South Africa–South West Africa, a bibliography, 1945–63* (Arnold Bergstraesser Institut, Freiburg, 1964).

TOYNBEE, A., *A Study of History* (Oxford University Press, London, 1935–54) 10 vols.

TREVELYAN, G. M., *English Social History* (Longmans, London, 1942/4).

TRIANDIS, H. C., DAVIS, E. E., AND TAZEKAWA, S., 'Some determinants of social distance among American, German and Japanese Students', *Journal of Personality and Social Psychology*, 2, no. 4 (1965), 540–51.

TRIEMAN, D. J., 'Status Discrepancy and Prejudice', *A.J.S.* 71, no. 6 (1966) 651–64.

TURK, R. T., 'The Futures of South Africa', *Social Forces*, 45, no. 3 (1967), 402–12.

TURNER, R. H., 'Contest and Sponsored Mobility: Modes of Social Ascent through Education', *A.S.R.* 25 (1960), 121–39.

—— *The Social Context of Ambition* (Chandler Publishing Co., San Francisco, 1964).

VAN DEN BERGHE, P. L., 'The Dynamics of Racial Prejudice: an ideal type dichotomy', *Social Forces*, 37 (1958), 138–41.

—— 'The Dynamics of Race Relations: an ideal-type case study of South Africa', unpublished Ph.D. Thesis, Harvard University, 1959.

—— 'Miscegenation in South Africa', *Cahiers d'Études Africaines*, 4 (1960), 68–84.

—— 'Race Attitudes in Durban, South Africa', *Journal of Social Psychology*, 57 (1962), 55–72. (*Reprinted in Africa: Social Problems of Change and Conflict* (van den Berghe ed., 1964), p. 254).

—— 'Some Trends in unpublished Social Science Research in South Africa', *International Social Science Journal* (1962).

—— 'Dialectic and Functionalism: Towards a Theoretical Synthesis', *A.S.R.* 28 (1963) 695–705.

—— *Caneville: The Social Structure of a South African Town* (Wesleyan University Press, Middletown, 1964).

—— *South Africa: A Study in Conflict* (Wesleyan University Press, Middletown, 1965).

—— *Race and Racism: a comparative perspective* (Wiley, New York, 1967).

VAN DER HORST, S. T., *Native Labour in South Africa* (Oxford University Press, London, 1942).

—— *The African Factory Worker in Cape Town* (Oxford University Press, London, 1964).

—— 'The Effects of Industrialization on Race Relations in South Africa' in Hunter, G. (ed.), *Industrialization and Race Relations* (Oxford University Press, London, I.R.R., 1965) pp. 97–140.

VAN EYK, H. J., 'Some Aspects of the South African Industrial Revolution', Hoernlé Memorial Lecture, 1951.

VANN WOODWARD, C., *The Strange Career of Jim Crow* (Oxford University Press, New York, 2nd. rev. edn. 1966).

VATCHER, W. H., *White Laager: the Rise of Afrikaner Nationalism* (Pall Mall, London, 1965).

WALKER, E. A., *A History of Southern Africa* (Longmans, London, 1957).

WARD, R. H., 'Discrimination, the market and the ethnic colony', paper delivered to the British Sociological Association, 28 Mar. 1969.

WATSON, S. G. S., AND LAMPKIN, H., 'Race and socio-economic status as factors in the friendship choices of pupils in a racially heterogeneous South African school', *Race*, 10, no. 2 (1968), 181–4.

—— *Passing for White: a study of racial assimilation in a South African School*, (Tavistock, London, 1970).

WAUGHRAY, V., 'The French Racial Scene: North African Immigrants in France', *Race*, 2, no. 1 (1960), 60–70.

WEBER, M., *The Theory of Social and Economic Organization* (trans. by Henderson and Parsons, Oxford University Press, New York, 1947).

—— *The Methodology of the Social Sciences* (trans. by Shils and Finch, Free Press, New York, 1949).

WEINGROD, A., *Israel—Group Relations in a New Society* (Pall Mall, London, 1965).

WEINSTOCK, S. A., 'A Note on the Value of Structural Explanations in the Study of Acculturation', *B.J.S.* 17, no. 1 (1966), 60–3.

WEISBROD, R. G., 'The Dilemma of South African Jewry', *Journal of Modern African Studies*, 5 (1967), 233–41.

WESTERGAARD, J. H., 'The Withering away of Class: A Contemporary Myth', in Anderson, P., and Blackburn, R., *Towards Socialism* (Fontana, London, 1965), pp. 77–113.

WESTIE, F. R., 'An American Dilemma: an Empirical Test', *A.S.R.* 30, no. 4 (1965).

WILENSKY, H. L., AND EDWARDS, H., 'The Skidder; ideological adjustments of downward mobile workers', *A.S.R.* 24 (1959), 215–31.

WILLIAMS, R. M., *Strangers next door: ethnic relations in American communities* (Prentice-Hall, Englewood Cliffs, 1964).

WILSON, B. R., 'An Analysis of Sect Development', *A.S.R.* 24 (1959), 3–15.

—— *Religion in Secular Society* (Watts, London, 1966).

—— 'A Typology of Sects in a Dynamic and Comparative Perspective', reprinted in Robertson, R. (ed.), *Sociology of Religion: selected readings* (Penguin, Harmondsworth, 1969), pp. 361–83.

WILSON, M., AND MAFEJE, A., *Langa, A Study of social groups in an African Township* (Oxford University Press, Cape Town, 1963).

WILSON, M., AND THOMPSON, L. M. (eds.), *The Oxford History of South Africa*. Vol. I, *South Africa to 1870* (Clarendon Press, Oxford, 1969). 2 vols.

WISEMAN, A. V., *Political Systems* (Routledge, London, 1966).

WISH, H. (ed.), *Ante-Bellum* (G. P. Putnams, New York, 1960).

WOLPE, H., 'The Sociology of Race Relations in South Africa', paper delivered to the British Sociological Association, 27 Mar. 1969.

WORSLEY, P., 'The Distribution of Power in Industrial Society', *The Sociological Review Monograph No. 8* (1964).

WRIGHT, P. L., *The Coloured Worker in British Industry* (I.R.R., Oxford University Press, London, 1968).

WRONG, D. H., 'The Over-socialized Conception of Man in Modern Sociology', *A.S.R.* 26 (1961), 184–93.

YOUNG, M., AND WILLMOTT, P., *Family and Kinship in East London* (Routledge, London, 1957).

ZAJONC, R. B., 'Balance, Congruity and Dissonance', in Jahoda, M., and Warren, N., *Attitudes* (Penguin, Harmondsworth, 1966), pp. 261–78.

ZINKIN, T., *Caste Today* (I.R.R., Oxford University Press, London, 1965).

ZUBAIDA, S. (ed.), *Race and Racialism* (Tavistock, London, 1970).

ZUBRZYCKI, J., *Polish Immigrants in Britain: a study in adjustment* (Martinus Nijhoff, The Hague, 1956).

Index

Abrams, M., 79, 80, 154, 210
Act of Union, 64, 120, 143
Africa, winds of change, 136
African Nationalism, 42
Afrikaans language, 119, 208–9
Afrikaner, 21, 34, 42, 191, 192, 218
Afrikaner élite, 43
Afrikaner Nationalist, 48
Afrikaner Nationalist Government, 144
Agar-Hamilton, J. A. I., 64
Albany settlement, 97, 105, 110
Algoa Bay, vii, 101, 112, 125
Aliens Act, 124
Allport, G. W., 23
Almond, G. A., 78
American Creed, 33
Anglo-Boer War, 73, 119, 143
Anti-semitism, 121
Apartheid, 43, 60, 66, 85, 137, 151, 156, 160, 166, 172, 174, 185, 191, 193, 211, 233, 249
  artisans and, 122–42
  attitudes to, 224–9
  concept of industrial relations, 58
  doctrine of, 39
  immigrants' attitude to, 152, 155, 158, 228, 236, 243
  in industry, 54
  in marriage, 74
  in religion, 76, 201, 202
  in trade unions, 199
  legislation, 48, 53
  support for, 238
Apartheid State, 75
Appleyard, R. T., 154, 175
Artisans and Apartheid, 122–42
Asiatic Law Amendments Act, 65
Assisted-passage scheme, 140, 163
Australia, 17, 32, 175, 252
Aycliff, Revd. J., 99

Baasskap, 39, 127
Ballinger, M., 64, 131, 132
Banton, M., 74, 79

Bantu, 52, 64, 71, 103, 114, 118, 144, 213
Bantu Affairs Department, 71
Bantu Education Act, 71
Bantu Laws Amendment Act, 60
Bantustans, 60, 63
Barrow, Sir John, 97
Berlin, I., 86
Bird, W., 98
Bloemfontein, 151
Boer War, 218
Boers, 104, 114, 118, 143
Bogardus social-distance test, 210
Botha, Gen., 121, 127
Botha's Land Settlement Act, 122
Bowker, J. M., 104
Boyle, Sir Edward, 68
Britain, and South Africa, contrasting social structures, 34–7
  coloured immigration to, 49, 60–2
  race relations, 47, 67–70
  social and geographical mobility, 162
  trade unions, 57, 197
British immigrant, acceptance of new values, 39
  apartheid, 239–40
  basic variables, age and family size, 157–7
    area of residence, 149–52
    length of residence, 157–9
    sex and marital status, 153–6
    social class and education, 159–61
  chronology of dates, 278–80
  conclusions, 252–3
  ease of integration, 29
  factors in integration, 83–5
  historical parallels, 109
  ideology, 240–1
  post-war exodus, 133
  post-war nadir, 136
  process of integration, 5
  quest for legitimacy, 37–9
  reactions to social mobility, 38
  results of status discrepancies, 31–2
  rise in social status, 37
  summary, 247–9

British Imperialism, 126
British migration, statistics, 136
Brockway, F., 67, 69
Brookes, E., 59, 64
Bryce, J., 117, 118, 119, 123, 205, 214,
    218, 247, 248, 253
Burchell, W., 97
Bureau of State Security Act, 42
Butler, Gen., 118
Byrne settlement, 105, 106, 107

Calley, M. J. C., 77
Calpin, G. H., 4
Campbell, E. Q., 33
Canada, 17, 252
Cape of Good Hope, 38, 92, 93, 248
Cape Colony, 118
    early British settlers, 92–109
    social composition of settlers, 100
Cape Coloureds, 21, 213–14
Cape Mounted Rifles, 114
Cape Town, 92, 110, 112, 151–2
Cardiff, 52
Carnegie Commission, Report of, 123
Carron, W., 56
Carter, G., 62
Citizenship Act (1949), 135
Collins, Col., 95
Coloured immigration to Britain, 49,
    60–2
Commonwealth Immigration Act, 72
    Amendment to, 69
Community Relations Commission,
    56
Contacts and visits, 171–2
Cousins, F., 56
Cox, O. C., 33, 39
Creswell, F., 51
Crewe, Sir Charles, 127
Crosse, Capt., 91

Dahrendorf, R., 36, 259
Daniel, W. W., 61
Danziger, K., 240
Davenport, R., 58
Deakin, N., 49, 63
De Beers, 115
de Klerk, Senator, 140
de Tocqueville, A., 17, 205
de Villiers, Gen., 134
de Villiers Graaff, Sir, 223
Diamonds, 113
Dollard, J., 259

Donges, Dr., 74, 134, 137
Douglas-Home, Sir Alec, 40
Doxey, G. V., 54
Drake, Sir Francis, 91
Durban, 168
Durkheim, E., 19, 31, 258
Dutch immigrants, 216, 232
Dutch Reformed Church, 75–6 196,
    200, 201

Eastern Cape Province, 274
Eastern Province, 112, 152
Eastern Frontier, 102, 105, 110
Economic integration, comparative
        prospects, education and chil-
        dren's opportunities, 187
    expectations and realities, 189
    frequency distribution, 188
    housing, 180–3
    occupational change, 183–4
    prospects and opportunities, 186–9
    standard of living, 186
    transport, 183
    working conditions, 184–5
Education, 70–3
    in Britain, 72
    in South Africa, 71
    integration and intolerance, 161
Eisenstadt, S. N., 16, 25, 164
    definition of migration, 12
    motivational basis of migration, 12–
        13
    theory of absorption, 13
Ellis, D. E., 56
Emigration, sociological process, 11
Empire Windrush, 47, 49
Employment, 50–8
England, Sons of, 28
Extension of University Education
        Act, 71, 72

Fagan report, 48, 59
Farewell, F. G., 105
Federale Raad van Skakelkomittees,
    28
Fifth Frontier War, 109
Fitzherbert, H., 92
Fitzhugh, G., 38
Fitzpatrick, Sir Percy, 122
Folk theory, 10
Fort Beaufort, 113
Franck, T., 157
Frantz, C., 7, 157

Frazier, E. F., 38
Free State, 151
Freedman, M., 35
Frelimo, 42
Fynn, H. F., 105, 108

Gans, H., 236
Gladstone, W., 105
Glesiner, J., 56
Goldthorpe, J. H., 40
Golightly, C. L., 33
Gordon, M. M., 36
Graham, Lieut.-Col. J., 95
Grahamstown, 110, 113
Grahamstown Journal, 12
Great Trek, 12, 14, 105
Grey, Sir George, 111
Griffen, J., 96–7
Griffiths, P., 69
Grobbelaar, A., 58
Grondwet, 13
Group Area Acts, 59, 183

Hall-Jones scale, 159
Hancock, W. K., 4, 26
Herstigte Nationale Party, 42
Hertzog, A., 42, 76, 196
Hertzog, Gen. J. B. M., 51
Hillbrow, 81, 224
Hockly, H. E., 100
Hofmeyr, J. H., 64, 127, 132
Holleman, J. F., 7
Hopetown, 113
Horwitz, R., 39
Host society, 25–30, 249, 251, 252
Hottentots, 102
Housing, 58–62, 180–3
    coloured immigrants in Britain, 60–2
    South African prices, 181
Hughes, H., 38

Immigrants, attitude-change or self-
        selection, 233–6
    attitudes towards African before and
        after emigration, 234
    behaviour changes, 22, 23
    conformity and ignorance, 236–8
    occupations, early 20th century, 120
    orientation towards host society, 251
    provincial distribution, 151
    quest for acceptance, 24–5
    residence intention and satisfaction,
        243

resocialization, 13
    social mobility and acceptance, 238–
        9
    see also British immigrants; Dutch
        immigrants
Immigration, decline, 121
    Department of, 139, 257
    interrelation with race relations, 11
    motivation statistics, 155
    regional differences, 150
Immigration Acts, 121, 122
Immigration Authorities, 171
Immigration Boards, 111–12
Immigration Selection committee, 134
Immorality Acts, 73, 74
In den Bosch, B. J., 157, 187
India, 133
Indians, 65, 122, 214
Industry, 51, 52
    in Britain, 51
        racial prejudice, 53–6
Inkeles, A., 78
Inquiries, 170–1
Integration, and outgroup scores by
        length of residence in South
        Africa, 158
    class distinction, 160
    social structure and culture, 20
Intermarriage, 74, 155
Interview schedule, 261–73
Israel, 14, 24, 43

Jews, 4, 122, 124, 211–12
Johannesburg, 152
Johnston, P., 168
Joost de Blank, 201
Jooste, C. J., 40

Kaffir War, 95
Kafirs, 118
Katz, E., 172
Kerr, C., 41
Keynes's dictum, 41
Kitchener, Lord, 119
Koornhof, P., 18, 28
Kruger, P., 26, 117, 218
Kuper, L., 22, 233

Labour Government, 166
Landes, R., 46
Langa, 67
Lapiere study, 79
Lazarsfeld, P. F., 172

Lever, H., 7, 81, 157, 210, 215, 224
Lieberson, S., 37
Little, K., 57
Liverpool, 52
Loedolff, J. F., 157, 216, 232
Lohman, J. D., 8
Lugard, F., 39

McCarran-Walter Act, 53
McCorkindale, A., 113
MacCrone, I. D., 8, 79, 81, 209, 210, 215
MacMillan, W. M., 103
Mafeje incident, 72
Maitland's bounty system, 110
Malan, Dr., 124, 130, 131, 134–5
Malherbe, E. G., 81, 124
Malvern, Lord, 27
Mannheim, K., 161, 240, 241, 259
Marais, J., 42
Marriages, mixed, 74, 155
Marx, Karl, 17, 50
Matanzima, Chief, 66
Memorial Settlers' Association, viii,
    18, 132, 135, 151, 172, 178, 197,
    242, 257, 275
  aims, 126
  artisan immigration, 129
  development, 126
  formation, 125
  post-war immigration, 129
  survey on immigrant motivation, 141
Merriman, J. X., 64, 113, 118, 131
Merton, R. K., 46, 80, 249
Michael X, 70
Migrant integration, typology, 249–52
Migrant statistics, 276–7
Migration, 17
  early, motives, 116
  first stage, 162–79
    agencies for mobilization, 178
    awareness of opportunities, 169–
      75
    contacts and visits, 171–2
    factors precipitating, 175–7
    incentive factor, 16–18, 163–9
    information, 172
  inquiries, 170–1
  knowledge, 173–5
  'means', 162–3
  motivating factors, 15–18
  precipitating factors, 18
  social controls, 179
  value-added perspective, 14–19

gestation period and precipitants,
  175
inquiries and alternative choices, 170
macro-social theory of, 12–14
motives, 164, 235
personal influence, 128
second and third stages, adjustment
  and integration, 19–32
  insecurity and conformity, 21–5
  social mobility and status dis-
    crepancies, 30–2
  social structure of host society,
    25–30
  see also Returning migrants
Milner, Sir A., 26, 117, 119, 125, 218
Milner's Law, 26
Mineral discoveries, 114
Mineworkers' Union, 57
Mixed marriages, 74, 155
Mondlane, Dr., 42
Moodie, B., 93–4
Moodie, J., 93
Moore, W. E., 38
Mosley, O., 69
Mulder, C. P., 28, 29
Myrdal, G., 5, 11, 33, 38, 39, 78, 247,
  248, 259

Napier, Lieut.-Col. E., 104
Natal, 92, 105–9, 114, 152, 248
National Party, 28, 47, 134, 137, 155,
  216, 223
Nationalist Government, immigration
  policy, 26–9
Nationalists, 136
Native Labour (Settlement of Disputes)
  Act, 58
Native Laws Amendment Act, 59, 75
Native (Urban Areas) Act, 1923, 58
Natives' Land Act, 75
New Zealand, 17, 252
Newcastle, Lord, 113
Newspapers, 115, 152, 197

Osborne, C., 67, 69

Pareto, V., 41
Paris, Treaty of, 92
Park, R. E., 24
Parsons, T., 12, 20, 41
Patterson, S., 62, 74
Pentecostalism, 77
Petersen, W., 16

Pettigrew, T. F., 8, 47, 79, 80, 154, 214, 215, 236
Philip, J., 76, 102
Phillips, L., 117, 127
Pietermaritzburg, 107
Plowden Report, 72
Pluralism, 83, 251
  definition, 3–4
  illustrations, 4
Political-cultural integration, Afrikaans language, 208–9
  attitudes to apartheid, 224–9
  citizenship, 215–17
  comparative political interest and allegiance, 220
  expectations and experience, 229
  group stereotypes, 209–15
  political orientations and affiliations, 219–24
  republicanism and national identification, 217–19
Popper, K. R., 86
Population Registration Act, 74
Port Elizabeth, vii, 112
Powell, E., 43, 57, 68, 69, 234
Prejudice, sociological definition, 23
Pretoria, 151
Pringle, T., 98, 100, 101, 103
Progressive Party, 223
Prohibition of Improper Interference Act, 63, 65
Prohibition of Mixed Marriages Act, 74
Promotion of Bantu Self-Government Act, 64

Quota Act, 124

Race, concept in sociological theory, 9
Race relations, America, 5–7
  and economics, 50–62
    employment, 50–8
    housing, 58–62
  and politics, 62–70
  and social institutions, 70–8
    education, 70–3
    family, 73–5
    religion, 75–8
  attitudes and values, 78–82
  Britain, 47, 67
  Cape Town, 151–2
  political basis, 64
  problem in sociological theory, 11

relation to social stratification, 9
significance of social groups, 8
structural and cultural aspects, 7
Race Relations Act, 54, 61, 62, 69
Racial prejudice, early immigrants, 116
  in Britain, 68–70
  multi-causality, 9
Racial structure, 26
Radio, 196
Railways, 114, 115
Rand, 53
Rand Revolt, 51
Raubenheimer, J., 4
Reitzes, D. C., 8
Religion, 75–8, 199–202
Republic, 65, 137, 218
Retief, P., 12
Returning migrants, 241–4
  case study of, 274
  motives, 243–4
  statistics, 242
Rex, J., 38
Rheinallt-Jones, J. D., 64
Rhodesia, 7, 42, 48, 124, 141
  Southern, 27
Richardson, A., 15, 17, 18
Richmond, A. H., 37, 39, 157, 163, 186 203, 242, 243
Rogers, C. A., 7, 157
Rogers, Capt., 92
Roman Catholics, 28, 29, 140
Rossi, P. H., 78

Sachs, S., 56
Samorgan, 172, 178
Sandys, D., 70, 74
Sauer report, 48
Schreiner, W. P., 64
Science Research Council, 259
Security Police, 42
Selborne, Earl, 125
Separate Representation of Voters Bill, 65
Separatist Churches 75, 76, 77
Seretse Khama, 74
Settlers, and the Frontier, 91–109
  economic motives, 95
Shaka, 108
Sharpeville, 27, 42, 67, 109, 137, 139, 140, 142, 225
Shearer, Dr., 138
Shepstone, Sir T., 48, 108
Shillinge, A., 92

Shils, E., 237
Simon's Bay, 110
Smelser, N. J., 14, 162, 164, 248
Smethwick, 68, 69
Smith, Sir Harry, 110
Smith, I., 42
Smit report, 59
Smuts, J. C., 39, 117, 125, 128, 131, 137
  immigration policy, 124, 130, 131–4
Smuts Government, 130
Smuts United Party, 48
Smythe, Sir Thomas, 91
Social developments, 144
Social integration, attitudes of fellow-workers to British immigrants, 202
  class-consciousness and social mobility, 203–7
  comparative ease of friendship and ethnic differences, 191
  comparative religious attendance, 199
  congruence of expectations and experience, 206
  frequency distribution, 207
  leisure-time adjustment and comparative social life, 193–7
  patterns of friendship, 191–3
  relations at work, 202–3
  religious associational activity, 199–202
  secular associational activity, 197
Social mobility and prejudice, 30
Social system, 3
Somerset, Lord Charles, 26, 95
South Africa, and Britain, contrasting social structures, 34–7
  concept of dilemma, 33–4
  conflicts of colour and culture, 26
  departure from Commonwealth, 137
  lack of revolutionary impetus, 42
  legal racial discrimination, 35
  power structure, 143–4
  reasons for decline in immigration, 139
  Republic, 65, 137, 218
  role of economic factors, 39–44
  segregation and integration, 21
  social structure, 3
South Africa House, 98, 172, 178
South African Citizenship Act, 1949, 26

South African Confederation of Labour, 57
South African ethnic groups, 210
South African Immigration Co. (Samorgan), 172, 178
South-West Africa, 124, 151
Southern African League, 28
Soviet Union, 41
Stallard doctrine, 58
Steenkamp, A., 12, 75
Stevens, T., 91
Stonequist, E., 21
Strydom, J. G., 130
Stultz, N., 65–6
Sumner, W. G., 7
Sumnerian doctrine, 35
Sundays River Settlement Company, 122–3
Sundkler, B. E. M., 75, 77
Swart Gevaar, 51

Table Bay, 112
Terblanche, H. J., 28
Thomas, W. I., 6, 11, 19, 25, 247
Tomlinson Commission, 138
Total integration, 230–2
  statistics, 231–2
Trade Union Council of South Africa, 58
Trade unions, 56–8, 117, 197
  Britain, 57, 197
Transvaal, 119, 120, 151, 152, 248
Trollip, Senator, 140
Trollope, A., 116
Tumin, M. M., 38

Uitenhage, 113
Uitlanders, 26, 110–21, 144, 250
Union, Act of, 64, 120, 143
  formation of, 121
United Nations, 137
United Party, 59, 130, 135, 136, 223
Unlawful Organizations Act, 63
Urban Areas Acts, 59

van den Berghe, P. L., 7, 41, 44, 215
van Hogendorp, Baron, 93
Van Riebeeck, J., 48, 92
Verba, S., 78
Verkrampte, 152
Verligte, 152
Verwoerd, Dr., 27, 43, 65, 71, 141, 174, 225

Viljoen Commission, 139
Viljoen, M., 58
Voortrekkers, 12

Wagner, O. J. M., 24
Weber, M., 144, 249
Weberian stratification continuum, 36

Western Cape, 113
Women, integration statistics, 153

Xhosa, 'Red', 21
  'School', 21

Zambesi, 27, 43
Znaniecki, F., 6, 11, 19, 25, 247